VIOLENCE, HOSPITALITY, AND THE CROSS

REAPPROPRIATING THE ATONEMENT TRADITION

HANS BOERSMA

Baker Academic

Grand Rapids, Michigan

© 2004 by Hans Boersma

Published by Baker Academic
a division of Baker Publishing Group
P.O. Box 6287, Grand Rapids, MI 49516-6287
www.bakeracademic.com

Paperback edition published in 2006

ISBN 0-8010-3133-8

Printed in the United States of America

The Library of Congress has cataloged the hardcover edition as follows:
Boersma, Hans, 1961–
     Violence, hospitality, and the cross : reappropriating the atonement tradition / Hans Boersma.
          p.   cm.
     Includes bibliographical references and index.
     ISBN 0-8010-2720-9
     1. Atonement. 2. Hospitality—Religious aspects—Christianity. 3. Violence—Religious aspects—Christianity. I. Title.
BT265.3.B64 2004
232′.3—dc22   2004007697

VIOLENCE, HOSPITALITY, AND THE CROSS

To my parents
—*guides into eschatological hospitality*—

Contents

Preface

It is not always easy to keep the hospitality of God in the center of our vision. Violence has a tendency to obscure this vision and to diminish our appreciation of divine hospitality. As in the title of this book—*Violence, Hospitality, and the Cross*—so in our personal lives and in our theological reflection, violence tends to take center stage, making it difficult to see the hospitality of God's grace that beckons us into the eschaton of peace. Today, perhaps more so than at any other period in the history of the Church, people struggle to give an account of the love of God in the face of so much senseless violence. We stand face-to-face with the question: Is it really possible to give a theological account of the hospitality of God? Or is such a notion a mere chimera, and are we inevitably and forever mired in violence?

This book gives an account, albeit indirectly, of my journey as I have grappled with these questions. The Reformed tradition, which continues to be my home, has especially been accused of complicity with violence. The centrality of predestinarian theology, the retributive character of substitutionary atonement theology, and the iron logic of Calvinist theological systems have all been the object of sharp criticism. This book makes clear that I believe some of this critique is justified. The heart of God does not harbor in exact parallel fashion love and wrath, mercy and justice, election and reprobation, hospitality and violence. The second chapter of this book, on divine election and limited atonement, illustrates where I believe such parallelisms in Calvinist predestinarian thought fall short. At the same time, however, I have become convinced that in significant ways the Reformed tradition occupies its rightful place within the broad tradition of the Church. Each of the three main atonement models—including, therefore, a penal view of the cross—have their roots in the ancient tradition of the Church.

9

Weary of the violence of past border clashes, we may be tempted to give up on our theological heritage altogether. But this would be a serious mistake. What I wish to do in this book is to reappropriate the tradition of atonement theology in an ecumenical attempt to contribute positively to what Thomas Oden has recently called "the rebirth of orthodoxy." I draw on what I have come to regard as positive elements in the historic Christian faith and in particular in the Reformed tradition. This comes to the fore in my reevaluation of violence as something that is not inherently negative; in my insistence that boundaries can function in wholesome ways and need at times to be defended; as well as in my argument that restorative justice can only function if we are willing to include the notion of punishment. I would describe my view of the atonement, therefore, as a modified Reformed position that wishes to draw on elements throughout the catholic tradition.

Many have contributed to this book over the past couple of years. I wish to mention particularly the invaluable support and generosity of the board members and friends of the Geneva Society on whose behalf I have been teaching at Trinity Western University for the past five years. Many of them have read and commented on (parts of) the book. A sincere thank-you, therefore, to Rick Baartman, Harry Boessenkool, Yolanda Bouwman, Dennis de Groot, Lee Hollaar, John Koster, Nick Loenen, Bert Moes, Margie Patrick, John Siebenga, Bart van der Kamp, Greg van Popta, Tako van Popta, Wilma Vanderleek, and Pieter Vanderpol. Without their support of my position as Geneva Chair and without their active interest in this research project, I would not have been able to bring it to completion. Also, I gratefully acknowledge the generous support for the Geneva Society by the Oikodome Foundation throughout this period.

The research for this book has benefited from two seminars. In 2000, I participated in a six-week seminar with Miroslav Volf as part of Calvin College's Seminars in Christian Scholarship program funded through the Pew Charitable Trusts. In many ways, Miroslav's book, *Exclusion and Embrace*, has been an inspiration for my project, and I deeply value his kind support and his encouragement to mine the Church's traditional teaching on the atonement. Two years later, Bob Webber and Dennis Okholm directed a theological faculty workshop at Wheaton College for the Council of Christian Colleges and Universities. Their enthusiasm and their love for the Christian tradition have contributed in meaningful ways to the ethos of my book as it draws from this broad Christian tradition. Needless to say, both seminars were not only great learning experiences but also have led to lasting friendships and memories.

Much of the material in this book stems from papers that I have presented at academic conferences. I appreciate the feedback that I received at meetings of the Association for Reformational Philosophy (in the Netherlands), the Canadian Evangelical Theological Association, the Canadian Theological Society, the Christian Theological Research Fellowship, and the Evangelical

Theology Group, the latter two at annual meetings of the American Academy of Religion. Although the chapters in this book have not been published before in their entirety, scattered throughout the book are both small and large segments of published essays. I appreciate the permission to republish essays from the following journals: *Journal for Christian Theological Research*, *Pro Ecclesia*, *Psyche en Geloof*, and *Scottish Journal of Theology*. I have listed each of these essays in the bibliography. Several of them are the result of grants from the Social Sciences and Humanities Research Council of Canada, channeled through the kind assistance of the research office at Trinity Western University.

The wonderful experience of teaching a course on atonement theology and thereby testing most of the material in this book will remain with me forever, and I hereby thank my students for their marvelous interaction. Thanks also to my friends and colleagues who have read and critiqued the book: Craig Allert, Kent Clarke, Ron Dart, Doug Harink, Tom Juchmes, Andrew Kaethler, Andy Reimer, Miroslav Volf, and Jens Zimmermann. I want to make special mention of Jamie Smith, to whom I am grateful both for friendship and dialogue. Also, I cannot believe the many hours of hard work that my students Vanessa Caruso and Joy Pecknold have poured into this project! It has certainly made a huge difference. And I wish to thank the people at Baker Academic, notably Brian Bolger and Jim Kinney, for their active interest and their great support throughout.

More than anywhere else, I continue to witness in my wife, Linda, the iconic presence of divine hospitality as she consistently supports me in my work.

Introduction

Richard J. Neuhaus, in his masterful collection of meditations on Jesus' words on the cross, comments that "all the theories of atonement are but probings into mystery, the mystery of a love that did not have to be but was, and is."[1] Neuhaus's thoughtful meditations prove that the "mystery of love" does not preclude "theories of the atonement." The mystery of love as God has expressed it in the sending of his Son does mean, however, that atonement theology needs a certain modesty or humility. I am not referring to the false humility to which John Milbank rightly alludes, and which results from an abdication of responsibility and a capitulation before the throne of human reason.[2] Instead, I am referring to a humility that acknowledges that love cannot, in the final analysis, be grasped or explained. "The heart has its reasons of which reason knows nothing," Blaise Pascal rightly commented in his *Pensées* (1670), echoing the divine truth underlying the love of God's election of Israel (cf. Deut. 7:7–8).

It is no secret that theologians have not universally heeded Neuhaus's cautionary remark. Most theologians, after all, are convinced that some truth claims are more adequate than others, and many will insist that they hold their opinions, however tentatively expressed, with universal intent. While I believe such claims are helpful, even necessary, theology's place of significance has often tempted theologians to analyze and comprehend divine realities fully and exhaustively. And it is certainly possible that I transgress these limits of epistemic humility also in this book. I have nonetheless attempted to impose some restraints to prevent undue individual theological hubris. Theology, I am convinced, is born in the Church and is nurtured by the faith of the Church.

---

1. Richard J. Neuhaus, *Death on a Friday Afternoon: Meditations on the Last Words of Jesus from the Cross* (New York: Basic, 2000), 8.
2. John Milbank, *Theology and Social Theory: Beyond Secular Reason* (Oxford: Blackwell, 1993), 1.

Thus, individual theologians, and also particular theological traditions, must allow for correction from the breadth of theological traditions in the Church.[3] In this study I discuss each of the three main atonement models not in order to exclude one or the other from the discussion, but in a genuine attempt to learn what each of these models may have to contribute to our appreciation of the mystery of God's love. I do not mean to suggest that we should simply adopt each and every theological element from the tradition. Some theologians and their contributions are more profound than others. And the historical meanderings of the various atonement theologies have their low points as well as their high points. Nonetheless, since the Church throughout the ages has particularly benefited from three atonement models (moral influence, penal representation, and Christus Victor), it would be foolhardy to exclude a priori any of these models from the discussion.

Broadening one's horizon to include perspectives from the various traditions also means that a reappraisal of the insights of the early Church may be of great benefit.[4] The acrimonious divisions throughout the history of the Church, and in particular since the time of the Reformation, cannot possibly be overcome when theologians simply look for confirmation of the views of their particular tradition by analyzing the thought of their own denominational heroes. Both my denominational and my academic background are rooted in the Calvinist Reformation. I trust that this study will make clear that I have appreciation as well as criticism for my tradition. But I have purposely gone back beyond the Reformation to the early Church—and to the second-century Church father Irenaeus, in particular—in order to explore the possibilities of an ecumenical grounding for atonement theology. Irenaeus's view of recapitulation holds out rich promise in overcoming seemingly insuperable polarities between the various models of the atonement. In other words, I am not going back to Irenaeus in order to avoid the difficulties and mutual conflicts involved in later atonement models. Instead, I believe that his recapitulation theory assists in exploring the way in which the various models might relate to one another.

The reappropriation of the early Church is only one aspect of recent evangelical development. Accompanying this appreciation for patristics is a realization that the Protestant Reformation arose within a particular historical context that has shaped subsequent Reformation beliefs and practices in ways that have not always been equally beneficial. More and more evangelical scholars are looking

3. Cf. Miroslav Volf's discussion of "double vision," by which we temporarily put ourselves into other people's skin in order to take on their perspective (*Exclusion and Embrace: A Theological Exploration of Identity, Otherness, and Reconciliation* [Nashville: Abingdon, 1996], 250–53).

4. Cf. Robert E. Webber, *Ancient-Future Faith: Rethinking Evangelicalism for a Postmodern World* (Grand Rapids: Baker, 1999); Christopher A. Hall, *Reading Scripture with the Church Fathers* (Downers Grove, Ill.: InterVarsity, 1998); Christopher A. Hall, *Learning Theology with the Church Fathers* (Downers Grove, Ill.: InterVarsity, 2002). The publication of the Ancient Christian Commentary on Scripture series, edited by Thomas C. Oden and published by InterVarsity, is also a tremendously encouraging development.

to Catholicism to correct some of the unhealthy emphases that have taken root among the heirs of the Reformation.[5] Various aspects of this book will make clear that I have benefited from the increased dialogue with Catholic scholars. In particular, evangelicals need to recover the Catholic emphasis on moral integrity and on the visible Church. Both of these elements come to the fore in various parts of this book. But my use of Catholic theology goes beyond a desire that Catholics and Protestants might learn from each other. My hope is ultimately ecumenical in character: the unity of the one, holy, catholic, and apostolic Church.[6] This ecumenical starting point does not imply that each and every theological tradition always has equally valid contributions to make. True dialogue across denominational and theological boundaries may, however, lead to surprising possibilities of convergence.

Most of us consider hospitality an important virtue. We want to be open to others around us, and we are intuitively aware that by sharing something of our lives with others both they and we ourselves are enriched. But the practice of hospitality is difficult. The busyness of our lives makes it hard to create time for others. When inviting people whose lives are in shambles, we are often painfully aware of the inequity between the hosts and the guests. The secret satisfaction we get out of hospitality makes us feel guilty: the altruistic character of our actions often doesn't stand up to honest self-evaluation. And then there is the fact that hospitality opens us up to potential abuse, so that we quickly erect boundaries that offer protection. Faced with the other, we feel called to practice hospitality, but we soon realize that face-to-face encounters result in complex situations. Genuine hospitality appears to be elusive; the violence of exclusion always lurks around the corner. So what are we to do when hospitality becomes an insurmountable problem?

This book doesn't focus primarily on questions of our individual practices of hospitality—the invitations we offer to strangers or the meals we share with friends—though such activities are never far from my purview, and the questions raised in this book also have direct relevance to such personal issues. Instead, in this book I want to deal with questions surrounding hospitality by a theological engagement with the heart of hospitality: God's work of reconciliation in Jesus Christ. This book is about atonement theology as an expression of God's hospitality toward us. Our hospitality only makes sense in light of God's prior hospitality toward us: God has come to us in Christ to

5. Carl E. Braaten, *Mother Church: Ecclesiology and Ecumenism* (Minneapolis: Fortress, 1998); D. H. Williams, *Retrieving the Tradition and Renewing Evangelicalism: A Primer for Suspicious Protestants* (Grand Rapids: Eerdmans, 1999); Thomas P. Rausch, ed., *Catholics and Evangelicals: Do They Share a Common Future?* (Downers Grove, Ill.: InterVarsity, 2000). The increasing convergence between evangelicals and Catholics is also encouraged by the Evangelicals and Catholics Together (ECT) project and by publications like *Pro Ecclesia, First Things,* and *Touchstone: A Journal of Mere Christianity.*

6. I very much appreciate Thomas C. Oden's discussion of "new ecumenism" in his recent book, *The Rebirth of Orthodoxy: Signs of New Life in Christianity* (New York: HarperSanFrancisco, 2003).

invite us into his presence so that we might share eternal fellowship with him. Christians throughout the centuries have looked to the cross and marveled at this expression of divine hospitality. It is in the cross, perhaps more than anywhere else, that we see the face of the divine host: the true love of God. This book is, therefore, about the face of God—his hospitality toward us in giving himself in Christ.

By moving from the human practice of hospitality to divine hospitality, however, we may merely seem to expand our difficulties. As God's chosen people, we may discern the divine face of hospitality in his electing love for us, but doesn't this election go hand in hand with the violent exclusion of others? As people saved by the blood of Christ, we may recognize the cruciform face of hospitality in Christ's atoning death for us, but doesn't this hospitality toward us go hand in hand with the violent exclusion and death of God's innocent Son on the cross? Can we really speak of divine hospitality and of cruciform hospitality? Or is the violence of exclusion always present, and does this violence render the cross the ultimate instance of divine violence rather than of divine grace? In that case, there is no hope that the communal practices of the Church (let alone the social, economic, and political practices outside the Church) could be manifestations of divine hospitality. In that case, the public face of hospitality disappears from our horizons. By structuring this book around the various faces of hospitality—its divine face (part 1), its cruciform face (part 2), and its public face (part 3)—I claim that despite our questioning, hospitality does have a face: a divine face, a cruciform face, and a public face. Violence does not destroy hospitality.

Not everyone believes that such a positive assessment of hospitality is realistic. Our postmodern climate is downright negative about the prospects of hospitality. Postmodern philosophers insist that we are always engaged in an inescapable web of violence, which makes hospitality—despite the demands that it makes—impossible. The Western legacy of control, mastery, and destruction are obvious indications of our inability to do justice to the faces of others we encounter. Indeed, many argue that Christianity is responsible for, or at least quite complicit in, the legacy of violence that the modern period has left behind. The exclusionary practices of the Christian Church, the violent suppression of internal dissenters throughout its history, and the collusion of the Church with the sword of the state all seem to illustrate the fact that violence, not hospitality, lies at the heart of the Church. And could the reason perhaps lie in the Church's theology? Could it be that violence and exclusion are inscribed in the very heart of the Church's faith: in the divine face of violence on the cross? It will not do to avoid these questions and merely reassert the love of God's hospitality. Only by facing the questions regarding hospitality and violence head-on will we do justice to the genuine concerns that many are expressing today about the Church's faith and about the possibility of hospitality. Throughout this book, therefore, I engage in discussion with the contemporary skepticism that questions the possibility of hospitality, and I do so in the confidence that the Church has not been misguided in trusting the face of God in Jesus Christ. Traditional atonement theology upholds the divine face, the cruciform face, and the public face of hospitality.

How, then, do we deal with the tension between hospitality and violence? Because of the mystery of love that drives theology, paradoxical tension is unavoidable in theology. The title of this book connects the atonement with the two elements of hospitality and violence. I look at hospitality as a metaphor for the love of God, as embodied in the life of Israel, the Church, and the world, and argue that this hospitality, while necessarily involving violence, retains its integrity as hospitality. No doubt, this paradox will not please everyone. It is the violence of the monotheistic religions that makes these religions offensive to many; it is the violence of conditional hospitality that makes postmodern philosophers demand that we open ourselves up completely, without limit, to the stranger; and it is the divine violence involved in the traditional atonement theologies that causes a number of theologians to look elsewhere. There is much in these concerns that I appreciate. In particular, I share the vision of the telos of peace and of absolute eschatological hospitality. I am not convinced, however, that the traditional atonement models need to be abandoned because of their (divine) violence. To the contrary, I claim that we need to affirm the paradox of redemptive violence in order to retain the vision of eschatological unconditional hospitality.

The starting point of my discussion lies in hospitality as a divine virtue. I have, therefore, titled part 1 "The Divine Face of Hospitality." I make clear at the outset in chapter 1 that we can only speak of the human virtue of hospitality inasmuch as God has opened himself up to us. This implies a different point of departure than is common in the postmodern philosophies of Emmanuel Levinas and Jacques Derrida. I discuss their insistence on absolute hospitality and argue that we need to take seriously the fact that God's hospitality has entered into a finite world already marked by injustice. Several contemporary approaches to atonement theology argue that the divine violence involved in each of the traditional models renders them problematic. Usually such arguments assume a definition of violence that already includes its negative character in the definition itself. I appeal instead to the Augustinian understanding of violence as any use of coercion that causes injury, whether that coercion is positive or negative. Toward the end of this chapter I set the stage for the remainder of the study by arguing that although acts of hospitality involve violence, this does not necessarily disqualify them as truly hospitable acts.

Chapters 2 and 3 form the theological backdrop to my discussion of atonement theology. Both chapters deal with divine election. In chapter 2 I discuss what I call "limited hospitality." Here I argue that the Calvinist emphasis on double predestination has been unable to avoid drawing violence into the heart of God, thereby making his eternal unconditional hospitality problematic. In

Calvin, and particularly in later Reformed scholasticism, double predestination functioned as an eternal, individual, and futuristic category. Calvinism's emphasis on double predestination meant that the violence of God's hidden will came to overshadow the hospitality of his revealed will. The harshness of this system became evident especially when Calvinism limited the redemptive value of Christ's work to the elect. Christ's death had no meaning at all for those outside the invisible Church of the elect. Calvinism came to highlight divine violence both in the idea that God powerfully overcame all resistance against his grace for his chosen ones and in the notion that certain individuals had been eternally excluded from his hospitality. The result was a limited hospitality that located violence in the very heart of God.

It is one thing, of course, to criticize the Reformed tradition for its violent tendencies. It is not as easy to avoid the biblical notion of election altogether. In chapter 3, therefore, I give a different interpretation of the notion of election, to which I refer as "preferential hospitality." I argue that the Deuteronomic understanding of election regards it as an act of sovereign grace in the history of God's people. This preferential hospitality is instrumental in character; that is to say, the election of God's people leads to a relationship with them: election is the foundation of the covenant. The question of divine violence is one that I believe cannot be avoided. There is simply no hospitality in our world without violence. This does not mean that we need to make the tension more pronounced than it is. The hospitality of God's election serves necessarily to safeguard monotheistic worship, and the violence against the nations is a divine response to their immorality. God's choice of Israel is a "preferential option for the poor." In the end this preferential hospitality serves a missiological purpose: it is meant to embrace also the other nations. This is not to say that we can rationally explain divine violence. I argue that it is only the resurrection light of God's eternal pure hospitality, the mystery of his ineffable love, that justifies the conditionality of his hospitality.

In chapter 4 I prepare the exposition of the various atonement models through a discussion of the role of metaphors and models. This is the beginning, therefore, of part 2, "The Cruciform Face of Hospitality." I begin by arguing that metaphors play a very important role. Not only do I believe that we can identify some specific roles that metaphors play in linguistic constructions, but I am also convinced that *all* language is metaphoric in character. Thus, we can never downplay the significance of metaphors as somehow less truthful than what we think of as literal descriptions. Since not all metaphors have equal weight, we need to choose among the various metaphors as we develop our atonement theology. Only some metaphors carry the kind of significance that permits them to function as the basis for a distinct model of the atonement. I regard hospitality as the soil in which the various models of the atonement can take root and flourish. Especially helpful in giving shape to these various atonement models is the notion of "recapitulation" (Irenaeus) or "reconstitution" (N. T. Wright). In everything Christ does—and in whatever models we may use to describe this—he functions as the representative of Israel and Adam who recapitulates or reconstitutes their life, death, and resurrection.

The next four chapters form the heart of this study. I begin in chapter 5 with a discussion of the moral-influence theory of the atonement, often associated with Peter Abelard. Contemporary apprehensions of self-sacrificial love notwithstanding, I present an extensive discussion of Irenaeus's view of recapitulation as the obedient retracing of Adam's creation, temptation, and death, which reverses the effects of the Fall and restores humanity on its road to incorruption and immortality. Drawing on Irenaeus, I argue that the subjective moral-influence theory rightly points us to Christ both as our teacher who rescues us from our forgetfulness of God and brings us to a true knowledge of God and as our example who "persuades" us to employ our free will to accept God's hospitality and to live in obedience to him. I conclude that the moral-influence theory offers an indispensable anchor for the hospitality of God.

This is not to say that all articulations of the moral-influence theory are equally helpful. A discussion of atonement and violence cannot avoid dealing with René Girard's increasingly influential theory of mimetic violence. In chapter 6 I make clear that despite some helpful aspects of this theory, it suffers from serious drawbacks. Girard attempts to dissociate God from all involvement in the cross by arguing that the violence of the mob turned Jesus into a scapegoat. Since the New Testament witness reveals the scapegoat mechanism, however, the cross becomes the revelation that lifts the ignorance surrounding the process of mimetic violence. While Girard also uses Christus Victor elements in his exposition of the atonement, he insists that it is when human beings become aware of the mimetic violence of the single-victim mechanism that redemption is accomplished. Unfortunately, Girard's explanation of the scapegoat mechanism implies that violence lies at the root of all human culture, which implies an "ontology of violence" (John Milbank) and makes it difficult for Girard to present the building blocks of a politics of hospitality.

Many regard the penal substitutionary view of the atonement as the most problematic of the traditional models. In chapter 7 I first discuss the idea that substitutionary models of the atonement, often associated with St. Anselm, are the result of the Constantinian arrangement. I show that the Church fathers already worked with substitutionary elements, and that these cannot be the result of fourth-century shifts in power arrangements. At the same time, however, I argue that the Calvinist tradition's understanding of penal substitution fell prey to juridicizing, individualizing, and de-historicizing tendencies that led to a view of the cross dominated by a strict economy of exchange that obscured the hospitality of the cross. With an appeal to the "new perspective on Paul," I show that the apostle viewed Christ's death on the cross as the divine punishment of exile. Since the exilic curse is a national punishment that takes place at a specific point in history, it is possible to insist on Christ's representative penal suffering while avoiding some of the drawbacks of the scholastic Reformed tradition.

Chapter 8 presents a discussion of the Christus Victor theme of the atonement. In a discussion of Gustaf Aulén's 1931 retrieval of this model, I express my regret at Aulén's inability to appreciate either the human dimension in the atonement or the contributions made by the other models of the atonement. Aulén rightly focuses on Irenaeus, however, as a protagonist of the Christus Victor model. When trying to answer the question of *how* Christ gained the victory, the early Church fathers presented several proposals. Gregory of Nyssa maintained that God had tricked the devil by blinding him to Christ's divinity, so that the devil overreached himself when he had Jesus crucified. Interestingly, Gregory justifies this divine deception by saying that it was for the sake of the telos of the eschaton. Feminist theologian Darby Kathleen Ray expresses her appreciation for Gregory's use of divine trickery as she makes a plea for a nonviolent understanding of the atonement. Although not all the current reappropriations of the Christus Victor theme are equally promising, and although it cannot stand on its own, it nonetheless reminds us that we need a limited metaphysical dualism, and that moral influence and penal representation ultimately serve the victory of Christ.

The last two chapters discuss some of the implications of divine hospitality both with regard to the Church (chapter 9) and with regard to questions of public justice (chapter 10). Together they form part 3 of this study, "The Public Face of Hospitality." I argue that since the Church is the continuation of Christ's presence in the world, the redemptive hospitality of the atonement continues in and through the Church. The Church publicly proclaims the hospitality of the gospel ("evangelical hospitality") and therefore needs to recover the public character of worship. Baptism, which Christians receive along with forgiveness and renewal, forges the boundaries of the Church ("baptismal hospitality"). As an act of hospitality toward those who believe, baptism is not indiscriminate and is not an unconditional form of hospitality. God's hospitality climaxes in the celebration of the Eucharist. Since we are merely recognizing God's hospitality when we open the table in intercommunion, we should extend "eucharistic hospitality" to all who through baptism are incorporated into Christ and his Church. Those who share in Christ need to confess their sins to those in authority to forgive them. Such "penitential hospitality" is a form of justice that protects the character of the Church as a hospitable community. If the Church, as the continuation of Christ, practices true hospitality, then persecution and suffering will likely follow. In this suffering the Church continues the redemptive suffering of Christ. Even the Church's "cruciform hospitality," therefore, plays a role in the hospitality of the cross.

The mystery of the Church as the continuation of Christ's hospitality in the world does not mean that hospitality and justice cannot be found beyond the boundaries of the Church. Chapter 10 presents a plea for justice as a public category. This runs counter to the movement of Radical Orthodoxy, which despite some of its gains to my mind confuses the centrality of the Church with the monopoly of the Church. I discuss the way in which liberation theology has appropriated some of the traditional atonement motifs (in particular the moral-influence and Christus Victor models) and has tried to make a contribution to public justice. To be sure, such public justice is never an autonomous end in itself and can only be pursued with a view to the eschatological public justice of God. Liberationists rightly remind us that we should pursue justice not only through forgiveness and "the refusal to cease suffering" (Daniel Bell). Justice can also be practiced through active prophetic involvement (which may well result in suffering) and through proactive government policies. I conclude that public justice may serve as a signpost of the resurrection and the end to violence.

Throughout this book the paradox of the relationship between hospitality and violence figures prominently. In the epilogue I raise the question of how we might envision the end to violence (in other words, a situation of absolute hospitality) without the loss of true humanness. Although Irenaeus does not really answer this question, I believe that his description of deification does justice to the New Testament witness, which insists both on the physicality of the resurrection body and on its glorified character. God's redemption in Christ will be complete when as deified human beings we will share in the absolute hospitality of the glory of God.

PART 1

The Divine Face
of Hospitality

1

The Possibility of Hospitality

Hospitality as a Divine Virtue

God "stretched out His hands on the Cross, that He might embrace the ends of the world; for this Golgotha is the very center of the earth," wrote Cyril of Jerusalem around A.D. 347.[1] His comment illustrates the fact that it is at the foot of the cross that we learn from God how hospitality is to function. The human practice of hospitality is, in the words of Reinhard Hütter, "both a reflection and an extension of God's own hospitality—God's sharing of the love of the triune life with those who are dust. At the very center of this hospitality stands both a death and a resurrection, the most fundamental enactment of truth from God's side and precisely therefore also the threshold of God's abundant hospitality."[2] According to the Christian understanding of

1. Cyril of Jerusalem, *Catechetical Lectures*, in *Nicene and Post-Nicene Fathers*, Second Series, trans. Edward Hamilton Gifford, ed. Philip Schaff and Henry Ware (repr., Peabody, Mass.: Hendrickson, 1994), 7:89 (XIII.28). Cf. Hans Urs von Balthasar, *Mysterium Paschale: The Mystery of Easter*, trans. Aidan Nichols (Grand Rapids: Eerdmans, 1993), 129–30.
2. Reinhard Hütter, "Hospitality and Truth: The Disclosure of Practices in Worship and Doctrine," in *Practicing Theology: Beliefs and Practices in Christian Life*, ed. Miroslav Volf and Dorothy C. Bass (Grand Rapids: Eerdmans, 2002), 219. Christine D. Pohl likewise comments that our hospitality is a "reflection and reenactment" of God's hospitality (*Making Room: Recovering Hospitality as a Christian Tradition* [Grand Rapids: Eerdmans, 1999], 29). Hospitality "reflects God's greater hospitality that welcomes the undeserving, provides the lonely with a home, and sets a banquet table for the hungry" (ibid., 16). Cf. also Patrick R. Keifert, *Welcoming the Stranger: A Public Theology of Worship and Evangelism* (Minneapolis: Fortress,

history, Christ's death and resurrection constitute the ultimate expression of God's hospitality and form the matrix for an understanding of all God's actions and as such also the normative paradigm for human actions.

In Cyril and Hütter's understanding, God has embodied his hospitality on the cross. The well-known parable of the prodigal son (Luke 15:11–32) functions as an icon of this embodied hospitality. The parable, often accused of lacking in Christology, in reality presents us with our crucified Lord. It depicts God's embracing welcome of sinners into his eternal home. Throughout the history of the Church, this parable has rightly functioned as a narrative description of God's grace of forgiveness and renewal. The story captures for us the amazing interplay between divine grace and human freedom. Divine grace enters the picture in a number of ways: a father who unceremoniously runs up to his lost son to receive him back and who ignores his dignity as the paterfamilias must have a very special place for his son in his heart.[3] A father who restores his prodigal son's position as a member in the community (offering him the best robe), who grants him authority (giving him a ring to wear), and who gives him freedom (putting sandals on his feet) is someone who manifestly revels in the celebration of fellowship between father and child. The parable of the prodigal son is, therefore, equally the parable of the hospitable father.

At the same time, God's hospitality does not nullify human freedom. The father's embrace does not force itself in tyrannical fashion on a son who has no choice but to endure the father's imposition of his love. Hospitality rejects the violence of a totalizing imposition of oneself on the other, the violence that forces the other to be shaped into one's own image. The father's love, says Henri Nouwen in his commentary on Rembrandt's painting of the prodigal son, "cannot force, constrain, push, or pull. It offers the freedom to reject that love or to love in return."[4] A forced embrace would mean the loss of hospitality through the violence of the imposition of the host on the stranger.[5] Even when we have lost our way and when our lives have come to an end,[6] God's hospitable grace requires that we enter voluntarily into his loving embrace.

1992), 11–12, 57–61; Brendan Byrne, *The Hospitality of God: A Reading of Luke's Gospel* (Collegeville, Minn.: Liturgical, 2000); Elizabeth Newman, "Hospitality and Christian Education," *Christian Scholar's Review* 33 (2003): 86.

3. Cf. Kenneth E. Bailey, *Poet and Peasant; and, Through Peasant Eyes: A Literary-Cultural Approach to the Parables of Luke* (Grand Rapids: Eerdmans, 1983), 181.

4. Henri J. Nouwen, *The Return of the Prodigal Son: A Story of Homecoming* (New York: Image-Doubleday, 1992), 95.

5. For a more elaborate "phenomenology of embrace" built on the parable of the prodigal son, see Miroslav Volf, *Exclusion and Embrace: A Theological Exploration of Identity, Otherness, and Reconciliation* (Nashville: Abingdon, 1996), 99–165. Cf. Scott Hahn, *Lord, Have Mercy: The Healing Power of Confession* (New York: Doubleday, 2003), 103–18.

6. Cf. the "lost and found" and "death and resurrection" language in Luke 15:24, 32.

With these introductory comments I am taking a distinctly Christian approach. Postmodern reflections on hospitality—those of Emmanuel Levinas and Jacques Derrida in particular—tend to focus on one's hospitality toward the other. This turn to the ethical and the religious in postmodern philosophy is fascinating and in many ways encouraging.[7] We need to probe further, however, and look for a divine transcendent warrant of our human responsibility.[8] Hospitality is not only or even primarily a human virtue, but it is a virtue that has a divine origin; it is a divine virtue. As a divine virtue, it gives expression to the very character of God. Already in the Old Testament, Israel's hospitable treatment of others was to function as "a reflection of the hospitable heart of Yahweh."[9] And particularly on the cross and in the resurrection, God has shown himself to be a God of hospitality. This book is a discussion of how human hospitality is underwritten by God's hospitality in Jesus Christ.

The backdrop for this discussion is twofold. First, there is the encouraging phenomenon of a renewed focus on human hospitality among postmodern philosophers. This book can be read as an interaction with this renewed quest for hospitality. Second, there is an increasing scrutiny among theologians of the role that the cross has played and continues to play in our society. Apprehension of the cross as a place of divine violence has led to a renewed debate about the traditional models of atonement theology. In this book I bring these two centers of contemporary discussion into contact with each other. I ask the question: With these two areas of scholarship in the background—postmodern philosophical discussions on hospitality and contemporary theological discussions on divine violence and the cross—is it possible to come to a renewed understanding of the cross as a place where God is truly hospitable and thus undermines violence and underwrites the prospects of human hospitality? Can we truly say with Cyril that on the cross God embraces the ends of the world?

The question facing Christian theology is what the divine welcome of strangers looks like. Is it a hospitality without violence? Is hospitality without violence even possible? After all, before opening the door we often glance through the peephole, and when we don't trust the person staring us in the face, we don't open the door. There are times that we set limits on our hospitality. There are occasions when we feel it is necessary to exclude others. What exactly is the relationship between hospitality and violence, especially as it comes to expression on the cross? And by way of extension, do we as human beings have

7. Cf. Simon Critchley, *The Ethics of Deconstruction: Derrida and Levinas*, 2nd ed. (West Lafayette, Ind.: Purdue University Press, 1999).

8. As we will see, the religious discourse of Levinas and Derrida has a sense of transcendence, but not in the classical theist understanding of the word.

9. Simon Morrison Steer, "Eating Bread in the Kingdom of God: The Foodways of Jesus in the Gospel of Luke" (Ph.D. diss., Westminster Theological Seminary, 2002), 40. Steer refers to Exod. 22:21; 23:9; Lev. 19:33–34; Deut. 10:17–19; 24:17–19; 26:5–9.

the right, and perhaps even the duty, to protect ourselves and others against strangers who might want to abuse our hospitality? Is the violence of exclusion a necessary counterpart to the practice of hospitality?[10]

Levinas, Derrida, and the Impossibility of Pure Hospitality

These questions lead us to the postmodern reflections on hospitality to which I have already alluded. Postmodern philosophers have alerted us to the presence of violent structures in Western thought that make it difficult for hospitality to flourish. Emmanuel Levinas (1906–95), in particular, has criticized Western thought for its violent tendencies and for its inability to respect others. The Western philosophical tradition, says Levinas, has had a penchant for ontological categories. The preoccupation with questions of being (ontology) has led to a tendency to understand, to grasp, and to master the exterior world. Western culture is built on attempts to analyze, scrutinize, dissect, explore, and utilize. As a result Western philosophy has encouraged a tendency toward violence. The imposition of rational categories on the exterior world has undermined all that is different or other than one's self. The alterity (otherness) of everything in the outside world gets suppressed. Our attempts to remake the world in our own image imply an inability to accept the other as other. The philosophical tradition is focused on sameness and totality: in a totalizing fashion, we have shaped everything that we see into our own image. Sameness (*le Même*) rather than alterity, totality rather than infinity, being rather than ethics lies at the basis of our modern society: "The ontological event accomplished by philosophy consists in suppressing or transmuting the alterity of all that is Other, in universalizing the immanence of the Same (*le Même*) or of Freedom in effacing the boundaries, and in expelling the violence of Being (*Être*)."[11]

Looming large in the background of Levinas's reflections is his experience with Nazism. As a Jew, Levinas was shocked to learn that the Freiburg philosopher Martin Heidegger (1889–1976) came out in support of Hitler's regime in the 1930s. Levinas had been a great admirer of Heidegger, but the

---

10. Caroline Westerhoff emphasizes the need for boundaries to counter possible abuse of hospitality (*Good Fences: The Boundaries of Hospitality* [Cambridge: Cowley, 1999]). Cf. also Thomas C. Oden's comment in his discussion on the need for boundaries: "A center without a circumference is just a dot, nothing more. It is the circumference that marks the boundary of the circle. To eliminate the boundary is to eliminate the circle itself. The circle of faith cannot identify its center without recognizing its perimeter" (*The Rebirth of Orthodoxy: Signs of New Life in Christianity* [New York: HarperSanFrancisco, 2002], 131). And cf. Volf, *Exclusion and Embrace*, 63–64.

11. Emmanuel Levinas, *Basic Philosophical Writings,* ed. Adriaan T. Peperzak, Simon Critchley, and Robert Bernasconi (Bloomington: Indiana University Press, 1996), 11. Cf. Bruce Ellis Benson, *Graven Ideologies: Nietzsche, Derrida, and Marion on Idolatry* (Downers Grove, Ill.: InterVarsity, 2002), 113.

latter's political alignment, as well as Levinas's five-year imprisonment by the Nazi regime (1940–45), caused him to reevaluate, both on a personal and on a philosophical level. Levinas came to view fascist totalitarianism as the natural outcome of the Western metaphysical tradition. Heidegger, who structured his philosophy around the concept of Being (*Dasein*), worked within this Western tradition with its desire to understand, to grasp, and so to control. Levinas came to see that a politics based on Western metaphysics naturally led to oppression and violence, because it had no room for the inbreaking of the other. The philosophical tradition had not been open to the alterity of the other and had thus suppressed hospitality toward the stranger. Levinas came to see the necessity of a radical break with the Western preoccupation with being and insisted that ethics—rather than ontology—must be the "first philosophy."

Levinas wants to upset the entire stage of Western metaphysics. In doing so, he takes his starting point in the face of the other who is knocking on the door. The alterity of the other places me immediately under the obligation of hospitality. I am no longer allowed to look through the peephole before opening the door: "[T]he other facing me makes me responsible for him/her, and this responsibility has no limits."[12] The face of the other places me under the ethical obligation of responding with hospitable love, before I can make any sort of rational, analytic judgment about the identity of the other. "The relation between the Other and me," says Levinas, "which dawns forth in his expression, issues neither in number nor in concept. The Other remains infinitely transcendent, infinitely foreign; his face in which his epiphany is produced and which appeals to me breaks with the world that is common to us, whose virtualities are inscribed in our *nature* and developed by our existence."[13] Thus, rather than trying to impose my rationality on the other, my primary attitude should be one of absolute openness and hospitality.[14]

Several theologians have found elements in Levinas's Jewish philosophy that are useful for Christian reflection. Hospitality is, after all, a virtue with a venerable tradition, both in the biblical witness and throughout the Christian tradition. Levinas's ethical concerns have especially come to the fore, however, through their appropriation by Jacques Derrida (b. 1930). Scattered throughout his writings, one finds reflections on the virtue of hospitality. To a large extent Derrida builds on Levinas. Deconstruction, the term with which Derrida is

12. Adriaan Peperzak, *To the Other: An Introduction to the Philosophy of Emmanuel Levinas* (West Lafayette, Ind.: Purdue University Press, 1993), 22.

13. Emmanuel Levinas, *Totality and Infinity: An Essay on Interiority,* trans. Alphonso Lingis (Pittsburgh: Duquesne University Press, 1969), 194.

14. Levinas realizes that this radical hospitality implies the possibility, perhaps even the necessity, of violence. Thus, he refers to our responsibility for another as "an interruption of essence, a disinterestedness imposed with a good violence" (*Otherwise than Being: Or Beyond Essence,* trans. Alphonso Lingis [Pittsburgh: Duquesne University Press, 1998], 43; cf. ibid., 15). With thanks to my colleague Jens Zimmermann for pointing out to me Levinas's acceptance of the notion of "good violence."

often associated, is for Derrida not a matter of arbitrary, nihilistic destruction. Rather, as the title of Simon Critchley's book *The Ethics of Deconstruction* indicates, deconstruction is an ethical demand. Ethics is more than just a branch of philosophy; it is a way of doing philosophy. An "ethical moment," says Critchley, "is essential to deconstructive reading and that ethics is the goal, or horizon, towards which Derrida's work tends."[15]

If Derrida's postmodern philosophy is intimately connected with ethics, we need to ask what this ethics looks like and how hospitality is tied in with Derrida's ethics. Perhaps the best way to describe Derrida's understanding of hospitality is by characterizing it as an eschatological concept. This is not to say that Derrida expects a Jewish messiah to arrive one day. As we will see, he is rather fearful of any particular kind of messianic figure claiming that the kingdom has arrived. Derrida rejects all particular or determinate messianisms in favor of a messianicity that we may view as a stance of absolute openness to the future. Derrida describes this eschatological vision of messianicity as "the opening to the future or to the coming of the other as the advent of justice, but without horizon of expectation and without prefiguration."[16] This quotation highlights three characteristics of Derrida's eschatological vision and, by extension, of his concept of hospitality: Derrida's hospitality is absolute in character; it requires an indeterminate future; and it can never be realized.

First, when Derrida speaks of an "opening to the future," he means a radical, absolute kind of opening. Derrida's messianicity, his hospitality, entails an unreserved and absolute or unconditional openness toward the future, no matter what this future may look like. We need a radical openness to the advent (*invention*) of the wholly other (*tout autre*). In line with Levinas, he insists that pure hospitality means that I forego all judging, analyzing, and classification of the other. It means that I am summoned to forego all violence that tries to shape the other into my own image. By consequence, it also entails the refusal to judge, condemn, or penalize the other. Hospitality, for Derrida, is an attitude of utter openness and a readiness to give, unconditionally, all my possessions to the stranger knocking on my door. Hospitality means self-sacrifice rather than a sacrificing of the other. Even the possibility of the stranger violating my hospitality may not pose a restriction on that hospitality. Derrida is quite aware that "the other and death—and radical evil—can come as a surprise at any moment."[17] The result of this hospitality may be terrible, Derrida acknowledges, "because the newcomer may be a good person, or may

---

15. Critchley, *Ethics*, 2.

16. Jacques Derrida, "Faith and Knowledge: The Two Sources of 'Religion' at the Limits of Reason Alone," in *Religion*, trans. Samuel Weber, ed. Jacques Derrida and Gianni Vattimo (Stanford, Calif.: Stanford University Press, 1998), 17 (italics omitted).

17. Ibid.

be the devil."[18] Hospitality is unconditional, to the point of teetering on the brink of violence and chaos.

Hospitality must therefore be absolute, pure, or unconditional.[19] Derrida criticizes Immanuel Kant (1724–1804) for the limitations that the philosopher from Königsberg places on hospitality. Kant's "universal hospitality," described in his essay on *Perpetual Peace* (1795), was a hospitality that carried conditions: the stranger must behave peaceably in another's country, and he is only given the right to visit, not the right to stay.[20] Derrida rejects the lack of openness, the determinacy, and the horizon of expectation, each of which are involved in a Kantian hospitality. His motivation is a laudable desire to escape the violence inherent in the particularities of determinate messianisms and of modern politics. When we restrict hospitality along Kantian lines, it seems impossible to avoid violence: we will ward off, violently if needed, any unacceptable behavior of the stranger. Derrida rejects the violence of a conditional hospitality in favor of pure hospitality, even though this pure hospitality may ultimately require openness to the devil himself.

Derrida is not entirely oblivious to charges that his pure hospitality is mere pie in the sky (since his messianic future is entirely indeterminate and since there is no horizon of expectation) or perfectionistic (since nobody is capable of being hospitable in an absolute sense). So he eases the tension at times and makes concessions to Kant's "universal" (conditional) hospitality. Derrida suggests, for instance: "Just hospitality breaks with hospitality by right; *not that it condemns or is opposed to it,* and it can on the contrary set and maintain it in a perpetual progressive movement; but it is as strangely heterogeneous to it as justice is heterogeneous to the law to which it is yet so close, from which in truth it is indissociable."[21] Derrida wants to engage in the practice of hospitality

---

18. Jacques Derrida, "Hospitality, Justice, and Responsibility: A Dialogue with Jacques Derrida," in *Questioning Ethics: Contemporary Debates in Philosophy,* ed. Richard Kearney and Mark Dooley (London: Routledge, 1999), 70. Cf. John D. Caputo, *The Prayers and Tears of Jacques Derrida: Religion without Religion* (Bloomington: Indiana University Press, 1997), 145; Jacques Derrida, with Alexander Garcia Düttmann, "Perhaps or Maybe," in *Responsibilities of Deconstruction,* ed. Jonathon Dronsfield and Nick Midgley, *PLI: Warwick Journal of Philosophy* 6 (1997): 9, 13; Jacques Derrida, *Of Hospitality: Anne Dufourmantelle Invites Jacques Derrida to Respond,* trans. Rachel Bowlby (Stanford, Calif.: Stanford University Press, 2000), 77; John D. Caputo, *On Religion* (London: Routledge, 2001), 11.

19. Derrida often describes "pure hospitality" as a hospitality that has no limits or conditions whatsoever. See, for instance, Derrida, "Hospitality, Justice, and Responsibility," 70; Derrida, *Of Hospitality,* 77; Caputo, *Prayers and Tears,* 145. He also calls this pure hospitality the "hospitality of visitation," which he contrasts with the "hospitality of invitation," which we extend on our own terms and is conditional. See Brian Russell, "Developing Derrida: Pointers to Faith, Hope, and Prayer," *Theology* 104 (2001): 406. Elsewhere, Derrida refers to pure hospitality as "just hospitality," which he contrasts with "hospitality by right" (*Of Hospitality,* 24–25).

20. Immanuel Kant, *Perpetual Peace,* ed. Lewis White Beck (Indianapolis: Bobbs-Merrill, 1957), 20–21.

21. Derrida, *Of Hospitality,* 24–25 (italics added). Cf. Jacques Derrida, *Points . . . : Interviews, 1974–1994,* ed. Elisabeth Weber, trans. Peggy Kamuf et al. (Stanford, Calif.: Stanford University Press, 1995), 199.

despite the conviction that he will never truly attain it. His eschatology bumps up against the realities of the created order.[22] Put in Levinasian terms: infinity must make concessions to totality.

We need to keep in mind, however, that the Derridean concessions to the violence of a conditional hospitality remain just that: concessions, and incidental ones at that.[23] In theological terms we could say that Derrida suffers from an over-realized eschatology. The messianic future so dominates the landscape of his philosophy that he is insufficiently attuned to the wisdom that recognizes that hospitality takes place within the limited conditions of time and space and must of necessity, therefore, be limited in its character.[24] Derrida's understanding of hospitality is first and foremost one that centers on the demand of unconditionality and an openness without any boundaries whatsoever.

Second, this absolute openness implies that Derrida is never sure what the messianic future might hold. It is indeterminate in character. There is no "prophetic anticipation," says Derrida. In other words, we cannot look to the prophets of the eighth or of the sixth century B.C. to see what will be in store for us. Just as we don't know who the unexpected visitor might be, so we don't know what the messianic future might look like. To be sure, justice and democracy characterize the messianic future, but this justice and this democracy are so entirely different from justice and democracy as we know them today that we cannot say anything particular or determinate about them. It is precisely fear of the violence of particular messianisms—Judaism, Christianity, and Islam—that has set Derrida on the course of his quest for an indeterminate messianicity.[25] There is a structural similarity, therefore, between Derrida's eschatological understanding of hospitality and the Eastern Orthodox methodology of apophatic, or negative, theology:[26] just as in negative theology the

22. Cf. James K. A. Smith, with reference to Caputo's observations on Derrida: "Despite the fact that Derrida insists that it is a faith without dogma or content, 'the Derridean messianic does have certain determinable features,' such as an affinity for democracy and the prophetic tradition of justice; that is, 'Derrida's messianic has emerged under determinate historical conditions and takes a determinate form'" ("Determined Violence: Derrida's Structural Religion," *Journal of Religion* 78 [1998]: 206–7).

23. Mark Dooley seems to overemphasize the Derridean concessions to the conditional hospitality and to an economy of exchange ("The Politics of Exodus: Derrida, Kierkegaard, and Levinas on 'Hospitality,'" in *Works of Love,* ed. Robert L. Perkins [Macon, Ga.: Mercer University Press, 1999], 167–92).

24. Cf. Thomas W. Ogletree's comment, in his discussion of Levinas, that we need "full appreciation for the fact that the eschatological horizon is not yet as well as already. To demand self-sacrifice from those who are not yet capable of it is not to further moral maturity but to use moral appeals to violate and assault persons. Should such a demand win compliance, the compliance would more likely express self-hatred and resentment than love and justice" (*Hospitality to the Stranger: Dimensions of Moral Understanding* [Philadelphia: Fortress, 1985], 52).

25. Jacques Derrida, *Specters of Marx: The State of the Debt, the Work of Mourning, and the New International,* trans. Peggy Kamuf (New York: Routledge, 1994), 59.

26. In the face of God's transcendence, apophatic theology only negates and denies: we can only say what God is *not.* Kataphatic theology, on the other hand, positively or affirmatively states what God is like. Although

future of deification transcends the boundaries of language, so also Derrida's hopes for a messianic future cannot be captured in words.[27] Just as in Eastern Orthodoxy the apophatic (God's welcome to us) implies at least a sense in which we are taken up into the divine life and so are transformed,[28] so also in Derrida our welcome of the other implies a hospitality or openness that is entirely unconditional or complete and that impinges, therefore, on the integrity of our individual identity.[29]

Third, for Derrida the demand of hospitality is an impossible demand. He insists that our openness to the future is "without horizon of expectation." Hospitality, always entirely indeterminate in its radical openness, is a messianic ideal that will never and can never be realized in a violent world. For Derrida violence is so intricately interwoven with the fabric of the created order itself that all legal structures carry the seed of violence, and their application constantly requires that they be deconstructed for the sake of justice. Justice is in the end the only thing that is undeconstructible. The law never captures this justice in its entirety. Justice, therefore, must always do more than calculate mere statistical evidence. The injustices of historical, positive laws mean that they are always subject to revision or deconstruction, whereas the notion of justice itself cannot be deconstructed. As Derrida puts it:

> The structure I am describing here is a structure in which law (*droit*) is essentially deconstructible. . . . The fact that law is deconstructible is not bad news. We may even see in this a stroke of luck for politics, for all historical progress. But the paradox that I'd like to submit for discussion is the following: it is this deconstructible structure of law (*droit*), or if you prefer of justice as *droit*, that also insures the possibility of deconstruction. Justice in itself, if such a thing exists, outside or beyond law, is not deconstructible. No more than deconstruction itself, if such a thing exists. Deconstruction is justice.[30]

---

apophatic theology has also influenced mystical strands of Western theology, Western apophatic theologians have tended to be marginal. In Eastern Orthodoxy apophatic theology has always been central.

27. Cf. Harold Coward and Toby Foshy, eds., *Derrida and Negative Theology* (New York: State University of New York Press, 1992).

28. It remains, of course, a question of debate whether the Eastern notion of deification is appropriate to describe this transformation or whether it compromises the integrity of the Creator-creation distinction.

29. This is not to say there are no differences between Derrida's philosophy and Eastern Orthodox apophaticism. Derrida, in a sense, radicalizes apophaticism in a Gnostic direction. See Hans Boersma, "Irenaeus, Derrida, and Hospitality: On the Eschatological Overcoming of Violence," *Modern Theology* 19 (2003): 163–80.

30. Jacques Derrida, "Force of Law: The 'Mystical Foundation of Authority,'" in *Deconstruction and the Possibility of Justice,* ed. Drucilla Cornell, Michel Rosenfeld, and David Gray Carlson (London: Routledge, 1992), 14–15. While affirming Derrida's distinction between law and justice (as well as the deconstructibility of the former and the undeconstructibility of the latter), I am more hopeful than he is about the presence of justice within concrete historical legal constructs and therefore see more of an overlap between law and justice than he does.

Justice does not blindly apply the law but looks at the particular situation and so comes to a particular decision. John D. Caputo, Derrida's interpreter, rightly comments: "Whenever a legal system has been good, whenever it has been something more than a blind and flexible tyrant, whenever laws have protected the weak against the strong and prevented the winds of injustice from sweeping across the land, then the law has been deconstructible."[31] In our pursuit of justice we deconstruct the law, in the full awareness that we will never attain this state of nonviolence, of justice, and of pure hospitality. Hospitality implies a messianicity whose eschatological future always remains to come (à venir). In Caputo's words, "If the tout autre ever won the revolution, if the Messiah ever actually showed up, if you ever thought that justice has come—that would ruin everything."[32]

Derrida refers in this context to narcissistic tendencies that we all have and that necessarily lead to insincerity in hospitality. He characterizes our practice of hospitality as a "hospitable narcissism."[33] He means that there are always some strings attached to our deeds. Our actions are always tinged with a degree of self-love. We cannot affirm the other without at the same time affirming ourselves. When we open the door to let the stranger come in, we invite him or her into our home. Lurking behind the simple reality that we have a home to open up and have hospitality to offer is at least some injustice. In the past we haven't always shared as much as we should have. There have already been shortcomings, both in our personal lives and more broadly in worldwide social and economic structures.[34] Furthermore, when we give, we always do so with at least some desire of return, even if it is merely in the form of gratitude on the part of the stranger. Hospitality, in other words, is always part and parcel of an "economy of exchange." Gift giving is never purely altruistic.[35] Hospitality lies embedded in a context of violence. Violence is omnipresent in the time-space conditions of our existence. Derrida, writes James K. A. Smith, "deconstructs the notion of violence as an accident befalling a fundamental goodness. Rather, the proper name represents the first violence."[36] For Derrida (as for Levinas)

31. Jacques Derrida, *Deconstruction in a Nutshell: A Conversation with Jacques Derrida,* ed. John D. Caputo (New York: Fordham University Press, 1997), 130.

32. Caputo, *Prayers and Tears,* 74.

33. Derrida, *Points,* 199. Cf. Dooley, "Politics of Exodus."

34. Marjorie Hewitt Suchocki goes so far as to suggest: "Whether subtle or raw, each act of violence spreads throughout the whole race, conditioning what and how each member of the race can be. We are each participants in every act of violence, whether or not we are aware of these acts" (*The Fall into Violence: Original Sin in Relational Theology* [New York: Continuum, 1994], 105–6). This account of the pervasiveness of violence would make the victim at least partially guilty of the perpetrator's act of violence. Even though Suchocki has difficulty retaining the distinction between victim and perpetrator, she is nonetheless right to point out that every human act is already embedded in a context infested with violence.

35. Cf. Jacques Derrida, *Deconstruction,* 140–51.

36. James K. A. Smith, *The Fall of Interpretation: Philosophical Foundations for a Creational Hermeneutic* (Downers Grove, Ill.: InterVarsity, 2000), 122.

violence is inscribed in the very nature of things and cannot ever be avoided. As soon as we subject the outside world to our intellectual powers of analysis and comprehension, we inevitably violate them.[37]

Derrida's messianic longings, as well as his understanding of violence, contain valuable aspects, which Christians can affirm. All activities that we undertake in our present historical circumstances are indeed necessarily accompanied by inhospitality, by a kind of violence.[38] Derrida is right to suggest that our actions always and necessarily involve violence and boundaries that we are willing to enforce. For example, with a potentially infinite number of strangers to which I am summoned to respond, and with only a limited amount of time available, I can only stretch myself so far. I end up making choices that limit and exclude. The quest for justice necessarily means getting "messed up" in legal structures and arrangements that never quite fully correspond to the particularities of the given situation.[39] The structural situation of the created order—its materiality and temporality—implies limits to my ability to extend hospitality.[40] Real-life decisions cannot be avoided, however, and hospitality needs to be practiced despite the violence that these decisions may entail.[41]

But Derrida, as a man of "prayer and tears," laments this violence as he longs for a messianic future that he believes will never materialize. I am not sure that this necessary violence is lamentable and that we always stand condemned by the demand of pure hospitality. It is not clear to me why our adherence to the limitations and boundaries of the created order would have to be branded as negative. Could it perhaps be possible that the violence involved in the conditions of the created order is actually a positive thing? Even if it were possible to extend "pure hospitality," I would argue that the result would be more violence rather than less: one might end up welcoming devils rather than saints. Hospitality is an art that is impossible to practice when we refuse to challenge evil. When Derrida pleads for an absolute or "pure hospitality" in which the stranger "may be a good person, or may be the devil," he

37. Ibid., 126.

38. For my understanding of violence, see the last section of this chapter ("Violence as Harm or Injury").

39. Cf. Volf: "There is no escape from noninnocence, either for perpetrators or for victims or for a 'third party'" (*Exclusion and Embrace,* 84). "In a world of evil . . . we cannot dispense with an imperfect and therefore essentially unjust justice" (ibid., 223). Although I agree with Volf that violence is inescapable, I would disagree that this entails a loss of innocence and justice.

40. I am deeply appreciative of Jamie Smith for our discussions on this point. Smith does not want to associate finite existence as such with violence (*Fall of Interpretation*). I affirm with him that the eschaton should be seen as a renewed and perfected nonviolent created order. Unlike both Derrida and Smith, however, I am not convinced that all violence is negative, and so I am less hesitant to affirm that violence is inherent in the creational structures as we know them. We might like to know what a nonviolent created order would look like—either in Eden or in the hereafter—but the boundaries of the Fall and of the final resurrection make this an epistemological impossibility.

41. Cf. Derrida, *Deconstruction,* 138–40.

knowingly runs the danger of giving violence and injustice free reign.[42] Such "pure hospitality" seems to be the result of an inability to take seriously the particularities and the limitations that we experience in this world, and it may well betray a Gnostic touch.[43]

Derrida's notion of "pure hospitality" is in itself a valuable notion. The problem is not with this idea as such. Christians have always affirmed that God is love or pure hospitality. The difficulty with Derrida's unconditional hospitality is that it is the logical outcome of his loss of the God of a determinate religion. There is for Derrida no God who at some point will usher in the eschatological messianic future and deal with all violence that we have witnessed and participated in throughout our lives. It is as though the lack of a transcendent warrant for human hospitality (i.e., the God of the cross and the resurrection) creates a utopian impatience in Derrida that insists we introduce pure hospitality here and now. What is tragic about this insistence is Derrida's awareness that this hospitality remains an impossibility.

The ultimate messianic justice lies beyond the eschatological equation and still awaits us. Christians affirm that such hospitality—no longer tinged with any violence whatsoever—is an eschatological reality that is to come (*à venir*) and will be realized in a future characterized by a new historical reality, namely, that of the resurrection.[44] Miroslav Volf speaks about that reality when he comments that in a world of perfect justice "[t]he blindfold would be taken from the eyes of *Justitia* and she would delight in whatever she saw; she would lay aside the scales because she would not need to weigh and compare anything; she would drop her sword because there would be nothing to police. *Justitia* would then be like the God of justice in a world of justice—the God who is nothing but perfect love (1 John 4:8)."[45] God did not enter such a world of perfect justice. He has entered into a world about which we at times despairingly exclaim that "not a single one is wise, not a single one seeks God. . . . Their feet quick to shed innocent blood, wherever they go there is havoc and ruin" (Rom. 3:11, 15–16). Under such historical conditions, it is impossible to extend acts of hospitality without at the same time being involved in some kind of violence. Historically enacted hospitality cannot possibly avoid it. In Jesus Christ, God steps into a world that is already beset by violence, injustice, and inhospitality. In this world God aims for undeconstructible justice and a

---

42. Cf. Ogletree's criticism of Levinas that the latter's decentering of the self doesn't promote just relationships: "The criticism of Levinas . . . is that he seems to resolve the moral issues raised in the encounter wholly in favor of the other" (*Hospitality*, 55). Ogletree rightly argues that "the oppressed could not on Levinas's terms legitimately assert their rights against their oppressors" (ibid., 56).

43. I explain this more fully in "Irenaeus, Derrida, and Hospitality," 164–68.

44. I refer to the eschaton as a "historical reality" to indicate that despite the absence of all violence from this eschatological, pure hospitality, it is the present creation that will be renewed, so that language, time, and space will somehow continue.

45. Volf, *Exclusion and Embrace*, 223.

situation of pure hospitality. And the Christian faith claims that such a situation will one day be realized, once heaven and earth are reunited. In the meantime, incarnation and crucifixion mean getting involved and getting "messed up" in the quirks and quarks of a thoroughly inhospitable situation. We can readily grant Derrida that violence is part and parcel of the world as we know it, and that even God is willing to employ violence. Traditional atonement theologies—of whatever stripe!—have always maintained that *God* is the one who "gave up" (*paredōken*) his Son for our sake (Rom. 8:32).[46] My disagreement with Derrida comes from his reluctance to accept that this violence will ever be overcome and his opinion that "pure hospitality" always remains a mirage, a mere specter.

Whereas Levinas and Derrida speak of *our* hospitality toward the other, I want to speak first of all of God's hospitality toward us. Of course, there are differences between divine hospitality and human hospitality that need to be discussed at this point. God's hospitality is not restricted by the "narcissism" involved in human hospitality. That is to say, although God may employ violence as he extends his divine hospitality, he never uses it for selfish reasons. God's hospitality is never narcissistic in character. That is one reason why I am uncomfortable with the Derridean phrase "hospitality of narcissism": God's hospitality on the cross may have limitations because of its entry into a finite world that is already marked by injustice, but Christians will want to confess that when God acts in this world—even when he acts through violent means, whether it be the ban (*ḥerem*) on the Canaanites or his punitive justice on the cross—he does not have ulterior, narcissistic motives.[47]

Such divine violence may well serve the interests of God's eschatological hospitality—what Derrida calls "undeconstructible justice." It is at least possible that God steps into a violent world, that on the cross he performs an act of amazing hospitality (which is also attended by violence), and that he thus reaches the eschatological goal of pure, unconditional hospitality. Our postmodern eyes are perhaps trained to see the violence of the cross more clearly than its hospitality. But it is theologically quite conceivable that this divine act of delivering Christ to the cross will one day prove to be an act justified by

46. This is also a way to deal with the difficult issue of divine violence in the Old Testament. God's entry in restricted and inhospitable surroundings required the use of violence. The theodicy question, as I will suggest later, is answered eschatologically rather than just rationally.

47. The term "hospitable narcissism" also implies that a human act can never be characterized as an act of hospitality. Derrida appears to intimate that human acts don't really deserve the status of the noun "hospitality" and can only get the miserly adjective "hospitable" in front of the noun "narcissism." It seems to me that many acts of love and hospitality—though they are not without exclusion and violence—nevertheless ought to be described as acts of hospitality rather than as acts of violence. Generous invitation and gracious reception characterize the heart of such acts; the violence and exclusion are no more than annotations in the margin. Such acts of hospitality are undertaken with a minimum of violence and with a clear view to the goal of eschatological, unconditional hospitality.

the eschatological hospitality that awaits us. If we dare say this about so many human actions (despite the violence involved), why not have the courage to say it about God as well? Barbara Brown Taylor, struggling with the questions raised by divine violence and by the terror that we encounter in our lives, finally concludes: "If we are tempted to draw back from it and seek an easier way, we are not alone. The world is full of former disciples. 'Do you also wish to go away?' Jesus asks the handful who are left him in the sixth chapter of John (6:67). 'Lord,' Simon Peter answers him, 'to whom can we go? You have the words of eternal life.'"[48]

Divine Violence and Traditional Atonement Theories

The practice of hospitality on this side of the resurrection—including the hospitality that God extends to his people—is always accompanied by violence. This assertion raises an important issue. Many people have instinctively negative reactions to the word "violence." The word itself often has a morally negative connotation, so that to act violently seems the same as to act in an evil fashion. And indeed, the Scriptures themselves seem to support this in their negative characterization of violence: "Yahweh examines the upright and the wicked, the lover of violence he detests" (Ps. 11:5). Yahweh is the God who redeems his people from violence: "Violence will no longer be heard of in your country, nor devastation and ruin within your frontiers. You will call your walls 'Salvation' and your gates 'Praise'" (Isa. 60:18). But do these references imply that all violence is inherently negative? When we say that hospitality is accompanied by violence, are we saying that it is accompanied by something negative or morally insidious?

There is no denying that the cross is a place of violence. Few punishments are as harsh and cruel as crucifixion. Jack Miles comments graphically: "The crucifix is a violently obscene icon. To recover its visceral power, children of the twenty-first century must imagine a lynching, the body of the victim swollen and distorted, his head hanging askew above a broken neck, while the bystanders smile their twisted smiles. Then they must imagine that grisly spectacle reproduced at the holiest spot in whatever edifice they call holy."[49] The horrendous character of crucifixion has often made the physical sufferings of the Savior a key focus of Christian meditation. Some types of piety

48. Barbara Brown Taylor, "Preaching the Terrors," in *Exilic Preaching: Testimony for Christian Exiles in an Increasingly Hostile Culture,* ed. Erskine Clarke (Harrisburg, Pa.: Trinity Press International, 1998), 90. Other theologians have also drawn attention to the impossibility of explaining evil. Leo D. Lefebure, for example, comments: "Massive evil is a surd that resists explanation. There are only practical responses of resistance" (*Revelation, the Religions, and Violence* [Maryknoll, N.Y.: Orbis, 2000], 15).

49. Jack Miles, *Christ: A Crisis in the Life of God* (New York: Knopf, 2001), 3–4. Cf. Martin Hengel, *Crucifixion in the Ancient World and the Folly of the Message of the Cross* (Philadelphia: Fortress, 1977), 22–32.

have fixed their gaze on the gaping holes in Jesus' hands and feet and on the spear wound that one of the soldiers inflicted on his side. Devoted Christians throughout the centuries have adored the stigmata of Jesus—the result of his violent death—as evidence of the hospitable love of their Lord. But Christian spirituality must go beyond the physical brutality inflicted on Jesus in his crucifixion. Jesus was not the only one to undergo this type of punishment. Two fellow convicts accompanied him, one on his left and one on his right. Many slaves and insurrectionists underwent the same horrible punishment that Jesus experienced. It is not, therefore, his physical suffering by itself that calls for our meditation and devotion. The brutal character of Jesus' crucifixion stands out because he suffered as an innocent, perfectly faithful human being, as someone the Church has confessed is the eternal Son of God. The judicial procedures leading to his crucifixion as we find them described in the Gospel accounts highlight the injustice of the conviction of an innocent man. The coalescence of the political scheming of the religious leaders, the face-saving concerns of the civil authorities, and the furious clamoring of the mob ensured a travesty of justice. The outrageous injustice of Jesus' punishment adds to the brutal nature of this particular crucifixion.

Even the injustice of Jesus' brutal death, however, is not sufficient to explain the unique character of the violence of his death. Christian theology has traditionally probed further and seen in the death of Jesus a mixing of various motivations and purposes. Violent, evil people had a hand in the death of Jesus. But why does the Church see the death of Jesus as salvific? How is it possible that this violent death has become an instrument by which God ensures the arrival of the kingdom of peace? Numerous answers to these questions have been given throughout the history of the Church. Theologians have used different metaphors, different pictures, to explore the depth of meaning of the cross. The cross has been seen as a sacrifice, a purchase, a victory, a punishment, and a cleansing. These various metaphors have been combined and developed into theories or models of the atonement.[50] Some theologians, tracing their roots to the twelfth-century theologian Peter Abelard (1079–1142), have pictured God as sending his Son to die for the world as a demonstration of God's love, which was meant to evoke a response of faith and love among people who were alienated from the love of God. This understanding of the cross has been particularly popular among nineteenth-century liberal theologians. Others, both Catholics and Protestants, taking their stand in the tradition of Abelard's older contemporary St. Anselm (1033–1109), have argued that sin infringed on God's honor or law and that the balance had to be redressed. The cross thus became a way of restoring the balance, a method designed to satisfy God's honor,

---

50. For the relationship between metaphors and models, see A. H. Van Veluw, *De straf die ons de vrede aanbrengt: Over God, kruis, straf en de slachtoffers van deze wereld in de christelijke verzoeningsleer* (Zoetermeer, Neth.: Boekencentrum, 2002), 23–28. I discuss the role of metaphors in more detail in chapter 4.

his justice, or his law. This line of thinking has long been the majority view in Western theology. Again other theologians, in particular a number of early Church fathers, interpreted the death of Jesus as the climactic battle between God and Satan—a battle won by God, either by means of a transaction or by means of deception. Various versions of this early Christus Victor view of the atonement are once again gaining in popularity today.[51]

These three strands of interpretation differ in significant ways. Yet it is important to note that regardless of how we associate God with the cross— demonstrating his love, punishing his Son, battling the devil—God somehow is associated with violence. Each of the three main theological traditions of the Christian faith appears to associate God with violence.[52] In recent discussions on violence and the atonement, the penal substitutionary view of the atonement (which we could describe as the Reformation's submodel of the Anselmian satisfaction model) in particular bears the brunt of the criticism. It is often seen as responsible for the retributive character of the Western judicial system,[53] as well as for various other forms of oppression and abuse.[54] Since the Anselmian tradition has been a main player in Western atonement theology, it is, of course, understandable that the fingers point in its direction. And it is certainly true that the Anselmian model (and penal substitution) involves God in violence. In this model God sends his Son to the earth in order to punish him for the sins of the world.[55] But also the classical model of the atonement (the Christus Victor model) involves God in violence. Here we have God making a deal with the devil (paying him a ransom for the freedom of human

51. Gregory Boyd, *God at War: The Bible and Spiritual Conflict* (Downers Grove, Ill.: InterVarsity, 1997), 238–68; Robert E. Webber, *Ancient-Future Faith: Rethinking Evangelicalism for a Postmodern World* (Grand Rapids: Baker, 1999), 49–61; Darby Kathleen Ray, *Deceiving the Devil: Atonement, Abuse, and Ransom* (Cleveland: Pilgrim, 1998); J. Denny Weaver, *The Nonviolent Atonement* (Grand Rapids: Eerdmans, 2001).

52. J. Denny Weaver, advocating a nonviolent understanding of the atonement, acknowledges his departure from the broad tradition of the Church by insisting that all three traditional models involve God in violence (*Nonviolent Atonement,* 71–74, 226).

53. Timothy Gorringe, *God's Just Vengeance: Crime, Violence, and the Rhetoric of Salvation* (Cambridge: Cambridge University Press, 1996); T. Richard Snyder, *The Protestant Ethic and the Spirit of Punishment* (Grand Rapids: Eerdmans, 2001).

54. Aaron Milavec, "Is God Arbitrary and Sadistic? Anselm's Atonement Theory Reconsidered," *Schola* 4 (1981): 45–94; Simon S. Maimela, "The Atonement in the Context of Liberation Theology," *International Review of Mission* 75 (1986): 261–69; Rita Nakashima Brock, *Journeys by Heart: A Christology of Erotic Power* (New York: Crossroad, 1988), 50–57; Joanne Carlson Brown and Rebecca Parker, "For God So Loved the World?" in *Christianity, Patriarchy, and Abuse,* ed. Joanne Carlson Brown and Carole R. Bohn (New York: Pilgrim, 1989), 1–30; Joanne Carlson Brown, "Divine Child Abuse?" *Daughters of Sarah* 18 (3) (1992): 24–28; Cynthia S. W. Crysdale, *Embracing Travail: Retrieving the Cross Today* (New York: Continuum, 1999); Joel B. Green and Mark D. Baker, *Recovering the Scandal of the Cross: Atonement in New Testament and Contemporary Contexts* (Downers Grove, Ill.: InterVarsity, 2000); Weaver, *Nonviolent Atonement.*

55. Some might object that punishment does not necessarily mean violence. This depends, of course, on one's understanding of violence. According to my understanding of violence, which I discuss in the next section of this chapter ("Violence as Harm or Injury"), punishment necessarily involves violence.

beings), deceiving him (tricking the devil into thinking that Jesus was a mere human being), or actually fighting with and conquering the powers and principalities on the cross. Even the Abelardian moral-influence theory, though it may seem to be the most hospitable, involves God in the violence of the cross. It is by sacrificing his Son that God intends to evoke a human response of love and wants to draw human beings into his reconciling love.[56] Only by radically limiting Christ's redemptive role to his life (so that his life becomes an example to us) or by absolutely dissociating God from any role in the cross (turning the crucifixion into a solely human act) can we somehow avoid dealing with the difficulty of divine violence. All traditional interpretations of the cross must in some way give an account of the relationship between divine violence and the atonement.

It may seem incongruous to link God to violence. God is the hospitable God, the God of peace. How is it possible to link him with violence—especially the violence of the cross of his Son? It is understandable that the notion of divine violence has not found universal acceptance. The second-century antagonist of orthodoxy Marcion (c. 85–160) is probably both the best known and the most radical opponent of the idea. Appalled by the notion that the God we worship could be a violent God, Marcion introduced a sharp division between the Old and the New Testaments. The former was the book of the violent Creator God. He was the God of wrath, the God of war. The latter was the book of the peaceful God of redemption. He was the God of love, the God of Jesus Christ. Marcion may have been apprehensive of divine violence, but he did not remove the cross from the Gospel accounts. It kept a central place in his theology. According to Marcion it was the Creator God, the God of the Jews, who was responsible for Jesus' death on the cross: "It was because by bringing about the death of Jesus the God of the Jews—the generally just but not benevolent Demiurge—had violated his own laws, that it became just for the true and benevolent God to set man free from the Demiurge."[57] The injustice of the Creator God putting Jesus Christ to death became paradoxically the way for the Savior God to redeem his people. Marcion's scheme has the advantage of neatly categorizing love and wrath, justice and injustice, hospitality and violence. Violence, injustice, and wrath are restricted to the Creator God, while hospitality, justice, and love are ours through the God of the New Testament.

The same reluctance to hold God responsible for violence was a major factor in the allegorical excesses that were rampant among the Gnostic sects of the

---

56. Of course, the Abelardian motivation for the death of Christ (to evoke a response of love) may seem more laudable than the Anselmian motivation (satisfaction of God's honor or law). From the perspective of the victim, however, the motivation for violence may not make a great deal of difference.

57. Hastings Rashdall, *The Idea of Atonement in Christian Theology: Being the Bampton Lectures for 1915* (London: Macmillan, 1919), 245. Cf. Jaroslav Pelikan, *The Emergence of the Catholic Tradition (100–600)*, vol. 1 of *The Christian Tradition: A History of the Development of Doctrine* (Chicago: University of Chicago Press, 1971), 75–76.

second century and that unfortunately also affected some of the Church fathers, most notably Clement of Alexandria († c. 215) and Origen (c. 185–253).[58] The Alexandrian school of theology in particular had a hard time accepting the historical narratives of the Old Testament at face value: "Its anthropomorphisms, its improbabilities, the sanction which it seemed to give to immoralities, the dark picture which it sometimes presented of both God and the servants of God, seemed to many men to be irreconcilable with both the theology and the ethics of the Gospel."[59] As a result, theologians were often tempted to work with a split between the sensible world and the intelligible world, a split that entered into the theological realm via the first-century Jewish philosopher Philo of Alexandria (c. 20 B.C.–A.D. 50).[60] The difficulty with such allegorizing was always the detachment of the biblical stories from their original historical setting. Timeless truths tended to replace the historical events of salvation. In T. F. Torrance's words: "Once these motifs and types became detached from history or were extracted from their setting in the actual narrative or context, they tended to become timeless ideas which could be artificially associated with or read into other texts through the allegorical principle of letting one idea stand symbolically for another."[61]

The concerns about divine violence in the atonement—both ancient and contemporary—are significant and should not be ignored. Contemporary contextual situations may alert us to certain aspects of the Christian faith that have been either underdeveloped or misconstrued in the past. If traditional atonement models have, perhaps unwittingly, contributed to cycles of abuse and brutality, it is imperative that we face the issues theologically. Even if we conclude that the charges against traditional atonement theology are based on caricatures or misunderstandings, this still does not absolve us from the responsibility to deal with the issues. The sheer number of articles and books in the last few decades implicating traditional models of the atonement in brutality and abuse make it necessary for us to reflect carefully on the issue.

Aware of the need to revisit atonement theology, a variety of scholars across the theological spectrum have attempted either to devise largely new ways of interpreting the cross or to revise elements from earlier theories so as to make them more palatable to a contemporary mind-set. Followers of René Girard, for instance, have presented an ingenious—albeit speculative—alternative un-

58. See R. M. Grant, *The Letter and the Spirit* (London: SPCK, 1957), 85–104; Bertrand de Margerie, *The Greek Fathers*, vol. 1 of *An Introduction to the History of Exegesis,* trans. Leonard Maluf (Petersham, Mass.: Saint Bede's, 1994), 79–116; Leo D. Lefebure, *Revelation*, 113–15.

59. Edwin Hatch, *The Influence of Greek Ideas and Usages upon the Christian Church*, ed. A. M. Fairbairn, 5th ed. (Peabody, Mass.: Hendrickson, 1995), 77.

60. Thomas F. Torrance, *Divine Meaning: Studies in Patristic Hermeneutics* (Edinburgh: T&T Clark, 1995), 22–25.

61. Ibid., 105.

derstanding of the cross, based on a mimetic anthropology.[62] Some scholars in the Anabaptist tradition have adopted a largely Abelardian approach but have attempted to remove the divine involvement in the cross from this approach in order to focus radically on the life of Jesus and his resurrection as the answer to human violence.[63] I question some of these attempts to solve the difficulties. But the critics correctly sense that if we want to have a God who is in no way associated with violence, we must at the very least revise significant elements of the three main atonement models in which God either makes a deal with the devil, deceives him, or himself gives his innocent Son over to die on the cross. We can only shield God from the violence of the cross at the cost of parting ways with the tradition of the Church.

Violence as Harm or Injury

When theologians express fear of "implicating" God in violence, such implication is clearly understood as a negative thing. It seems unthinkable—perhaps particularly in our late modern context—to associate God with violence. The problem of God and violence appears to us analogous to the problem of God and evil. We find it just as impossible to worship a God who is implicated in violence as to worship a God who is the author of evil. The underlying assumption in many discussions of divine violence appears to be that violence is inherently evil and immoral: a violent God necessarily leads to a violent society, since "what happens above happens below."[64] I suggest, however, that we need to test our sensibilities. In particular we need to ask whether violence is, under any and all circumstances, a morally negative thing.

The history of the Christian Church has hardly shown a consensus on the inherent negativity of violence. This is already evident in that none of the traditional atonement models have felt the need to absolve God from all violence. And by far the majority of theologians have argued that human violence also can, under certain circumstances, be justified and even be regarded as an act of love. St. Augustine (354–430), St. Thomas Aquinas (1225–74), and John Calvin (1509–64) all agreed that under certain circumstances acts of violence—such as war—are not only permitted but are required as acts of love.[65] To be sure, they

---

62. Walter Wink, *Engaging the Powers: Discernment and Resistance in a World of Domination* (Minneapolis: Fortress, 1992); James G. Williams, *The Bible, Violence, and the Sacred: Liberation from the Myth of Sanctioned Violence* (Valley Forge, Pa.: Trinity, 1995); Raymund Schwager, *Jesus in the Drama of Salvation* (New York: Crossroad, 1999); Anthony W. Bartlett, *Cross Purposes: The Violent Grammar of Christian Atonement* (Harrisburg, Pa.: Trinity, 2001). For further discussion, see chapter 6.

63. John Driver, *Understanding the Atonement for the Mission of the Church* (Scottdale, Pa.: Herald, 1986); Weaver, *Nonviolent Atonement*.

64. Wink, *Engaging the Powers*, 15.

65. Darrell Cole, "Good Wars," *First Things* 116 (October 2001): 27–31.

would distinguish between divine and human violence and between vengeance of the state (as a divine agent) and vengeance of individuals. Not all human violence and vengeance can be justified by an appeal to divine vengeance.[66] All the same, just-war theories stem from the assumption that sometimes violence is not only unavoidable but also positively required. Such an ethical stance likely grates our contemporary sensibilities, and it may therefore be helpful to subject our understanding of violence to some analysis.

Donald X. Burt defines a violent act as "any act which *contravenes the rights* of another. It can also be described as an act which *causes injury* to the life, property, or person of a human being, oneself, or others."[67] This definition makes clear that violence is extremely pervasive. First of all, there is both physical and nonphysical violence. We may contravene someone's rights and cause injury to someone in numerous ways. These means of violence need not necessarily be physical. Emotional abuse can be just as damaging as physical abuse—and at times even more so.[68] This point is crucial, because insistence on absolute nonviolence is often based on an arbitrary understanding of violence as something physical, so that we are willing to accept our involvement in other forms of coercion and force that often are no less invasive. Second, violence is not necessarily a direct act committed by one individual against another. Structures and institutions can be violent as well. Violence can be either personal or systemic. Political, legal, and economic systems can and do contribute to horrible suffering, so that violence pervades all areas of life. "No human beings can decide whether they even want to begin with violence," German theologian Wolfgang Huber writes, "for there is no situation totally devoid of violence."[69] People are involved in violence not only as the result of their individual decisions. They also are born in situations of violence and continue to perpetuate violent structures in their daily lives.

While it may never be fitting to contravene someone's rights, there may well be occasions when it is justifiable to injure someone. In his *Confessions,* Augustine argues that physical punishment may cause pain and may thus be

66. Miroslav Volf distinguishes between divine and human violence, justifying the former and rejecting the latter (*Exclusion and Embrace,* 301–4). He does not, however, distinguish between the role of the state and the role of the individual in delivering punishment (or vengeance) as a particular mode of violence. It seems to me that the Catholic and mainstream Protestant traditions rightly made the latter distinction, thereby justifying at least some human violence.

67. Donald X. Burt, *Friendship and Society: An Introduction to Augustine's Practical Philosophy* (Grand Rapids: Eerdmans, 1999), 162 (italics in the original).

68. Cf. Wolfgang Huber: "And even if physical injury is at the forefront of the concept of violence, the aspect of intentional mental injury can never be completely eliminated" (*Violence: The Unrelenting Assault on Human Dignity,* trans. Ruth C. L. Gritsch [Minneapolis: Fortress, 1996], 128). Leo D. Lefebure, relying on Craig L. Nessan's definition of violence, speaks of it as "the attempt of an individual or group to impose its will on others through any nonverbal, verbal, or physical means that inflict psychological or physical injury" (*Revelation,* 13).

69. Huber, *Violence,* 129.

injurious, but it is not therefore immoral. Reflecting on the punishment he received in his childhood, Augustine comments: "As a boy I began to pray to you, 'my help and my refuge' (Ps. 93:22), and for my prayer to you I broke the bonds of my tongue. Though I was only a small child, there was great feeling when I pleaded with you that I might not be caned at school. And when you did not hear me, which was so as 'not to give me to foolishness', . . . adult people, including even my parents, who wished no evil to come upon me, used to laugh at my stripes, which were at that time a great and painful evil to me."[70] We may or may not agree that physical punishment is a proper mode of discipline. The point remains the same: most people would agree that at least some punishments—whether physical or nonphysical—function in positive ways in the upbringing of our children. This discipline will invariably involve some immediate (nonphysical) injury; even a minor scolding causes some degree of emotional discomfort. But most of us recognize that a properly administered punishment is a good thing in the overall process of bringing up our children.

Am I right, however, in referring to corrective discipline—whether physical or nonphysical—as violence? Is it right to define *all* acts that cause some kind of injury as acts of violence? When I physically restrain my wife from crossing the street because I suddenly see a car speeding around the corner, am I acting violently? Or, to move to a nonphysical example, when the government forces my thirteen-year-old to attend school regularly, is the government acting violently? Some theologians don't think so. J. Denny Weaver, in his recent defense of a nonviolent atonement, offers a definition of violence similar to mine. He sees violence as causing harm or damage. This includes for him "physical harm or injury to bodily integrity" as well as systemic forms of violence, such as racism, sexism, and poverty. In other words, he does not restrict violence to physical violence. Remarkably, however, Weaver's understanding of violence does not include active nonphysical resistance (economic boycotts, strikes, etc.) or positive physical and nonphysical coercion, such as "physically restraining children from running into the street, knocking a person out of the path of a vehicle, and physically restraining a person attempting suicide."[71] Thus, Weaver wants to retain the possibility of active resistance without describing such activity as violent.

Weaver's advocacy of nonviolent resistance builds on Walter Wink's well-known advocacy of nonviolence in his book *Engaging the Powers*.[72] Here Wink attempts to establish a third way between just-war theories associated with

70. Aurelius Augustine, *Confessions*, trans. Henry Chadwick (Oxford: Oxford University Press, 1992), I.ix.14.

71. Weaver, *Nonviolent Atonement*, 9.

72. See also Wink's popularized version, *The Powers That Be: Theology for a New Millennium* (New York: Galilee-Doubleday, 1998).

Augustine and a radical pacifism or nonresistance that rejects all use of force or coercion. The cycle of revenge, argues Wink, is inherent in the use of violence: "Violence inculcates the longing for revenge, and for what the losers call 'justice.' And they will have learned from our example how to use violence more efficiently. *Violence can never stop violence because its very success leads others to imitate it.*"[73] Wink opposes all use of what he terms "redemptive violence." Still, he does not believe that this rejection of violence leaves us without any means of opposing evil. He argues that Jesus' "third way" beyond just war and pacifism is not "averse to using coercion. His way aims at converting the opponent; failing that, it hopes for accommodation, where the opponent is willing to make some changes simply to get the protesters off his back. But if that too fails, nonviolence entails coercion: the opponent is forced to make a change rather than suffer the loss of power, even though he remains hostile. But Jesus' way does not employ *violent* coercion."[74] Wink's nonviolent coercion takes on a rather militaristic tone when he not only speaks of "coercion" as a legitimate part of Jesus' "third way" but also refers to it as a "militant nonviolence" and a "highly aggressive nonviolence."[75] In fact, despite his opposition to the Augustinian just-war theory, Wink even wishes success to those who in desperation resort to counterviolence![76]

Two critical comments seem in order. First, it is not clear to me why Wink and Weaver insist so strongly on limiting active resistance to nonphysical methods, while condoning physical interference in other cases (such as stopping a child from crossing the street). By what standard would one term physical resistance to an enemy violent but physical interference to stop a person from committing suicide nonviolent? If my interference with a suicide takes the form of a physical encounter, is this not a form of violence? Most people would probably justify their (physical) interference with an appeal to the greater good of rescuing the suicidal person from death. In other words, some minor degree of physical harm may be necessary in this instance to avoid what we consider the horrible prospect of death. The physical harm that one inflicts in the process may well be justifiable, but that doesn't make it nonviolent. Clearly there are situations in which most people believe inflicting physical harm or injury is justified.

Second, Weaver argues that social structures that impose poverty are violent (and hence morally wrong), while economic boycotts and strikes can be acceptable nonviolent acts of resistance. Again, I might well agree with Weaver's moral evaluation in specific instances, but by what standard is the former

73. Wink, *Engaging the Powers,* 216 (italics in the original).

74. Ibid., 192 (italics in the original).

75. Ibid., 227.

76. Wink's suggestion that the victory of counterviolence might "usher in a better society" (ibid., 224) clashes with his notion that all violence is mimetic in character and is therefore always self-defeating.

violent and the latter nonviolent? Do economic boycotts not cause harm? Do strikes not cause harm? It seems to me that they do.[77] In fact, we employ these means precisely *because* they inflict harm. The point is that we find the harm acceptable under certain circumstances. It would be possible, of course, to refer only to morally reprehensible or unacceptable harm as violence—as long as we acknowledge that there are situations in which both physical and nonphysical harm are acceptable and even morally required. For the sake of consistency I think we should refer to *all* such acts of damage or injury (including the morally acceptable ones) as violence.

Any use of force or coercion that involves some kind of hurt or injury—whether the coercion is physical or nonphysical—is a form of violence. But it is not therefore morally reprehensible. Following St. Augustine, Burt suggests that violence may under certain circumstances be an act of "ordered love." The key is that the person performing the violent act must have in mind the lessening of violence: "For example, mandatory vaccination against small pox ('injurious' in the sense of being an invasion of bodily integrity and a lessening of individual freedom) may prevent a much greater quantity of 'injury' coming from a deadly plague."[78] Burt does not intend to glorify violence, but in true Augustinian fashion he argues against the notion that violence always begets more violence. In an imperfect world violence (the infliction of harm or injury) is at times the only option and as such a moral obligation and an act of love.

Even if the use of violence is necessary, it is, of course, still possible that people use it with the wrong motivation or in the wrong fashion. In his *Reply to Faustus the Manichaean,* St. Augustine comments: "The real evils in war are love of violence, revengeful cruelty, fierce and implacable enmity, wild resistance, and the lust of power, and such like; and it is generally to punish these things, when force is required to inflict the punishment, that, in obedience to God or some lawful authority, good men undertake wars, when they find themselves in such a position as regards the conduct of human affairs, that right conduct requires them to act, or to make others act in this way."[79] Augustine decries here the *love* of violence—not every act of violence as such—as something that must be opposed.[80] The Augustinian perspective would unequivocally condemn people engaging in violence out of purely sadistic pleasure or for the

---

77. Cf. Leo D. Lefebure, "Victims, Violence, and the Sacred: The Thought of René Girard," *The Christian Century* 113 (December 11, 1996): 1229: "At what point do economic sanctions that result in the deaths of children become an act of war? Buddhists pondering the First Precept note that if you boil water, you commit an act of violence against the microorganisms in it."

78. Burt, *Friendship and Society,* 164.

79. Aurelius Augustine, *Reply to Faustus the Manichaean,* in *Nicene and Post-Nicene Fathers,* First Series, trans. Richard Stothert, ed. Philip Schaff (1887; repr., Peabody, Mass.: Hendrickson, 1994), 4:301 (XXII.74).

80. Cf. C. S. Lewis, *Mere Christianity* (New York: Simon & Schuster, 1996), 107–8 (chap. 7).

satisfaction that retribution may offer. Not all violence is justified. Marjorie Suchocki makes a similar point when she argues that violence is sinful whenever it is unnecessary.[81] Violence may be unavoidable and even morally required under certain circumstances. But it should be avoided and countered as much as possible. Unnecessary injury is morally reprehensible. Justified violence, in an Augustinian paradigm, can be an act of love. What this means is that the practice of hospitality does not exclude all violence. Levinas and Derrida have already alerted us to the fact that in our world it is, strictly speaking, impossible to extend hospitality without at the same time also engaging in some violence. Now we see that a significant theological tradition argues that the use of this violence is not always wrong. If hospitality is to be practiced, doing so requires a certain degree of violence.

When we understand hospitality in this more fragile and limited sense, we can also make some sense of God's wrath in the biblical narrative. To be sure, if we see God's wrath simply as something that opposes his love, we end up with an arbitrary or even schizophrenic God in whom good and evil have positions of equal significance. God's hospitality and faithfulness would be compromised because of his anger and wrath. But fears of such a dualist understanding of God should not tempt us into ignoring the biblical expressions of God's wrath. It won't do, for instance, to interpret God's wrath as a metaphor that does not truly bespeak a reality. Joel Green and Mark Baker go in this direction when they suggest that "perhaps we attribute 'anger' to God only because we have no language other than human language with which to comprehend God."[82] But the restrictions of human language cannot so easily be reserved for particular characteristics of God that we find less appealing. To say that anger as applied to God is metaphorical sounds as if it were *just* metaphorical and hence somehow less real. But isn't all language about God metaphorical?[83] Can we speak about God at all without using metaphorical language? In the next chapters I discuss notions of victory, of exchange, of punishment, and so on. In the use of all these words, we employ metaphors derived from our everyday lives. The various models of the atonement all base themselves on these metaphors. The biblical use of metaphors to describe the meaning of the cross does not somehow make them less valuable or less real. They are not *just* metaphors. Colin Gunton has argued cogently that in metaphors we encounter "linguistic usages which demand a new way of thinking about and living in the world. Here is *real* sacrifice, victory and justice, so that what we thought the words meant

---

81. Suchocki, *Fall into Violence*, 95. I have my reservations about Suchocki's underlying foundation of process theology.

82. Green and Baker, *Recovering the Scandal*, 54.

83. Cf. Tony Lane, "The Wrath of God as an Aspect of the Love of God," in *Nothing Greater, Nothing Better: Theological Essays on the Love of God*, ed. Kevin J. Vanhoozer (Grand Rapids: Eerdmans, 2001), 145.

is shown to be inadequate and in need of reshaping by that to which the language refers."[84] It is the same when we speak about God's wrath. Here is "real" wrath that in turn forges the way in which we understand "wrath" in our everyday lives.[85]

It is probably more fruitful, therefore, to understand the relationship between God's love and his wrath along the same lines as the relationship between divine hospitality and divine violence. Just as divine hospitality requires at least some violence to make it flourish, so also God's love requires that he become angry when his love is violated. For God not to get angry when he is rejected by people made in his image (and redeemed in Christ) would demonstrate indifference, not love. When God steps into a world of injustice, he shows his love in particular ways. H. G. L. Peels therefore comments in his study on the wrath of God: "It would show little love for his people if the ruler were to ignore the lot of his subjects. . . . This is also evident in the vengeance texts."[86] Love, it seems, requires passionate anger toward anything that would endanger the relationship of love.

God's hospitality requires violence, just as his love necessitates wrath. This is not to say, of course, that God's violence and wrath are his essential attributes. God *is* love, not wrath; he *is* a God of hospitality, not a God of violence. There is an absolute primacy, therefore, of hospitality over violence. Hospitality bespeaks the very essence of God, while violence is merely one of the ways to safeguard or ensure the future of his hospitality when dealing with the humps and bumps of our lives. Divine violence, in other words, is a way in which God strives toward an eschatological situation of pure hospitality. To use Derrida's terminology, conditional hospitality is necessary in this life to safeguard the eschatological reality of pure, unconditional hospitality. All limitations in the expressions of God's hospitality here on earth will be overcome once we share in his eternal hospitable love.

Earlier I criticized postmodern reflections on hospitality for their impatience. Derrida works with a utopian understanding of hospitality structured around a messianicity that rejects any conditionality, any determinacy, and any horizon of expectation. Derrida, like Levinas, insists on the eschaton here and now. Both replace ontology with eschatology.[87] Levinas and Derrida place us before the impossible demand of a pure hospitality that, from a Christian perspec-

84. Colin E. Gunton, *The Actuality of Atonement: A Study of Metaphor, Rationality, and the Christian Tradition* (Grand Rapids: Eerdmans, 1989), 51–52.

85. For a more in-depth discussion on the role of metaphors, see chapter 4.

86. H. G. L. Peels, *The Vengeance of God: The Meaning of the Root NQM and the Function of the NQM-Texts in the Context of Divine Revelation in the Old Testament*, trans. William Koopmans (Leiden: Brill, 1995), 293.

87. Cf. Patrick R. Keifert on Levinas: the "face-to-face presents the other as the inbreaking of the Infinite, the eschatological rather than being or becoming" ("The Other: Hospitality to the Stranger, Levinas, and Multicultural Mission," *Dialog* 30 [1] [1991]: 39).

tive, is still to come—and, in fact, *will* come. But this hospitality remains, in important ways, a future reality.

Although we should not follow Levinas and Derrida in essentially substituting eschatology for ontology, it is nonetheless true that eschatology helps us to give shape to hospitality in our lives. Christ is the first fruits of a resurrection harvest that has already begun (Rom. 8:23; 1 Cor. 15:23). In isolation the cross is not enough to bring about God's absolute or pure hospitality. On this side of the eschaton, God's hospitality consistently entails violence. The resurrection ensures that this divine violence, including God's violence on the cross, is a redemptive violence. The age to come—God's pure hospitality—has already broken into the present age by means of the resurrection of Christ. The violence of the cross thus finds its ultimate justification in the resurrection of Christ—the inbreaking of God's absolute hospitality.

The consequence of this irruption of God's eschatological hospitality is that believers find themselves in the overlap of the ages.[88] While the limits of the present age still place their conditions on this hospitality, through the Spirit believers already share in Christ's resurrection life—in the eschatological, absolute hospitality of the age to come. The Christian thus always lives in a tension between the "already" and the "not yet." As James Dunn puts it: "Fundamental to Paul's conception of the process of salvation . . . is his conviction that the believer has not yet arrived, is not yet perfect, is always *in via,* in transit. It is this which determines the experience of 'being saved' as a process of 'eschatological tension'—the tension between a work 'begun' but not 'complete,' between fulfillment and consummation, between a decisive 'already' and a still to be worked out 'not yet.'"[89] The eschatological tension means that, on the one hand, Christians continue to operate with the limitations and the violence of the present age, while on the other hand, the Christian community is a community stamped by the resurrection life of Jesus Christ. "Since you have been raised up to be with Christ, you must look for the things that are above, where Christ is, sitting at God's right hand" (Col. 3:1). God's absolute hospitality in Christ keeps beckoning us. It must give shape to the Christian life, though in a way that is moderated by the present conditions. The absolute nonviolence of God's eschaton—his pure hospitality—is always calling us to implement a hospitality that reduces violence as much as possible and promotes the kingdom of eternal justice and peace.

So far, I have argued that we need to practice hospitality with an eye to the future of God's pure hospitality in which violence will no longer have a place. Such a practice necessarily involves violence. But that does not turn our acts of hospitality into acts of violence. The same is the case with God's activity in the world. Although his acts of hospitality involve violence, this does not

88. James D. G. Dunn, *The Theology of Paul the Apostle* (Grand Rapids: Eerdmans, 1998), 464–65.
89. Ibid., 465.

mean that they are so permeated by violence that we can no longer recognize the beckoning future of God's eternal, pure hospitality. As long as we restrain violence as much as possible and only employ it in the interest of God's eschatological, undeconstructible justice, violence is a necessary and acceptable accompaniment both of God's and of our practice of hospitality. Throughout the remainder of this book, I argue that this is what we see on the cross: divine hospitality, despite the presence also of divine violence. Before we turn to a discussion of the various models of the atonement, however, we need to ask whether biblical expressions of hospitality leading up to the cross are truly examples of hospitality, or whether we are forced to admit that the historical expressions of divine hospitality do not rise above the level of "hospitable narcissism." Is the sovereignty of God's electing grace toward some—and his exclusion of others—compatible with the relationship between hospitality and violence as I have sketched it here? Or does predestination yield a God who violently forces his grace on some, while tyrannically rejecting others? In the next two chapters, I discuss several questions surrounding the triad of election, violence, and hospitality.

2

Limited Hospitality

Election and Violence in Eternity

Divine Violence and Predestination

Divine violence may at times be necessary to ensure a hospitable future. The account of the Fall teaches us that God is not involved with a pristine humanity whose moral integrity has remained unscathed. In Jesus Christ he confronts a world that is prone to violence and sin. To expect that in such historical circumstances God could correct evil in consistently nonviolent ways is to underestimate the persistence and power of evil. In certain situations the only morally upright act would be for God to forcefully oppose violence. Particularly when human beings violently flaunt their rejection of God's hospitality, God needs to set boundaries, precisely in the name of hospitality. We could go even further and argue that when God enters into time and space (under the conditions of the present age), he accepts its limitations, including the limitations to hospitality. I argued in chapter 1 that hospitality in our world can only be hospitality when it is accompanied by the violence of certain boundaries, including those of time and space.[1] Thus, when God extends his hospitality

---

1. I want to make clear that time and space necessarily involve violence *only* in the current historical circumstances. I believe (against Gnosticism) that in our glorified eschatological mode of existence, time and space continue—but they are no longer accompanied by any restrictions (or violence) because of the presence (the unconditional hospitality) of God.

to us, it is a hospitality characterized by some conditionality and violence. The violence resulting from the implementation of creational boundaries is necessary for God to embody hospitality in our world.

The Christian faith does not, however, commit to a God who has violence inscribed in the heart of his being. The God who encounters us in the cross of Jesus is a hospitable God, a God who avoids violence wherever possible. The essence of God is unbounded love, pure hospitality. God intends to embody this hospitality wherever possible and works toward its full eschatological realization. Theology, therefore, should not reify divine violence in the sense of locating it in the heart of God. The circumstances under which divine violence might be justified need to be clearly delineated. It would be difficult to worship a God who would engage in violence at whim. Attempts to justify divine violence could easily degenerate into a plea for divine arbitrariness. This would make it impossible for us to rely on God's faithfulness and trustworthiness in Jesus Christ and would squelch our hope of sharing in God's unconditional eschatological hospitality.

The meaning and purpose of the cross are often traced back to God's eternal plan of predestination. Thus, the cross can easily be overshadowed by our belief in predestination. When this happens, divine violence overtakes and ultimately eliminates divine hospitality. This is by no means an imaginary problem. Radical predestinarian theology has been a consistent and influential subculture within the larger Christian tradition. Notions of predestination and election are usually associated with the theology of John Calvin (1509–64) and with later Calvinist theology. Calvin's God appears to many as a harsh, arbitrary God, eternally choosing some for salvation (election) and condemning others to damnation (reprobation). The violence this implies seems replicated in the violent way in which Calvin disposed of those who disagreed with him, either on the issue of predestination or on other theological matters.[2] It seems clear that the place of election and reprobation in Calvin and in later Calvinism has done little to boost Calvinism's popular image.

There are nonetheless some important reasons to sound a cautionary note before engaging in a critique of Calvinist notions of predestination. First, the Calvinist understanding of predestination stands in a long tradition that emphasizes the sovereignty of God's grace and the human inability to attain salvation simply by means of natural endowments and merely external assistance. Calvin's emphasis goes back at least to the father of the Western Church, Augustine (354–430), while Thomas Aquinas (1225–74) also held to double predestination.[3] In the late Middle Ages several theologians in the Augustinian

2. Cf. Philip C. Holtrop, *The Bolsec Controversy on Predestination from 1551 to 1555: The Statements of Jerome Bolsec, and the Responses of John Calvin, Theodore Beza, and Other Reformed Theologians* (Lewiston, N.Y.: Edwin Mellen, 1993), 275–95.

3. Double predestination is the view that from eternity God has decreed the ultimate destiny of each individual, whether eternal life (election) or eternal damnation (reprobation).

tradition emphasized double predestination in their opposition to what they saw as Pelagian tendencies in the nominalist school of thought.[4] Furthermore, Calvin was not the only Reformer holding to double predestination. As is well known, Luther's comments on the topic could be quite strong and uncompromising as well. Even Arminius (1560–1609) held to double predestination from eternity, although he didn't accept the way in which Calvinists lined up the order of God's eternal decrees.[5] Calvin and his followers are essentially the heirs to the right wing of the Augustinian tradition, a tradition that has always had a place—and at times a prominent one—in the universal Church.

Second, in any critique of the Calvinist understanding of predestination it is necessary to do justice at least to its intention. An important function of the doctrine of election is precisely to safeguard the hospitality of God. Divine election is God's determination to extend his grace, so it is the sovereignty of *grace* that Calvin is concerned with when he discusses predestination. The doctrine of predestination exalts, for Calvin, the mercy of God, who accepts alienated strangers into fellowship with him and so brings them into his eternal home. In the very first paragraph of his discussion on election, Calvin comments: "We shall never be clearly persuaded, as we ought to be, that our salvation flows from the wellspring of God's free mercy until we come to know his eternal election."[6] Calvin rejects the idea that God elects people on the basis of foreseen faith precisely because of his desire to uphold God's hospitality. A strict economy of exchange would base election on human works or holiness. Calvin, in opposition to what he considers Roman Catholic notions of works righteousness, insists that our relationship with God is not based on human merit. Instead, God is the hospitable God who sovereignly and graciously adopts us and brings us into fellowship with him. There is for Calvin no rationale for God's election beyond his generous hospitality: "[T]he cause does not appear except that Moses, to cut off from posterity any occasion to boast, teaches that they excel solely by God's freely given love."[7]

Third, we also need to remember that the difficulty of divine violence, which seems implied in double predestination, does not necessarily disappear by giving up this notion altogether. Some of the alternatives may seem more palatable, but they do not necessarily resolve the issue of divine violence. We may be tempted, for example, to give up the idea of reprobation as the dark side

---

4. I am following the common denotation of the theology of medieval theologians like William Ockham and Gabriel Biel as "nominalist." McGrath has pointed out that this appellation may not be entirely accurate. See Alister E. McGrath, "The Anti-Pelagian Structure of 'Nominalist' Doctrines of Justification," *Ephemerides Theologicae Lovanienses* 57 (1981): 107–19.

5. Cf. Stanley J. Grenz and John R. Franke, *Beyond Foundationalism: Shaping Theology in a Postmodern Context* (Louisville: Westminster John Knox, 2001), 262–65.

6. John Calvin, *Institutes of the Christian Religion*, ed. John T. McNeill, trans. Ford Lewis Battles, 2 vols. (Philadelphia: Westminster, 1960), III.xxi.1.

7. Ibid., III.xxi.5.

of predestination, but this would still leave us with an eternal divine decision to choose some people out of the mass of the human race and to give them (and only them!) eternal life. Another avenue—one that I will pursue in the next chapter—is to redefine election in historical rather than eternal terms. Such a solution indeed relieves us of the harsh violence implied in eternal double predestination, but we may still be left wondering whether it gives us the universal equality and justice that we hope to find in the God to whom we render our worship and entrust our lives.

There is something about the particularity of the biblical account that allows us neither to circumvent nor to solve disconcerting questions about violence and election. One of the laudable elements of Calvin's theology is his awareness of the need for humility in the face of the mystery of God's being.[8] Therefore, although my exploration of the interface between violence and election will lead to some serious criticism of Calvin and in particular of later Calvinism, this criticism is not directed against the notion that God is involved with violence. The only way to solve the problem of violence and election logically in an absolutely consistent fashion is by adopting some kind of neo-Marcionite position and by radically opposing the God of peace whom we know in Jesus to the Old Testament warrior god, Yahweh. Calvinism has at least realized that the question of violence and election cannot be solved by means of a rationally satisfying theodicy.

In this chapter I discuss the relationship between divine hospitality and the Calvinist understanding of double predestination. I argue that the Calvinist understanding of double predestination draws divine violence from history into the heart of God and thereby undermines his unconditional hospitality. I begin with an exposition of predestination in Calvin and later high Calvinism, where election (as something eternal, individual, and futuristic in orientation) has become the driving force of much theologizing. I argue that especially in later Calvinism the violence of God's absolute will overshadows the hospitality of his revealed will. Next, I discuss how, as a result, Calvinist theologians have limited God's hospitality on the cross to those whom he has elected from eternity (limited atonement). I conclude that for high Calvinism, God's love is a violent love that forces some individual strangers into the Father's mansions while excluding others from his hospitality because of his eternal decree of reprobation.

Calvin and Later Calvinism on Predestination

John Calvin describes predestination as "God's eternal decree, by which he compacted with himself what he willed to become of each man. For all are

---

8. Ibid., III.xxi.1.

not created in equal condition; rather, eternal life is foreordained for some, eternal damnation for others."[9] This brief definition contains three significant characteristics. First, predestination is an eternal decree of God. That is to say, predestination is not an act of God in time or in history. It is not that Calvin does not know about historical election or does not refer to it. In fact, he distinguishes three stages (*gradus*) of election: the first is God's election of the nation Israel, the second is his election of individual Israelites, and the third is his eternal election of individuals to salvation.[10] Whereas the first two are historical choices, the latter is an eternal decision made by God. And it is this decision from eternity that constitutes predestination in the proper sense of the word. Calvin employs the eternal character of predestination by way of an anti-Catholic polemic. If election is from eternity, then God does not elect or reprobate people after they have been born and have made all sorts of positive and negative moral commitments. Calvin discusses at length the Pauline example of Jacob and Esau and cautions his readers not "to evade the apostle's contention that the distinction between the brothers depends not upon any basis of works but upon the mere calling of God, because it was established between them before they were born."[11] Neither God's election of Jacob nor his reprobation of Esau had anything to do with their actions. The timing of election—"before the world was made," according to Ephesians 1:4—implies for Calvin that "Paul sets 'God's good pleasure' over against any merits of ours."[12] Salvation, in other words, is not based on good works. Calvin is clearly concerned to stave off any moralizing Catholic sentiments from his doctrine of election.

Second, predestination is for Calvin an individual matter. "God compacted with himself what he willed to become *of each man*," Calvin maintains. Again, the Genevan Reformer is aware of the Old Testament background of election, in which the *nation* of Israel is the object of God's electing love: "The separation is apparent to all men: in the person of Abraham, as in a dry tree trunk, one people is peculiarly chosen, while the others are rejected."[13] But Calvin does not let this corporate sense of election determine his exegesis of the New Testament. While he does not deny the historical election of Jacob and Esau as ancestors of particular nations, these two individuals nonetheless take on the function of types or models of individual election and reprobation: "God willed by an earthly symbol to declare Jacob's spiritual election, which otherwise lay hid in his inaccessible judgment seat." Jacob's election was a "spiritual elec-

9. Ibid., III.xxi.5.
10. Ibid., III.xxi.5–7.
11. Ibid., III.xxii.4.
12. Ibid., III.xxii.1.
13. Ibid., III.xxi.5 (italics added).

tion," and the rights that came to him along with the position of the firstborn referred to "the age to come."[14]

Interpreting Jacob and Esau as types of individual predestination means that Calvin not only embraces election as the positive aspect of predestination, but that he also accepts reprobation as its negative counterpart: "For all are not created in equal condition; rather, eternal life is foreordained for some, eternal damnation for others." Calvin is convinced of double predestination (*predestinatio gemina*) since "election itself could not stand except as set over against reprobation."[15] In other words, the notion of election logically demands the notion of reprobation. Calvin is also convinced that certain biblical texts—seen through the lens of individual predestination—imply an eternal decree of reprobation (Rom. 9:22–23; 1 Pet. 2:8).

Third, Calvin's definition has an emphatically futuristic orientation. The purpose or telos of election and reprobation is salvation and damnation, respectively. God decreed "what he willed to become" of each individual, whether that be "eternal life" or "eternal damnation." It is not as though Calvin rejects intermediate goals and denies that elect individuals have a responsibility to do good works; the work of the Holy Spirit and sanctification play an important role in his theology, and Calvin recognizes that there is a sense in which "election has as its goal holiness."[16] Nonetheless, this purpose is at the most an intermediate purpose. It speaks volumes that Calvin feels the need to defend himself against the objections that predestination would destroy all zeal for an upright life and that it would make admonitions useless.[17] In the overall pattern of his thought, predestination is not geared toward the Christian life but toward the eternal future of every individual.

To be sure, Calvin's theology contains several elements that soften the impact of his approach. He does not put all his cards on the secret will of God, which has cast in stone the eternal future of each and every individual. While confessing and also preaching predestination as the ultimate and hidden will of God, Calvin refuses to let this hidden will of God's good pleasure (*voluntas beneplaciti*) set the agenda for the preacher. Calvin wants to give due acknowledgment also to the presence of God's revealed or signified will (*voluntas signi*). Calvin inherited this distinction between God's hidden and his revealed will from medieval scholastic theologians. Throughout his *Institutes* the Reformer attempts to tread the fine line between these two aspects of God's will.[18] Despite the prominence of predestination in Calvin's preaching as well as in his

14. Ibid., III.xxii.6.
15. Ibid., III.xxiii.1.
16. Ibid., III.xxiii.12.
17. Ibid., III.xxiii.12–13.
18. Calvin explicitly rejects separating these two aspects of God's will into two separate wills, though the tension is palpable throughout his writings. Cf. John Calvin, *Concerning the Eternal Predestination of God*, trans. J. K. S. Reid (Louisville: Westminster John Knox, 1997), 182–83.

political struggles, it would not be entirely fair to say that it is the unifying element behind his theology. Predestination is not the controlling element that binds together his thinking. Calvin centers his *Institutes* on the doctrine of the Trinity—one book for each Person of the Trinity—and this prevents his theology from being entirely consumed by predestinarian concerns.

This impression is reinforced by the fact that Calvin never loses sight of Jesus Christ in connection with election. As the second Person of the Trinity, Christ is the electing God, the subject or "author" of election. As mediator Christ is the elect, the chosen object of God's election. God makes our election certain through Christ's role as mediator. We should, therefore, never view our election as separate from Christ's election. God has united us to Christ, which means that Christ is the "mirror" of our election.[19] This christological concern explains Calvin's repeated warnings against too much curiosity and speculation about election. These warnings are not meant to imply that predestination is a doctrine about which he is unsure and therefore does not want to speculate. We have already seen that Calvin is quite explicit in his assertions about double predestination. Rather, his reticence stems from a pastoral sensitivity. Aware that his stark theory of predestination may conjure up fears of an arbitrary and violent God of whose favors we can never be sure, Calvin cautions against "wandering in forbidden bypaths,"[20] against the "labyrinth of predestination."[21] Thus, Calvin adjures his readers to cling to what God has revealed about himself in his Word: "And let us not be ashamed to be ignorant of something in this matter, wherein there is a certain learned ignorance [*docta ignorantia*]."[22]

Calvin may not be the harsh predestinarian theologian he is sometimes portrayed to be, but it is nonetheless clear that later high Calvinism could build on much of his thought and did not have to alter his understanding of predestination a great deal in order to make it the driving force of later Reformed orthodoxy.[23] The much debated shift from Calvin to later Calvinism is probably less a change in predestinarian doctrine as such than a shift in the

---

19. Calvin, *Institutes*, III.xxi.7; xxv.5. Cf. Jaroslav Pelikan, "The Mirror of the Eternal," in *Jesus through the Centuries: His Place in the History of Culture* (New Haven, Conn.: Yale University Press, 1985), 157–67; C. Graafland, *Van Calvijn tot Barth: Oorsprong en ontwikkeling van de leer der verkiezing in het Gereformeerd Protestantisme* (The Hague, Neth.: Boekencentrum, 1987), 35–41.

20. Calvin, *Institutes*, III.xxi.1.

21. John Calvin, *The Gospel according to St. John 1–10,* trans. T. H. L. Parker, ed. David W. Torrance and Thomas F. Torrance (Grand Rapids: Eerdmans, 1959), 162 (*Comm.* John 6:40). Cf. François Wendel, "Justification and Predestination in Calvin," in *Readings in Calvin's Theology,* ed. Donald K. McKim (Grand Rapids: Baker, 1984), 166.

22. Calvin, *Institutes*, III.xxi.2.

23. High Calvinism developed out of Calvinism in the late sixteenth and seventeenth centuries and is usually understood to indicate a theological emphasis that (1) turned predestination into the central theological doctrine; (2) strictly limited Christ's atonement to the elect only; (3) developed clearly defined outlines of the order of salvation (*ordo salutis*); and (4) tended toward a doctrine of assurance of faith based on so-called practical and mystical syllogisms.

relative significance accorded to this doctrine in the late sixteenth and early seventeenth centuries.[24]

Already in Calvin we find the notion that God's hidden will determines the actual events in history and is, in a real sense, the "true will" of God.[25] Although there is a general election of the people of Israel, this does not determine the ultimate salvation of individuals in the nation of Israel. This general election merely belongs to the revealed will of God. It is God's special election of individuals that in the end counts for one's salvation.[26] Just as there is a general and a special election, so there is also a twofold calling. The one is merely external, by the Word. Not everyone who hears the Word receives true faith. To be effective, the external calling of the Word needs to be coupled with an internal calling of the Spirit.[27] The former is an expression of God's common grace.[28] The latter is an extension of his special grace to the elect only. Those who never experience the working of the Spirit may have the general adoption as children of God, but they do not have the special adoption that comes through the gift of the Spirit and enables them to call on God as their Father.[29] The conclusion must follow that God extends dual grace: a common, externally offered grace and the special, internal grace of the Holy Spirit. This consistent oscillating between general and special election, between external and internal calling, between general and special adoption, and between common and special grace can be traced back to Calvin's distinction between the hidden and the revealed will of God (table 1).

Whereas God's revealed will is communal (with God wanting everyone to follow his law), his hidden will concerns the outcome of the lives of specific individuals. Whereas the external preaching of the Word extends to many (though not all), the inward working of the Spirit is limited to those who have been chosen from eternity. Whereas the outward call merely leads to a general

24. For the debate on the relationship between Calvinism and later Calvinism, see Basil Hall, "Calvin against the Calvinists," in *John Calvin,* ed. G. E. Duffield (Grand Rapids: Eerdmans, 1966), 19–37; Brian G. Armstrong, *Calvinism and the Amyraut Heresy: Protestant Scholasticism and Humanism in Seventeenth-Century France* (Madison: University of Wisconsin Press, 1969); Tony Lane, "The Quest for the Historical Calvin," *Evangelical Quarterly* 55 (1983): 95–113; Richard A. Muller, "Calvin and the 'Calvinists': Assessing the Continuities and Discontinuities between the Reformation and Orthodoxy," *Calvin Theological Journal* 30 (1995): 345–75; 31 (1996): 125–60.

25. Calvin repeatedly argues that God merely accommodates himself to us in his revealed will. See Hans Boersma, "Calvin and the Extent of the Atonement," *Evangelical Quarterly* 64 (1992): 348–49.

26. Anthony Hoekema, "The Covenant of Grace in Calvin's Teaching," *Calvin Theological Journal* 2 (1967): 151.

27. Calvin, *Institutes,* III.xxiv.8. Calvin makes the point, however, that the Spirit "also causes those whom he illumines only for a time to partake of it [i.e., the special, inward call]."

28. Since God does not make the preaching of the gospel common to everyone, there are differences of degree even within common grace. Cf. Calvin, *Eternal Predestination,* 109; *Institutes,* II.iii.4.

29. Cf. C. Graafland, *Van Calvijn tot Comrie: Oorsprong en ontwikkeling van de leer van het verbond in het Gereformeerd Protestantisme* (Zoetermeer, Neth.: Boekencentrum, 1992), 1:99–101.

Table 1
Calvin and the Twofold Will of God

Revealed Will	Hidden Will
Communal	Individual
External (Word)	Internal (Spirit)
Impersonal	Personal
Conditional	Unconditional

adoption and thus remains impersonal, adoption through the gift of faith means an intimate and mystical union with Christ. Finally, whereas the preaching of God's revealed will is always accompanied by the demand of faith, God's electing will is unconditional and absolutely certain, so that all who have been granted the special grace of God's Spirit will persevere till the end.

The hidden will of God may not be the unifying element of Calvin's thought, but in a real sense this hidden will is his ultimate concern. The hospitality of God is constantly in danger of being overshadowed by the violent tyranny of the hidden will of God looming over the heads of the faithful. Calvin is aware of the objection that reprobation "is more like the caprice of a tyrant than the lawful sentence of a judge." In his defense, Calvin makes the will of God his ultimate court of appeal: "For God's will is so much the highest rule of righteousness that whatever he wills, by the very fact that he wills it, must be considered righteous."[30] God appears to will things not because they are just, but they are just because God wills them. It is difficult to escape the idea that God stands outside the law (*ex lex*).[31] Certainly, by exalting God's will in such an absolute fashion, Calvin obscures the hospitality of God in Christ. The hidden will takes precedence over the revealed will. Violence trumps hospitality.[32]

It was up to Calvin's successors to take these developments one step further. Not content with keeping predestination as the ultimate concern of God's hidden will, they turned it into the unifying element of their theology. This shift is perhaps most dramatically illustrated by a well-known "table" in Theodore Beza's 1555 publication, *Summa totius Christianismi* (figure 1). In this diagram Calvin's successor in Geneva, Theodore Beza (1519–1605), summarized the entire Christian faith under the rubric of predestination. It is worthwhile to pay some attention to this chart, because it provided the faithful with a handy catechetical tool that assisted them in quickly grasping the central truths of the Reformed faith. Its popularity was guaranteed when in 1590 the Elizabethan Puritan William Perkins

30. Calvin, *Institutes,* III.xxiii.2.

31. Cf. Graafland, *Van Calvijn tot Barth,* 28.

32. I do not mean to give the impression that I equate God's revealed will with a Derridean type of absolute hospitality (which I take to be reserved for the eschaton). I do, however, want to argue that God's revealed will expresses something that we legitimately call "hospitality" despite the necessity of it being tinged with violence under the conditions of our current time/space universe.

(1558–1602) adopted it with minor modifications in his *Golden Chaine.* Beza refers to the diagram, which takes its starting point in double predestination, as a "summary of the entire Christian faith." By turning predestination into the heart of Reformed theology, Beza placed the emphasis where Calvin's Trinitarian theology had never quite located it.[33] In his chart Beza outlined an entire order of salvation (*ordo salutis*), beginning with God's eternal decrees and ending with eternal life for the elect and eternal death for the reprobates. Calvin had always stopped short of outlining a standard order of salvation.[34] Beza, however, systematized his predecessor's thought and carefully worked his way from election, via calling, conversion, faith, justification, and sanctification, to glorification and eternal life. The result was an emphasis on the observable interior psychological development of the Christian life, which would lead to a great deal of psychological self-assessment and self-examination among later Puritan and Reformed believers. The lack of assurance and the trepidation about participating in communion that crept in among the high Calvinist segments of the Reformed tradition can be traced directly to Beza's emphasis on an observable order of salvation. His chart gave the theological justification for this inward turn.

The uncertainty and fear of being on the wrong side of the chart were reinforced by the notion of an "ineffectual calling," which Beza connected with temporary faith. Reprobates might have many signs that would appear to indicate God had called them, too. Yet in reality this calling was not a true calling. Their love of God's Word, their desire for Christian fellowship, and their zeal to do good works might all seem to indicate the presence of God's special grace and effectual calling, but these visible signs were merely the result of an ineffectual calling that did not lead to true conversion and true faith. In due time this would become evident, when people with an ineffectual calling would harden their hearts and thereby show that they had never been inwardly called by the Spirit of God. Their call had merely been an external one. Those who were truly and inwardly called would always and necessarily persevere in their faith.[35] The horribly difficult question now became "how to distinguish a weak but true faith from a strong but temporary one."[36] As a

---

33. Graafland, *Van Calvijn tot Barth,* 53. The Canons of Dort (1619) are closer to Calvin than to Beza with regard to double predestination. They adopt an explicitly infralapsarian approach, placing the eternal decree of reprobation after the decrees of Creation and the Fall (I.15), thereby moderating somewhat the impression of arbitrary divine violence.

34. C. Graafland, "Heeft Calvijn een bepaalde orde des heils geleerd?" in *Verbi Divini Minister,* ed. J. van Oort (Amsterdam: Bolland, 1983), 109–27; J. Von Rohr, *The Covenant of Grace in Puritan Thought* (Atlanta: Scholars, 1986).

35. Again, all these notions (temporary vs. true faith, outward vs. inward calling, perseverance of the saints) had already been taught by Calvin but had not been placed in a highly systematized scheme centering on the doctrine of predestination.

36. Peter White, *Predestination, Policy, and Polemic: Conflict and Consensus in the English Church from the Reformation to the Civil War* (Cambridge: Cambridge University Press, 1992), 21.

Figure 1
Theodore Beza's *Tabula* (1555)

The sum total of the Christian faith,

Or a description and distribution of the causes of election and reprobation, gathered from the Holy Scriptures

God, whose ways are incomprehensible

His eternal and immutable purpose, preceding also in order all causes, whereby in himself he decreed from eternity certain persons to his glory

| Election to salvation in Christ | Creation of humankind in an upright but mutable state | Reprobation to damnation through their own fault |

Man's corruption spontaneous and contingent

| God's gratuitous love for those corrupt in themselves, but freely destined in Christ to election and salvation. | God's just hatred for those corrupt in themselves through the propagation of sin through Adam. |

Effectual calling

| No calling | Ineffectual calling |

Softening or conversion out of pure grace

Spontaneous hardening

Faith

| Ignorance of the gospel | Contempt of the offer of the gospel |

Justification by imputation and incomplete sanctification

Unrighteousness and pollution

God's judgment on both

| Glorification of the justified in Christ | Just damnation of sinners |

God's judgment on both groups

| Eternal life by crowning in Christ's members also his obedience freely imputed to them | Just punishment of eternal death by penalizing sinners |

The glory of God, the supremely merciful and the supremely severe, in accordance with his eternal decree

O depth of God's judgments! Who has first given to him that he would recompense it to him?
Rom. 11:36.

result of this Bezan approach, a nagging doubt began to creep in among the Reformed communities.

Limiting Atonement and Hospitality: John Calvin

By emphasizing the revealed will of God and by encouraging his readers to turn to Christ for the grounding of their election, Calvin injected into his theology an element of hospitality for which he is not often known. I remember being startled when, in my undergraduate studies, I first came across R. T. Kendall's 1979 publication, *Calvin and English Calvinism to 1649*. Growing up in the Reformed tradition, I had simply assumed that Calvin taught limited atonement. Kendall challenged this assumption with the claim, made at the outset of his study, that in Calvin's view Christ died for every single individual: "Fundamental to the doctrine of faith in John Calvin (1509–64) is his belief that Christ died indiscriminately for all men. Equally crucial, however, is his conviction that, until faith is given, 'all that He has suffered and done for the salvation of the human race remains useless and of no value for us.'"[37] Kendall assumes that Calvin makes a sharp distinction between Christ's death (being universal), on the one hand, and the human appropriation of the value of Christ's death (being limited), on the other hand.[38]

The initial shock about what Calvin may actually have taught has disappeared through a more in-depth study, both of Calvin's teaching on this issue and of the larger historical developments within which Calvin made his contribution. Indeed, further exploration of Calvin studies quickly shows that Kendall's bold statement has by no means gone unchallenged. Calvin scholars have embarked on a heated debate on the question of limited versus universal atonement, especially since the publication of Kendall's book. The reason, both for my initial bewilderment and for the heated nature of the discussions, is obvious. If Calvin indeed taught universal redemption, this would place him in the Arminian rather than in the Calvinist camp—at least on the question of the extent of the atonement. The underlying question is, therefore, Was Calvin really a Calvinist?[39]

---

37. R. T. Kendall, *Calvin and English Calvinism to 1649*, rev. ed. (Carlisle, UK: Paternoster, 1997), 13. Kendall's quote is taken from Calvin, *Institutes,* III.i.1.

38. It is important to distinguish between universal atonement (or universal redemption) and universal salvation. The former means that Christ died for everyone, and the latter goes a step further and says that everyone will reach eternal salvation. While some scholars will argue that Calvin held to universal atonement, none argue that he believed in universal salvation.

39. This rhetorical question pertains only to the question of the extent of the atonement. There is no real disagreement among scholars that Calvin clearly held to the other Calvinist distinctives, such as total depravity, unconditional election, irresistible grace, and perseverance of the saints.

Much of the discussion has unfortunately focused on explicit statements of Calvin that would illustrate either a limited or a universal position.[40] The discussion does not allow for easy solutions, because Calvin makes few, if any, explicit statements on the issue. All too often this fact is disregarded, probably because many of the participants in the debate are too keen on enlisting Calvin's support for their own particular opinion. Calvin remains an unwilling victim for such personal theological agendas. Sometimes the absence of any discussion in Calvin on the extent of the atonement is taken as evidence that the debate was a later in-house Calvinist issue that arose with the growth of Reformed scholasticism. But this is too easy a way out. There is little doubt that Calvin must have been aware of differences of opinion on this matter. He must have given the question at least some thought, if for no other reason than that the question of the extent of the atonement is at least as old as the ninth century. At that time Gottschalk of Orbais († c. 869), a strict Augustinian, pressed the predestinarian doctrine of Augustine further by insisting on limited redemption. God had not only restricted the number of people he had chosen, but Christ's work was similarly limited to the elect. Gottschalk operated with what Jonathan Rainbow has helpfully called a "two-worlds concept."[41] For Gottschalk the biblical notion of "world" could either refer to the world of the elect or to the world that is opposed to Christ. The "world" of 1 John 2:2 ("He is the sacrifice to expiate our sins, and not only ours, but also those of the whole world") and the "everyone" of 1 Timothy 2:4 ("he wants everyone to be saved and reach full knowledge of the truth"), in Gottschalk's mind, clearly referred to the world of the elect.[42] This radical Augustinianism was condemned by the Synod of Quiercy (849), and Gottschalk himself was imprisoned. But the debate over the extent of redemption carried on beyond the ninth century. Gottschalk and his followers had touched on an issue that was directly connected to one's views on predestination. Once predestination had been allowed to set the boundaries of divine hospitality, the implications for God's love in Christ could hardly be avoided. No longer could God's character unequivocally be characterized as "pure hospitality."

Thomas Aquinas, reluctant to adopt such a radical limitation on God's hospitality in the cross, attempted a resolution by distinguishing between God's

40. Alan C. Clifford adduces no less than ninety statements from Calvin's writings in an attempt to prove that Calvin held to universal atonement (*Calvinus: Authentic Calvinism: A Clarification* [Norwich, UK: Charenton Reformed, 1996]).

41. Jonathan H. Rainbow, *The Will of God and the Cross: An Historical and Theological Study of John Calvin's Doctrine of Limited Redemption* (Allison Park, Pa.: Pickwick, 1990), 26. Rainbow traces this "two-worlds concept" to Augustine. While it may be true that Augustine worked with this distinction, this does not mean that he actually taught limited atonement, as Rainbow alleges.

42. Ibid., 29. For the controversy surrounding Gottschalk, see also Jaroslav Pelikan, *The Growth of Medieval Theology (600–1300)*, vol. 3 of *The Christian Tradition: A History of the Development of Doctrine* (Chicago: University of Chicago Press, 1978), 80–95.

antecedent and his consequent will. By his antecedent will, God wanted literally everyone to be saved. In this sense Christ died sufficiently for all. Thomas
was thus able to affirm the prima facie meaning of texts such as John 12:32,
1 Timothy 2:4, and 1 John 2:2. God's antecedent will was universal. He really did want all people to be saved. Only if people rejected God's hospitality
could we start to speak of God's consequent will, by which Christ had died
effectively only for the elect: "God wills all men to be saved by His antecedent
will, which is to will not simply but relatively; and not by His consequent will,
which is to will simply."[43]

The extent of the atonement may not often have occupied the center of
theological discussion, but it was always out there as an issue tied in with
questions about predestination. If the notion of double predestination already
elicited fears of a violent God, the obvious restriction on divine hospitality in
the notion of limited atonement was the ultimate confirmation that concerns
about Augustinianism were not entirely ill founded. The radical wing of the
Augustinian tradition would always have difficulty battling the impression of
a tyrannical God.

Calvin must have been familiar with the issue of the extent of the atonement not only because of its lengthy past history but also because his mentor
in Strasbourg from 1538–41, Martin Bucer (1491–1551), had engaged in a
public debate on this very question in 1526 with the Anabaptist theologian
Hans Denck (1495–1527)—with Bucer wanting to limit the hospitality on
the cross to the elect only. The result was Denck's expulsion from the city. A
few years later, in 1533, the universalist views of another Anabaptist leader,
Melchior Hoffman († 1543), were examined by the Strasbourg Synod, and
Hoffman spent the remaining ten years of his life in prison.[44]

But Calvin's familiarity with the problem did not result in a strong commitment to either side of the debate. The few comments that he makes on the issue
are often vague and can be interpreted in different ways. In his commentary
on 1 John 2:2, for instance, Calvin states:

> But here the question may be asked as to how the sins of the whole world have been expi-
> ated. I pass over the dreams of the fanatics, who make this a reason to extend salvation to
> all the reprobate and even to Satan himself. Such a monstrous idea is not worth refuting.
> Those who want to avoid this absurdity have said that Christ suffered sufficiently for the

43. Thomas Aquinas, *Summa theologica*, trans. Fathers of the English Dominican Province, vol. 1 (Westminster, Md.: Christian Classics, 1948), 128 (I.xxiii.4). Cf. Rainbow, *Will of God,* 35. The sufficiency/efficiency
distinction did not originate with Thomas; it was common in medieval scholasticism.

44. Rainbow, *Will of God,* 49–63; Alvin J. Beachy, *The Concept of Grace in the Radical Reformation*
(Nieuwkoop, Neth.: De Graaf, 1977), 16–17; Klaus Deppermann, *Melchior Hoffman: Social Unrest and
Apocalyptic Visions in the Age of Reformation,* trans. Malcolm Wren, ed. Benjamin Drewery (Edinburgh:
T&T Clark, 1987), 268–311. G. Michael Thomas, *The Extent of the Atonement: A Dilemma for Reformed
Theology from Calvin to the Consensus* (Carlisle, UK: Paternoster, 1997), 7–8.

whole world but effectively only for the elect. This solution has commonly prevailed in the schools. Although I allow the truth of this, I deny that it fits this passage. For John's purpose was only to make this blessing common to the whole Church. Therefore, under the word "all" he does not include the reprobate, but refers to all who would believe and those who were scattered through various regions of the earth. For, as is meet, the grace of Christ is really made clear when it is declared to be the only salvation of the world.[45]

I have already noted that Calvin's distinction between sufficiency and efficiency had been common throughout the Middle Ages, particularly since Thomas Aquinas employed it. But Calvin's acceptance of the distinction is not nearly as clear as it may at first seem. What does Calvin mean by affirming that Christ died sufficiently for the whole world? Does he mean to include the reprobate in "the whole world"? Or is he perhaps speaking of "the whole world" as the elect who are scattered throughout the world? Even if he is not just talking about the elect—and I suspect he is not—what is it exactly that makes Christ's death sufficient for the whole world? What does Calvin positively mean by this sufficiency? These questions are not without their significance. As we will see shortly, debates among later Reformed theologians opened up a variety of understandings of the sufficiency of Christ's death for all. For better or for worse, Calvin does not commit himself to a clear position on what he means by the sufficiency of Christ's death. He seems rather reluctant to enter the debate.

We may never know the exact reasons for this reluctance. I suspect, however, that it reflects an inner tension in Calvin's theology. On the one hand, he must have realized that limited atonement was the logical result of a strongly predestinarian thought pattern. The violence of exclusion conjured up by his radically Augustinian position fit, in many ways, with a limitation of divine hospitality on the cross.[46] Thus, Calvin's focus on the secret will of God as his real will probably did not allow him to explicitly teach universal redemption. On the other hand, Calvin was at pains to do justice also to the revealed will of God and so to portray God as a hospitable God. Commenting on 2 Peter 3:9 (The Lord is "being patient with you, wanting nobody to be lost and everybody to be brought to repentance"), Calvin states:

> This is His wondrous love towards the human race, that He desires all men to be saved, and is prepared to bring even the perishing to safety. . . . It could be asked here, if God does not want any to perish, why do so many in fact perish? My reply is that no mention is made here of the secret decree of God by which the wicked are doomed to their own

45. John Calvin, *The Gospel according to St. John 11–21 and the First Epistle of John,* trans. T. H. L. Parker, ed. David W. Torrance and Thomas F. Torrance (Grand Rapids: Eerdmans, 1959), 244 (*Comm. 1 John 2:2*).

46. Elsewhere I have argued that Calvin's emphasis on the unity of Christ's work of redemption, on the substitutionary understanding of Christ's work, and on God's secret will would all have predisposed him to the position of limited atonement as explicitly taught by later high Calvinists. See Boersma, "Calvin," 333–55.

ruin, but only of His loving-kindness as it is made known to us in the Gospel. There God stretches out His hand to all alike, but He only grasps those (in such a way as to lead to Himself) whom He has chosen before the foundation of the world.[47]

Echoing the well-known "universalist passages" of the Bible, Calvin affirms that God wants "all men" to be saved, does not want "any" to perish, and in fact stretches out his hand "to all alike." The warm, inviting discourse shines through in this as well as in many other passages throughout Calvin's writings. I suspect that it reflects his desire to hold on to God's revealed will and thereby to affirm the hospitality of God, particularly in the context of God's promise and his offer of grace. G. M. Thomas puts it well, as he draws attention to the importance of the twofold will in Calvin's theology: "From Calvin's comments on this formula [the sufficiency/efficiency distinction] it is plainly apparent that he was willing to place the work of Christ in conjunction with the electing purpose of God, and so present the atonement as having a particular as well as a universal aspect. Which of these facets was more prominent at any time depended on the context. Particular redemption appears in the context of election, while universal atonement is usually set forth in the context of promise."[48] Calvin's theology displays a constant tension between the forceful and even violent character of God's secret will and the hospitable extension of grace in his revealed will.

Limiting Atonement and Hospitality: The Synod of Dort

If Calvin stretched the tension between the two aspects of God's will, his successors eliminated it altogether. We have already seen how Beza and Perkins took God's absolute will both as their starting point and as the center of their theological enterprise. Beza "was far more consistent than Calvin, and much more thorough in giving God's *voluntas signi* only secondary importance. He was careful to warn that the name 'will' must not lead us to think of it as God's will, strictly speaking."[49] This unambiguous emphasis on divine sovereignty could not but raise apprehensions concerning the violence of God: Would God's power eclipse his hospitality?

The question of the extent of the atonement would come to a head in intense discussions at the Synod of Dort (1618–19). Convened to deal with the

47. John Calvin, *The Epistle of Paul the Apostle to the Hebrews and the First and Second Epistles of St. Peter,* trans. William B. Johnston, ed. David W. Torrance and Thomas F. Torrance (Grand Rapids: Eerdmans, 1963), 364 (*Comm.* 2 Pet. 3:9).

48. Thomas, *Extent,* 31. In his recent study, Kevin Dixon Kennedy is so insistent on Calvin holding to universal atonement that he largely overlooks this tension, which Thomas documents so well (*Union with Christ and the Extent of the Atonement in Calvin* [New York: Lang, 2002]).

49. Ibid., 54.

Calvinist-Arminian divide in the Netherlands, this synod formed the pinnacle of Reformed orthodoxy. The attempt to drum up ecclesiastical and political support for the more radical stream of Augustinianism reached a significant victory: Arminianism was outlawed, and its proponents were exiled, jailed, or forced underground. The confessional outcome, the Canons of Dort (1619), was destined to shape the future of international Calvinism.

On one side of the debate stood the Arminians, who held that Christ died for everybody and that faith is required if people are to benefit from this death: "The price of the redemption which Christ offered to God the Father is not only in itself and by itself sufficient for the redemption of the whole human race but has also been paid for all men and for every man, according to the decree, will, and grace of God the Father; therefore no one is absolutely excluded from participation in the fruits of Christ's death by an absolute and antecedent decree of God."[50]

The Arminian terminology of the "antecedent decree" went back to the traditional Thomist position on the issue. The Calvinists were hesitant about tracing the sufficiency of Christ's death to such a decree of God. To trace the universal "sufficiency" of Christ's death to a divine decree would seem to imply that God wanted all individuals to be saved, a notion unacceptable to high Calvinists.

The opponents of the Arminian faction were by no means united among themselves. Some of the English and other foreign delegates at Dort expressed serious reservations about the restrictions that some of the high Calvinists placed on God's hospitality in Christ. At one point the emotions ran so high that one of the Dutch high Calvinist proponents, Gomarus (1563–1641), challenged the German delegate Martinius (1572–1630) to a duel, "though they parted for that night without blows!"[51] The synod nearly disintegrated over the sharp disagreements on the issue. Gomarus and some of the other Dutch delegates opined that God's will in the decree of predestination determined whether or not Christ had died for someone. Christ simply died for the elect only. Even the traditional sufficiency/efficiency distinction, affirmed by Calvin, came under critique.[52] Delegates like Martinius, as well as some of the English delegates, particularly John Davenant (1576–1641) and Samuel Ward (1571–1641), argued that atonement is, at least in a sense, universal and that Christ died for all individuals. The sufficiency of Christ's death was somehow tied to God's will and to his desire and intention to save all people:

---

50. Quoted in Peter Y. De Jong, *Crisis in the Reformed Churches: Essays in Commemoration of the Great Synod of Dort, 1618–1619* (Grand Rapids: Reformed Fellowship, 1968), 224.

51. John Hales, *Golden remains, of the ever memorable Mr. John Hales of Eaton-Colledge, &c.,* ed. John Pearson (1659; 3rd ed. London, 1688), 456. See William Robert Godfrey, "Tensions within International Calvinism: The Debate on the Atonement at the Synod of Dort, 1618–1619" (Ph.D. diss., Stanford University, 1974), 151–53.

52. Godfrey, "Tensions," 172, 195.

"Davenant was adamant that the Father and the Son had some intention to save all, though that intention was conditional and not absolutely efficacious. . . . Davenant constructed a parallel order of decrees: one set with a universal though conditional character, and the other with a particular and efficacious character."[53] The specific concern of this moderate Calvinist position at Dort was the desire to retain the hospitality of God, seen in his desire to offer entry into the kingdom to all who find themselves estranged from it. Davenant and others wanted to reaffirm "the importance of the universal offer of the Gospel. The Christian preacher must be able to declare the offer of salvation unreservedly to all who would believe."[54]

The majority at the synod took a mediating position that maintained the traditional distinction between the sufficiency (for all) and the efficiency (for the elect) of the atonement. Still, they were careful not to link the universal aspect to God's will or intent that all be saved. The carefully drafted final statement in the Canons of Dort expressed the following consensus in its second head of doctrine:

> ART. III. The death of the Son of God is the only and most perfect sacrifice and satisfaction for sin; is of infinite worth and value, abundantly sufficient to expiate the sins of the whole world.
>
> ART. IV. This death derives its infinite value and dignity from these considerations; because the person who submitted to it was not only really man and perfectly holy, but also the only-begotten Son of God, of the same eternal and infinite essence with the Father and Holy Spirit, which qualifications were necessary to constitute him a Saviour for us; and because it was attended with a sense of the wrath and curse of God due to us for sin.
>
> ART. V. Moreover the promise of the gospel is, that whosoever believeth in Christ crucified shall not perish, but have everlasting life. This promise, together with the command to repent and believe, ought to be declared and published to all nations, and to all persons promiscuously and without distinction, to whom God out of his good pleasure sends the gospel.[55]

The Dort pronouncement evidently took into account the concerns of Martinius, Davenant, and others to maintain the hospitality of God, at least in the sense that there was a human obligation to offer God's hospitality universally. The promise "ought to be declared and published to all nations, and to all persons promiscuously and without distinction." Predestinarian concerns should not overshadow the practice of hospitality. Dort sought to underwrite divine hospitality by an appeal to the "infinite worth and value" of Christ's

---

53. Ibid., 184–85.

54. Ibid., 232.

55. Philip Schaff, *The Creeds of Christendom: With a History and Critical Notes*, rev. David S. Schaff (New York: Harper & Row, 1931; reprint, Grand Rapids: Baker, 1996), 2:586.

death. Without explicitly resorting to the sufficiency/efficiency distinction, this is clearly what Dort has in mind in article II.3.

Was this enough, however, to safeguard divine hospitality? Several problems must be noted in this regard. First, one may wonder whether the mere assertion of the duty to preach the gospel "promiscuously and without distinction" is sufficient. Dort's second head of doctrine as a whole is preceded by the first head, which explicitly maintains double predestination. We already saw that double predestination leads to fears of the introduction of violence and tyranny into the very heart of God. We should not forget that even the most moderate representatives at Dort belonged to the right wing of the Augustinian tradition and wholeheartedly affirmed eternal double predestination as a key ingredient of their theology. I suspect that many will not find it convincing to argue that God is a hospitable God when his eternal plan has already excluded the reprobate.

Second, Dort explicitly avoids linking the hospitality of God—the free offer of grace—to his desire or intent that all people be saved. What Dort doesn't say here is as interesting as what it does say. The reason for the omission of God's desire (his will) to save everyone is clear: most of the delegates at Dort did not believe that God wanted all people to be saved. They refused to attach the universal sufficiency of Christ's death to any kind of decree or will of God. The disagreement among the delegates on this issue explains why the Canons studiously avoid addressing the link between the sufficiency of Christ's death and God's will or decree.

When Dort explains what the sufficiency of Christ's death means, it begins with the comment that his death is "sufficient to expiate the sins of the whole world." This statement may seem obvious in its implication: Christ died—at least sufficiently—for all people. But this would be too hasty a conclusion. Delegates at Dort debated at length the meaning of the expression "the whole world" (*totius mundi*). Did it mean "all individuals"? Or did it merely refer to God's chosen ones throughout the whole world? Dort is at least open to the interpretation that Christ's death is sufficient only for the elect.[56] Such a limited hospitality makes sense when we look at how Dort further explains the sufficiency of Christ's death. As we saw, this sufficiency has to do both with the person of Christ and with the eternal wrath of God (art. II.4). A consideration that is conspicuously absent is the love of God for all people. Christ's death is sufficient for the whole world simply because of who Christ is and because of what he suffered. Dort does not add that his death is sufficient for the whole world because it actually extends to the entire world.[57]

---

56. Godfrey, "Tensions," 170–73.

57. A number of high Calvinists, including Beza, Perkins, and John Owen, strictly limited the sufficiency of Christ's death to the elect, thereby significantly altering the traditional understanding of the

Conclusion

Because of the high Calvinist concern to safeguard eternal double predestination, it tended toward a concept of God that involved unnecessary (arbitrary) violence. To be sure, it was Calvinism's express intent to safeguard the hospitality of God. Double predestination removed the burden of merit from human beings: the relationship between God and his people should not fall under the auspices of an "economy of exchange." The notion of divine election (or at least the way it functioned in Calvinism) ensured that God's hospitable grace was prior to any human action. God did not invite human beings on the basis of any standard or any prior analysis. At the same time, the single-minded emphasis on the vigorous character of this divine hospitality was problematic, for the decree of election itself functioned in high Calvinism as an inexorable, eternal force that irresistibly drew the elect into his presence.[58] Eternal election ensured that all the elect were inescapably and irresistibly drawn to God and to his eternal salvation. The high Calvinists strongly opposed the Arminians' insistence on free will and on conversion by means of "moral persuasion." For God to be truly God he had to have the capacity and the will to override any human resistance to his love. God's love had to be a powerful love, a love that violently overtook the hearts of his chosen ones.[59]

What is more, by complementing the notion of election with that of reprobation, Calvinism endangered the very hospitality that it so zealously attempted to protect. God was from eternity not just a God of love but also a God of wrath. Here his hospitality was certainly not absolute or pure hospitality. The protracted debates around the question of the extent of the atonement illustrate the difficulty that scholastic Calvinists came to experience as they struggled to maintain the hospitality of God in the face of the idea of an eternally determined exclusion of certain individuals. With images of power and violence solidly in place, divine hospitality was marginalized, as is clear from

---

sufficiency/efficiency distinction. See Hans Boersma, *A Hot Pepper Corn: Richard Baxter's Doctrine of Justification in Its Seventeenth-Century Context of Controversy*, 2nd ed. (Vancouver, B.C.: Regent College Publishing, 2004), 215–17. Whereas medieval theologians had regarded the sufficiency of Christ's death as being for everyone, these high Calvinists saw the sufficiency and the efficiency of Christ's death as applying to one and the same category: the elect only. Cf. Owen's comment that Christ's sacrifice was "sufficient in itself for the redeeming of all and every man, if it had pleased the Lord to employ it to that purpose" (John Owen, *Death of Death in the Death of Christ* [1647], in *The Works of John Owen*, ed. William H. Goold [1850–53; repr., London: Banner of Truth, 1965–68], 10:296). The conditional clause renders the notion of "sufficiency" all but meaningless.

58. For an insightful discussion of the Catholic/Protestant divide on the relationship between nature and grace, see Jaroslav Pelikan, *Reformation of Church and Dogma (1300–1700)*, vol. 4 of *The Christian Tradition: A History of the Development of Doctrine* (Chicago: University of Chicago Press, 1984), 374–85.

59. Cf. by contrast Timothy Ware's suggestion: "God knocks, but waits for us to open the door—He does not break it down. The grace of God invites all but compels none" (*The Orthodox Church*, rev. ed. [London: Penguin, 1964], 222).

the agonizing in-house debates over the extent of the atonement. God's love was a powerful and violent love,[60] a love that forced the stranger to enter into the Father's mansions, and one that excluded those who fell under the spell of God's eternal decree of reprobation. High Calvinism was insufficiently attuned to the fact that the host who forces rather than welcomes the stranger into his home runs the risk of changing his home into a prison. Thus, Calvinism's limited hospitality, drawing violence into the heart of God, ended up undermining the unconditional hospitality of God.

---

60. Speaking of mortification as an aspect of repentance, Calvin notes that we must be "violently slain by the sword of the Spirit and brought to nought" (*Institutes*, III.iii.8).

3

Preferential Hospitality

Election and Violence in History

Deuteronomy and Divine Election

God's involvement with human existence implies geographical boundaries, historical determinations, and national and ethnic particularities. His rescue and restoration of the created order demands that God get involved with violence. God's gracious involvement with his creation never excluded the possibility of angry and even violent intervention in creation. Recognition of the tensions involved in divine hospitality will make us aware of the need to respect boundaries, to protect space, and, under certain circumstances, even to use violence. As we have seen, Calvinism has historically taken these limitations and boundaries extremely seriously. It has regarded election and reprobation, mercy and justice, love and wrath, as complementary, not as mutually exclusive. In the previous chapter I criticized the right wing of Augustinianism for carrying the limitations of time and space into the realm of eternity, thereby locating the violence of divine exclusion at the very core of God's character and of the Christian faith. For scholastic Calvinism there is no such thing as absolute or pure hospitality. Hospitality is conditional or limited, even in the heart of God.

In this chapter I want to explore a possible way of looking at election that avoids compromising the unconditional hospitality that lies at the heart of

God's character. I intend to present an understanding of predestination as an embodiment of God's hospitality in Jesus Christ. I particularly explore the exclusionary limitations of God's election and argue that they are necessary to maintain its hospitable character. There are several reasons why I refer to this hospitality as "preferential hospitality." First, although the adjective "preferential" circumscribes and even limits God's elective acts in history, the limitations to God's hospitality are not essential to his character. God's preferential hospitality stems from an unconditional, eternally absolute hospitality that describes what God is truly like. Second, like the expression "preferential option for the poor," so the expression "preferential hospitality" is a positive term. I want to underscore that despite its violent connotations, election is a positive expression of divine hospitality. Third, by using the term "preferential," I want to indicate that we are dealing with historical realities: poor *versus* rich people, marginalized people *versus* oppressors, and so on. In this chapter, therefore, I present an understanding of election that is historical, corporate, and instrumental in character. I argue that the violence of "reprobation" accompanying this election is meant to safeguard monotheism, to counter immorality, to protect the poor, and ultimately to draw all nations into God's absolute, unconditional eschatological hospitality. The violence of reprobation is necessary to protect the hospitable character of God's actions in history and will ultimately be justified by the mystery of our eternal life in God's presence.

The Calvinist divines of the sixteenth century were, of course, not the ones to dream up the idea of election. This concept has played a significant role throughout the history of the Church, for the simple reason that it goes back to the biblical testimony itself. The notion of election does not even start with St. Paul, however much we have come to associate it with his letters. It is important to recognize that when St. Paul speaks of election, he does not draw on Greek philosophical notions but rather on his Jewish background. Thoroughly immersed in the Old Testament literature through his Pharisaic training, St. Paul developed his theology against the backdrop of the Old Testament. Western theology has tended to read the Pauline epistles through the lens of its Greek philosophical heritage. The timeless, individual, and futuristic reading of election that has dominated much of Western theologizing—and particularly the Calvinist tradition—amounts to a decontextualizing of St. Paul. In some ways he has been read through the lens of Greek philosophy rather than the lens of the Old Testament. This is illustrated dramatically in the Canons of Dort (1619) as the touchstone of international Calvinism, from which the Old Testament is remarkably absent.[1] In the last few decades the Jewish background of the theology of St. Paul has made somewhat of a

---

1. Cf. Klaas Runia, "Recent Reformed Criticisms of the Canons," in *Crisis in the Reformed Churches: Essays in Commemoration of the Great Synod of Dort, 1618–1619,* ed. Peter Y. De Jong (Grand Rapids: Reformed Fellowship, 1968), 165, 179 n. 21.

comeback. Biblical scholars are realizing that it is impossible to read the Pauline letters without taking their Old Testament background into consideration. This shift in Pauline studies is a wholesome one that cannot but positively affect our appreciation of divine hospitality.

Among the Old Testament writings, the Deuteronomic literature in particular is suffused with the idea of election. In the book of Deuteronomy the notion of election (*bahar*) occurs no less than thirty-two times. Nearly always it is a matter of God "choosing" or "electing." He chooses Israel; he chooses a place for worship; he chooses a king; and he chooses Levites.[2] The predominant emphasis, therefore, is on God choosing a nation and certain individuals within this nation.

This divine election has at least four characteristics that are significant in light of the discussion in the preceding chapter. First—and this point has rightly been emphasized in the Augustinian tradition—election is an act of *sovereign grace.* God's choice of Israel has nothing to do with any qualification of Israel, whether it be its numerical growth ("for indeed you were the smallest of all"—Deut. 7:7); its economic success ("Remember Yahweh your God; he was the one who gave you the strength to act effectively like this"—Deut. 8:18); or its high moral standards ("for you are an obstinate people"—Deut. 9:6). In traditional theological terminology, the Israelites could not possibly prepare themselves for God's election by means of their natural capacities. The idea that by living up to their natural abilities (*facere quod in se est*) people can somehow prepare themselves for their election and for grace has rightly been viewed with suspicion in the Augustinian tradition of the Church.[3]

Second, this election is an act of God *in history.* God's choice means that he liberates the Israelites from slavery in Egypt: "Because he loved your ancestors and, after them, chose their descendants, he has brought you out of Egypt, displaying his presence and mighty power" (Deut. 4:37; cf. 7:8).[4] This act in history is, moreover, an act by which God chooses not just certain individuals, but a nation. Election is in the third place, therefore, a *corporate act:* "For you are a people consecrated to Yahweh your God; of all the peoples on earth, you

---

2. Cf. Deut. 4:37; 7:6–7; 10:15; 14:2 (regarding Israel); Deut. 12:5, 11, 14, 18, 21, 26; 14:23–25; 15:20; 16:2, 6–7, 11, 15–16; 17:8, 10; 18:6; 26:2; 31:11 (regarding a place of worship); Deut. 17:15 (regarding a king); and Deut. 18:5; 21:5 (regarding Levites).

3. Cf. H. A. Oberman, *The Dawn of the Reformation: Essays in Late Medieval and Early Reformation Thought* (Grand Rapids: Eerdmans, 1986), 84–103, 204–33; Karlfried Froehlich, "Justification Language and Grace: The Charge of Pelagianism in the Middle Ages," in *Probing the Tradition: Historical Studies in Honor of Edward A. Dowey, Jr.,* ed. Elsie Anne McKee and Brian G. Armstrong (Louisville: Westminster John Knox, 1989), 21–47; Heiko Augustinus Oberman, *The Harvest of Medieval Theology: Gabriel Biel and Late Medieval Nominalism* (1963; repr., Grand Rapids: Baker, 2000), 128–45.

4. Cf. Horst Dietrich Preuss, *Old Testament Theology,* trans. Leo G. Perdue (Louisville: Westminster John Knox, 1995), 1:37: "'Election' in the Old Testament refers not to some kind of supratemporal or primeval divine decree but rather to a historical action of YHWH."

have been chosen by Yahweh your God to be his own people" (Deut. 7:6; cf. 14:2). This element of community and of a communal identity as a chosen nation can hardly be overemphasized. God does not choose certain individuals out of the mass of uncreated humanity, but he chooses a nation, a people. Even when he does on occasion choose particular individuals, this choice is always intimately connected to God's choice of a nation. When he chooses, for instance, a king (Deut. 17:15), this king is emphatically seen as in no way superior to his brothers (Deut. 17:20) and thus as the representative of the nation. And when God chooses Levites, he chooses them to stand before Yahweh, "to bless in Yahweh's name" (Deut. 18:5), so that the purpose of this choice is for them to be instrumental in maintaining the relationship between Yahweh and the entire nation.

Finally, this election is *instrumental* in character. Deuteronomic history closely ties together the notions of election and covenant. Election is not futuristic in the sense that it determines who in the end will be saved. Rather, election has in view the maintenance of the covenant relationship and is therefore instrumental in character. If election indicates God's unilateral choice of his people, the covenant refers to the bilateral maintenance of the relationship. Whereas election is unconditional, the covenant is conditional. E. P. Sanders presents an appropriate characterization of the relationship between election and covenant in his landmark 1977 publication, *Paul and Palestinian Judaism.* Here Sanders argues that Palestinian Judaism held to a worldview of "covenantal nomism." According to this rabbinic position, God's initial act of grace was unconditional, so that salvation was never "earned." God's election of Israel was in no way a matter of human merit or good works. Legalism was, therefore, foreign to Palestinian Judaism. But once God had graciously chosen his nation and had liberated her from the oppressive powers of paganism, he did require obedience. God meted out blessings and curses depending on Israel's response to God's covenant law. Sanders summarizes the structure of Judaism's "covenantal nomism" as follows:

> (1) God has chosen Israel and (2) given the law. The law implies both (3) God's promise to maintain the election and (4) the requirement to obey. (5) God rewards obedience and punishes transgression. (6) The law provides for means of atonement, and atonement results in (7) maintenance or re-establishment of the covenantal relationship. (8) All those who are maintained in the covenant by obedience, atonement and God's mercy belong to the group which will be saved. An important interpretation of the first and last points is that election and ultimately salvation are considered to be by God's mercy rather than human merit.[5]

5. E. P. Sanders, *Paul and Palestinian Judaism: A Comparison of Patterns of Religion* (Philadelphia: Fortress, 1977), 422.

Put succinctly, *getting in* was a matter of grace and thus unconditional, but *staying in* required a human response of obedience to the precepts of the Law and was thus conditional.[6] This understanding of the relationship between election and covenant holds true not only for the Judaism that held sway around the time of Jesus and Paul, but it is also the pattern of the Deutero-nomic understanding of the relationship between Israel and her God. After mentioning God's gracious election of his people, Moses continues with the words: "Hence, grasp this today and meditate on it carefully: Yahweh is the true God, in heaven above as on earth beneath, he and no other. Keep his laws and commandments as I give them to you today, so that you and your children after you, may prosper and live long in the country that Yahweh your God is giving you for ever" (Deut. 4:39–40). While the initiation of the covenant relationship had its basis in God's gracious election alone, the flourishing of the covenant depended on obedience to God's covenant law.

Hospitality and the Violence of Reprobation

This understanding of election implies that God is not the only one who chooses. Although Yahweh is by far the most frequently mentioned subject of the verb "to choose" (*bahar*), toward the end of his life Moses enjoins Israel to choose God in response: "I am offering you life or death, blessing or curse. Choose life, then, so that you and your descendants may live, in the love of Yahweh your God, obeying his voice, holding fast to him" (Deut. 30:19–20). Israel's choice is a choice to love Yahweh and to obey the Law. It is the choice to maintain the covenant relationship that God has established by means of his gracious election. Divine hospitality thus initiates a response of human hospitality, which in turn leads to divine acceptance and joy and therefore implies a genuine reciprocity and openness in the divine-human relationship.

Using a musical analogy, Jeremy Begbie describes election in terms of improvisation when he comments that in election "[t]here is coherence but there is also contingency and openness. This is the metaphysics of grace, not determinism. Improvisation's coherent patterns of open-ended give and take, imbibed with a high degree of contingency, can go a long way to challenging discussions which are tempted too easily to resort to the categories of necessi-

---

6. It will be obvious that this understanding has implications for our understanding of justification and for the relationship between faith and works in justification. I do not have the space here to elaborate significantly on this. Suffice it to say that I believe recent rapprochements between Catholics and Protestants are most encouraging. For an elaboration on the Pauline understanding of issues surrounding justification, see N. T. Wright, *What Saint Paul Really Said: Was Paul of Tarsus the Real Founder of Christianity?* (Grand Rapids: Eerdmans, 1997), 95–133.

tarianism, while at the same time helping us to evade any downplaying of God's consistency."[7] God's hospitable election in no way forces Israel's hand; rather, it is meant to lead to a continuous process of mutual hospitality in which the relationship (in Deuteronomic language referred to as "covenant") flourishes without stifling oppression or determination. God's hospitality toward Israel wants to keep violence at bay as much as possible.

The instrumental function of election (serving to establish the mutual covenant relationship between God and Israel) is closely connected with Israel's role as a missionary nation. Israel's election was never for its own sake. Not only was election in no way based on Israel's prior condition (whether in terms of numerical size, economic growth, or moral integrity), but also the purpose of election reached beyond Israel. God had in mind more than just the salvation of Israel. Underlying the Deuteronomic theology of election is the realization that God had already called Abraham, as Israel's ancestor, with a view to bringing salvation to the world. Abraham's call implied that "all clans on earth" would bless themselves through him (Gen. 12:3).[8] God's hospitality extended beyond the borders of Israel. Israel was chosen to extend this hospitality to the nations, in order to woo them back into a relationship with God and thus bring salvation to the entire world. Israel was God's means to undo the effects of the Fall.

The gracious hospitality of God's election did not force Israel's hand. The prospect of either blessing or curse presupposes a freedom that could potentially mean the failure of Israel's missionary purpose. "The reality of human freedom . . . implies that the harmonious vision may or may not be realized," writes Gordon McConville.[9] Israel's obedience was meant to be a showcase for the nations, who would admire Israel's wisdom and would exclaim, "No other people is as wise and prudent as this great nation!" (Deut. 4:6; cf. 28:10). Conversely, if Israel would not live up to the relationship established by God, "all the nations [would] exclaim, 'Why has Yahweh treated this country like this? Why this great blaze of anger?'" (Deut. 29:23).[10]

The book of Deuteronomy, despite its fiercely covenantal approach, is not in doubt about the outcome of Israel's election and of its missionary role. In chapter 27, Moses guides the people in making a covenant with Yahweh, when they enter the Promised Land west of Shechem, with six tribes occupying the northern Mount Ebal and the other six tribes facing them on the southern Mount Gerizim. With the priests and the ark in between the mountains, the people on Mount Ebal are instructed to pronounce curses and affirm them

7. Jeremy S. Begbie, *Theology, Music, and Time* (Cambridge: Cambridge University Press, 2000), 265.

8. Cf. Gen. 18:18; 22:18; 26:4; 28:14.

9. Gordon McConville, *Grace in the End: A Study in Deuteronomic Theology* (Grand Rapids: Zondervan, 1993), 131.

10. Cf. Deut. 28:37; 1 Kings 4:34; 8:60.

with their "amens." This chapter, with twelve curses—known as the "twelve commandments" or the "dodecalogue"—contains no blessings at all, but only curses, climaxing in verse 26: "Accursed be anyone who does not make the words of this Law effective by putting them into practice" (cf. Gal. 3:10).[11] The preponderance of curses is evident also in chapters 28 and 29. The prospect of curse includes disease, ecological disaster, defeat in war, ruined harvests, and even people eating their own children. This train of events will climax in Israel's destruction and exile: "For not having obeyed the voice of Yahweh your God, just as Yahweh used to delight in making you happy and in making your numbers grow, so will he take delight in ruining you and destroying you. You will be torn from the country which you are about to enter and make your own. Yahweh will scatter you throughout every people, from one end of the earth to the other; there you will serve other gods made of wood and stone, hitherto unknown either to you or to your ancestors" (Deut. 28:62–64; cf. vv. 36–37, 49–52).

The emphasis on the covenant curses is indicative of the covenant's anticipated outcome. The hospitality of election notwithstanding, God warns that if Israel rejects his hospitality, it will face the violence of his reprobation. Therefore, when at the end of his life Moses is instructed to teach the Israelites a song—depicting Israel's unfaithfulness against the backdrop of God's gracious election—this song is to function as a legal witness in Yahweh's court case against his people (Deut. 31:19, 21). The prospect of such self-indictment is not in doubt. Yahweh confides to Moses: "You will soon be sleeping with your ancestors, and this people is about to play the harlot by following the gods of the foreigners of the country, among whom they are going to live. They will desert me and break my covenant, which I have made with them" (Deut. 31:16; cf. v. 29). Israel's disobedience, and hence the curse of exile, is never in doubt. Instead of serving as a missionary nation to the surrounding peoples, the Israelites will end up serving other gods. God's hospitality will inexplicably be rejected by a nation that will prefer to live outside the boundaries of divine grace. Yahweh's purpose with Israel thus seems to end in failure.[12] The elect people of God become—in history—the reprobate people as "instruments of his retribution" (Rom. 9:22).[13] Divine violence is here the result of the rejection of divine hospitality.

11. See chapter 7 for an interpretation of Gal. 3:10.

12. Deut. 30:1–10 holds out the prospect of a new covenant and of life beyond exile. Despite all appearances to the contrary, God's purposes with Israel do not end in failure.

13. For a historical reading of this text, often used in defense of double predestination from eternity, see N. T. Wright, *The Climax of the Covenant: Christ and the Law in Pauline Theology* (Minneapolis: Fortress, 1992), 239.

No Hospitality without Violence

If Israel's election is not based on her inherent worthiness, the question becomes: What are God's reasons for choosing Israel? Behind this question lurks our fear that this choice might be arbitrary, and that we end up with a tyrant who with one violent sweep chops up humanity into elect and reprobate nations. In other words, election may not be timeless, individual, and futuristic, but is this sufficient to put us at ease and to assure us of divine hospitality? Regina M. Schwartz, in the preface of a book linking biblical monotheism to arbitrary violence, addresses the issue of election. She comments how one day she was teaching about the exodus in one of her undergraduate classes. She told the class that the story was a deeply inspiring one about liberation from slavery. As Schwartz puts it:

> I added some remarks about class consciousness and liberation theology to make the story more contemporary, and lingered over the fact that this story has now come to have urgent political force in Latin America and South Africa as it had during the U.S. civil rights movement. Then, in the midst of this celebration, the student raised his hand and asked simply, "What about the Canaanites?" Suddenly all the uncomfortable feelings I had been repressing about the Bible for years flooded me. Yes, what about the Canaanites? And the Amorites, Moabites, Hittites? . . . I now began to see some complicity, for over and over the Bible tells the story of a people who inherit at someone else's expense.[14]

What is the motivation behind God's election of Israel? And does the violence that he unleashes against the surrounding nations not make clear that election cannot possibly be redeemed, regardless of how we construe such a notion? Doesn't divine hospitality for the one entail excruciating divine violence for the other? We may want to discard eternal election and reprobation, but don't the historical examples of divine hospitality and violence confront us with similar difficulties?

The Jewish people have pondered the mystery of divine election for centuries. Loath to admit that God's election was a pure act of his will, at times they centered their search for a divine motive around the worthiness of Abraham or Israel. In Second Temple Judaism the notion was not uncommon that God chose Abraham because of his favorable response to God's initial call.[15] Placing

---

14. Regina M. Schwartz, *The Curse of Cain: The Violent Legacy of Monotheism* (Chicago: University of Chicago Press, 1997), ix–x. Robert Allen Warrior expresses similar apprehensions about the exodus story. As a Native American, he laments that "the narrative tells us that the Canaanites have status only as the people Yahweh removes from the land in order to bring the chosen people in" ("A Native American Perspective: Canaanites, Cowboys, and Indians," in *Voices from the Margin: Interpreting the Bible in the Third World*, ed. R. S. Sugirtharajah [Maryknoll, N.Y.: Orbis, 1991], 291. Cf. also Magi Abdul-Masih, "The Challenge of Present-Day Palestine to Contemporary Theology," *Studies in Religion* 29 (2000): 439–51.

15. Cf. Sanders, *Paul and Palestinian Judaism*, 87–101. Note, however, Sanders's cautionary remark: "Even if the view that God chose Israel only because of some past or present or future merit were Rabbinic

the emphasis on Abraham's personal attitude and making it the ground of election would indeed enable us to overcome apprehensions of violence in divine election. God's choice would then no longer be arbitrary. He would not step in arbitrarily to impose his salvific will forcefully and violently on the people of Israel. But hospitality is threatened not only by means of violent imposition. When we take the other extreme and squarely place the responsibility for the initiation of fellowship on the shoulder of the stranger or the alien, we still end up undermining hospitality—this time not through the violence of imposition, but through the violence of neglect, indifference, and chaos. For hospitality to flourish, the host somehow needs to embody the desire for fellowship. When election is made dependent on human merit, the divine quest for fellowship loses its hospitable character.[16]

God's electing hospitality is not based on human merit. Nonetheless, God does give us some insight into what motivates both his hospitality toward Israel and the accompanying violence against the surrounding nations. The danger of syncretism is prominent here. Moses explains to the Israelites that Yahweh places the nations surrounding Israel under a ban (*herem*). He then comments:

> You must not intermarry with them; you must not give a daughter of yours to a son of theirs, or take a daughter of theirs for a son of yours, for your son would be seduced from following me into serving other gods; the wrath of Yahweh would blaze out against you and he would instantly destroy you. Instead, treat them like this: tear down their altars, smash their standing-stones, cut down their sacred poles and burn their idols. For you are a people consecrated to Yahweh your God; of all the peoples on earth, you have been chosen by Yahweh your God to be his own people. (Deut. 7:3–6)

The election of Israel is intimately connected with God's demand that he alone be worshipped. The confession of monotheism, as expressed in the Shema of Deuteronomy 6:4–6, constitutes the background to the notion of election. God wants to keep Israel separate as a nation with a view to monotheistic worship (cf. Deut. 20:16–18). At stake is the purity of worship.

Election, and the accompanying notion of conquest, is also related to the immorality of the nations that Israel is uprooting. We have already seen that election has nothing to do with Israel's uprightness. The obverse of this implies that "it is because of their wickedness that Yahweh is dispossessing these nations

---

doctrine—which it is not—this would still not prove that individual Israelites had to earn salvation. Even if the election had been earned in the past, there is no thought that subsequent Israelites must continue to earn their place in the covenant as individuals" (101).

16. I do not mean to discard all talk of "merit." There is a difference between meriting initial grace (in election or conversion) and meriting within an already established covenant relationship. There is also a difference between condign merit (which, properly speaking, earns the reward) and congruous merit (where a value higher than the inherent or proper value is ascribed to human acts).

for you" (Deut. 9:5). The conquest has, at least partially, a penal basis (cf. Gen. 15:16). Precisely because God's hospitality takes place within a history that is already marred by human violence, his hospitality cannot be pure or universal in character. God's hospitality is concerned to put an end to human sin and violence. Giving universal, unconditional affirmation would mean that God would let human violence run amok. Divine hospitality and violence must be viewed in the context of a world that God is not content to leave mired in violence and oppression. His violence against the Canaanites may seem harsh to us, but we need to remember that it is enacted in a judicial, penal context.

It may still seem arbitrary for God to extend hospitality to Israel and to unleash violence against the Canaanites. The Canaanites may have deserved punishment, but so did the Israelites. This is perhaps the most difficult question in connection with divine hospitality. The problem is not just the violence itself, but the fact that it has hospitality as its counterpart. It seems inherently unfair to us to punish one party when both are guilty. By pointing out Israel's lack of achievement and status, however, Deuteronomy is intimating something about the hospitality of God. This hospitality is not one that invites the powerful and the strong, but it is one that has a special predilection for the poor and the underprivileged. Along with Israel, other marginalized people may look to God's electing grace. God looks for the weak and vulnerable in society. He provides a place for Abraham, the "wandering Aramaean" (Deut. 26:5); he chooses the younger brother over the elder (Mal. 1:3; cf. Rom. 9:13); he hears the cry of a nation without resources as it is oppressed by Pharaoh in Egypt (Exod. 3:7–8); he makes Pharaoh obstinate in his arrogant and violent treatment of a tribe of strangers within his borders (Exod. 4:21); he angrily opposes the inhospitable refusal of Edom to let Israel travel peacefully through its land (Num. 20:14–21). God's hospitality toward Israel is not an arbitrary and violent choice of one nation at the cost of others. His hospitality always expresses a "preferential option for the poor."[17] We may perhaps want to describe this hospitality as discriminatory. But it is a discrimination that sides with the poor and oppressed over against the rich and violent. God's election of Israel and Israel's conquest of Canaan do not take place in a vacuum, so as to justify our asking, "What about the Canaanites?" All people may be implicated in violence and sin, but it is important to retain the distinction between oppressor and victim, violator and violated. God's choice of Israel is a choice that favors the marginalized and oppressed over those who reject his hospitality.

17. Cf. Pope John Paul II's encyclical *Sollicitudo rei socialis* (1987): "Here I would like to indicate one of them [i.e., the magisterium's guidelines]: the *option* or *love of preference* for the poor. This is an option, or a *special form* of primacy in the exercise of Christian charity, to which the whole Tradition of the Church bears witness" (*The Encyclicals of John Paul II*, ed. J. Michael Miller, 2nd ed. [Huntington, Ind.: Our Sunday Visitor, 2001], 412–13 [42.2]; italics in the original). The expression has its origin in liberation theology. See Gustavo Gutiérrez, *A Theology of Liberation*, trans. and ed. Caridad Inda and John Eagleson, rev. ed. (Maryknoll, N.Y.: Orbis, 1988), xxv–xxviii.

God's preferential hospitality toward the poor implies that he measures Israel by her response to his hospitality. Divine hospitality must lead to human hospitality. The Torah's concern for justice—concern for the stranger and the sojourner—is a concern for hospitality rooted in Israel's own experience of violence and oppression: "Love the stranger then, for you were once strangers in Egypt" (Deut. 10:19; cf. Exod. 22:21). The Israelites' experience of being oppressed as aliens and strangers should lead to an attitude of love and compassion toward the stranger. Not only should the Israelites look at their own experiences of oppression, but they should also remember God's intervention in the situation: "Remember that you were once a slave in Egypt and that Yahweh your God redeemed you from that" (Deut. 24:18; cf. 15:15). God's concern for Israel as a tribe of strangers should in turn lead to the Israelites' compassionate and hospitable treatment of aliens and strangers in their midst. The practice of human hospitality derives from divine hospitality.

God's preferential hospitality toward the poor means that Israel can never use her election to claim some kind of absolute and inviolable status with God. Israel is not beyond divine punishment and even abandonment. In a dramatic passage Leviticus draws a direct line from God's punishment of the Canaanites to that of the Israelites: "Do not make yourselves unclean by any of these practices, for it was by such things that the nations that I am driving out before you made themselves unclean. The country has become unclean; hence I am about to punish it for its guilt, and the country itself will vomit out its inhabitants. . . . If you make it unclean, will it not vomit you out as it vomited out the nations there before you?" (Lev. 18:24–28). If Israel does not accept God's provision of space, the consequence cannot but mean the loss of the land as the concrete embodiment of God's hospitality for his people.[18] Slightly altering the geographic metaphor, we could say that Israel's abandonment of divine presence will lead to God's abandonment of Israel. Yahweh forewarns Moses: "They will desert me and break my covenant, which I have made with them. That very day, my anger will blaze against them; I shall desert them and hide my face from them" (Deut. 31:16–17). Of course, the land's vomiting out of the people of Israel and their desertion by God lead to the question of how this can be squared with God's faithfulness. Does God's hospitality toward Israel come to nothing when it is faced with rejection? This question of divine reliability is one of the core questions underlying Pauline theology. But the point that I want to make here is that the Israelites' status as the elect people of God does not give them a special claim to divine favor, irrespective of their response. Divine punishment is not restricted to those who

18. Cf. Walter Brueggemann, in commenting on Yahweh's violence in connection with the conquest: "[L]and-by-violence is a primary claim for this God [Yahweh]. It turns out to be a costly claim for Israel, who learned that land taken for Israel in violence by Yahweh can also be taken from Israel by Yahweh's violence" (*Theology of the Old Testament: Testimony, Dispute, Advocacy* [Minneapolis: Fortress, 1997], 382–83).

once were the oppressors but may be directed equally toward God's people, if they forget their place as "strangers and guests" who are entirely dependent on God's hospitality in allowing them to live in a land that belongs to him (Lev. 25:23; cf. Ps. 39:12).

These motivations of divine choice—concern for monotheism, aversion to pagan immorality, concern for the marginalized, and punishment of evil—do not constitute a rational basis for election. Since Israel's moral superiority was not the reason for her election, Israel could hardly be expected to provide a guarantee for upholding monotheism. The wilderness wanderings, and the Israelites' response as wandering strangers to Yahweh's hospitality, hardly give reason for optimism. Indeed, the Deuteronomic motivations of purity of worship and of punishment of the Canaanites do not imply divine confidence in Israel; rather, they are invoked because of a prior relationship between God and his people. Thus, Moses appeals to God's "pact which he swore" to Abraham, Isaac, and Jacob (Deut. 9:5). It is the Abrahamic covenant that makes God look at Israel as his agent to ensure both monotheistic worship and punishment of foreign nations.[19] The Abrahamic covenant thus becomes the fallback position as the rationale for Israel's election.

Discussions about a divine rationale for election and reprobation (hospitality and violence) cannot have recourse to a foundationalism that argues on purely rational grounds for God's choice of Israel. The covenant is a relationship of love, and love ultimately does not allow itself to be explained: "Yahweh set his heart on you and chose you . . . because he loved you and meant to keep the oath which he swore to your ancestors" (Deut. 7:7–8). The tautology could hardly be more blatant: God bases his love on his love. Indeed, this statement in Deuteronomy is an acknowledgment that election cannot ultimately be explained. It is not the logic of rationality but the logic of love that is at work in divine election.

Why Abraham? Why Israel? There are no reasons beyond those of love and fidelity. This is not to argue, however, that nothing can be said about the *purpose* of God's election. The missiological or teleological drive of election has often been pointed out.[20] When one is drawn into divine fellowship by God's gracious hospitality, this affects one's relationship with others. Divine hospitality and human hospitality are, therefore, inseparable. God's call of Abraham was an act of hospitality not just to his descendants but also to all other nations (Gen. 12:3). The nation of Israel had as its calling the embodiment of God's hospitality so as to draw all nations into a relationship with him. We have

19. Cf. Th. C. Vriezen, *De verkiezing van Israël volgens het Oude Testament* (Amsterdam: Bolland, 1974), 44–52.

20. E.g., Jack W. Cottrell, "Conditional Election," in *Grace Unlimited*, ed. Clark H. Pinnock (Minneapolis: Bethany, 1975), 54; Stanley J. Grenz, *Theology for the Community of God* (Nashville: Broadman & Holman, 1994), 590–91.

already seen that the book of Deuteronomy has a deep concern for the nations' reactions to Israel's hospitality and to the lack thereof. The surrounding nations could either stand in awe of God's hospitality toward Israel and her response to God, or they could respond in astonishment to Israel's rejection of God's hospitality. The purpose of divine hospitality is ultimately not just to draw Israel into a relationship with God but also to restore the intimacy of love with all humanity and with the entire created order.

Justice involves discrimination. The Hebrew notion of justice (*ṣĕdāqâ*) is rather different from that of the blindfolded Roman goddess, Justitia. Miroslav Volf rightly comments: "If *Justitia* is just, then Yahweh is patently unjust."[21] God's hospitality discriminates in favor of the poor and the oppressed. It takes shape in the particularity of nations that carry names, of geographical locations that are contested, and of temporal and cultural situations that carry the burdens of historical development. "God's purpose of salvation," comments missiologist Lesslie Newbigin, "is not that we should be taken out of history and related to him in some way which bypasses the specificities and particularities of history. His purpose is that in and through history there should be brought into being that which is symbolized in the vision with which the Bible ends—the Holy City into which all the glory of the nations will finally be gathered."[22]

Without doubt, the particularity of history of which Newbigin speaks can be offensive. Newbigin asserts that it is a scandal particularly to a "certain kind of cosmopolitan mind."[23] Indeed, the universalizing rationalism of the modern mind-set finds it difficult to accept the particularities of time and space. The very notion that God needs history to bring a good creation toward eternal fellowship with him seems suspicious to those who search for a Cartesian mathematical certainty that escapes the complications of time and space. Today's concerns about divine involvement with violence—whether in connection with the conquest of the nations or with Christ's suffering on the cross—are strongly impacted by modern apprehensions of anything that is particular.

But can we use cultural apprehensions of historical particularity to explain or justify the violence toward the non-Israelites that accompanies God's hospitality for his people? When we are told that the divine "curse of destruction" (*ḥerem*) required the annihilation of entire cities—"men, women and children" (Deut. 2:34; 3:6)—the conflict between this apparent barbarity and our cultural sensitivities becomes nearly unbearable.[24] When King Saul kills the Amalekites—"man and woman, babe and suckling, ox and sheep, camel and donkey"

---

21. Miroslav Volf, *Exclusion and Embrace: A Theological Exploration of Identity, Otherness, and Reconciliation* (Nashville: Abingdon, 1996), 221.

22. Lesslie Newbigin, *The Gospel in a Pluralist Society* (Grand Rapids: Eerdmans; Geneva: WCC, 1989), 87.

23. Ibid., 88.

24. Cf. Preuss, *Old Testament Theology,* 136–37.

(1 Sam. 15:3)—and nonetheless gets dethroned because he has extended clemency toward King Agag, we again tend to side with Western apprehensions of unnecessary cruelty toward a defeated enemy. Saul's failure to kill Agag is a failure to comply with Yahweh's implementation of the curse of destruction (*herem*) on the Amalekites. It is a failure to comply with the requirements of a "holy war." No matter how we try to reinterpret the biblical text to justify our sense of pity for King Agag, such attempts remain awkward and forced.[25] The biblical text seems to condemn unequivocally Saul's hesitancy in fulfilling the *herem*'s demands. Can we really shrug off our sensibilities toward the idea of a holy war with the suggestion that those sensibilities are historically conditioned? This is difficult, not merely because it is impossible to sidestep our historical particularity, but also because there is strong biblical backing for the idea that life is to be valued. The *herem* seems to be an instance where divine violence directly conflicts with divine hospitality. Whatever motivations God may have—whether it be purity of worship or punishment of evil—doesn't his violence ultimately jeopardize his hospitality? It remains difficult to reconcile God's preferential hospitality for the poor with the mandated total destruction of women and children in a holy war. The God who appears to us in the biblical text does not allow himself to be molded and shaped according to our sense of morality.

Violence and Authorial Intent

We may ask, of course, whether we want to restrict ourselves to the intent of the biblical authors. Perhaps we should read in the margins of the text and so deconstruct the original, intended meaning of certain passages. Phyllis Trible, in her well-known book *Texts of Terror*, takes this approach. She discusses four violent incidents: Hagar's banishment (Gen. 16; 21:9–21), Tamar's rape (2 Sam. 13:1–22), the concubine's rape, murder, and dismemberment (Judg. 19), and the sacrifice of Jephthah's daughter (Judg. 11:29–40). In each of these passages Trible sees misogynist oppression and violation of marginalized women. These passages "are tales of terror with women as victims."[26] Trible engages in an interpretive process that takes place on several levels. First, she regards these four women as "Christ figures" and so applies to them the Suffering Servant songs of Second Isaiah, as well as the passion narratives of the Gospels and the

---

25. This is the (in my opinion unsuccessful) approach of Robert A. Burt, who argues that the text of 1 Sam. 15 looks with sympathy on Agag's agony ("Reconciling with Injustice," in *Transgression, Punishment, Responsibility, Forgiveness,* ed. Andrew D. Weiner; and Leonard V. Kaplan, *Graven Images,* vol. 4 [Madison: University of Wisconsin Law School, 1998], 109–11).

26. Phyllis Trible, *Texts of Terror: Literary-Feminist Readings of Biblical Narratives* (Philadelphia: Fortress, 1984), 1.

Eucharistic segments of the Pauline epistles.[27] Hagar "was wounded for our transgressions; she was bruised for our iniquities."[28] Tamar was a "woman of sorrows and acquainted with grief."[29] The concubine's "body was broken and given to many."[30] We cry out for Jephthah's daughter, "My God, my God, why hast thou forsaken her?"[31]

Trible presents a detailed literary-critical analysis of these four biblical passages. She points out how various elements of the biblical text confront and condemn the terrible acts of violence committed against these women. When she finds herself unable to account for at least some of the violence in the biblical text, however, she takes a second significant interpretive move. She considers both the biblical narrator and the God of the biblical story implicated in at least some of these wanton crimes. She comments, for instance, that the storyteller who narrates the rape and murder of the concubine from Bethlehem "cares little about the woman's fate"[32] and has a perspective that "does not direct its heart to her."[33] When the biblical author shows no compassion or attention to victimized women, Trible argues that it is necessary "to interpret against the narrator, plot, other characters, and the biblical tradition."[34]

Chris Heard, in an article on the prophetic book of Habakkuk, takes a similar approach.[35] The book takes the form of a complaint in which the prophet argues that Yahweh must put an end to the violence that takes place among the people of Judah: "How long, Yahweh, am I to cry for help while you will not listen; to cry, 'Violence!' in your ear while you will not save? Why do you make me see wrong-doing, why do you countenance oppression? Plundering and violence confront me, contention and discord flourish" (Hab. 1:2–3). In response Yahweh promises to put an end to Judah's violence by raising up the Babylonians: "They are dreadful and awesome, a law and authority to themselves. . . . They are all bent on violence" (1:7, 9). Habakkuk then questions Yahweh's use of violence to end violence: the solution seems to be worse than the plight (1:12–17). Yahweh's second, lengthy response indicates that he will use even more violence in order to deal with the evil of the Babylonians: "For the violence done to the Lebanon will overwhelm you [Babylonians] and the

27. Ibid., 3.

28. Ibid., 8.

29. Ibid., 36.

30. Ibid., 64.

31. Ibid., 92.

32. Ibid., 76.

33. Ibid., 84. Similarly, Trible comments that by praising Jephthah's faith, the Epistle to the Hebrews has "violated the ancient story" (ibid., 108; cf. Heb. 11:32–34).

34. Ibid., 86.

35. Chris Heard, "Hearing the Children's Cries: Commentary, Deconstruction, Ethics, and the Book of Habakkuk," *Semeia* 77 (1997): 75–89. With appreciation to J. Richard Middleton for directing my attention to this article.

massacre of animals will terrify you, because of the bloodshed and violence done to the country, to the city and to all who live in it" (2:17). The cycle of violence seems unending. In Heard's words, "When YHWH walks, the earth shakes, mountains are toppled, dry land is flooded, all in the service of retributive justice."[36] The problem with this picture, argues Heard, is that it implicates not only the Babylonians but also Yahweh in violence. Appealing to Jacques Derrida and Simon Critchley, Heard makes the point that in a deconstructive reading the text opens itself up to a wholly other reading that sees one's ethical obligation toward those outside the margin. Taking his cue from the mention of children in Psalm 109:9–13, Heard wants us to pay attention to the children whom we have lost from sight in our desire for revenge: "The text didn't say anything about the oppressors having children! But now that the psalmist mentions it—now that this intertext exposes the heartfelt desires of the vengeful—I see them there. Right over there, just outside the margins of the text. Punished for the sins of their fathers. Branded. Outcast. Homeless. Naked. Starving. If, that is—and what a big 'if' this is!—if the Chaldeans didn't just kill them outright."[37] Heard's sudden recognition that the book of Habakkuk expresses no concern for the children leads him to charge the book with muffling the children's cries.[38] He argues that a deconstructive reading of Habakkuk, while implicating Habakkuk in the injustice of violence, might perhaps—in the interest of undeconstructible justice—allow us to hear anew the cries of the Judahite and Babylonian children.

The deconstructive readings presented by Trible and Heard have a certain appeal in our postmodern context. They allow us to hear the suffering victims cry. Our hermeneutical glasses have too long been tinted by the modernist assumptions of the dominant structures of society. Our so-called objective understanding of Scripture has often reflected dominant Western cultural assumptions, shaped by centuries of theological and cultural development. Deconstructive reinterpretations of the story are helpful when they allow us to look at the biblical story—and at the violence in the story—with different glasses, so as to modify or enlarge our vistas.

Still, when we are asked to deconstruct the biblical text in our pursuit of justice, we must ask: Just what does this justice look like? Trible maintains that it means the liberation of women from oppressive situations. Heard argues that it consists of resistance against the violence enacted against children. These are instances of justice, they argue. And I certainly would not want to belittle these causes. But are we, by adopting a postmodern framework, really warranted to hold up these causes as instances where people struggle for justice? Can justice ever take on concrete particularity in a Derridean understanding of deconstruc-

36. Ibid., 79.
37. Ibid., 86.
38. Ibid., 87.

tion? Is it possible for justice ever to enter into the historical realm of time and space? As we saw in chapter 1, Derrida argues that justice and hospitality can never be embodied in time and space. They relate to a messianic future that is always still to come (*à venir*).[39]

A deconstructive reading of the text has a tendency to become overly subjective, even arbitrary. This is not to say that a historical-critical reading is no longer important for postmodern philosophers. For Derrida the deconstructive move does not take place until *after* a careful reading of the text in its original context.[40] Both Trible and Heard engage in a careful exegetical analysis of the text. It is not clear, however, on what basis Trible sees the suffering women as types of Christ and on what basis Heard feels justified in pulling the suffering children inside the margins of the text. Presumably, the response of both authors would be that they do so in deference to justice. But this again brings us back to the question of how we determine—and whether, in fact, we are able to determine—what justice is in any given historical context.[41] We may desperately want to avoid blaming the God whom we worship for the violence in his story. But knowingly interpreting the biblical text against the intention of the author and the biblical tradition is an unsatisfying way of coping with the divine violence that we meet in the pages of the Bible.

Living with the Violence of Hospitality

In a sense we have come full circle. I have pointed out some of the weaknesses in the Calvinist understanding of hospitality and violence. The problem here is that it hardly does justice to God's gracious hospitality in Jesus Christ. By mak-

39. John D. Caputo, *The Prayers and Tears of Jacques Derrida: Religion without Religion* (Bloomington: Indiana University Press, 1997), 145. Derrida does, of course, have some concrete ideals in terms of what justice looks like. This seems incongruous with his strong apprehension about the possibility of the embodiment of justice. Cf. James K. A. Smith, "Determined Hope: A Phenomenology of Christian Expectation," in *The Future of Hope: Essays on Christian Tradition amid Modernity and Postmodernity*, ed. Miroslav Volf and William Katerberg (Grand Rapids: Eerdmans, forthcoming).

40. Cf. Bruce Ellis Benson, *Graven Images: Nietzsche, Derrida, and Marion on Modern Idolatry* (Downers Grove, Ill.: InterVarsity, 2002), 129–30.

41. J. Richard Middleton and Brian J. Walsh argue that Trible's approach allows us to escape from Scripture as a "tyrannical authority to be imposed from the outside" (*Truth Is Stranger Than It Used to Be: Biblical Faith in a Postmodern Age* [Downers Grove, Ill.: InterVarsity, 1995], 186). They are concerned to be faithful to the Scriptures, and they rightly point out that we need to improvise an ending to God's ongoing drama of salvation and that this improvisation needs to be consistent with the script as it has developed thus far and with the author's plot intentions, insofar as we know them (182). It is not clear how this concern allows the authors to appropriate Trible's willingness to interpret against the narrator, the plot, and the biblical tradition (184). Moreover, opposition to the violence described in the book of Judges in no way requires us to deconstruct the authorial intent of Judges. Trible ignores the fact that the author does not condone the situation of lawlessness but rather looks forward to a time in which a Davidic king will put an end to the chaos and violence described in the book.

ing this hospitality subservient to an eternal double decree that is solely based on the will of God, the Calvinist notion of hospitality becomes a forced, even tyrannical "hospitality." Here the cross does not just *enable* salvation; instead, it actually *determines* salvation. The cross is not just a hospitable opening up; rather, it forces people to enter. The necessary corollary is a narrowing of the hospitable intent of the cross to the elect only (limited atonement), with all the attendant problems for a meaningful and robust understanding of hospitality. By locating divine violence at the heart of God's character, Calvinism makes absolute or pure hospitality an eternal impossibility. In its essence God's hospitality is a limited hospitality.

The violence that accompanies a Calvinist view of hospitality is not easily overcome, however. I have commented that while the alternatives to Calvinism may seem more attractive, they do not necessarily resolve the issue of divine violence. Indeed, it is one of Calvinism's strengths that it refuses to resolve the issue of divine violence by rejecting it in favor of absolute nonviolence. No matter how much we analyze biblical narratives, it appears impossible to expunge all references to God's involvement with violence.[42] Such attempts to remove all violence from God often contrast Jesus' apparent nonviolence to the violent picture of the Old Testament God. But we can only interpret Jesus' life as a life of nonviolence if we take a narrow view of violence as the use of physical harm. When we take violence in the broader sense in which I have defined it in chapter 1, Jesus' temple "cleansing" turns out to be a rather violent action, which upset the tables of the moneychangers and the seats of the dove sellers (Mark 11:15).[43] Also, many of Jesus' words and actions were offensive to many and encroached on people's personal space and well-being. The Gospel of Matthew displays an ever-increasing tension between Jesus and those who trust in their ethnicity to save them, with Jesus threatening that "the children of the kingdom will be thrown out into the darkness outside, where there will be weeping and grinding of teeth" (Matt. 8:12) and proclaiming that it will be "more bearable for Sodom on Judgement Day" than for Capernaum (Matt. 11:24). Even the Gospel of Luke, which continually emphasizes hospitality in the context of meals and feasts, presents Jesus as favorably comparing a prostitute to a Pharisee (Luke 7:36–50), as berating Pharisees and lawyers in forceful language (Luke 11:37–52), and as upsetting important visitors at the house of a leading Pharisee (Luke 14:1–24). Apparently, the hospitable context of dinner parties does not exclude at least verbally violating the boundaries and comfort zones of the leaders of the people. By appealing to Jesus' apparent nonviolence, we end up stretching the discontinuity between the Old and the New Testaments beyond the warrant of the biblical text.

---

42. Cf. Brueggemann: "In the end, a student of the Old Testament cannot answer for or justify the violence, but must concede that it belongs to the very fabric of this faith" (*Theology,* 381).

43. See the last section of chapter 1 ("Violence as Harm or Injury").

This is not to say that Jesus merely affirms everything in the Old Testament and that the approach to violence and hospitality remains exactly the same in the New Testament. Jesus is not content with the Old Testament lex talionis ("eye for eye and tooth for tooth") and sharpens the demand for hospitality (Matt. 5:38–42).[44] To the degree that the attitude toward hospitality and violence changes in the New Testament, we could say that there is an increase in the urgency to strive for hospitality and to avoid violence. God has never expressed his hospitality as openly and has never extended it as universally as he has done in Jesus Christ (Heb. 1:1–2). Election in New Testament thought is no longer the choice of one nation, but is God's choice of a Church made up of Jews and Gentiles. Through Christ, it is the Church that now becomes "*a chosen race, a kingdom of priests, a holy nation, a people to be a personal possession* to sing the praises of God" (1 Pet. 2:9, italics added). Election is no longer tied to ethnicity; it is now election *in Christ* (Eph. 1:4). Much of the violence accompanying the election of Israel is overcome in the election of the Church in Jesus Christ. More than ever before, God demonstrates that it is hospitality rather than violence that characterizes the heart of all his actions.

As we have seen, however, absolute hospitality—hospitality without any boundaries or limits whatsoever—is impossible in the created order as we know it, both because of creational limitations and because of the influence of sin. Therefore, when people arbitrarily limit the boundaries of the Church, God's hospitality shows that it has a violent edge. The Judaizing Law party in Galatia, wanting to place ethnic restrictions on divine hospitality (Gal. 2:11–14; 4:17) and violently persecuting Gentile believers (Gal. 4:29; 5:11), find themselves outside the fellowship of the community. *"Drive away that slave girl and her son,"* St. Paul insists, identifying the Law party with Hagar and her son (Gal. 4:30; cf. Gen. 21:10). He even makes the violent suggestion that those who insist on circumcision should "go further and mutilate themselves" (Gal. 5:12). This is not some arbitrary barbaric suggestion but has the distinct purpose of excluding the Law party from a legitimate place in the hospitable community: the Law regulated that castration excluded one from the assembly of Yahweh (Deut. 23:1; cf. Lev. 21:20). Even the hospitality of election in Christ has a particularity that entails boundaries and violence. To be sure, this violence does not predominate, and neither does it have the final say. But to insist on "pure hospitality" in an impure world would mean to give it over to the forces of inhospitality and violence. Put provocatively, God's hospitality in Christ needs an edge of violence to ensure the welcome of humanity and all creation.

---

44. Jesus contrasts his teaching here not just with the oral tradition but also with the Law itself. See Richard B. Hays, *The Moral Vision of the New Testament: A Contemporary Introduction to New Testament Ethics* (New York: HarperSanFrancisco, 1996), 319–29; Christopher D. Marshall, *Beyond Retribution: A New Testament Vision for Justice, Crime, and Punishment* (Grand Rapids: Eerdmans; Auckland: Lime Grove, 2001), 84–89.

We tend to view this edge of violence as something negative—hence our hesitations about the divine violence of election issuing ultimately in the violence of the cross. In this chapter, I have used several strategies to lessen the tension: I have substituted a historical, corporate, and instrumental view of election for one that tends to be eternal, individual, and futuristic. Also, I have argued that the hospitality of election is not an arbitrary decision but is God's way of safeguarding monotheism, while the violence against other nations functions as a divine response to their immorality, so that the election of Israel expresses God's "preferential option for the poor." Since God's hospitality is not inviolable, the fairness of election is enhanced by the possibility that Israel, as God's elect nation, might receive the same treatment as the reprobate nations around it. Perhaps most significantly, I have argued that election always serves God's missiological purpose to embrace all the nations, not just the nation of Israel, in his hospitality.

Despite all our attempts at a theodicy, in the end we still wonder: Why this historical journey of hospitality? Why violence at all? Why not absolute hospitality, both now and forever? Is the violence really worth it? Do we really dare attribute to God's actions in history—his salvific act in Christ—the term "hospitality"? Do we really dare call God's election of Israel and the Church an act of hospitality, despite the violence that it entails? Though I believe the arguments from the biblical narrative presented in this chapter are helpful (even necessary), our rational reflection on the biblical story cannot suffice. Our reflections and thought patterns are limited by the very same limitations that stamp all our actions. Violence intrudes into our very minds and hearts. St. Paul reminds us of our epistemic limitations when he calls out, "How rich and deep are the wisdom and the knowledge of God! We cannot reach to the root of his decisions or his ways" (Rom. 11:33). This confession of human inadequacy in probing the mystery of divine election at the end of three profound chapters on the topic should function as a reminder that election is a matter of praise and adoration first—and only then one of theological reflection. The charts of high Calvinists like Beza and Perkins, outlining the historical outworking of election and reprobation, certainly had their shortcomings.[45] But Beza was right to conclude at the bottom of his chart with a reference to Romans 11:33. A rational explanation attempting to justify divine violence will always have its limitations. It always runs into what Calvin terms the divine "labyrinth," and which I would prefer to call simply the "mystery" of God's presence. This is not the labyrinth of an absolute will that may be quite at odds with God's revealed will. Rather, it is the mystery of God's ineffable love, whose hospitable character will draw us ever deeper into his divine life of glory. It is only the light of the pure hospitality awaiting us that can deal with the darkness of all violence and inhospitality that we now experience. In

---

45. For Beza's chart, see chapter 2.

the end it is less a matter of rationally justifying than of having the courage to live with the violence that accompanies hospitality. The courage to denote particular actions—God's choice of Israel and his involvement in the cross—as hospitable awaits future eschatological justification. Only to the degree that we share in God's absolute hospitality can we truly appreciate also the need for conditional hospitality.

PART 2

The Cruciform Face
of Hospitality

4

Atonement, Metaphors, and Models

The Linguistic Web of Metaphors

When we speak about the atonement in terms of hospitality, we are, of course, already using a metaphor. Likewise, when we speak of divine violence, we are using metaphorical language. Indeed, the way in which I have framed the question of this entire study (the relationship between hospitality and violence in connection with the cross) is metaphorical. And we don't escape the metaphorical character of our language when we "unpack" (yet another metaphor) the hospitality of the cross in terms of imitation, victory, and punishment. Chapters 5–8 deal with three different models of the atonement: the moral-influence model, the model of representative punishment, and the Christus Victor model. Each of these models works with different metaphors. Some of the most prominent metaphors that Scripture uses to describe the meaning of the cross center on sacrifice, financial exchange, slave trade, healing, reconciliation, and military battle.[1] In this book I do not explore each of these in detail. Rather, in the next four chapters I ask the question how the theme of hospitality relates to some of these metaphors and to the three models in Christian atonement theology that are based on them. Are the three traditional models of the atonement expressions of God's hospitality, or are we inescapably

---

1. Cf. Scott Hahn, *Lord, Have Mercy: The Healing Power of Confession* (New York: Doubleday, 2003), 95–97.

bound to a violent God? Is it possible to retain these models in a world that seems increasingly concerned with the issue of religious violence?

By looking at atonement models in terms of hospitality, I am not suggesting that hospitality is the "literal" or "uncontaminated" essence lying behind the metaphoric embodiments of the various models. The notion of hospitality is itself a metaphor. Viewing the atonement from the perspective of the hospitality theme thus cannot mean an escape from metaphor into the world of literal truth. As will become clear in this chapter, I am not convinced that we can make such an escape, nor do I believe that such an escape should be our goal.

We are delving into issues surrounding language, metaphors, and models. Indeed, the question of divine hospitality in relation to the cross is intimately connected with general questions surrounding the theory of knowledge (epistemology) and the nature of theology. When we make certain theological claims, what exactly are we doing? Are we making statements that relate with absolute transparency to objective realities that are out there? Do we, in other words, have immediate access to objective reality? Modern realist theories of knowledge have tended to emphasize the possibility of direct and complete access to the empirical realities outside us. Postmodern philosophers, however, have drawn attention to our inability to escape the linguistic web in which we find ourselves and have been far less certain that there is an objective reality that we can access by means of our senses. The question of the function of language (does it correspond to a reality that exists independent of our perception and of our linguistic capacities?) is both more significant and more difficult in connection with theological language. The question takes on greater significance in the sense that theological language touches on the core of our being. Our ability to speak truthfully about God—and about the restoration of his relationship with us—impinges directly on our ability to attribute meaning and value to our existence. The question becomes more difficult in the sense that theological language—including atonement theology—makes statements about a reality that we do not access by means of our five senses. The claims of faith are not empirically based in the same sense as other claims.[2]

Not only the overarching concepts of hospitality and violence but also the various traditional ways of approaching atonement theology are obviously metaphorical. It is important, therefore, to clarify what we understand by a metaphor. Perhaps the meaning of the word is best described in terms of its root meaning. The Greek origin of the word tells us that something is carried across (*meta,* across; *pherein,* to carry). In the case of a metaphor, it is the meaning of a word that is carried over from one semantic field to another. For

---

2. This is not to deny that faith underlies nontheological claims. I am merely suggesting that God language takes us beyond the creational or natural realm into the supernatural realm.

example, when I say that God is my shepherd, I am transferring the meaning of the word "shepherd" from the area of a particular seminomadic way of making a living to the area of God's care for his people. Likewise, when I say that Jesus paid a heavy price for our salvation, I am transferring the meaning of a monetary price from the field of finances and trade to the area of salvation. Metaphors take words out of their original contexts and use them in new, seemingly inappropriate ways. As Sallie McFague puts it: "Most simply, a metaphor is seeing one thing *as* something else, pretending 'this' is 'that' because we do not know how to think or talk about 'this', so we use 'that' as a way of saying something about it."[3] In other words, metaphors have an "as if" structure. We carry the meaning of certain words over from one area into another *as if* those words still held the same meaning.

We all realize that the use of metaphors introduces a certain tension. We may say that God is our shepherd, but certain things can be said of shepherds that cannot be said of God. Shepherds in first-century Palestine belonged to a rough, poor, and despised class of society. We don't mean to draw attention to these features of a shepherd when we use this term for God. Instead, we intend to refer to God's "pastoral" (i.e., loving and caring) character traits. Likewise, when we say that Christ paid a heavy price, we don't mean to suggest that he has just concluded an extensive process of negotiation with someone and has finally bought human souls as a commodity on some kind of a divine (or diabolic) market. All we likely mean to say is that Jesus' suffering and death for us was immensely difficult. What this means is that metaphors introduce a certain tension. They don't just open up the meaning of something by associating it with something else, but in the process they also limit and circumscribe. Not all aspects of shepherds are transferable to God, and not all aspects of a purchase can be appropriately connected to the death of Christ. Sallie McFague refers to this limiting characteristic of metaphors when she says that they "always contain the whisper, 'it is *and it is not.*'"[4] By ignoring or forgetting that metaphors don't have the ability to transfer every aspect of the original meaning, we run into serious problems. We make claims that are entirely unwarranted, such as the claim that God is a rough, poor, and despised individual, or the claim that in return for the souls of the lost the devil extracted a certain monetary price from Christ.[5]

---

3. Sallie McFague, *Metaphorical Theology: Models of God in Religious Language* (Philadelphia: Fortress, 1982), 15. Cf. Sallie McFague, *Models of God: Theology for an Ecological, Nuclear Age* (Philadelphia: Fortress, 1987), 33.

4. McFague, *Metaphorical Theology,* 13. Cf. McFague, *Models,* 33; Vincent Brümmer, *The Model of Love: A Study in Philosophical Theology* (Cambridge: Cambridge University Press, 1993), 8.

5. Cf. Ian G. Barbour, *Myths, Models, and Paradigms: A Comparative Study in Science and Religion* (New York: Harper & Row, 1974), 12: "'The lion is king of the beasts', but it has only some of the attributes of royalty. 'Love is a fire', but we do not expect it to cook a meal. There is a tension between affirmation and negation, for in analogy there are both similarities and differences."

Functions of Metaphors

It is clear, then, that there are certain pitfalls in the use of metaphorical language. Perhaps we feel that it is safer, therefore, to avoid metaphors and instead to use literal language as much as possible. In this way we might avoid the imprecision and the ambiguities of metaphorical language. The more rational and objective we become, the less chance we have of using our metaphors in erroneous ways or of drawing outrageous conclusions from our use of them. It is easy to develop a degree of unease with "metaphorical" language and to favor "literal" language instead. Conservative Christians have often had a keen distrust of metaphorical interpretations of Scripture.[6] I suspect this stems from the notion that literal language is rational, whereas metaphorical language is creative. Literal language, therefore, is often considered more trustworthy in describing reality and relating historical events. In evangelical circles it is still a popular hermeneutical dictum that Scripture needs to be interpreted literally whenever possible.

Although there are indeed differences between what we call "literal" and "metaphorical" language,[7] this does not mean that we can understand literal language as "more rational" and hence "more real" and therefore as giving better descriptions of reality. Metaphors have at least four important functions in our dealings with reality. First, a picture is worth a thousand words. Metaphors can give quick, pithy characterizations in ways that other (more literal) descriptions cannot. I can describe God as someone who protects me against attacks, who provides me with physical and spiritual needs, who warns me when I am tempted to fall away from him, and who brings me safely to my ultimate destination, but this is a lengthy description that I can avoid by referring to God as my shepherd. What is more, the image of God as a shepherd has an emotive "extra" that a more literal representation does not carry. The pastoral scene of a shepherd with his sheep does not just pass on information; it conveys an atmosphere that no other description captures quite as adequately. No matter how carefully we try to analyze and unwrap the meaning of the metaphor, we can never quite give a literal description that conveys the exact same sense as the metaphor. Just as an explanation of a piece of art can never quite capture the full richness of the artwork, so also every attempt to unpack the metaphor will be only partially successful.

---

6. Cf. A. L. Th. de Bruijne, "Hermeneutiek en metaforie," in *Woord op schrift: Theologische reflecties over het gezag van de bijbel,* ed. C. Trimp (Kampen, Neth.: Kok, 2002), 109–60.

7. I will argue later that all language is metaphorical. It remains true, however, that in some instances we transfer words from one linguistic field into another more consciously and more obviously. The metaphorical character of words and expressions can become so ingrained that we speak of "flat" metaphors or don't recognize them as metaphors at all.

The "extra" that is contained in metaphors derives from the way in which metaphors evoke our imagination and creativity. We associate the metaphor of a shepherd with certain well-known biblical passages. We think of the "tranquil streams" of Psalm 23, of David snatching a sheep from the jaw of a lion or a bear in 1 Samuel 17, and of Jesus physically functioning as the reassuring gate in front of the sheepfold in John 10. We readily associate metaphors with stories that we know and with other elements of our world of experience. As interpreters, therefore, we bring meaning to bear on the metaphors that we encounter. Metaphors are not just out there, separated from us by an imaginary glass screen and waiting for us to analyze them in a clinical fashion. It is in our encounter with metaphors that they become alive and begin to function in certain ways.[8]

Metaphors are dependent on human creativity and imagination. What is more, they enable our creativity and imagination to flourish in ways that "ordinary" language does not. A second function of metaphors, therefore, is that they create room for enrichment and allow for a creative engagement with our surroundings. Through the odd and seemingly awkward and inappropriate use of language, new vistas are opened up. I once heard the story of a poet who read one of his poems in a public setting. When asked to interpret it, he responded by reading it again. His point was that art cannot be reduced to strictly objective propositional statements. Instead it asks us to work with it, play with it, and so enhance it in creative and imaginative ways. John Franklin has rightly commented that "the imagination never simply reproduces the reality it encounters. It always adds something. At its best, it is not an addition that distorts reality, but enhances it, and gets us to see it in a fresh and fuller way. Imagination does a productive work, it helps us create the world we know."[9]

Because of this connection between metaphors and our ability to creatively interpret and give meaning to our world, metaphors allow us to influence and shape our environment. The third function of metaphors, therefore, is that they have transformative power. Vincent Brümmer argues that by interpreting our experience of the world in terms of religious models (which, as we will see, are closely connected with metaphors), "believers come to see which actions and attitudes are called for in relation to the world and in the various situations in which they have to act."[10] Metaphors don't just present certain propositional truths; they first of all relate normatively how we want to view the world around

8. This is not to say that metaphors are entirely dependent on the individual interpreter. The meaning of words, including the meaning of metaphors, is dependent on conventions established through social-linguistic patterns of transmission. These patterns become the normative framework setting certain guidelines and boundaries for interpretation. The only point I am making is that the guidelines and boundaries are not cast in stone and always remain fluid.

9. John Franklin, "Arts, Imagination, and Theology," *Canadian Evangelical Review* 21 (2001): 5.

10. Brümmer, *Model of Love,* 16.

us and how we believe the world should change.[11] From a Christian perspective, this role of metaphors is highly significant. Since metaphors give direction to the future, the ethical Christian life cannot do without metaphors. They help us envision a future in which the justice of God's hospitality holds sway.

A final function of metaphors is that they are a divinely given means to avoid idolatrous claims of knowledge. Metaphors are nonliteral descriptions of reality. They are an acknowledgment that we need to access the world around us in an indirect fashion, and that the idea of direct and complete access is an arrogant illusion that violates the multifaceted integrity of the created world.[12] Levinas's opposition to the Western emphasis on ontology may be overstated, but he is right in arguing that our claims of knowledge have functioned in totalizing and idolatrous ways. Knowledge implies power, and the human quest for objective knowledge is often accompanied by a desire to reduce difference, to overcome the alterity of the other, and to shape our environment in accordance with our desires. When human claims of knowledge are overstated, and when we don't acknowledge the need for metaphorical associations and creativity, the result is a prideful claim of divinity. Claims of absolute knowledge don't take into account the Creator/creature distinction and fail to acknowledge that our understanding is always colored by our backgrounds and experiences and is therefore partial at best. The use of metaphors implies that interpretation and the expansion of our epistemic horizon is only possible by means of mental associations with linguistic experiences that we have already had and that are already part of our horizon.[13]

The Universality of Metaphors

The various positive functions of metaphors show that the common parlance of metaphors as "just" metaphors is highly questionable. When we say that something is "just" a metaphor, we most likely mean that metaphors are less significant and are an accommodation to our inability of expressing ourselves accurately. At the very least, references to metaphors as "only" metaphors are meant to place them at a lower level than literal descriptions. Most likely such statements are also meant to suggest that metaphors are somehow less accurate and less truthful than literal descriptions. Colin Gunton argues that

11. The transformative power of metaphors is reason for Paul Trudinger to question "fight talk" (as well as metaphors of divine "maleness" and of the cross): "[I]f we continue making the assertion 'Edmund Hilary conquered Everest', we shall likely continue to have wars" ("Biblical Metaphors and Symbols: Handle with Care!" *Faith and Freedom* 43 [1993]: 45).

12. Cf. James K. A. Smith, *The Fall of Interpretation: Philosophical Foundations for a Creational Hermeneutic* (Downers Grove, Ill.: InterVarsity, 2000), 26–27, 148. Smith argues that interpretation is constitutive of human creaturehood and, therefore, good (and, he continues, nonviolent).

13. Cf. Barbour, *Myths*, 50; McFague, *Metaphorical Theology*, 20–23.

because the world can be known only indirectly, metaphor is really "the most appropriate form that a duly humble and listening language should take. In all this, there is a combination of openness and mystery, speech and silence, which makes the clarity and distinctness aimed at by the rationalist tradition positively hostile to the truth. Thus the tables are turned: metaphor rather than being the cinderella of cognitive language becomes the most rather than the least appropriate means of expressing the truth."[14] Metaphors, suggests Gunton, are a reminder that a rationalist position that places the cognitive or analytical faculties above our emotional and creative abilities is untenable. Metaphors are the most appropriate way of accessing the world.

In fact, we could go even further. Metaphors are not only the best, they are the *only* way of describing the world around us. All human language is metaphorical. To be sure, there is a difference between saying that God is a shepherd and saying that he is dependable. But the difference is not simply that the former statement is metaphorical and the latter literal. If it is true that all language derives its meaning from a large field of associations, then in a strict sense there is no such thing as "literal" language. Sallie McFague puts it this way: "Far from being an esoteric or ornamental rhetorical device superimposed *on* ordinary language, metaphor *is* ordinary language. It is the *way* we think. We often make distinctions between ordinary and poetic language, assuming that the first is direct and the second indirect, but actually both are indirect, for we always think by indirection."[15] We are often tempted to think that a particular word or expression is meant literally simply because the associations that person X makes with a certain word are very similar to the associations that person Y makes.

The necessity of metaphorical language is given with the structure of the created order. All interpretive access is indirect, by means of association. Our language about God and about his actions in the world, therefore, is necessarily metaphorical as well. Whether we speak about the atonement in terms of imitation, of justice, or of battle, we are speaking metaphorically. This is not to say that we are "just" using metaphors and are therefore not speaking truthfully. Quite the contrary! God has designed the world in such a way that by means of metaphor we are able to access—albeit in an indirect, creaturely manner—something about the way in which God redeems the world. Just because all language is metaphorical, it does not follow that God cannot enter into this process by means of revelation. The human capacity for association

---

14. Colin E. Gunton, *The Actuality of Atonement: A Study of Metaphor, Rationality, and the Christian Tradition* (Grand Rapids: Eerdmans, 1989), 37–38. Cf. N. T. Wright, *The New Testament and the People of God*, vol. 1 of *Christian Origins and the Question of God* (Minneapolis: Fortress, 1992), 63; A. H. Van Veluw, *'De straf die ons de vrede aanbrengt': Over God, kruis, straf en de slachtoffers van deze wereld in de christelijke verzoeningsleer* (Zoetermeer, Neth.: Boekencentrum, 2002), 146.

15. McFague, *Metaphorical Theology,* 16. Cf. Brümmer, *Model of Love,* 8.

(and hence for using metaphors) may perhaps look like an exclusively human process, but this is merely because we are capable of observing only our own associations. The human embeddedness of language in metaphor may, in fact, function as a divine means of revelation.[16]

Of course, the problem of incoherence or subjectivism is a real one. If language didn't really refer to some objective reality out there, our position would finally become "completely subjectivist or even solipsist."[17] Deconstructionist philosophy at times runs this risk. Derrida's notion that there is nothing outside the text is highly problematic. Of course, this comment is often quoted out of context,[18] but the danger of solipsism remains. "If there is only text, or writing," says McFague, "this means there is only the play of words, interpretation upon interpretation, referring to nothing but other words, an endless spiral with no beginning or end."[19] Human language may be inherently metaphorical and may thus require a humble epistemology, but this does not mean that there is no objective world that can, in some indirect fashion, be interpreted. In other words, while our language and interpretive process are necessarily metaphorical, the created order itself is not.

What I am really pleading for here is some kind of "critical-realist" epistemology that claims there truly is an objective world out there and that also asserts that some understandings are better than others. Certain interpretations may even be flat wrong. If I didn't believe that my statements were true or at least had a certain likelihood of being true, it would make no sense to make any truth claims at all: "It would be incoherent to live my life as a life in the presence of God," says Vincent Brümmer, "if I were to deny that there really is a God in whose presence I live."[20] A critical-realist epistemology says there is something beyond the metaphor. Even if we have only an incomplete and partially erroneous understanding of this reality, this does not mean that it does not exist. N. T. Wright, in his discussion of a critical-realist epistemology, makes the comment:

> Once again Story comes to the rescue. Recognition of god-language as fundamentally metaphorical does not mean that it does not have a referent, and that some at least of the metaphors may not actually possess a particular appropriateness to this referent. In fact, metaphors are themselves mini-stories, suggesting ways of looking at a reality which

---

16. There is no need, therefore, to deny the metaphorical character of revelation (pace De Bruijne, "Hermeneutiek en metaforie," 145–49). Since God is the one who has created the human capacity of developing a web of linguistic associations, he is also capable of entering into this web by means of divine revelation.

17. Gunton, *Actuality of Atonement,* 41.

18. Cf. Bruce Ellis Benson, *Graven Ideologies: Nietzsche, Derrida, and Marion on Idolatry* (Downers Grove, Ill.: InterVarsity, 2002), 129–30.

19. McFague, *Models of God,* 23.

20. Brümmer, *Model of Love,* 18.

cannot be reduced to terms of the metaphor itself. As has become more widely recognized in recent writing, such metaphors and stories are in fact *more* basic within human consciousness than apparently "factual" speech, and recognizing the essentially storied nature of god-talk is therefore no bar to asserting the reality of its referent.[21]

A critical-realist perspective acknowledges, on the one hand, our inability to have a God's-eye view of the world and our inability to use literal language that escapes the web of human associations and to access the world directly in a rational way; on the other hand, critical realism asserts that the metaphorical character of all language in no way precludes the possibility of divine revelation and is as such a dependable way of interpreting the world and also a trustworthy way of speaking about God and about his actions in the world.[22]

Using Metaphors Appropriately in Atonement Theology

This twofold conclusion is important for our further discussion of atonement theology. First, we may be tempted to press our metaphors too far. This is the danger of reductionism. Since not every aspect of a metaphor is transferable to its new linguistic context, we need to take care how we explicate and work with particular metaphors. Although Scripture and tradition have used juridical metaphors to describe the divine-human relationship, this does not mean that we can press the metaphor to the extent that we can reduce our relationship with God to a legal relationship. Likewise, although Scripture calls on us to imitate Jesus, this does not mean that Jesus can be reduced to an example of what our true humanity looks like. Certainly more is involved. Metaphors are pressed too far also when we expand or generalize their application. This happens, for instance, when we use the commercial metaphor of redemption (the freeing of slaves by means of payment) to argue that it is the devil or God the Father who demands payment. Such generalizing does not take into account the limited scope of the metaphor.[23] Either way—whether by reductionism or generalization—we push the metaphor too far, and we fail to acknowledge humbly that our use of metaphors binds us to a limited perspective.

Second, it is also possible to downplay the importance of particular metaphors. We cannot simply ignore biblical metaphors because we feel that they

21. Wright, *New Testament*, 129–30. Cf. ibid., 135.

22. John G. Stackhouse, in similar fashion, sails between the Scylla of doubt and the Charybdis of despair ("Why Christians Should Abandon Certainty," in *Living in the LambLight: Christianity and Contemporary Challenges to the Gospel*, ed. Hans Boersma [Vancouver, B.C.: Regent College Publishing, 2001], 33–42). See also Janet Martin Soskice, *Metaphor and Religious Language* (Oxford: Clarendon, 1985), 131–32.

23. Cf. Youssouf Dembele, "Salvation as Victory: A Reconsideration of the Concept of Salvation in the Light of Jesus Christ's Life and Work Viewed as a Triumph over the Personal Powers of Evil" (Ph.D. diss., Trinity Evangelical Divinity School, 2001), 266–67, 278–81. Cf. also note 4 of this chapter.

don't really reflect the way things are or should be. Disturbed by the biblical notion that God can become angry and at times inflicts punishment, some authors deal with this issue by arguing that "perhaps we attribute 'anger' to God only because we have no language other than human language with which to comprehend God."[24] I would certainly agree that "anger" or "wrath" is not an independent characteristic of God. God is not wrath, but he is love (1 John 4:8). Does this mean, however, that we need to understand God's wrath metaphorically, while we understand his love literally? I seriously doubt it. When we use metaphors to describe the meaning of the atonement, we are not thereby reverting to "mere" metaphors that are bereft of real content. We can misuse metaphors not only by reductionism and generalization but also by emptying them of real content.

These pitfalls draw our attention to an important fact in our use of metaphors. We cannot develop an atonement theology by simply listing a number of metaphors. Not every metaphor is of equal significance. Some are only used incidentally in Scripture or in the tradition and therefore have no "staying power."[25] Neither is it a matter of adding up a number of passages and seeing which metaphor has the largest number of occurrences. Some metaphors are particularly useful because they can function as an overall paradigm, an umbrella under which we can place a number of other metaphors that seem to fit in the same group. The complexity of the atonement requires that we use constellations of metaphors. These constellations can be gathered under the umbrella of the most suggestive metaphors of the group, so-called root metaphors, which are particularly appealing in terms of describing the atonement.[26] Some or more of the various functions of these metaphors appear to excel when we apply them. Root metaphors, in other words, are more helpful than other metaphors (1) in the way that they can give a quick or pithy description of the atonement; (2) in their particularly strong appeals to our creativity and imagination; (3) in their ability to give an impetus for the Christian walk of faith; or (4) in their ability to create an awareness that we have only a partial insight into God's dealings with human beings. Root metaphors thus become models. A model incorporates a number of other metaphors and thus forms a

---

24. Joel B. Green and Mark D. Baker, *Recovering the Scandal of the Cross: Atonement in New Testament and Contemporary Contexts* (Downers Grove, Ill.: InterVarsity, 2000), 54. Cf. the helpful discussion in Tony Lane, "The Wrath of God as an Aspect of the Love of God," in *Nothing Greater, Nothing Better: Theological Essays on the Love of God*, ed. Kevin J. Vanhoozer (Grand Rapids: Eerdmans, 2001), 138–67. See also Hans Boersma, "The Disappearance of Punishment: Metaphors, Models, and the Meaning of the Atonement," *Books & Culture* 9 (2) (March/April 2003): 32–34.

25. Sallie McFague uses this expression as a description of a model: "The simplest way to define a model is as a dominant metaphor, a metaphor with staying power" (*Metaphorical Theology*, 23).

26. For "root metaphors," see Barbour, *Myths*, 65; Earl R. MacCormac, *Metaphor and Myth in Science and Religion* (Durham, N.C.: Duke University Press, 1976), 93–101; McFague, *Metaphorical Theology*, 27–28, 104; McFague, *Models of God*, 34. Brümmer speaks of "key models" (*Model of Love*, 20–22).

complex structure that can function as a paradigm or lens through which we can look at a particular doctrine. One fundamental way in which we look at the doctrine of sin, for instance, is through the metaphor of pride, while a very significant model for our understanding of God is the metaphor of father.[27]

In developing various atonement models, we ask ourselves which of the metaphors are particularly suitable as "root metaphors." This is an important step because it safeguards us from relying on metaphors that are less than suitable for the development of atonement theology. Vincent Brümmer, in his discussion of the use of theological models, describes four different criteria for such models, which I think are helpful.[28] The first is that of "consonance with tradition." A particular metaphor proves its use through the frequency with which the Church's creeds and theologians have appealed to it. "Choice of models is not unconditioned," maintains Janet Martin Soskice. "[W]e do not choose the model of God as shepherd over that of God as poultry keeper or cattleman at random. A favoured model continues to be so in virtue of its own applicability certainly, but also because the history of its application makes it already freighted with meaning."[29] Since not every metaphor has the same potential, believers throughout the tradition have emphasized certain metaphors and models. The analysis of the three atonement models in the next three chapters is based in large part on the awareness that these models have proven their staying power throughout the history of the Church. I must admit to some discomfort with discarding all too easily the traditional models that have held sway in the Church for centuries.[30] Whatever we want to do with these models, we owe it to the tradition that we give a careful account as to why we approach them in the way that we do.

The Dutch theologian C. J. den Heyer in his book on the atonement comments with regard to satisfaction theories of the atonement that he can no longer identify with the "old confessions and dogmas": "I know the old and familiar truths of faith, but they no longer move or inspire me. The words and images have lost their significance. The excitement has slowly ebbed away."[31] Faced

---

27. The metaphor of father is, in fact, so significant, that several scholars have argued that "father" is not a metaphor of God, but a proper name. Cf. J. B. Torrance, *Worship, Community, and the Triune God of Grace* (Downers Grove, Ill.: InterVarsity, 1996), 121–25; John Cooper, "Is God Our Mother? The Bible and Inclusive Language for God," in *Living in the LambLight: Christianity and Contemporary Challenges to the Gospel,* ed. Hans Boersma (Vancouver, B.C.: Regent College Publishing, 2001), 109–25. While I am not convinced that this argument is correct, it illustrates the importance and abiding value of the appellation of "father" for God.

28. Brümmer, *Model of Love,* 22–29.

29. Soskice, *Metaphor,* 158.

30. Avery Dulles argues that one of the differences between the use of models in theology and in the experimental sciences is the objective historical norms given by Scripture and tradition (*Models of the Church,* rev. ed. [New York: Image-Doubleday, 1987], 25).

31. C. J. den Heyer, *Jesus and the Doctrine of the Atonement: Biblical Notes on a Controversial Topic,* trans. John Bowden (Harrisburg, Pa.: Trinity, 1998), 132.

with what he considers the confusion of a "cacophony of different voices" in the biblical account, den Heyer takes the liberty to simply discard one particular blend of choral voices: the Anselmian tradition. Green and Baker, though they give a far more careful reckoning of the various traditional metaphors, are still far too reckless with the tradition when they comment that "in many societies . . . people have different concepts of justice, so that for them, penal substitution is simply unintelligible."[32] Arguing that the meaning of Christ's death "in the end cannot be captured by language or images," they propose that "we, following in the footsteps of Peter or Paul, cast about for metaphors and models that speak of this mystery to the people around us." What is required is that we learn from Scripture and the tradition "the theological and missionary task, not that we mimic their words and repeat their metaphors."[33] It seems to me, however, that the Church has always seen the need to use the very words, metaphors, and models that are handed down to us by the biblical witness. It is necessary to do this in order to safeguard the tradition that has been entrusted to the Church. Atonement theology can only claim to stand in continuity with the tradition if it, in fact, continues to build on the models that are rooted in Scripture and tradition. As we struggle with questions of violence in connection with the atonement, we do well to heed Colin Gunton's advice to "treasure our metaphors, particularly those which have, over the centuries, commended themselves as especially illuminating."[34]

Brümmer's second criterion for theological models is that of "comprehensive coherence." With this he means that theological models must have logical consistency. I will return to this element later in this chapter, as it raises the question of how we relate the various models of the atonement to one another. Third, theological models must have "adequacy for the demands of life." Theology is always in interaction and conversation with the culture in which it develops. The importance of tradition for the development of theological models does not mean that theology should become static. I mentioned earlier that one of the functions of metaphors is their ability to enable our imagination and creativity to flourish, which in turn allows for metaphors to function in transformative ways. It is precisely our awareness and appreciation of the tradition that allow us to employ theological models in ways that are culturally relevant. Walter Brueggemann, in his book *Hopeful Imagination,* comments that people in the Babylonian exile suffered from amnesia, so that they could "remember nothing except the present arrangement." He links this lack of memory with

---

32. Green and Baker, *Recovering the Scandal,* 148.

33. Ibid., 114; cf. ibid., 111. Presumably, this explains why Green and Baker discard penal substitution as a model despite acknowledging its presence in 2 Cor. 5:14–6:2 and Gal. 3:1–14 (ibid., 58, 60, 64).

34. Gunton, *Actuality of Atonement,* 39. Cf. ibid., 48. Cf. John McIntyre's helpful comments in cautioning against a "historical relativism" where the historical context becomes too determinative of the contents of the models that we choose (*The Shape of Soteriology: Studies in the Doctrine of the Death of Christ* [Edinburgh: T&T Clark, 1992], 57–60).

a conservatism that is unable to envision new historical possibilities: "People without historical sense and a proper practice of tradition are so bound in the 'eternal now' that they finally end in despair."[35]

The need to work with the traditional models in new ways and to relate them in a culturally relevant fashion is always necessary, and in the case of atonement theology, we are emboldened to do so because the Church has consistently shied away from giving creedal affirmation to one particular model only. Whereas our understanding of the Trinity and of the Person of Christ has received formal conciliar expression through the Nicene Creed (381) and the Chalcedonian Formula (451), this is not the case with atonement theology.[36] The various models have always existed side by side, and different emphases and new ways of expression have continually come to the fore in the history of the Church. As Stephen Evans puts it, "The fact that no single theory of the atonement has won universal acceptance does not show that the story is one that lacks power and relevance today. It is rather confirmation of the fact that the work the Church claims God accomplished in Christ is both complex and mysterious."[37] While there is unanimous acceptance of the significance of the atonement, to insist on the static continuity of one particular expression would be to strangle the tradition.

This last point implies, finally, that individual believers may find particular models of the atonement more helpful than others. Brümmer refers to this as the criterion of "personal authenticity." Without disregarding the wisdom of the tradition or of the community of faith, he acknowledges that individual circumstances differ, and it is necessary for every person to be in active engagement with the various models that are embraced within the Church. This is not to advocate a subjectivism that avoids careful theological scrutiny but rather to recognize the embeddedness of metaphors within the variety of backgrounds and circumstances in which people may find themselves.

Relationships among Traditional Models

By affirming the various traditional atonement models as possible ways of speaking about the significance of Christ's death, we naturally raise the question of how they might possibly relate to one another.[38] It is, of course, difficult to discuss this question at this stage, prior to a discussion of the three atonement

---

35. Walter Brueggemann, *Hopeful Imagination: Prophetic Voices in Exile* (Philadelphia: Fortress, 1986), 123.

36. See the interesting account of this historical peculiarity in McIntyre, *Shape of Soteriology,* 1–25.

37. C. Stephen Evans, *The Historical Christ and the Jesus of Faith: The Incarnational Narrative as History* (Oxford: Clarendon, 1996), 96–97.

38. For an extensive discussion of this question, listing seven different possibilities of relating the various atonement models, see McIntyre, *Shape of Soteriology,* 26–87. Cf. Van Veluw, *Straf,* 156–59.

models themselves. I will restrict myself, therefore, to some tentative comments on the relationship between the various models, touching on their contents only insofar as it is necessary to discuss their relationship.

At the heart of this study lies the conviction that the cross expresses the hospitality of God. This assumes that whatever model we use to describe the atonement, the welcoming love of God must shine through in it. That is to say, an internal criterion for the viability of each of the atonement models is the way in which they are able to account for the hospitality of God, inviting his creation into eternal fellowship with him. After all, "it is proof of God's own love for us, that Christ died for us while we were still sinners" (Rom. 5:8). Any atonement model in which violence obscures God's hospitality needs some kind of reevaluation. Not only is the metaphor of hospitality useful to point out the divine motivation for the atonement, but hospitality also bespeaks the eschatological future. Hospitality, like love, refers to the very character of God to which believers look forward through Christ's work of redemption. Thus, God's hospitality forms the backdrop that precedes the atonement, as well as the horizon that the atonement anticipates in turn. The metaphor of hospitality is, therefore, more foundational than any of the three metaphors of traditional atonement theology.[39] God's hospitality is like the soil in which the process of reconciliation is able to take root and flourish. At no point can we separate what takes place in the atonement from the beckoning love of God.

My understanding of the atonement has been shaped particularly by two theologians, one from the early Church (Irenaeus) and one who takes his place among contemporary students of New Testament theology (N. T. Wright). Irenaeus's understanding of the atonement is often described as "recapitulation": Christ taking the place of Adam and of all humanity and as such giving shape to the genesis of a new humanity. N. T. Wright's understanding of the atonement, centering on the term "reconstitution," is quite similar. He regards Christ as the messianic representative of Israel and, as such, of all humanity. In his person he reconstitutes Israel and all humanity, so that his life and death overcome the failure of Israel and of Adam and restore Jews as well as Gentiles to covenant fellowship with God.

One of the exciting elements in the notion of recapitulation is that it coheres well with all three traditional models. It does so because recapitulation itself is a formal rather than a material concept. When we say that Christ recapitulated Israel and Adam, we haven't yet said *in which way* Christ recapitulated them. This is where the three atonement models come in. As the representative of Israel and Adam, Christ instructs us and models for us the love of God (moral influence). As the representative of Israel and Adam, Christ suffers God's judg-

---

39. With this comment I don't mean to place the traditional models into question. The love of divine hospitality as such does not define or describe what happens in the atonement. Rather, the atonement is enfolded by and is an expression of divine hospitality.

ment on evil and bears the suffering of the curse of the Law (penal representation). As the representative of Israel and Adam, Christ fights the powers of evil, expels demons, withstands satanic temptation to the point of death, and rises victorious from the grave (Christus Victor). One of the most intriguing elements of Irenaeus's atonement theology is his ability to combine the various atonement models by means of his understanding of recapitulation.[40]

Recapitulation means that through Christ the Church becomes the transformed beneficiary of his work of redemption. Each of the three atonement models describes something of Christ's work of redemption for the sake of the Church as the new humanity. Anticipating our discussion of each of the three models, the moral-influence model tells us that Christ as teacher imparts to us the knowledge of salvation (illumination) and that Christ as the incarnation of God's hospitable love motivates us to open our arms in love for God and creation and so be reconciled to God. The penal model shows us God's anger with human sin and tells us that through the cross God frees us from the penalty of the Law, so that we can receive forgiveness of sin and can again be made righteous before God. The Christus Victor model tells us that God in Christ unshackles us from the slavery that holds us in bondage to the principalities and powers of this world (liberation), adopts us as his children, and so raises us up with Christ to a new life in eternal fellowship with God.

It is by no means easy to describe the relationship between the three models. They should not be conceived as separate, hermetically sealed areas. It would not be quite right to argue that the traditional atonement models describe three different tasks or roles of Christ. The models are not complementary in the sense that they each describe a different aspect of Christ's work. It would be better to say that the three models each describe the same atoning work of Christ from a different viewpoint or perspective.[41] And even this way of understanding the relationship between the various models isn't quite satisfactory. The three perspectives are not each equally significant or foundational. The French Reformed theologian Henri Blocher has made the point that the penal model forms the foundation for the Christus Victor model and that the victory is gained both through obedience and through penal suffering.[42] In other words, according to Blocher's exegetical analysis, notions of obedience in the face of temptation, as well as divine punishment and sacrifice, explain the "how" of the victory. This is a valuable insight. On the one hand, it safeguards the penal character of the cross. God's judgment against sin forms in a significant sense

---

40. Cf. Hans Boersma, "Redemptive Hospitality in Irenaeus: A Model for Ecumenicity in a Violent World," *Pro Ecclesia* 11 (2002): 207–26.

41. Christ's perfect life, for instance, is both an example for us (moral influence) and a weapon in his fight against the devil.

42. Henri Blocher, "*Agnus Victor:* The Atonement as Victory and Vicarious Punishment," in *What Does It Mean to Be Saved? Broadening Evangelical Horizons of Salvation,* ed. John G. Stackhouse (Grand Rapids: Baker, 2002), 67–91.

the foundation for life in fellowship with God. Legal categories have a place in atonement theology. On the other hand, Blocher does not overemphasize the penal character of the cross. Its role is merely instrumental. The legal metaphor has a place, but it is restorative in nature. Punishment always looks beyond itself to the restoration and flourishing of the community.

There is a sense, then, in which Christus Victor is the ultimate atonement metaphor. We could describe obedience and sacrifice as the divine means of warfare, leading to the final victory. Victory over sin does not mean, however, that atonement theology can ultimately be reduced to the warfare metaphor. The Bible does not present a "warfare worldview" but a hospitality worldview.[43] Of course, the element of warfare—and hence the element of violence—is present. The warfare metaphor has an important place in atonement theology. Since God expresses his hospitality to us on this side of the eschatological equation, Christ's recapitulation of our existence and of our plight leads to a victory. The metaphor of victory remains a way of speaking about what God does in this world—on this side of the eschatological equation—to redeem his creatures. His hospitality is a *conditional* hospitality, entering into a world of sin and violence. Nonetheless, the biblical worldview cannot simply be described as a "warfare worldview." Behind each of the models (including the Christus Victor model) lies God's hospitality—his absolutely unconditional desire to draw us into eternal fellowship with him. We have some inkling of what this absolute hospitality of eternal life is like because of the resurrection of Jesus Christ. While the cross is still marred by the inescapable conditionality of violence, the resurrection brings us to the other side: we enter into the full shalom of the pure hospitality of God.

43. Pace Gregory A. Boyd, *God at War: The Bible and Spiritual Conflict* (Downers Grove, Ill.: InterVarsity, 1997), whose sole focus on the Christus Victor model and on the "warfare worldview" of Scripture does insufficient justice to the hospitality of God.

5

Modeling Hospitality

Atonement as Moral Influence

Moral Influence and the Problem of Violence

The various atonement theories are not mutually exclusive. It is quite possible to combine elements of the various theories into a coherent whole. This is best done by resisting the temptation of looking at the cross in isolation, as though Jesus' death were unconnected to the history of Israel and of the Church. If we regard Jesus' life, death, and resurrection as the recapitulation of Israel and so of all humanity, we are able to see how each of the three traditional atonement models can contribute to a full-orbed appreciation of the meaning of redemption. In this chapter I want to look specifically at the moral-influence theory of the atonement, to which traditionally the name of Peter Abelard (1079–1142) has been connected. Abelard, as is well known, argued in his commentary on the letter to the Romans that the cross is the ultimate demonstration of the love of God and as such makes an appeal to us to respond in kind. Speaking about the death of Christ, Abelard commented, "It is evident that all this was done in order that he [i.e., Christ] might show how great love he had for men, and so inflame them to greater love in return."[1]

---

1. Peter Abelard, *Exposition of the Epistle to the Romans, The Epitome of Christian Doctrine,* 25, quoted in H. D. McDonald, *The Atonement of the Death of Christ: In Faith, Revelation, and History* (Grand Rapids: Baker, 1985), 176.

Abelardian theories of the atonement are primarily subjective. They explain how our alienation from God can be remedied by the restoration of our love for God and others. This gives Abelardian-type theories their strong appeal. The renewal of our relationship with God does not depend solely on the death of Christ. Abelardian notions pull us away from divine punishment and wrath and from the requirement of the death of Christ as a condition for God to reconcile himself to humanity. If Christ's role is primarily that of someone who teaches us the knowledge of God or of one who by his life shows us what true love is like and so, by means of moral persuasion, encourages us to do the same, we end up with a less harsh understanding of God. God's hospitality, rather than his violence, takes center stage.

Already with the early Church fathers apprehension of divine violence was a key factor in emphasizing Christ's role as our teacher and model. Writing between A.D. 182 and 188, Irenaeus commented that God redeemed "His own property, not by violent means . . . but by means of persuasion, as became a God of counsel, who does not use violent means to obtain what He desires."[2] *The Epistle to Diognetus,* likewise, maintained that God sent his Son as a Savior "and as seeking to persuade, not to compel us; for violence has no place in the character of God."[3] Also Gregory of Nyssa († 385) argued that "if any one out of regard for the person who has so sold himself should use violence against him who has bought him, he will clearly be acting unjustly in thus arbitrarily rescuing one who has been legally purchased as a slave."[4] It is apprehension of violence that encouraged the early Fathers to emphasize what has become known as the moral-influence perspective. They were concerned to safeguard the hospitality of God in the life and death of Christ.

We need this emphasis on illumination and moral persuasion. Christ is not just priest and king; he is also prophet and teacher. The emphasis in the early Church on morality and the corresponding prominence of Christ's role in illuminating and modeling God's love for us ensure that talk about Christ's victory is not just empty rhetoric. Salvation in Christ only overcomes the bondage of sin and violence if our lives begin to reflect the life of Jesus Christ. Atonement, in other words, remains a forensic fiction unless it receives a subjective telos in the lives of Christians today. If Christ is teacher and example, then the Church benefits through illumination and reconciliation, and God's hospitality and love triumph over violence and hatred. Without the element of moral influence we do justice neither to Christology (the prophetic office

2. Irenaeus, *Irenaeus against Heresies* (hereafter *AH*), in *The Ante-Nicene Fathers,* ed. Alexander Roberts and James Donaldson (1885; repr., Peabody, Mass.: Hendrickson, 1994), 1:527 (V.1.1).

3. *The Epistle of Mathetes to Diognetus,* in *The Ante-Nicene Fathers,* ed. Alexander Roberts and James Donaldson, rev. A. Cleveland Coxe (1885; repr., Peabody, Mass.: Hendrickson, 1994), 1:27 (VII).

4. Gregory of Nyssa, *The Great Catechism,* in *Nicene and Post-Nicene Fathers,* Second Series, trans. William Moore and Henry Austin Wilson, ed. Philip Schaff and Henry Wace (1892; repr., Peabody, Mass.: Hendrickson, 1994), 5:492–93 (XXII).

of Christ) nor to soteriology (the subjective pole of the atonement). We end up missing a significant element of the hospitality of the cross.

Does this mean, however, that a moral-influence theory of the atonement is sufficient to ban all fear of violence from our understanding of the cross? Should we perhaps exclude all metaphors of battle and victory and of divine punishment in order to protect the hospitality of God? I am not sure that this would work. In the first place, we can only exclude all violence from moral-influence theories if we categorically exclude any divine involvement in the crucifixion. As soon as a moral-influence theory introduces any divine purpose at all into the crucifixion, an element of violence or exclusion is introduced into our understanding of the cross. J. Denny Weaver rightly comments: "For the moral theory, God appears quite specifically as the agent of Jesus' death. In this motif, God the Father sent his most precious possession to die in order to display an ultimately loving act. Apparently the death of Jesus has no salvific purpose in this motif if it is not God-intended."[5] Moral-influence theories have always tended to emphasize the salvific value of the *life* of Christ. Christ's teaching throughout his life and his exemplary humiliation throughout his life are meant to restore us to the image of Christ. But these theories have generally recognized that—with divine intent—Christ's life culminated on the cross.[6] A moral theory of the atonement only truly avoids the problem of divine violence if it focuses entirely on the life of Christ, so that there is no way in which God uses the death of Christ as a redemptive event.

The New Testament speaks too often and too emphatically about the redemptive function of the cross and of the blood of Christ for us to focus solely on his life. "We were reconciled to God through the death of his Son," St. Paul writes in Romans 5:10 (cf. Col. 1:22). To the elders in Ephesus, he says that God bought the Church "with the blood of his own Son" (Acts 20:28; cf. Rom. 3:25; Eph. 1:7). Also on two occasions the book of Acts rejects the either/or scenario that sees the cross either as the result of human scheming or of divine purpose. The first time, Peter addresses the Jewish crowds about Jesus: "This man, who was put into your power by the deliberate intention and foreknowledge of God, you took and had crucified and killed by men outside the Law" (Acts 2:23). The second time, the apostles are praying to God about the plotting of Herod and Pontius Pilate "*together* with the gentile *nations*

---

5. J. Denny Weaver, *The Nonviolent Atonement* (Grand Rapids: Eerdmans, 2001), 73.

6. Brock and Parker, in their recent biographically shaped dialogue with atonement theology, steadfastly refuse to acknowledge any involvement of God in the cross. Comments Brock, "To say that Jesus' executioners did what was historically necessary for salvation is to say that state terrorism is a good thing, that torture and murder are the will of God" (Rita Nakashima Brock and Rebecca Ann Parker, *Proverbs of Ashes: Violence, Redemptive Suffering, and the Search for What Saves Us* [Boston: Beacon, 2001], 49). Although I mention Brock and Parker in this context, they actually place themselves beyond the Abelardian tradition and do little to construct a positive theory of the atonement.

and the *peoples* of Israel, against your holy servant Jesus whom you *anointed,* to bring about the very thing that you in your strength and your wisdom had predetermined should happen" (Acts 4:27–28). At the very least the cross is not an event that is separated from divine intentionality. Also moral-influence theories of the atonement need to account for God's involvement in the death of Christ.

A number of theologians object to moral-influence theories of the atonement precisely because they believe that these theories result in violence. They object not just to God's violence on the cross, but they believe that the moral-influence theory encourages human violence today. If Christ voluntarily suffered and sacrificed himself to the point of death, does this not lead to human self-sacrifice? Does this not necessarily perpetuate abusive structures? Feminist theologian Darby Kathleen Ray rejects the Abelardian tradition because "the salvific values of suffering, self-sacrifice, and obedience are too easily distorted into a theological tool of subjugation."[7] Rita Brock and Rebecca Ann Parker also reject this tradition because of its glorification of suffering. Says Parker, "My religious community, most of all, could not see violence against children because it could not name clearly the violence that happened to Jesus. Even liberal Protestantism called Jesus' death on the cross an example of love that disciples were to imitate."[8]

These objections are seriously exaggerated. The notion of self-sacrifice is by no means in all circumstances a negative one. Self-sacrifice is asked not just of the oppressed and the marginalized but also of those who are in power. It is hard to believe a society could operate without any element of self-sacrifice. In a world where no one is willing to give up his or her own interests for the sake of others, power struggles and constant violence would dominate the scene. Hospitality becomes impossible when self-giving love is repudiated. Still, these feminist theologians do remind us that in our world an insistence on absolute hospitality would encourage violence. As we saw in chapter 1, we would open ourselves to abuse, since the devil himself might be entering through the door. In order to function, our hospitality must be moderated by some limitations. Likewise, the moral atonement theory of the cross needs more than Christ's model of absolute self-sacrifice. The pattern of Christ can be found also in his courageous voice that stands up for the victims of power and violence. The pattern of Christ can be found also in his readiness to question and oppose the religious and political powers that are in control and in his prophetic call to choose the worship of God over against all idolatrous human tendencies.

7. Darby Kathleen Ray, *Deceiving the Devil: Atonement, Abuse, and Ransom* (Cleveland: Pilgrim, 1998), 58.

8. Brock and Parker, *Proverbs,* 199. Cf. ibid., 41.

Irenaeus and the Fall

Thus, moral-influence theories, despite their emphasis on hospitality, are not so easily dissociated from violence. God's involvement in the cross seems to imply violence, and our imitation of Christ's self-sacrifice may also lend itself to the perpetuation of violence. This is not to say that the Abelardian theme does not have a rightful place at the table. But it does mean that we need to raise a cautionary voice. We are not avoiding the problem of violence by taking the Abelardian tradition on board. It also matters *how* we incorporate the moral-influence theory. It is not the be-all and end-all of atonement theology. We need to keep in mind the other theories and find ways of integrating them into a coherent whole. For that reason I now want to focus on Irenaeus. The second-century bishop of Lyons masterfully weaves together different elements from the various theories by means of his concept of recapitulation. In his refutation of the Gnostic and Marcionite sectarians, he combines elements that later theologians have often tended to regard as mutually exclusive. This makes him into an ecumenical paradigm of sorts. Irenaeus is a particularly valuable resource if we wish to develop an atonement theology that is ecumenical in its breadth, taking account of all the major traditions of atonement theology, as well as ecumenical in its background, returning beyond the atonement theologies of denominational traditions to the theology of the early Church.[9] The various atonement theories all have a place within the Church, and we need not exclude the one at the expense of the other.

Perhaps it is helpful first to see what, for Irenaeus, forms the backdrop to the atonement. The significance of the Fall plays a large role in the discussions surrounding Irenaeus's view of salvation. There is a sense in which the Fall constitutes a relatively minor event. Creation, according to Irenaeus, may have been good, but it was not perfect. Rather, creation set human beings on a course to perfection—a perfection that was reached, in principle, in the joining of the human and divine natures in the incarnation. Christ, therefore, was the climax of the human path toward salvation. Irenaeus argues that God did not "exhibit man as perfect from the beginning." Adam and Eve could not possibly endure such perfection, because they were still children.[10] They were created as immature infants who didn't even have "understanding of the procreation of children."[11] Slowly but surely, Irenaeus believes, the human race would have received a "faculty of the Uncreated, through the gratuitous bestowal of eternal existence upon them by God." This required

9. Cf. Hans Boersma, "Redemptive Hospitality in Irenaeus: A Model for Ecumenicity in a Violent World," *Pro Ecclesia* 11 (2002): 207–26.

10. Irenaeus, *AH,* 1:521 (IV.38.1).

11. Ibid., 1:455 (III.22.4). Cf. Irenaeus, *Proof of the Apostolic Preaching* (hereafter *Dem.*), trans. Joseph P. Smith (New York: Paulist, 1952), 12: "But the man was a little one, and his discretion still undeveloped, wherefore also he was easily misled by the deceiver." Cf. ibid., 14.

man making progress day by day and ascending towards the perfect, that is, approximating to the uncreated One. For the Uncreated is perfect, that is, God. Now it was necessary that man should in the first instance be created; and having been created, should receive growth; and having received growth, should be strengthened; and having been strengthened, should abound; and having abounded, should recover . . . ; and having recovered, should be glorified; and being glorified, should see his Lord. For God is He who is yet to be seen, and the beholding of God is productive of immortality, but immortality renders one nigh unto God.[12]

Irenaeus's description is one of near-uninterrupted progress toward perfection.[13] The story of salvation is an evolutionary one. The result is a relatively minor role for the Fall in Irenaeus's thought. In Nielsen's words, the Fall was "hardly more than an intermezzo."[14]

The intermezzo of the Fall nonetheless became the occasion for God to display his grace. God was able to use humanity's weakness to acquaint humankind with the power of God: "For how could a man have learned that he is himself an infirm being, and mortal by nature, but that God is immortal and powerful, unless he had learned by experience what is in both? For there is nothing evil in learning one's infirmities by endurance; yea, rather, it has even the beneficial effect of preventing him from forming an undue opinion of his own nature (*non aberrare in natura sua*)."[15] This amazing comment from Irenaeus almost seems to suggest that the fall into sin was a good thing. At the very least, God used it toward a good purpose. Likewise, the death that God had threatened to execute if Adam and Eve ate from the tree of knowledge turns out to be an act of mercy for Irenaeus. God removed Adam from the tree of life, not out of envy, "but because He pitied him" and did not want "the sin which surrounded him [to] be immortal, and evil interminable and irremediable."[16] It is not Adam and Eve, but Satan who bears the brunt of Irenaeus's indictment, so that he emphatically states that God did not curse Adam personally, while "the curse in all its fullness fell upon the serpent which had beguiled them."[17]

12. Irenaeus, *AH,* 1:522 (IV.38.3).

13. Robert F. Brown disputes that Irenaeus's "recovery" language here is a reference to the Fall. Even if Brown is wrong on this particular exegetical point, he is right in concluding, "The goal of human perfection is attained only by passing through all the stages of the series. This passage occurs in time, that is, in human history" ("On the Necessary Imperfection of Creation: Irenaeus' *Adversus Haereses* IV, 38," *Scottish Journal of Theology* 28 [1975]: 20).

14. J. T. Nielsen, *Adam and Christ in the Theology of Irenaeus of Lyons: An Examination of the Function of the Adam-Christ Typology in the Adversus Haereses of Irenaeus, against the Background of the Gnosticism of His Time* (Assen, Neth.: Van Gorcum, 1968), 62.

15. Irenaeus, *AH,* 1:529 (V.3.1).

16. Ibid., 1:457 (III.23.6).

17. Ibid., 1:456 (III.23.3).

The immaturity and imperfection of human beings before the Fall is more than an interesting Irenaean idiosyncrasy. On the one hand, in opposition to his Gnostic and Marcionite opponents, Irenaeus wants to maintain that God created the world good, and that time and matter are not to be despised. Thus, the vocabulary that Irenaeus uses to describe creation is fascinatingly down-to-earth.[18] The God of redemption is also the God of creation, and this is a fact to be celebrated, not something to acknowledge grudgingly. On the other hand, Irenaeus is keenly aware that God's immanence, his direct involvement with the created order, brings him face-to-face with imperfection and immaturity, with creational limitations, identities, and boundaries that are shaped in particular ways. One might even wish to argue that violence and death are necessarily a part of the created order with its historical and temporal limitations, so that perfection and deification would mean not just human maturation but also the overcoming of the violence and death inherent in creation itself. Irenaeus does not go quite this far, perhaps at the cost of some consistency.[19] Nonetheless, as long as the created order is not yet fully drawn into the light of the presence of God, creation remains in a state of immaturity and imperfection that Irenaeus believes needs God's hospitality to open up possibilities of renewal and perfection.[20]

Irenaeus and Recapitulation

Irenaeus is often associated with the Christus Victor theme of the atonement—and rightly so.[21] We will look at this element of Irenaeus's theology in some detail in chapter 8. There are also other notions, however, that feature in *Adversus haereses*. In chapter 7 we will see that the more objective notions of sacrifice and propitiation also have a place in his theology. In this chapter I discuss Irenaeus as a significant protagonist of an exemplarist understanding of the atonement. He is able to give all these elements a place in his theology because of the overarching concept of recapitulation (*anakephalaiōsis*).[22] Reca-

18. Irenaeus often speaks about creation using terms such as *plasma, plasmatio, caro, artifex Verbum, plasmare, fabricare*. See Nielsen, *Adam and Christ*, 16–17. Irenaeus's reluctance to admit that creational limitations imply mortality and violence may tie in with his fear of a Gnostic devaluation of time and matter.

19. F. Altermath argues unpersuasively (ignoring passages like *AH*, V.23.1–2 and *Dem.*, 15) that Irenaeus sees man as created mortal and that he sees death as part of the natural prelapsarian situation ("The Purpose of the Incarnation according to Irenaeus," *Studia Patristica* 13 [1975]: 63–68).

20. Interestingly, Marjorie Hewitt Suchocki appeals to Irenaeus for an evolutionary understanding of violence (*The Fall to Violence: Original Sin in Relational Theology* [New York: Continuum, 1994], 86–87).

21. Gustaf Aulén, for instance, devotes a separate chapter to Irenaeus (*Christus Victor: An Historical Study of the Three Main Types of the Idea of the Atonement*, trans. A. G. Hebert [London: SPCK, 1970], 16–35).

22. For explanations of Irenaeus's concept of recapitulation, see John Lawson, *The Biblical Theology of Saint Irenaeus* (London: Epworth, 1948), 140–98; William P. Loewe, "Myth and Counter-Myth: Irenaeus' Story of Salvation," in *Interpreting Tradition: The Art of Theological Reflection*, Annual Publication of the

pitulation encapsulates each of the three elements of the atonement. Christ's work of recapitulation has a prophetic element (moral influence), a priestly element (representative punishment), and a royal element (Christus Victor). Here I will look at Irenaeus's understanding of recapitulation from the perspective of Christ as prophet: the moral-influence theory of the atonement.

The term "recapitulation" stems from the letter to the Ephesians, which explains that God "would bring everything together under Christ, as head, everything in the heavens and everything on earth" (Eph. 1:10)—though Irenaeus works out this notion in far more detail than does the Pauline letter.[23] The idea of bringing all creation together under Christ as head—the word "recapitulation" stems from the Latin caput, meaning "head"—turns out to be a fruitful theme for Irenaeus's understanding of the atonement. The theme of recapitulation is a way of expressing the idea of representation or reconstitution. For Irenaeus, Christ represents all Adamic humanity. As humanity's representative, he takes the position of humanity.[24]

The notion of recapitulation results in a high regard for the incarnation. The incarnation makes recapitulation possible. Through the incarnation Christ becomes humanity's representative. Irenaeus suggests that the Word took on human flesh in order to present human beings to God: "For in what way could we be partakers of the adoption of sons, unless we had received from Him through the Son that fellowship which refers to Himself, unless His Word, having been made flesh, had entered into communion with us?"[25] Irenaeus is consistently and strongly antidocetic. Christ must have taken on true human flesh, for salvation is impossible without his having done so. Irenaeus comments, for example: "For it behoved Him who was to destroy sin, and redeem man under the power of death, that He should Himself be made that very same thing which he was, that is, man; who had been drawn by sin into bondage, but was held by death, so that sin should be destroyed by man, and man should go forth from death."[26] Clearly, Irenaeus regards the incarnation

---

College Theology Society, vol. 29, ed. Jane Kopas (Chico, Calif.: Scholars, 1983), 46–52; Christopher Smith, "Chiliasm and Recapitulation in the Theology of Ireneus," *Vigiliae Christianae* 48 (1994): 313–31.

23. For an argument pleading for an Irenaean reading of Eph. 1:10, see John McHugh, "A Reconsideration of Ephesians 1.10b in the Light of Irenaeus," in *Paul and Paulinism: Essays in Honour of C. K. Barrett*, ed. M. D. Hooker and S. G. Wilson (London: SPCK, 1982), 302–9.

24. I am open to referring to this representation as vicarious or substitutionary as long as it is clear that Christ is not simply replacing human beings as a third party but includes all others in his recapitulation, so that it really is a reconstitution of Adamic humanity itself in Jesus Christ.

25. Irenaeus, *AH*, 1:448 (III.18.7). Cf. 1:448–49 (III.19.1); 1:454–55 (III.22.1–2); 1:527 (V.1.2); 1:541 (V.14.1).

26. Ibid., 1:448 (III.18.7). See also Irenaeus, *Dem.*, 31: "*So the Word was made flesh*, in order that sin, destroyed by means of that same flesh through which it had gained mastery and taken hold and lorded it, should no longer be in us" (italics in the original). Cf. H. E. W. Turner, *The Patristic Doctrine of Redemption: A Study of the Development of Doctrine during the First Five Centuries* (London: Mowbray; New York: Morehouse-Gorham, 1952), 52–53.

as necessary to "destroy" sin, to overcome the "power" or "bondage" of death. Incarnation and recapitulation ultimately lead to victory.

The close connection between incarnation and redemption has been the main reason that a number of theologians have gone even further and argued that for Irenaeus the incarnation itself is already salvific and by itself is enough to give people eternal life.[27] I am not convinced that Irenaeus in fact holds to such a "physical" soteriology, which would logically lead to a position of universal salvation.[28] Important though it may be, the incarnation by itself is not enough for Irenaeus to render the human race immortal. He does not go quite so far as to make the incarnation *by itself* (i.e., in isolation) redemptive in nature. Aulén helpfully points out the limitations of this "naturalistic" or "physical" understanding of Irenaeus. The gift of immortality, comments Aulén correctly, is not the result of the incarnation in and of itself.[29] The incarnation had as its aim the victory over Satan: "In Irenæus' thought, the Incarnation is the necessary preliminary to the atoning work, because only God is able to overcome the powers which hold man in bondage, and man is helpless."[30] This victory over the powers of evil is the result of Christ's obedience: "By His obedience Christ 'recapitulated' and annulled the disobedience. The obedience is the means of His triumph."[31] Aulén makes some important observations here.[32] The incarnation remains subordinate to something that is even more significant: Christ's ultimate victory by means of his obedience.[33] By living as

27. For interpretations that more or less fall into this category, see Demetrios J. Constantelos, "Irenaeos of Lyons and His Central Views on Human Nature," *St. Vladimir's Theological Quarterly* 33 (1989): 351–63; Gabriel Daly, "Theology of Redemption in the Fathers," in *Witness to the Spirit: Essays on Revelation, Spirit, Redemption,* ed. Wilfrid Harrington (Dublin: Irish Biblical Association; Manchester: Koinonia Press, 1979), 137–39.

28. So also Andrew J. Bandstra, "Paul and an Ancient Interpreter: A Comparison of the Teaching of Redemption in Paul and Irenaeus," *Calvin Theological Journal* 5 (1970): 56; Trevor A. Hart, "Irenaeus, Recapitulation, and Physical Redemption," in *Christ in Our Place: The Humanity of God in Christ for the Reconciliation of the World,* ed. Trevor A. Hart and Daniel P. Thimell (Exeter: Paternoster; Allison Park, Pa.: Pickwick, 1989), 155. See also Terrance L. Tiessen, *Irenaeus on the Salvation of the Unevangelized,* ATLA Monograph Series, no. 31 (Metuchen, N.J.: Scarecrow, 1993), 161–62: "It is frequently recognized, therefore, that although Irenaeus's doctrine of recapitulation might logically lead to universal salvation, for Irenaeus it does not conclude that way." The common terminology of a "physical" understanding of redemption is somewhat confusing and unfortunate. The term, coined by Harnack, describes the notion that the physicality of the union of the two natures in the incarnation magically effects a redemption that is described in the language of ontological transformation—deification.

29. Aulén, *Christus Victor,* 18.

30. Ibid., 20.

31. Ibid., 29.

32. Aulén is too critical, however, both of the "physical" and of the "juridical" interpretations of Irenaeus. For Irenaeus both the incarnation and propitiation have salvific value. It is just that they are not salvific by themselves.

33. Aulén seems to me quite wrong to interpret the Christus Victor theme in the sense that human beings cannot save themselves, so that instead God himself saves us. Aulén wrongly argues that for Irenaeus Christ's obedience is not a "human offering made to God from man's side" (*Christus Victor,* 33). Irenaeus precisely

the obedient, true human being, Jesus Christ is able to place us once again on the road from which we have strayed, so that we are restored in fellowship with God and receive incorruption and immortality. The incarnation functions as the prelude to Christ's obedient life of recapitulation. All the same, of course, the incarnation is emphatically present as a necessary precondition for the restoration of fellowship with God. And although it does not give immortality all by itself, nonetheless, as part of Christ's recapitulation, the incarnation contributes to our redemption.

The reason for the close relationship between incarnation and recapitulation lies in the fact that in the incarnation the Word comes to us as the second Adam. Recapitulation thus emphatically includes for Irenaeus the *life* of Jesus Christ. The incarnation itself is part of his recapitulation: just as Adam was molded from untilled virgin soil (Gen. 2:5), so Christ was born of a virgin.[34] The only reason that Christ was not taken directly from dust (as Adam had been), but was born from a human being, was that Christ had to have the same humanity that Adam had—"the very same formation should be summed up"—so that recapitulation would truly be that of the human race.[35]

It is the Fall that makes the incarnation, as well as the entire process of the recapitulation of Adamic humanity, necessary. The Word became incarnate, Irenaeus maintains, in order that Christ might recapitulate Adam's temptation and be victorious over sin.[36] Irenaeus therefore mines the temptation narratives for analogies between Christ and Adam.[37] Especially in this context we see the Christus Victor theme figuring prominently: "He [i.e., Christ] has therefore, in His work of recapitulation, summed up all things, both waging war against our enemy, and crushing him who had at the beginning led us away captives in Adam, and trampled upon his head."[38] The way in which the battle is fought, however, leads Irenaeus away from military metaphors. Christ's recapitulation—here a retracing and reversing—of Adam's disobedience takes place by means of his obedience. Christ's obedience in the face of temptation is for Irenaeus a significant part of the answer to the question of *how* Christ gains the victory over Satan, sin, and death. Christ gains the victory not by employing counterviolence but by faithful obedience in the face of satanic temptation. The theory of recapitulation clearly implies that it is not only the death of Christ but also the life of Christ that has redemptive significance.

---

emphasizes the reality of the incarnation and the obedience of Christ as the second Adam. It appears that Aulén's Lutheranism precludes him from seeing Irenaeus's rather obvious emphasis on the human obedience of Christ (see chapter 8 under the heading "Gustaf Aulén: A Lutheran Christus Victor").

34. Irenaeus, *AH,* 1:448 (III.18.7); 1:454 (III.21.10); *Dem.,* 32.

35. Irenaeus, *AH,* 1:454 (III.21.10).

36. Ibid., 1:448 (III.18.7).

37. Ibid., 1:548–50 (V.21.1–3). Cf. D. Jeffrey Bingham, *Irenaeus' Use of Matthew's Gospel in Adversus Haereses,* Traditio Exegetica Graeca, no. 7 (Louvain: Peeters, 1998), 274–81.

38. Ibid., 1:548 (V.21.1).

So far we have seen that both the incarnation and Christ's obedient life are key elements of his work of recapitulation. But recapitulation also involves his suffering on the cross. Irenaeus elaborates on Christ's retracing of Adam's temptation by repeated analogies between the tree of knowledge and the tree of the cross. The record of our debt has been fastened to the cross for the remission of sins, "so that as by means of a tree we were made debtors to God, [so also] by means of a tree we may obtain the remission of our debt."[39] Christ had to die on the sixth day of the week, Irenaeus argues, for Adam and Eve had sinned and died also on the sixth day. Christ recapitulated in himself the entire day, "thus granting him [Adam] a second creation by means of His passion, which is that [creation] out of death."[40] Christ himself "points out the recapitulation that should take place in his own person of the effusion of blood from the beginning," says Irenaeus with a reference to the blood of the martyrs of the Old Testament.[41]

By retracing the creation, temptation, and death of Adam, Christ as the new humanity reversed the effects of the Fall and restored humanity. But he not only took on the same flesh as Adam; he also retraced every age of all human beings:

> For he came to save all through means of Himself—all, I say, who through Him are born again to God—infants, and children, and boys, and youths, and old men. He therefore passed through every age, becoming an infant for infants, thus sanctifying infants; a child for children, thus sanctifying those who are of this age, being at the same time made to them an example of piety, righteousness and submission; a youth for youths, becoming an example to youths, and thus sanctifying them for the Lord. Likewise, He was an old man for old men, that He might be a perfect Master for all, not merely as respects the setting forth of the truth, but also as regards age, sanctifying at the same time the aged also, and becoming an example to them likewise. Then, at last, He came on to death itself, that He might be "the first-born from the dead, that in all things He might have the pre-eminence," the Prince of Life, existing before all, and going before all.[42]

For Irenaeus, Christ had to go through every stage of human existence because he functioned as the vicarious representative of humanity. It seems as though Christ, simply by recapitulating every age group, sanctified those age groups. Recapitulation implies that the incarnation, obedience, and death of Christ are *themselves* ways in which he defeats the devil.

39. Irenaeus, *AH,* 1:545 (V.17.2). Cf. 1:544 (V.16.3); 1:545 (V.17.3); 1:547 (V.19.1); *Dem.,* 34; *Fragments from the Lost Writings of Irenæus,* in *The Ante-Nicene Fathers,* ed. Alexander Roberts and James Donaldson (1885; repr., Peabody, Mass.: Hendrickson, 1994), 1:28.

40. Irenaeus, *AH,* 1:551 (V.23.2).

41. Ibid., 1:541 (V.14.1).

42. Ibid., 1:391 (II.22.4). Cf. 1:448 (III.18.7); 1:521 (IV.38.2). With an appeal to tradition and John 8:56–57, Irenaeus argues that Jesus reached the age of fifty (*AH,* 1:391–92 [II.22.5–6]; cf. George Ogg, "The Age of Jesus When He Taught," *New Testament Studies* 5 [1958–59]: 291–98).

The concept of recapitulation is similar to N. T. Wright's "reconstitution" of Israel.[43] It is *by* being the faithful Israel (or Adam) that Christ in principle restores humanity and places it on the course to recovery. For Irenaeus, Christ is not simply another human being (albeit the divine Logos at the same time), but in his person he retraces the steps of Adam himself and so of all humanity. Christ, as it were, functions as a corporate personality.[44] He includes all humanity in his person, so that when he overcomes the temptation of sin, humanity—at least in principle—has overcome the temptation of sin. Of course, this still leaves open the question of punishment. But the notion of recapitulation or reconstitution is at least a partial answer.[45]

Christ as the Teacher of God

Redemption is more, however, than recapitulation or reconstitution. In the earlier quotation, Irenaeus did not just assert that Christ retraced all ages of all human beings, but he also insisted that Christ became an example for each of these age groups. In other words, although Christ's work of recapitulation means that the victory is his and can be located in his incarnation, his obedient life, and his suffering, the atonement also contains a subjective element. God's redemptive move of hospitality can only have the desired effect of homecoming if and when human beings look to Christ as their example. There needs to be a positive subjective human response if redemption is to be completed.

How does this subjective element function? This is where Christ's roles as a teacher and as a model of obedience come into play. These elements figure prominently in Irenaeus's understanding of what it is that makes up the process of recapitulation. The prophetic aspect of Christ as teacher and moral example answers for Irenaeus at least in part *how* exactly Christ gains the victory, *how* he robs the strong man and destroys death. We will see in chapter 8 that the Christus Victor theme is important for Irenaeus. But it does not describe the "how" or the method of the victory. To describe the means of the victory, Irenaeus has recourse to different models, the most important one of which is the prophetic office of Christ: Christ as teacher and model.

---

43. See, for instance, N. T. Wright, *Jesus and the Victory of God,* vol. 2 of *Christian Origins and the Question of God* (Minneapolis: Fortress, 1996), 169.

44. I do not mean hereby to endorse every aspect of Robinson's use of the concept of "corporate personality." Cf. H. Wheeler Robinson, *Corporate Personality in Ancient Israel,* rev. ed. (Philadelphia: Fortress, 1980).

45. It may well be possible to combine the elements of Christ's obedient recapitulation and his suffering the punishment for human sin as ways in which reconciliation is accomplished. This would be strikingly similar to the scholastic Reformed distinction between Christ's active obedience (whereby he perfectly and obediently fulfills the Law) and his passive obedience (whereby he vicariously suffers the punishment for human sin).

Irenaeus wants nothing to do with a Gnostic escapism that regards knowledge as salvation from time and matter. This is not to say that in reaction he resorts to a strictly Western or Augustinian view of salvation as forgiveness. Despite his strenuous opposition to Gnostic soteriology, Irenaeus is unwilling to abandon knowledge as lying at the heart of redemption. The full title of his main work is significant: *A Refutation and Subversion of Knowledge Falsely So Called*.[46] One does not gain true knowledge through the esoteric teachings of the heretics but through the public revelation of Jesus Christ.

William P. Loewe has drawn particular attention to Irenaeus's emphasis on revelation and knowledge and has gone so far as to characterize his thought as a type of "noetic soteriology." Loewe points out that the idea of God creating Adam and Eve as immature infants implies that a pedagogical element is part and parcel of Irenaeus's doctrine of creation. Our first parents still had to grow in knowledge and maturity.[47] Even though the Fall was a negative episode in the course of human existence, God nevertheless used it to bring his children to greater knowledge and maturity. The "pedagogical value" of the Fall was that it "offered human beings a first-hand taste of the misery of evil and of their own powerlessness, preparing them to appreciate all the more gratefully the rescuing hand of God who alone can confer life and immortality."[48]

Over against the Gnostic notion of secret knowledge imparted to an elite segment of believers, Irenaeus insists that the revelation of the Word is public.[49] Indeed, the entire history of redemption is one in which God reveals himself ever more clearly. Not only is it the case that the Word of salvation is present wherever God speaks in the Old Testament narratives, but the Word also continuously reveals God the Father:

> And for this reason did the Word become the dispenser of the paternal grace for the benefit of men, for whom He made such great dispensations, revealing God indeed to men, but presenting man to God, and preserving at the same time the invisibility of the Father, lest man should at any time become a despiser of God, and that he should always possess something towards which he might advance; but, on the other hand, revealing God to men through many dispensations, lest man, falling away from God altogether, should cease to exist. For the glory of God is a living man; and the life of man consists in beholding God. For if the manifestation of God which

---

46. For knowledge and Gnostics "falsely so called," see also Irenaeus, *AH,* 1:348 (I.23.4); 1:426 (III.11.1); 1:468 (IV.6.4); 1:513 (IV.35.1); 1:525 (IV.41.4); 1:526 (V.pref.); 1:555 (V.26.2).

47. Loewe, "Myth and Counter-Myth," 45–46.

48. Ibid., 46.

49. Cf. Philip J. Lee's contrast between the private, secret illumination of Gnosticism and the public, open character of revelation in orthodox Christianity (*Against the Protestant Gnostics* [New York: Oxford University Press, 1987], 101–14).

is made by means of the creation, affords life to all living in the earth, much more does that revelation of the Father which comes through the Word, give life to those who see God.[50]

The entire history is the *oikonomia* of the Word that continuously and progressively reveals God. This process of revelation climaxes in the incarnation of the Word, and it leads finally to the *visio Dei* in the kingdom of God.[51]

Loewe points out that the temptation narratives play an important role in Irenaeus.[52] Whereas Adam had succumbed to Satan's temptation in paradise, Christ stood firm. When Christ rebuffed Satan the third time, "there was done away with that infringement of God's commandment which had occurred in Adam, by means of the precepts of the law, which the Son of man observed, who did not transgress the commandment of God."[53] It is thus Christ's obedience that rendered Satan powerless, gave Christ the victory, and redeemed humanity. In a passage that is full of martial imageries, Irenaeus argues that Satan was crushed (cf. Gen. 3:15) when Christ made his threefold appeal to the Law. It is the words of the Law, therefore, that showed Satan for who he truly was, so that he was "exposed in his true colours, and vanquished by the Son of man keeping the commandment of God."[54] Loewe aptly summarizes Irenaeus's intentions: "Christ's obedience wins a more than personal victory; it decisively subdues Satan, leaving him bound and powerless. How? By exposing him in his true colors. His power was based on a lie, a false promise of immortality, and the exposure of that falsehood leaves Satan bound with the same fetters with which he had bound humanity, namely, judgment as a sinner by the Word of God. With this exposure of his identity as a liar and sinner, his promises lose their allure, and thus his power is broken."[55] Human beings, says Loewe, needed to be rescued from their "forgetfulness" of the true God and come to a true knowledge of God, which only Jesus Christ, as the Word of God, imparts to us. Christ, in other words, is the revealer or teacher who alone gives us the knowledge of God.[56]

50. Irenaeus, *AH*, 1:489–90 (IV.20.7). The entire chapter is relevant to the notion of God's increasing self-revelation through his Word and Spirit. Cf. also 1:469 (IV.6.6).

51. See Mary Ann Donovan, "Alive to the Glory of God: A Key Insight in St. Irenaeus," *Theological Studies* 49 (1988): 283–97; Tiessen, *Irenaeus,* 86–87.

52. Loewe, "Myth and Counter-Myth," 50–51; William P. Loewe, "Irenaeus' Soteriology: *Christus Victor* Revisited," *Anglican Theological Review* 67 (1985): 6–8.

53. Irenaeus, *AH,* 1:549–50 (V.21.2).

54. Ibid., 1:550 (V.21.3).

55. Loewe, "Irenaeus' Soteriology: *Christus Victor* Revisited," 7–8.

56. Loewe exaggerates when he characterizes Irenaeus's understanding of redemption as "noetic soteriology." After all, the moral element of Christ's example also features prominently. Moreover, despite Loewe's protestations to the contrary, both of these elements are instrumental in the defeat of Satan and thus subservient to the Christus Victor theme.

Moral Persuasion and Hospitality

Christ's role as teacher does not mean that Irenaeus has succumbed to the esoteric understanding of salvation that his Gnostic opponents put forward. Sin is not mere forgetfulness for Irenaeus, and salvation is more than intellectual knowledge. Christ's obedience in the face of temptation doesn't just expose Satan's true colors; it also inspires us to live in obedience to the only true God. One way in which Christ conquers sin and death is by gaining followers who are persuaded by his teaching and example. In the paragraph where Irenaeus speaks about "seeing our Teacher and hearing His voice," he also makes the comment that the Word of God "did righteously turn against that apostasy, and redeem from it His own property, not by violent means, as the [apostasy] had obtained dominion over us at the beginning, when it insatiably snatched away what was not its own, but by means of persuasion, as became a God of counsel, who does not use violent means to obtain what he desires; so that neither should justice be infringed upon, nor the ancient handiwork of God go to destruction."[57] The Word redeemed his property by means of "persuasion," maintains Irenaeus. He does not identify the exact object of the persuasion; the most likely interpretation is that the revelation of God in Christ convinces people of the truth of the gospel. God persuades people of the truth. This element of persuasion thus introduces a subjective element in Irenaeus's understanding of the atonement.

The emphasis on knowledge and teaching does not stand on its own. For Irenaeus the key question is what we do with this knowledge. We can hear pre-Abelardian rumblings when Irenaeus comments that "we could have learned in no other way than by seeing our Teacher, and hearing His voice with our own ears, that, having become imitators of His works as well as doers of His words, we may have communion with Him, receiving increase from the perfect One, and from Him who is prior to all creation."[58] Irenaeus clearly connects Christ's role as our teacher to his role as our model. Christ is our teacher who requires our imitation.[59]

God's revelation and teaching throughout the one economy of redemption, climaxing in Christ, requires a human response. This means that the future of human beings is not determined according to the various Gnostic types (pneumatic, psychical, and material).[60] Irenaeus emphatically defends the freedom of the human will, both before and after the Fall. Redemption means that God does not use violence, but "persuades" human beings. This implies

---

57. Irenaeus, *AH,* 1:527 (V.1.1).

58. Ibid., 1:526 (V.1.1).

59. Cf. Turner, *Patristic Doctrine,* 38; Nielsen, *Adam and Christ,* 63.

60. For the Gnostics only the future of the psychical class of human beings was open. The future of the pneumatic and material classes was determined by their nature.

a true freedom of the will, since "there is no coercion with God."[61] To be sure, the "ancient law of human liberty" is no occasion for pride. Irenaeus adduces a number of Old Testament passages that illustrate that "not by ourselves, but by the help of God, we must be saved."[62] Nonetheless, the emphatic presence of free will in Irenaeus makes it fair to conclude that salvation is ultimately the result of a synergy of divine and human powers.[63] Thus, while Irenaeus insists on specifying divine hospitality as an entering into the historical and material particularities of human life, this hospitality does not result in an unjustified violence of divine coercion. While hospitality is not afraid to express itself concretely by identifying with the other and by sharing in the other's situation, hospitality would turn into hostility if characterized by mere force.[64]

The importance of the human response is seen also in the place of faith and works in Irenaeus. He regards Abraham as the father of all who follow the example of his faith and in this way are saved.[65] This does not mean that Irenaeus, in proto-Reformation fashion, opposes faith to works.[66] He consistently keeps the two together.[67] Apprehensive of any Gnostic devaluation of the significance of moral choice and good works, he warns of the moral relativism inherent in the Gnostic position[68] and insists that by definition Christians have changed lives.[69] Repeatedly Irenaeus warns of the danger of losing the Spirit of God, after which there is no further forgiveness of sins, but only the loss of the kingdom of heaven.[70] Irenaeus even goes so far as to suggest that it is not sacrifices but

61. Irenaeus, *AH*, 1:518 (IV.37.1).

62. Ibid., *AH*, 1:450 (III.20.3). Cf. 1:446 (III.18.2). Tiessen puts it too strongly when he states that "Irenaeus clearly affirmed the necessity of God's grace prior to human choice of the good and the decision of faith in God" (*Irenaeus*, 219). Irenaeus does not express any logical or temporal priority, either to the work of the Spirit or to the human response.

63. Constantelos, "Irenaeos of Lyons," 360.

64. Cf. Miroslav Volf's comment: "In an embrace a host is a guest and a guest is a host. Though one self may receive or give more than the other, each must enter the space of the other, feel the presence of the other in the self, and make its own presence felt. Without such reciprocity, there is no embrace" (*Exclusion and Embrace: A Theological Exploration of Identity, Otherness, and Reconciliation* [Nashville: Abingdon, 1996], 143).

65. Irenaeus, *AH*, 1:467 (IV.5.3–5); 1:481 (IV.16.2); *Dem.*, 24.

66. Irenaeus, *Dem.*, 2: "For what is the use of knowing the truth in word, while defiling the body and accomplishing the works of evil? Or what real good at all can bodily holiness do, if truth be not in the soul? For these two rejoice in each other's company, and agree together and fight side by side to set man in the presence of God." Cf. *AH*, 1:467 (IV.5.3–4); *Dem.*, 3, 41.

67. Irenaeus does not oppose faith to works but to the Mosaic Law specifically. It is the Law—with the exception of the Decalogue—that has lost its prescriptive role (*Dem.*, 35, 87, 89, 95–96). This emphatic assertion of normative discontinuity is all the more remarkable considering that Irenaeus opposes Marcion with a consistent appeal to the unity of the Old and the New Testaments.

68. Irenaeus, *AH*, 1:324 (I.6.2–3); 1:348 (I.23.3); 1:350–51 (I.25.3); 1:408 (II.32.1). Cf. 1:351 (I.25.4): "So unbridled is their madness that . . . they maintain that things are evil, or good, simply in virtue of human opinion."

69. Irenaeus, *Dem.*, 61.

70. Irenaeus, *AH*, 1:499 (IV.27.2); 1:535 (V.9.3); 1:536 (V.10.1).

doing justice for the oppressed, the fatherless, and the widow that "propitiates" God.[71] Those who consistently refuse to do this and reject Christ will be given over to eternal judgment as the consequence of their choice.[72]

The human response, for Irenaeus, is part and parcel of God's redemptive action in Christ. Redemption does not consist solely of a physical union of the human and the divine in the incarnation of the Word, something that would imply universal redemption.[73] Redemption needs more than incarnation. Even knowledge, by itself, does not save, as the Gnostics erroneously propose. For Irenaeus revelation and knowledge are intimately tied to Christ as the teaching *model* that requires *imitation*. Hence, persuasion, free will, faith, morality, and judgment all have their integral place within the whole of Irenaeus's thought. Human maturity and perfection can only be reached by means of faith and obedience. The consequences of the Fall must be undone by Christ's victory as it is completed in the human response that prepares believers for the eternal kingdom.[74]

Of course, this implies that redemption is for Irenaeus not something that only took place objectively in Christ's own life and death. Redemption has a subjective pole in the lives of those who become persuaded by God's revelation in Christ.[75] Recapitulation of Adamic existence—creation, temptation, and death—is indeed the means by which Christ gains the victory. But this decisive victory of Christ requires implementation in the lives of Christians. The new

71. Ibid., 1:482–83 (IV.17.1–2).

72. Ibid., 1:330–31 (I.10.1); 1:347 (I.22.1); 1:408 (II.32.2); 1:417 (III.4.2); 1:459 (III.25.4); 1:466 (IV.4.3); 1:468–69 (IV.6.5,7); 1:500 (IV.27.4); 1:501 (IV.28.1–3); 1:516–17 (IV.36.4,6); 1:523–24 (IV.40.1–3); 1:556 (V.27.1–2). This emphasis on judgment is somewhat softened by the fact that God's goodness takes precedence over his justice (*AH*, 1:459 [III.25.3]) and by the fact that in judgment God is simply honoring people's own moral commitments and choices (*AH*, 1:468 [IV.6.5]; 1:556 [V.27.2]). Cf. William P. Loewe, "Irenaeus' Soteriology: Transposing the Question," in *Religion and Culture: Essays in Honor of Bernard Lonergan, S.J.*, ed. Timothy P. Fallon and Philip Boo Riley (Albany: State University of New York Press, 1987), 177; Denis Minns, *Irenaeus* (Washington, D.C.: Georgetown University Press, 1994), 128. Terrance Tiessen raises the question whether for Irenaeus the unevangelized also can be saved, a question that he maintains cannot be answered conclusively ("Irenaeus on Salvation and the Millennium," Διδασκαλια 3 [April 1991]: 2–5; cf. Tiessen, *Irenaeus*, 168–70).

73. Cf. Emil Brunner, *The Mediator: A Study of the Central Doctrine of the Christian Faith*, trans. Olive Wyon (London: Lutterworth, 1934), 255; Tiessen, *Irenaeus*, 155–58.

74. Cf. Hart's similar conclusion: "Thus we must give sufficient recognition to the fact that man's plight is described by Irenaeus in relational language as well as that which has been termed 'physical'" ("Irenaeus," 157). Likewise, Thomas Finger wants to hold the "ethical" and the "spiritual" together in Irenaeus ("Christus Victor and the Creeds: Some Historical Considerations," *Mennonite Quarterly Review* 72 [1998]: 49).

75. The theme of "persuasion" plays a prominent role throughout *Against Heresies*. Some of the most significant examples for the topic under discussion are the instances where, on the one hand, Satan "persuades" Adam and Eve (1:458 [III.23.8]; 1:549 [V.21.2]), the Antichrist "persuades" people (1:553 [V.25.1]), and the Gnostics "persuade" people of lies (1:324 [I.6.4]; 1:344 [I.19.1]; 1:358 [I.31.3]; 1:378 [II.14.8]); and where, on the other hand, Jesus Christ (1:352 [I.27.2]), the disciple John (1:426 [III.11.1]), John the Baptist (1:427 [III.11.4]), Philip (1:436 [III.12.15]; 1:495 [IV.23.2]), the apostles (1:495 [IV.23.2]), the angel speaking to Mary (1:547 [V.19.1]), and Irenaeus himself (1:460 [III.25.7]) "persuade" people of the truth.

humanity has its initiation in the life, death, and resurrection of Christ. But this resurrection life continues in the life of the Church. Christ's teaching and example are unique, but the Church's mission needs to implement the victory that his teaching and example have secured.

It is altogether mistaken, therefore, to argue that moral theories of the atonement encourage us to accept the status quo (after all, we should passively accept the lot that God gives us) or that they result in a masochistic glorification of suffering (after all, if Christ accepted suffering, so should we). What the moral theory of the atonement asks us to imitate is Christ's obedience and faithfulness. This may well involve suffering.[76] Cross bearing is a central New Testament concept that we need not avoid at all cost. But such suffering is always the result of faithfulness to the obedient call of the gospel, never a timeless concept that we are asked to pursue for its own sake.

Some may find it a weakness in the moral theory of the atonement that it requires the human or subjective pole for its completion. I believe that this is rather God's way of taking the human response seriously. He is not a God who harbors violence at the heart of his being and so forces us to enter into his kingdom. Rather, he is a God who welcomes us into his presence by means of persuasion.[77] Irenaeus shows that the moral theory of the atonement contains valuable aspects that we cannot afford to ignore. Without the moral theory we lose sight of the freedom of the human response, of the significance of human action, and ultimately of the love of God itself. The moral theory is an indispensable anchor for the hospitality of God.

76. See chapter 9 (the section titled "Cruciform Hospitality: *Salvifici Doloris*").

77. Jaroslav Pelikan alludes to Bernard of Clairvaux's answer to the question of the contribution of free will to salvation. The answer is: "It is saved. Take away free will, and there is nothing that needs to be saved; take away grace, and there is no way to save it" (*The Growth of Medieval Theology [600–1300]*, vol. 3 of *The Christian Tradition: A History of the Development of Doctrine* [Chicago: University of Chicago Press, 1978], 156).

6

Atonement and Mimetic Violence

René Girard: Cultural Anthropology and Nonviolence

Few people have had as significant an impact on questions surrounding violence and atonement as René Girard (b. 1923). This impact is all the more remarkable considering the fact that Girard is not a theologian. Trained as a historiographer, Girard soon turned to literary criticism and cultural anthropology. Through his studies of well-known literary giants, such as Cervantes, Flaubert, and Dostoevsky, as well as of Greek tragedies, Girard came to interpret human rivalry about objects of desire as the genesis of religion and culture. Girard's publications—of which *Violence and the Sacred* (1972; Eng. trans., 1977), *Things Hidden since the Foundation of the World* (1976; Eng. trans., 1987), *The Scapegoat* (1982; Eng. trans., 1986), and *I See Satan Fall like Lightning* (1999; Eng. trans., 2001) are the most well known—combine to present an audacious and ingenious attempt at constructing a metanarrative, just when we thought we were done with all grand explanations of the universe.

Not only is Girard not a professional theologian, but he also was not a Christian when in 1959 he put forward the key elements of his theory of mimetic rivalry. It was not until the 1970s that his Catholic convictions started to influence his writings and Girard became convinced that as a non-Christian he had stumbled across the generative principles of human culture. He then set out to interpret the Scriptures of the Church from his newly found perspective. Here was a grand scheme with an amazing internal coherence and an interdisciplinary character that derived its merit not from theological considerations alone but from a source outside the faith community, from a scholar with prestigious positions at Johns Hopkins University and Stanford University. Girard soon attracted scholarly disciples, who now organize the annual Conference on Violence and Religion (COV&R), publish the annual journal *Contagion: Journal of Violence, Mimesis, and Culture,* as well as the bi-annual bibliographical *Bulletin.*[1] Numerous theologians have built on Girard and have applied his conclusions to their own particular areas of interest.[2] The commitment to exploring the implications of Girard's insights at times leads to what one scholar has called "Girardianism."[3] The all-encompassing character of Girard's thought makes it tempting either to accept his framework in its entirety or to dismiss it completely. Some of the more careful students of Girard have resisted these temptations. Walter Wink (*Engaging the Powers,* 1984), Raymund Schwager (*Must There Be Scapegoats? Violence and Redemption in the Bible,* 1978; Eng. trans., 1987; *Jesus in the Drama of Salvation,* 1990; Eng. trans., 1999), Leo Lefebure (*Revelation, the Religions, and Violence,* 2000), and Anthony Bartlett (*Cross Purposes: The Violent Grammar of Christian Atonement,* 2001) have explored the meaning of the cross in the light of Girard's findings in particularly creative and independent ways.

Girard's understanding of the atonement can best be described as a variant of the moral-influence theory. He argues that the only violence associated with the cross is human violence and that God uses the cross to bring about a nonviolent society. Clearly, there is a potential in Girard to view the cross as a place of divine hospitality. By exposing human violence on the cross, God works toward democracy, justice, and equality. According to Girard, God's absolute nonviolence and hospitality on the cross secure the future of a peaceful eschaton. In this chapter I discuss the potential of Girard's contribution to the development of atonement theology. I first explain his understanding of the scapegoat mechanism and the origins of human culture. I then specifically enter into a discussion of the cross as the unmasking of satanic violence. I argue along with John Milbank that Girard's theology of the cross has its foundation in an ontology of violence rather than in an ontology of hospitality. This causes several problems for our ability to construct a theology of

---

1. See the COV&R website: http://theol.uibk.ac.at/cover/.

2. For theological applications of Girard, see, in addition to the titles mentioned in this paragraph, Robert G. Hamerton-Kelly, *Sacred Violence: Paul's Hermeneutic of the Cross* (Minneapolis: Fortress, 1992); Robert G. Hamerton-Kelly, *The Gospel and the Sacred: Poetics of Violence in Mark* (Minneapolis: Fortress, 1994); Gil Bailie, *Violence Unveiled: Humanity at the Crossroads* (New York: Crossroad, 1995); James G. Williams, *The Bible, Violence, and the Sacred: Liberation from the Myth of Sanctioned Violence* (Valley Forge, Pa.: Trinity, 1995); James Alison, *Raising Abel: The Recovery of the Eschatological Imagination* (New York: Crossroad, 1996); *The Joy of Being Wrong: Original Sin through Easter Eyes* (New York: Herder, 1998); Cheryl Kirk-Duggan, *Misbegotten Anguish: A Theology and Ethics of Violence* (St. Louis: Chalice, 2001); Cheryl Kirk-Duggan, *Refiner's Fire: A Religious Engagement with Violence* (Minneapolis: Fortress, 2001).

3. J. Bottum, "Girard among the Girardians," *First Things* 61 (March 1996): 42–45.

culture. Furthermore, I argue that Girard's nonsacrificial reading of the gospel leads to a depreciation of the Old Testament and of the juridical categories of the atonement. Thus, whereas chapter 5 outlined a positive appropriation of elements of moral influence (Irenaeus), this chapter functions as a cautionary note. Despite its positive elements, Girard's speculative theory is ultimately not the positive contribution that we need for the construction of a moral theory of the atonement.

The Violence of the Scapegoat Mechanism

Girard argues that the only way to appreciate the radical nature of the gospel and of the cross is to understand the backdrop of violence that constitutes the origin of all culture. He paints a distressingly inhospitable picture of the origins of human culture. When human beings first attained the ability of speech and of self-reflexive conscience, they became aware also of their desires, which conflicted with the desires of others. Michael Hardin helpfully explains this rivalry by means of the following analogy:

> Picture two children in a room full of toys. As soon as one of them reaches out for a toy, and not before that, that one toy becomes the object of desire. The first child becomes a model. The second child imitates the first. As the two children focus their attention on the toy, a rivalry ensues. The model issues a double-bind in his act of reaching. On the one hand, he makes the toy an object of desire by reaching for it, occasioning mimesis [imitation]. On the other hand, as soon as he reaches for the toy an implied prohibition is expressed; the toy belongs to him since he reached for it first. The rivalry, as most parents can attest, inevitably turns to violence. This violence ends with the expulsion or victimizing of one of the two rivals vying for the toy.[4]

Girard argues that the desire for the object is only there because another person already desires the object. In other words, the other individual becomes the mediator or model of one's desires. The cause of one's desire lies not in the object itself, but in the fact that someone else already desires the object. Strictly speaking, people don't just desire objects, but they desire other people's desires. There is not just a twofold relationship between the individual and the object of desire, but rather a threefold relationship between the individual, the model, and the object of desire. Girard speaks, therefore, of "triangular desire."[5] He makes clear that desire is intimately connected to cultural value systems. The reasons we value some things rather than others has a great deal to do with

---

4. Michael E. Hardin, "Violence: René Girard and the Recovery of Early Christian Perspectives," *Brethren Life and Thought* 37 (1992): 108.

5. René Girard, *Deceit, Desire, and the Novel: Self and Other in Literary Structure*, trans. Yvonne Freccero (Baltimore: Johns Hopkins University Press, 1965), 1–52.

the way in which other people evaluate particular objects of desire. The higher the value that others place on certain items, the greater the likelihood that a person will take them as his or her models and will desire these same items. The principle of "one-upmanship" ensures that one's desires are determined, at least to a degree, by mimesis: one imitates the desire of others.

With his notion of mimetic desire, Girard touches on a universally observable principle. It is highly questionable, however, whether all desire can be reduced to the process of imitation. Such reductionism fails to appreciate that some things have worth in and of themselves. Girard doesn't appear to accept that many desires and wants may be quite legitimate.[6] The idea that we never value objects of desire because they are truly and inherently valuable seems seriously problematic. It betrays, as John Milbank rightly sees, a "modern, liberal grid" through which Girard interprets the origin of religion in primitive societies.[7] Such a modern grid is unable to take its starting point in the revelatory religious claims of a particular tradition. This makes it difficult to make truth claims about the inherent desirability of particular objectives.[8]

It is often impossible to realize mimetic desires. The model possesses a certain object and so becomes an obstacle to the imitator. The other becomes a rival. The other, concerned about the imitator's desire for the object of the other's desire, reacts by trying to ensure that the imitator does not attain his or her desire. Thus, argues Girard, the imitator turns into a model for the other person. The result is a continuous cycle of rivalry: "The antagonists are caught in an escalation of frustration," says Girard. "In their dual role of obstacle and model, they both become more and more fascinated by each other. Beyond a certain level of intensity they are totally absorbed and the disputed object becomes secondary, even irrelevant."[9] The process of mimetic rivalry welds the individuals together in such a way that they become "mimetic doubles" who derive their identity from each other. People are never individuals. Their social or continuous mimetic derivation implies that they are always "interdividual."[10]

As the cycle of mimetic rivalry continues, it spreads to others by means of "mimetic contagion" or "mimetic snowballing." To prevent this process from

---

6. George L. Frear, "René Girard on Mimesis, Scapegoats, and Ethics," *The Annual of the Society of Christian Ethics,* ed. Harlan Beckley (1992): 124.

7. John Milbank, *Theology and Social Theory: Beyond Secular Reason* (Oxford: Blackwell, 1993), 394.

8. Of course, Girard accepts the notion of revelation, and nonviolence is his ultimate value. Significantly, however, both of these ideas derive from his cultural anthropology. For Girard theology has only secondary status.

9. René Girard, *The Girard Reader,* ed. James G. Williams (New York: Crossroad, 1996), 13.

10. René Girard, *Things Hidden since the Foundation of the World,* trans. Stephen Bann and Michael Metteer (Stanford, Calif.: Stanford University Press, 1987), 299–305. Cf. René Girard, *I See Satan Fall like Lightning,* trans. James G. Williams (Maryknoll, N.Y.: Orbis; Ottawa: Novalis; Leominster, UK: Gracewing, 2001), 137.

getting out of hand and leading to an outburst of violence and thus of self-destruction, the group subconsciously looks for a way out and finds this in a scapegoat. Girard views the "scapegoat mechanism" as the identification of a particular individual as the source of unrest, disorder, sickness, or other societal ills. The group is transformed into a mob and lets off steam against the victim, who becomes the substitute for the mimetic rivals. Usually this "surrogate victim" is someone who is somewhat different from the rest of society—someone who is lame (like Oedipus), is his father's favorite (like Joseph), is plagued with calamities (like Job), or stands out in some other way—for example, witches, slaves, children, kings, or strangers. The odd character of the scapegoat enables the community to think that the victim is truly guilty and that the violent expulsion or execution is justified. At the same time, the scapegoat must have some similarity to the community, or else the victim cannot attract the violent impulses.[11] By unanimously transferring the disorder and troubles from the real cause (one's own mimetic rivalry) to the surrogate victim, the crowd does not act deceptively. It truly believes that the victim is responsible for its woes and that violence is the only means to ensure the restoration of order and peace. The mob lynching can only function because of the ignorance (*méconnaissance*) of the scapegoat mechanism.

Ironically, the scapegoat mechanism works. Once the crowd has vented its frustrations, its violent impulses subside, resulting in peace and harmony. This peaceful situation can only be attributed to the victim. Whereas the crowd had earlier killed the victim in rage, it now ascribes divinity to this same scapegoat. Oedipus becomes king, the brothers bow down before Joseph, and Job is restored to glory. The people argue that only a god could have brought an end to their troubles and disorder. This divinization is a second transference, this time not the transference of disorder and misery onto the scapegoat, but instead the transference of the peaceful effects to the sacralized victim. It is this second transference that "covers up the demonic and conceals from human eyes" what the community has done.[12]

Violence and the Development of Culture

For Girard, then, violence lies at the origin of human culture. People try to contain their violent impulses by blaming and murdering innocent victims. They subsequently attempt to capitalize on the resulting peace by institutionalizing and containing violence by means of religion. First, religious communities engage in ritualistic sacrifices that are reenactments of the original act of murder.

---

11. Girard, *Reader*, 81, 88, 119.

12. Girard, *I See Satan*, 72. Cf. René Girard, *The Scapegoat*, trans. Yvonne Freccero (Baltimore: Johns Hopkins University Press, 1986), 50, where Girard speaks of a twofold "transfiguration."

Second, people tell one another mythological accounts that retell the primal murder. These are stories told from the perspective of the murderer. Since people are unaware either of the mimetic crisis or of the double transference that has taken place, they tell stories that cover up the hideous character of the murder of an innocent victim. Mythology always obscures the real nature of the violence committed against the victim. Finally, religious prohibitions or taboos ensure that the mimetic rivalry stays within bounds and does not escalate again beyond acceptable proportions. Thus, religious rituals, myths, and prohibitions ensure the peace of the community.

Girard's project is eminently modern. He operates with broad strokes on a metanarratival canvas. Assuming an evolutionary paradigm, Girard argues that over time the mythological framework has started to fall apart. Many societies have replaced lynch mobs with judicial systems. The punitive justice systems of modern society are thus merely a refined form of mimetic violence: "Vengeance is a vicious circle whose effect on primitive societies can only be surmised. For us the circle has been broken. We owe our good fortune to one of our societal institutions above all: our judicial system, which serves to deflect the menace of vengeance. The system does not suppress vengeance; rather, it effectively limits it to a single act of reprisal, enacted by a sovereign authority specializing in this particular function."[13] For Girard the judicial system is religious in origin and functions as an instrument of social control. It prevents the escalation of violence. As Ted Peters puts it: "Today's judicial system replaces yesterday's sacrificial system. Both share the goal of ending the cycle of violence."[14] Competitive sports are likewise religious in origin. By dislodging them from their ritualistic origins, we have secularized our contests and have obscured their mimetic origins.[15] In the same way, political power has its origin in "sacred monarchy." A king may have an exalted position, but he really is a type of scapegoat. He only differs from other scapegoats in that the community doesn't immediately kill him but "defers his execution." In other words, in the case of king-victim, the sacralizing process does not wait until after his execution. The king's "fate as a future sacrifice confers religious authority on him."[16] Our secularized democracies may conceal the violent and religious origins of political power, but this doesn't make them any less real.

Girard regards the secularization of religious rituals and the disappearance of religious taboos as highly effective means of controlling and suppressing violence. But there is more at stake than mere secularization. The Christian faith,

13. Girard, *Reader*, 84–85.

14. Ted Peters, "Atonement and the Final Scapegoat," *Perspectives in Religious Studies* 19 (1992): 173–74. Cf. Robert G. Hamerton-Kelly, "Religion and the Thought of René Girard," in *Curing Violence*, ed. Mark I. Wallace and Theophus H. Smith (Sonoma, Calif.: Polebridge, 1994), 19–20.

15. Girard, *Reader*, 22–23.

16. Girard, *I See Satan*, 92.

according to Girard, has also had a tremendous impact on Western culture. The result has been a subversion of traditional mythology. Whereas Western secularism has merely sublimated the religious and mythical underpinnings of societal order and peace, Christianity has actually subverted traditional mythology. The result has been a flourishing of democracy, a thoroughgoing equality, and an unparalleled concern for victims.[17] The only victims left, Girard ruefully observes, are the Christian faith and its biblical texts that are blamed for the violence of our past. While only Christianity and its Scriptures have functioned to unmask violence, our postmodern society holds precisely them responsible for the violence that has characterized the modern period.[18]

The Cross as Unmasking of Satanic Violence

But are contemporary critics of Christianity altogether mistaken in their criticism of the Christian faith as complicit in violence? How is it that Girard believes Christianity and the Bible have contributed to a more peaceful society? Is he justified in this assertion? This brings me to Girard's application of the "single-victim mechanism" of the cross and so to his understanding of the atonement in general. What happens when we apply Girard's cultural anthropology to this key element of Christian doctrine? Girard feels that he can clear the Christian faith, and in particular the atonement, of the charge of violence by presenting an unequivocally nonviolent interpretation of the cross. He maintains that in Jesus Christ, the Bible presents us with a nonviolent God. The myths of ancient cultures invariably portrayed a reality that valorized power, vengeance, scapegoating, and sacrifice. What is more, since myths do not just give us literary artifacts describing timeless, abstract truths but have a basis in historical reality, they describe actual instances of mob justice and murder and hold these up as models for us to emulate: "In the myth, the victim is always wrong, and his persecutors are always right."[19] On the cross we witness quite the opposite. Here the only violence is human violence—the violence of the mob, transferring its anxieties onto Jesus as the ultimate scapegoat.[20]

---

17. Ibid., 161–69.

18. Girard, *Reader,* 275; Girard, *I See Satan,* 178–81.

19. Girard, *I See Satan,* 109.

20. Girard's understanding of the revelatory power of the cross leads to a position of religious exclusivism: Christianity escapes the mimetic violence of the other world religions; only the cross is able to subvert or deconstruct the mimetic power at work in the false mythology of pagan religions. Several authors, even those otherwise sympathetic to Girard, have expressed reservations on this point. Is Christianity the only religion that carries the seeds of nonviolence? Leo D. Lefebure, for example, in a book relating a Girardian analysis to religious dialogue, comments that Girard "does not do justice to the complexity of the relationship between Israelite religion and other ancient traditions" (*Revelation, the Religions, and Violence* [New York: Orbis, 2000], 31). See also Walter Wink, *Engaging the Powers: Discernment and Resistance in a World of*

Girard's attempt to dissociate God from the violence of the cross appeals to many who advocate an ethical position of strict nonviolence. Peace initiatives and penal reforms in search of a theological basis for the rejection of violence get strong and ingenious support from a Girardian analysis. But Girard's theological rationale for nonviolence comes at a hermeneutical price. He has difficulty maintaining a clear line of continuity between the Old and the New Testaments. Especially his earlier writings posit a sharp disjunction between the two. In a 1979 essay on "Mimesis and Violence," for instance, Girard comments that the text of the Gospels "replaces the violent God of the past with a nonviolent one whose demand is for nonviolence rather than sacrifice. The Christ of the Gospels dies against sacrifice, and through his death, he reveals its nature and origin by making sacrifice unworkable, at least in the long run, and bringing sacrificial culture to an end. The word 'sacrifice' is not important in itself, but the singularity of the Passion is obscured if the same word is used for the Passion and for what takes place in sacrificial rituals."[21] Girard's notion that the text of the Gospels "replaces the violent God of the past" illustrates the difficulty he has incorporating the Old Testament stories of violence and sacrifice into a coherent theological model. Christoph Schroeder goes so far as to suggest that with his "opposition between the Old Testament God of persecutors and the New Testament God of victims, Girard follows the well-known tracks of Marcion."[22] To be sure, Girard does not simply posit a radical disjunction between the Old and the New Testaments. He repeatedly points to the narratives of Cain and Abel, Joseph, and Job to make the point that already in those instances, the authors are countermythical in choosing the side of the victim rather than of the oppressor. Girard regards the Old Testament prophets—and especially their antisacrificial discourse—as evidence of the breakdown of mimetic patterns of behavior.[23] And he has gradually become more explicit in asserting the unity of the Scriptures and explicitly disavowing a Marcionite position.[24] Nonetheless, his objections to Deuteronomic election theology (with its accompanying notions of violence and exclusion) and of sacrificial atonement have not fundamentally changed.

Domination (Minneapolis: Fortress, 1984), 154; Frear, "René Girard," 123, 127. Indeed, almost regardless of one's position on issues relating to religious dialogue, the radical discontinuity between Christianity and other religions seems to beg the question of how it is possible that any peace initiatives at all can be found among adherents of other religions.

21. Girard, *Reader*, 18.

22. Christoph Schroeder, "'Standing in the Breach': Turning Away the Wrath of God," *Interpretation* 53 (1999): 17. Cf. Margot Kässmann, *Overcoming Violence: The Challenge to the Churches in All Places* (Geneva: WCC, 1998), 26.

23. René Girard, *Violence and the Sacred*, trans. Patrick Gregory (Baltimore: Johns Hopkins University Press, 1977), 43 (Girard, *Reader*, 92); Girard, *Things Hidden*, 154–58 (Girard, *Reader*, 154–58).

24. Girard, *I See Satan*, 123, 129. See already in Girard, *Things Hidden*, 175–76 (Girard, *Reader*, 173).

Girard turns the nonviolence of the cross into the ultimate hermeneutical key and rejects anything that doesn't seem to fit this hermeneutic as a vestige of the mythology of mimetic rivalry and of the scapegoat mechanism.[25]

The Gospel accounts of Jesus' life and death are for Girard the documents that expose or reveal the violence of the myths of mimetic contagion and collective murder. The Old Testament, in many instances still in bondage to the mimetic cycle, contained the elements of mimetic crisis and collective violence, but the Old Testament never took the subsequent step of sacralizing the victims. Their monotheism prevented the Israelites from deifying their scapegoats.[26] In the Gospel accounts, however, we not only see the mimetic crisis and the collective violence surrounding Jesus' passion, but we are also privy to the element of the divinity of the collective victim: Jesus is proclaimed divine.[27] Thus, the similarities between the regular scapegoating process, with its feature of double transference, and the events leading to Jesus' death are striking.

But so are the differences: "There is no prior demonization behind the divinity of Christ. Christians don't ascribe any guilt to Jesus. Thus his divinity cannot rest on the same process as mythic deifications. Moreover, contrary to what happens in the myths, it is not the unanimous mob of persecutors who see Jesus as the Son of God himself; it is a rebellious minority, a small group of dissidents that separates from the collective violence of the crowd and destroys its unanimity."[28] The power of the Gospels lies, according to Girard, primarily in their revelatory ability. After Jesus' resurrection the disciples, who had earlier abandoned and betrayed their Master, came to see the scapegoat mechanism at work in the cross, as well as their own involvement in this process. The insight of the disciples after the resurrection broke the unanimity of the crowd. The myths, as "texts of persecution," are silent on the scapegoat mechanism. In Girard's view these documents of oppression are the products of the very people caught up in mimetic contagion. Unable to see the injustice of their own violence, they write accounts that necessarily cover up the violence and injustice that has been committed. The Christian Gospels, however, are the product of the witnesses of the resurrection, who have broken the unanimity of the crowd and are now in a position to expose the violence of the scapegoat mechanism against Jesus. The disciples now see that Jesus freely submitted to the violence of the mob and refused to be caught up in the spiral of mimetic contagion. As Girard puts it: "By submitting to violence, Christ reveals and uproots the structural matrix of all religion."[29] The effect of Christ's violent death is that "[n]o more myths can be produced to cover up the fact of per-

25. Girard, *I See Satan*, 119.
26. Ibid., 106–7.
27. Ibid., 121.
28. Ibid., 123.
29. Girard, *Things Hidden*, 178–79 (Girard, *Reader*, 176).

secution. The Gospels make all forms of 'mythologizing' impossible since, by revealing the founding mechanism, they stop it from functioning. That is why we have fewer and fewer myths all the time, in our universe dominated by the Gospels, and more and more texts bearing on persecution."[30]

So far Girard's explanation of the cross fits quite well within the moral-influence tradition of the atonement. It is the cross as revelation that saves people from the power of mimetic violence. Girard appeals to biblical texts that emphasize the ignorance of those who crucified Jesus (Luke 23:34; Acts 3:17) and comments, "The mythic process is based on a certain *ignorance* or even a *persecutory unconscious* that the myths never identify since it possesses them. The Gospels disclose this unconscious."[31]

Even though for Girard the power of the cross lies in its revelatory character, he does not hold to a typically Abelardian or liberal understanding of the cross. Girard's moral-influence theory has its own peculiarities. For one, he takes the divinity of Jesus seriously and emphasizes the close connection between the human and the divine natures. Thus, when Jesus suffers on the cross, God himself suffers. What makes the death of Christ unique is precisely that he is the divine Son of God.[32] It is his divinity that ensures that Jesus does not get caught up in the mimetic cycle of violence. As Collins puts it, for Girard "Jesus, being the Son of God, was the only one entirely outside the cultural system which is founded on the scapegoat mechanism. Hence Jesus was the only one not infected by human culture, which . . . is based on *concealment* of this mechanism."[33] The divinity of Jesus means for Girard that "God himself accepts the role of the victim of the crowd."[34]

Christ's submission to the single-victim mechanism of the crowd entails a second Girardian distinctive. As we have seen, Abelardian interpretations of the atonement usually regard the cross as the disclosure of God's love. Girard does not deny the love of God or of Christ on the cross, but he does not see this love as the focus of God's redemptive power. The cross saves because it displays mimetic violence, not because it displays God's love. The cross saves when human beings come to see the scapegoat mechanism operating in the crucifixion of Jesus Christ and when they become aware of the violent legacy of the mimetic process. The result is an emphasis on salvation as knowledge. In his foreword to Girard's most recent book, James G. Williams states: "The New Testament Gospels are the starting point for a new *science* or *knowledge* of humanity. This new *knowledge* begins with faith in Christ the innocent victim,

---

30. Girard, *Things Hidden,* 174 (Girard, *Reader,* 171–72).

31. Girard, *I See Satan,* 126 (italics in the original). Cf. Girard, *Scapegoat,* 111.

32. Girard, *I See Satan,* 43.

33. Robin Collins, "Girard and Atonement: An Incarnational Theory of Mimetic Participation," in *Violence Renounced: René Girard, Biblical Studies, and Peacemaking,* ed. Willard M. Swartley (Telford, Pa.: Pandora; Scottdale, Pa.: Herald, 2000), 136 (italics in the original).

34. Girard, *I See Satan,* 130.

and it becomes the leaven that will work itself out and expand to the point that the concern for victims becomes the absolute value in all societies molded or affected by the spread of Christianity."[35] Williams's repeated mentioning of "knowledge" as the key to salvation is indicative of a Girardian emphasis on the power of the cross to expose and so to teach awareness of the hideous character of the single-victim mechanism.

Girard does not argue, however, that the cross has this revelatory power in and of itself. One of the more encouraging elements in his approach is the way in which he connects crucifixion and resurrection. It is the resurrection of Christ that enabled the first Christians to break ranks with the crowd and to see the single-victim mechanism for what it is. "Until the resurrection," says Girard, "no one could foresee the reversal of the violent contagion that almost completely overcame the disciples themselves."[36] Atonement is the result of the combination of cross and resurrection.

Ontology of Violence or Politics of Hospitality

John Milbank has sharply criticized Girard for interpreting the cross as merely the revelation of the evil of mimetic violence. He feels that Girard's atonement theory cannot translate into a robust political theology. Since Girard approaches the issue of violence and nonviolence from a cultural anthropological perspective, he tends to focus on the origins and the insidious functioning of human violence. He pays a great deal of attention to mimetic rivalry and to the cross as the unmasking of human violence. But he is far less explicit when it comes to the question of how the cross can function positively in the construction of a hospitable and just society. John Milbank goes so far as to suggest that it is difficult to see what, for Girard,

> "the kingdom" could really amount to, other than the negative gesture of refusal of desire, along with all cultural difference. Girard does not, in fact, really present us with a theology of two cities, but instead with a story of one city, and its final rejection by a unique individual. This means that while his metanarrative does, indeed, have politically critical implications, these are too undiscriminating, because every culture is automatically sacrificial and "bad." At the same time, criticism cannot really be used to promote an alternative practice taking a collective, political form.[37]

Even if Milbank exaggerates, it remains true that Girard's description of the cross focuses on its critical function as unmasking the cultural foundations of

---

35. James G. Williams, foreword to *I See Satan,* by René Girard, xix (italics added).
36. Girard, *I See Satan,* 149; cf. 125, 133–36, 189.
37. Milbank, *Theology and Social Theory,* 395.

mimetic violence rather than on its positive role as revealing or introducing the hospitality of God's kingdom.

Girard may think that by breaking through the mimetic spiral, Jesus has revealed the scapegoat mechanism for what it is, but Milbank doesn't believe that such a critique of evil and of the origins of worldly power is enough. That's why he chastises Girard for only having "a story of one city, and its final rejection by a unique individual." In the terms of our study, Milbank hears Girard as saying no to the violence of the earthly city but doesn't hear him saying yes to the hospitality of the city of God. What does a politics of hospitality look like, positively? Milbank argues that we must find in Jesus an "exemplary practice which we can imitate and which can form the context of our lives together."[38]

Milbank draws our attention to an important question. What is, exactly, the redeeming power of the cross? Do we only find there a rejection of a human story based on violence and narcissism, or do we also locate there the love of divine hospitality? Girard's focus is certainly on the former, and Milbank's criticism is by no means unfounded. This is not to say that Girard entirely omits the positive role of the cross as the revelation of divine hospitality. Especially in his later writings, Girard acknowledges that mimesis not only has a negative function but can also play a positive role. In a 1992 interview he comments that he is not simply advocating a renunciation of mimetic desire, "because what Jesus advocates *is* mimetic desire. Imitate me, and imitate the father through me, he says, so it's twice mimetic. Jesus seems to say that the only way to avoid violence is to imitate me, and imitate the Father. So the idea that mimetic desire itself is bad makes no sense."[39] There is an element of imitation in Girard's understanding of the cross. He does not remain entirely stuck in an exposure of evil and violence as the basis of the human polis, as Milbank suggests. A politics of hospitality is not entirely out of sync with Girard's reading of the cross.

Girard may have an impetus toward a politics of hospitality, but is this hospitality of the cross (our imitation of Jesus and of God) sufficiently based in an ontology of hospitality? Here I have serious reservations. I argued in chapter 1 that violence is an integral part of what it means to be human, and that this is not necessarily and universally a negative thing.[40] Violence can be a

---

38. Ibid., 396.

39. Girard, *Reader,* 63. Cf. Girard, *I See Satan,* 13, 40; A. F. Lascaris, "De verzoeningsleer en het offerchristendom: Anselmus, Calvijn en Girard," *Nederlands Theologisch Tijdschrift* 42 (1988): 240.

40. On this point I disagree rather strongly with Milbank. While I appreciate his renewed emphasis on the role of theology, as well as his incisive criticism of nihilistic elements in postmodernism, I am not convinced of his equation of violence and evil as both inherently negative. Alyda Faber rightly points out that Milbank's own rhetoric is often rather bellicose ("Wounds: Theories of Violence in Theological Discourse" [Ph.D. diss., McGill University, 2001], 80–82). This underscores the impossibility of hospitality (Milbank's "ontology of peace") without some degree of violence.

positive expression of love. But this is not to say that violence is so pervasive as to lie at the heart of the created order or of human culture. Human (as well as divine) acts of hospitality may be characterized by the presence of some degree of violence, but these acts are still acts of hospitality as long as the violence is limited to that which is justifiable in the interest of the absolute hospitality of the eschatological future. Derrida, in characterizing all acts of hospitality as "hospitable narcissism," is so focused on the presence of violence in all human activity that he cannot see past our narcissism and see the practice of hospitality for the loving activity that it is. Girard, from quite a different angle, suffers from a similar preoccupation with violence. He argues that all human culture is the product of violence. The blood of the prophets has been shed "since the foundation of the world," comments Girard, with an appeal to Luke 11:50.[41] For Girard the origin of all civilization lies in the "mark of Cain." Society obtains the peace necessary for culture building only by means of the single-victim mechanism, which unites previous rivals first in their murderous scapegoating of the victim and then in their religious devotion to the divinized victim, a devotion maintained by sacrifices, myths, and taboos. Girard goes so far as to suggest, "At the origin not only of the Cainite culture but of all human cultures is ultimately the devil, namely, the bad contagion that results in violence and is expelled thanks to the unanimous misinterpretation of the founding murder."[42] According to Girard the evolution of life resulting in self-conscious human beings able to shape cultures implies a universal human association with Satan, the "murderer from the start" (John 8:44).[43] Girard locates the ontological origins of humanity and of human culture in violence rather than in hospitality.[44]

It is difficult to see how Girard's prioritizing of violence in terms of the origin of human culture fits with his notion of Jesus as the ultimate model of nonviolence. Is the hospitality of Jesus that we are to imitate a later intrusion into an essentially violent culture? Does Christ have nothing to do with the created order and with the development of culture? Girard, by separating the origin of culture (as violent) from the example of Christ (as hospitable), does not do justice to Christ as the Word through whom God spoke the world into being (Genesis 1; Colossians 2) and whose eternal hospitality forms the matrix for the exploration of culture and politics. Girard's anthropology leads to a theology of culture that is deeply troubling in its separation of culture,

41. Girard, *Things Hidden,* 159–60 (Girard, *Reader,* 159).

42. Girard, *I See Satan,* 87.

43. Craig L. Nessan builds on this association between the origin of human culture and violence. He combines evolutionary psychology with a Girardian anthropology to construct a nonviolent atonement theology ("Violence and Atonement," *Dialog* 35 [1996]: 26–34).

44. I find Fergus Kerr's defense of Girard against Milbank unconvincing at this point. Kerr wrongly states that "Girard denies any necessity to original violence" ("Rescuing Girard's Argument?" *Modern Theology* 8 [1992]: 397).

creation, and violence, on the one hand, and Church, redemption, and hospitality, on the other.

I See Satan Fall: Christus Victor Elements

Girard's understanding of the atonement is best classified as a type of moral-influence theory. His emphasis on the revelatory power of the cross, as well as his notion that we can now positively imitate Jesus rather than fall into patterns of mimetic rivalry, makes this a fitting classification. Interestingly, however, Girard combines his version of the moral-influence theory with elements of the Christus Victor theme. This comes to the fore especially in his recent book *I See Satan Fall like Lightning.* Here Girard appeals to the well-known Colossians 2 passage: God "has wiped out the record of our debt to the Law, which stood against us; he has destroyed it by nailing it to the cross; and he has stripped the sovereignties and the ruling forces, and paraded them in public, behind him in his triumphal procession" (Col. 2:14–15). Girard appeals to patristic understandings of Christ's victory over the devil by means of trickery, and he laments the loss of these traditional Christus Victor notions: "Western theology, in rejecting the idea of Satan tricked by the Cross, has lost a pearl of great price in the sphere of anthropology."[45] This is not to say that Girard blindly follows ancient notions of the divine trickery of Satan on the cross. Christ does not engage in immoral trickery but rather attains his victory on the cross precisely by his "renunciation of violence."[46] Because Christ submits to violence, this violence ends up revealing what it wants to conceal. "The trick that traps Satan does not include the least bit of either violence or dishonesty on God's part. It is not really a ruse or a trick; it is rather the inability of the prince of this world to understand the divine love." It is Satan himself who "transforms his own mechanism into a trap, and he falls into it headlong."[47] Satan's trickery, which had always managed to hide the violence of the single-victim mechanism behind the smoke of the alleged guilt of the victim, fails when applied to Jesus. Instead of covering up mimetic violence, the cross reveals and exposes it.

The divine nonviolence of Girard's version of the Christus Victor theme is not its only distinguishing feature. Girard also employs a revised demonology that removes the traditional personal characteristics of Satan and of the Pauline "principalities and powers." Satan, for Girard, is not "someone who really exists."[48] Satan is the very process of "violent contagion."[49] This process of

---

45. Girard, *I See Satan,* 150.
46. Ibid., 140.
47. Ibid., 152. Cf. Girard, *Things Hidden,* 49.
48. Girard, *I See Satan,* 45.
49. Ibid., 35, 43, 70.

mimetic contagion ultimately leads to the transference of misery and disorder onto the scapegoat. The mob's employment of the scapegoat mechanism is Satan's self-expulsion. "How can Satan drive out Satan?" asks Girard with a reference to Mark 3:23. The answer is that Satan first foments mimetic rivalry, and he then expels the disorder he has created by means of the single-victim mechanism.[50] If Girard sees Satan as the process leading up to the mob lynching of the victim, he interprets the "powers and principalities" as the political, social, and cultural phenomena that arise as the result of the peace that follows the murder of the victim. They are "the combination of material power and spiritual power" that stems from the founding murder.[51] Human culture cannot exist without them. They are "indispensable to the maintenance of order," so that St. Paul asks us to honor them.[52]

Girard sees the victory of the cross as the disarming and exposing of these "principalities and powers" that guarantee an order built on mimetic contagion. Alluding to the Colossians 2 passage, Girard comments: "In the triumph of a victorious general the humiliating display of those who are conquered is only a consequence of the victory achieved, whereas in the case of the Cross this display is the victory itself; it is the unveiling of the violent origin of culture. The powers are not put on display because they are defeated, but they are defeated because they are put on display."[53] It would be fair to say that for Girard the revelation of the scapegoat mechanism is the means of victory. He has combined, in an intriguing fashion, his own particular versions of the moral-influence and Christus Victor theories.[54] While his understanding of the actual functioning of the cross is that of revelation and imitation (moral influence), the revelatory power of the cross serves, and turns out to be, Christ's victory over Satan.

A Nonsacrificial Reading of the Cross

While Girard's version of the moral-influence theory of the atonement fits with a demythologized reading of the Christus Victor theme, it stands in

50. Girard's exegesis of Mark 3:23–26 is but one of many instances in which odd exegesis is made to fit his overall framework (*I See Satan*, 34–35). Cf. Girard, *Scapegoat*, 184–97.

51. Girard, *I See Satan*, 97.

52. Ibid., 98. Girard's understanding of the "principalities and powers" is very close to that of Walter Wink, who defines them as the "spirituality at the center of the political, economic, and cultural institutions" (*The Powers That Be: Theology for a New Millennium* [London: Galilee-Doubleday, 1999], 24). For a critique of Wink's position, see Marva J. Dawn, *Powers, Weakness, and the Tabernacling of God* (Grand Rapids: Eerdmans, 2001), 12–19.

53. Girard, *I See Satan*, 143.

54. Ted Peters also notes Girard's combination of the moral influence and Christus Victor models ("Atonement," 178).

sharp opposition to the Anselmian tradition and in particular to ideas that
God put forward his Son as a sacrifice or a scapegoat for sins to satisfy God's
justice or wrath: "There is nothing in the Gospels to suggest that the death of
Jesus is a sacrifice, whatever definition (expiation, substitution, etc.) we may
give for that sacrifice. At no point in the Gospels is the death of Jesus defined
as a sacrifice."[55] Sacrifices are society's method of covering up the primal murder of the innocent victim. For Girard God does not need to be reconciled,
but rather people need to become aware of their mimetic violence and so be
reconciled to God and to one another. The atonement is nonviolent from the
divine perspective. It is not God but the human mob that is violent. With
Jesus, therefore, we see the culmination of the prophetic questioning of the
need for sacrifices.

Unfortunately, argues Girard, soon after Christ's death Christians were
coopted by the powers and principalities and reinterpreted Jesus' death in a
mythological, sacrificial fashion. The Church soon came to interpret the very
death that was meant to expose mimetic violence and to introduce the end of
all sacrifice through the sacrificial lenses of the dominant culture. According
to Girard we see the beginnings of this sacrificial interpretation already in the
New Testament, in the letter to the Hebrews, and we see it particularly in the
Anselmian tradition, which has often explained the cross as a human sacrifice to
appease a wrathful God. Girard laments this dominant punitive and sacrificial
reading of the Christian tradition:

> Thanks to the sacrificial reading it has been possible for what we call Christendom to
> exist for fifteen or twenty centuries; that is to say, a culture has existed that is based, like
> all cultures (at least up to a certain point) on the mythological forms engendered by the
> founding mechanism. Paradoxically, in the sacrificial reading the Christian text itself pro-
> vides the basis. Mankind relies upon a misunderstanding of the text that explicitly reveals
> the founding mechanism to re-establish cultural forms which remain sacrificial and to
> engender a society that, by virtue of this misunderstanding, takes its place in the sequence
> of all other cultures, still clinging to the sacrificial vision that the Gospel rejects.[56]

Girard feels that the Christian tradition is complicit in the violence that lies
at the origin of all culture. The Church has not maintained the nonviolent
vision of the first disciples.

One cannot help but wonder at this point how the Church could have
made such a fatal mistake. If the cross is the obvious rejection of the scapegoat
mechanism that Girard claims it is, and if the biblical texts (in particular the
Gospels) are the unequivocal witness to a nonsacrificial, nonviolent religion
that Girard argues they are, how could the Church have taken such a radically

---

55. Girard, *Things Hidden,* 180 (Girard, *Reader,* 178). Cf. Girard, *Things Hidden,* 210, 213 (Girard,
Reader, 184, 186).

56. Girard, *Things Hidden,* 181 (Girard, *Reader,* 179).

erroneous direction? Girard states that the single-victim mechanism "has, to an extent, remained hidden after the Christian revelation up to our own time."[57] But again, if the violent origins of culture have been so hidden throughout the history of Western thought, how is it possible for Girard to claim that the Christian faith has placed an indelible stamp on Western democracy, equality, and justice (including concern for the victims of violence)? It cannot be that the scapegoating mechanism has been hidden throughout most of the history of the Christian Church *and* that the nonviolent principles of the Christian faith have been hugely influential. Girard cannot have his cake and eat it, too.

Girard has repeatedly been criticized for his disparagement of sacrificial language. Raymund Schwager and others have argued that the sacrificial language in the letter to the Hebrews need not be seen as part and parcel of a satisfaction theory of the atonement with Jesus' sacrifice appeasing the wrath of God. The sacrificial language of Hebrews could perhaps be seen as a reference to Jesus being "slaughtered by his violent opponents in the same way that the sacrificers led animals to the slaughter."[58] Perhaps, therefore, Jesus' death was a voluntary *self*-sacrificial act, which God's wrath never demanded.[59] Following Jesus might then entail that one be willing to take up one's cross and to suffer the effects of human violence. Would this not mean self-sacrifice for noble purposes? And wouldn't it imply that we should not throw out the concept of sacrifice altogether?[60] As a result of these attempts at a different reading of the letter to the Hebrews, Girard has changed his mind and become more open to notions of sacrifice. While this seems a positive development to me, Girard's modified position does not mean that he has come to accept a punitive or propitiatory view of the cross. Girard may accept the notion of sacrifice, but this sacrifice emphatically does not entail divine punitive justice.

To summarize our findings, one of the appealing elements in Girard's atonement theology is that it avoids an important (perceived) weakness of each of the traditional atonement theologies—that of divine violence. Girard's understanding of the cross is one that is radically nonviolent. There is neither divine trickery nor wrathful vengeance here. One of the main reasons that his theory continues to increase in popularity is that he helps Christians avoid the embarrassment of having to acknowledge that God is involved in violence, even as he expresses his most hospitable self on the cross.

57. Girard, *I See Satan*, 44.

58. Raymund Schwager, *Must There Be Scapegoats? Violence and Redemption in the Bible*, trans. Maria L. Assad (San Francisco: Harper & Row, 1987), 204.

59. Michael Hardin, "Sacrificial Language in Hebrews: Reappraising René Girard," in *Violence Renounced: René Girard, Biblical Studies, and Peacemaking*, ed. Willard M. Swartley (Telford, Pa.: Pandora; Scottdale, Pa.: Herald, 2000), 103–19; Marlin E. Miller, "Girardian Perspectives and Christian Atonement," in *Violence Renounced*, 39–40.

60. Cf. Frear, "René Girard," 128.

This gain carries the cost, however, of the denial of a good creation. Desire, as something underlying all cultural endeavor, is inherently mimetic and thus must lead to violence, Girard insists. But is it true that mimetic contagion explains all desire and that it accounts for all violence? Girard fails to acknowledge that we often desire certain objects because of their inherent value rather than simply because other models desire them. A theology of creation that affirms its inherent goodness will insist that desire can function in wholesome ways and stems not first of all from imitation but from the positive value of the created order. Girard's atonement theology is built on an ontology of violence that leads to a negative view of culture and is thus unable to function as a solid foundation for a positive politics of hospitality. Not only does Girard regard violence as the basis of human culture, but he also finds much of the Old Testament unworthy of the nonviolent God that we have come to know in Jesus Christ. The continuity between the two Testaments gets stretched to the breaking point.

What is more, as will become clear in the next chapter, the penal aspect of the cross needs to be retained for the sake of God's vision of eschatological hospitality. The complete absence of juridical categories from Girard's atonement theory implies a certain optimism. Girard doesn't talk much about sin, except, of course, in the sense that mimetic rivalry results in violence.[61] But even so, doesn't our violent past cause a problem of guilt? Should all juridical categories be declared contraband? I am not convinced that this is at all helpful. William Placher goes so far as to suggest that Girard "does not consider that we might retain some guilt and owe some penance for our evil past actions, even after we have turned away from scapegoating. He seems to assume that once we have understood the problem properly, it practically fixes itself."[62] In a similar vein, I would wish for more emphatic and consistent attention to the role of the Spirit.[63] Placher's comments serve as a reminder that, when left to their own devices, human beings have a hard time recognizing the revelation of God's hospitality in the cross. The victory of the cross is not assured without the enlightening revelation of the Spirit of God.

Girard's approach has structural similarities to Derrida's thought. Girard's understanding of the cross fits with what Derrida calls "pure hospitality." Girard has a radically nonviolent understanding of Jesus' actions and in particular of God's involvement with Jesus on the cross. But it is a hospitality without boundaries or punishment. That means it is a hospitality without recourse

---

61. I am not at all convinced that all sin can be reduced to violence. Violence may be one serious manifestation of sin, but Girard does not prove that "primal murder" lies at the root of all human misery.

62. William C. Placher, "Christ Takes Our Place: Rethinking Atonement," *Interpretation* 53 (1999): 9.

63. Girard does not deny the role of the Spirit in discerning how the single-victim mechanism operates in the crucifixion of Jesus. He describes the Spirit as the power "that triumphs over mimetic violence." It is "the Spirit of God that possesses [the disciples] and does not let them go" (Girard, *I See Satan,* 189).

for victims against violence. Where Girard overemphasizes the *vicious* role of violence in connection with the origin of human culture, he underestimates the *beneficial* role of violence in connection with redemption and a politics of hospitality. Girard is right to point to the ultimate victory of nonviolence and hospitality. And certainly the Christian faith looks forward to a future state of "pure hospitality." But by insisting that it be realized here and now through complete nonviolence (both on the cross and in the lives of Christians), in a world circumscribed by time and space, in a world that is characterized by a history of violence, we refuse to do what it takes to put a stop to violence. Thus we inadvertently give violence free reign. It would be immoral to shirk our responsibilities in the defense of hospitality.

7

Hospitality, Punishment, and the Atonement

The Anselmian Tradition and the Economy of Exchange

The relationship between penal views of the atonement and questions of hospitality and violence is a particularly sensitive one against the backdrop of the dominance of notions like sacrifice, substitution, judgment, and punishment in much of Western atonement theology. The questions multiply: Is it not true that penal theories of the atonement look at salvation as something imposed by means of a strict commercial transaction on the cross? Doesn't this reduce atonement to a harsh economy of exchange? Doesn't this mean that with its stern and uncompromising transactional understanding of the cross Western atonement theology has lost sight of God's unconditional hospitable invitation? Hasn't ethics given way to ontology, and infinity to totality? Hasn't the father forced his embrace on the prodigal and failed to respect the alterity of the son? Doesn't the Anselmian tradition (and especially the Reformed variant) turn redemption into an act of violence on God's part? It has repeatedly been argued in the last couple of decades that punishment and hospitality cannot possibly go hand in hand. According to this line of argument, the Anselmian tradition of atonement theology with its penal emphasis has lent itself to human violence rather than hospitality.[1] Many are concerned that penal views replace

---

1. Critics tend to focus on:

(1) The oppression or abuse of women: Joanne Carlson Brown and Rebecca Parker, "For God So Loved the World?" in *Christianity, Patriarchy, and Abuse,* ed. Joanne Carlson Brown and Carole R. Bohn (New York: Pilgrim, 1989), 1–30; Darby Kathleen Ray, *Deceiving the Devil: Atonement, Abuse, and Ransom* (Cleveland:

the celebratory mood of hospitality with a cold, calculating atmosphere of an Anselmian economy of exchange.[2]

In this chapter I present a model of penal representation that honors the death and resurrection of Jesus Christ as the climax of divine hospitality. I first discuss the view that Anselmian atonement theology is the result of a cozying Church-state relationship in the fourth century. As part of this discussion, I analyze some key moments in the pre-Reformation history of doctrine that have highlighted the theme of (penal) substitution.[3] I then present my own criticisms of the exchange model of the atonement as it has developed in Western thought. Building on contemporary New Testament theological developments, I present a framework of penal representation that avoids some of the tendencies of Western atonement theology (juridicizing, individualizing, and de-historicizing) that have rendered hospitality problematic. I argue that hospitality cannot be practiced without violence in the world as we know it; that the hospitality of the cross therefore necessarily involves (penal) violence; and that the justification of this violence in atonement is not merely found in a rational argument but in the eschatological reality of God's unconditional or pure hospitality.

Constantine and the Fall Model

Discussions on satisfaction and substitutionary models of atonement often take their starting point in the eleventh-century theologian St. Anselm

---

Pilgrim, 1998); Cynthia S. W. Crysdale, *Embracing Travail: Retrieving the Cross Today* (New York: Continuum, 1999); J. Denny Weaver, *The Nonviolent Atonement* (Grand Rapids: Eerdmans, 2001);

(2) The (American) retributive judicial system: Timothy Gorringe, *God's Just Vengeance: Crime, Violence, and the Rhetoric of Salvation* (Cambridge: Cambridge University Press, 1996); Pierre Allard and Wayne Northey, "Christianity: The Rediscovery of Restorative Justice," in *The Spiritual Roots of Restorative Justice*, ed. Michael L. Hadley (New York: State University of New York Press, 2001), 119–41; Christopher D. Marshall, *Beyond Retribution: A New Testament Vision for Justice, Crime, and Punishment* (Grand Rapids: Eerdmans; Auckland: Lime Grove House, 2001); T. Richard Snyder, *The Protestant Ethic and the Spirit of Punishment* (Grand Rapids: Eerdmans, 2001); Mark Lewis Taylor, *The Executed God: The Way of the Cross in Lockdown America* (Minneapolis: Fortress, 2001);

(3) Western imperialism and economic oppression: Leonardo Boff, *Passion of Christ, Passion of the World: The Facts, Their Interpretation, and Their Meaning,* trans. Robert R. Barr (Maryknoll, N.Y.: Orbis, 1987); James H. Cone, *God of the Oppressed,* rev. ed. (Maryknoll, N.Y.: Orbis, 1997); Ray, *Deceiving the Devil;* Weaver, *Nonviolent Atonement.*

Cf. also Joel B. Green and Mark D. Baker, *Recovering the Scandal of the Cross: Atonement in New Testament and Contemporary Contexts* (Downers Grove, Ill.: InterVarsity, 2000).

2. For an insightful overview of various postmodern attempts to replace an atonement model based on an economy of exchange with one based on an economy of excess, see Kevin J. Vanhoozer, "The Atonement in Postmodernity: Of Guilt, Goats, and Gifts," in *The Glory of the Atonement: Biblical, Theological, and Practical Perspectives,* ed. Charles E. Hill and Frank A. James (Downers Grove, Ill.: InterVarsity, 2004), 367–404.

3. This chapter will make clear that I prefer the term penal "representation" to "substitution," although I am willing to use the latter term depending on the understanding of it.

(1033–1109). And there is some justification for highlighting him as the protagonist par excellence of substitutionary atonement. In terms of logical rigor and clarity, his exposition of the meaning of Christ's death was unequaled at the time. This does not mean, however, that Anselm's *Cur Deus Homo* (1098) was the first treatise to bring to the fore the element of substitution. At times one gets the impression that the early Church interpreted the cross as Christ's victory over the principalities and powers, and that this theme disappeared into the background with the establishment of Constantinian Christendom, to be replaced by the harsh and violent Anselmian understanding of the cross as satisfaction.

Denny Weaver, for example, in his recent book *The Nonviolent Atonement* argues that the early Church's Christus Victor motif fell out of favor because of the Constantinian arrangement in the fourth century. Once the Church lost its sense of confrontation with the world, the Christus Victor imagery of confrontation no longer made sense. Although Anselm's theory of the atonement, propounded in his *Cur Deus Homo,* did not receive immediate universal consent, gradually it replaced the traditional Christus Victor model: "[A]lthough the change was gradual, there did come a time when discussing atonement in terms that assumed confrontation between church and social order no longer made sense. Narrative Christus Victor disappeared from the picture when the church came to support the world's social order, to accept the intervention of political authorities in churchly affairs, and to look to political authorities for support and protection."[4] Weaver argues that the change in atonement theology was the result of the Constantinianizing of the Church, which he sees particularly embodied in the Councils of Nicea (325) and Chalcedon (451). He maintains that these theological formulas meant the abandonment of ethics in favor of ontology and led to a focus on Jesus' death at the cost of a concern for what he did and taught throughout his life on earth. The outcome was an atonement theology that was juridicized (defining atonement with the help of a legal paradigm rather than focusing on ethical transformation), individualized (concerned only with individuals, no longer with systemic, structural problems), and de-historicized (ignoring the biblical narrative structure of salvation). Weaver, building in part on the work of John Howard Yoder, concludes that this "approach to atonement reflects a church that has reached accommodation of violence within the social order, a church in which the Christian life of ordinary lay people resembles the minimal expectations of polite society."[5] In the terminology of this study, according to Weaver, the Anselmian theory of the atonement, built on the Constantinian arrangement, is the culprit behind the loss of hospitality and has enabled violence to go unchecked.

4. Weaver, *Nonviolent Atonement,* 86–87.
5. Ibid., 91.

I appreciate Weaver's emphasis on narrative, on structural issues, and on ethical transformation. But his reconstruction contains several historical and theological flaws.[6] First, if the Constantinian arrangement of the fourth century was indeed responsible for the demise of the Christus Victor theme, why did it take until the eleventh century for the Anselmian model to appear as a viable alternative? One cannot help but wonder what happened in the intermediate seven hundred years of development. Furthermore, the Constantinian arrangement can hardly be held responsible for Nicea's and Chalcedon's alleged static or ontological approach to questions about the Person of Christ. The Arianizing party, denying the full divinity of Jesus Christ, was far cozier with the imperial powers than the Athanasian party, whose views were enshrined as orthodox. Those who held to the Nicene faith tended to be wary of the state's influence in the Church and particularly of the heterodox influence that tended to flourish in the context of a close Church-state relationship. In a couple of well-known articles in 1951, George Huntston Williams argued that the Arian party had difficulty accepting that the Church was ruled directly by Christ. The fourth-century bishop Eusebius (c. 260–340), not without sympathies for the Arian cause, "was unable to make a clear distinction between the Church founded by the Incarnate Logos and the Empire—once its ruler had become Christian."[7] Since the Arians saw Christ as merely *like* God, it became easier for them to view the position of Christ and that of the emperor as similar. The difference between the two was no longer quite as significant, and the emperor's authority in the Church was more readily accepted alongside the authority of Christ. All in all, the Arians tended to accept more easily than the Nicene party the power of the emperor also in Church affairs. According to Williams there is a connection "between the Arian preference for Christological subordination and the Arian disposition to subordinate the Church to the State."[8]

The fall model of historiography—the view that regards Constantine's embrace of Christianity as the fall of the Church—has undergone a detailed and careful critique in a recent publication by D. H. Williams. The author argues that the fall model is built on an erroneous understanding of the history of

6. For a careful critique of Weaver's position, see A. James Reimer, "Trinitarian Orthodoxy, Constantinianism, and Radical Protestant Theology," in *Mennonites and Classical Theology: Dogmatic Foundations for Christian Ethics* (Kitchener, Ont.: Pandora; Waterloo, Ont.: Herald, 2001), 247–71; Thomas Finger, "Christus Victor and the Creeds: Some Historical Considerations," *Mennonite Quarterly Review* 72 (1998): 31–51.

7. George Huntston Williams, "Christology and Church-State Relations in the Fourth Century," *Church History* 20 (3) (1951): 17.

8. Ibid., 10. For similar arguments, see Erik Peterson, "Der Monotheismus als politisches Problem," in *Theologische Traktate* (Munich: Kösel, 1951), 88–105; Yves Congar, "Classical Political Monotheism and the Trinity," *Concilium* 143 (1981): 31–36. Even John Howard Yoder, whose anti-Constantinian critique underlies that of Weaver, acknowledges this point in *Preface to Theology: Christology and Theological Method* (Grand Rapids: Brazos, 2002), 199.

the Church and has caused permanent historical damage.[9] He alleges that the renunciation of Constantinianism has meant "an abdication—tacitly or explicitly—from the theological and spiritual history of the post-apostolic church."[10] The fall model ignores the historical continuity between the patristic era and the period after Constantine. Much of the criticism of Constantinianism, says Williams, also "ignores the multiple ways [in] which Christian leaders and churches faithfully preserved doctrinal orthodoxy apart from, and sometimes in opposition to, prevailing imperial power."[11]

A curious illustration of the continuity of Constantinian Christianity with the faith of the early Fathers can be found in Constantine's use of the cross as a symbol of victory. Eusebius's well-known story of the emperor's conversion to Christianity, in his *Life of Constantine* (A.D. 337), relates the account of Constantine's vision on the eve of the battle at the Milvian Bridge: "[Constantine] said that about noon, when the day was already beginning to decline, he saw with his own eyes the trophy of a cross of light in the heavens, above the sun, and bearing the inscription, CONQUER BY THIS. At this sight he himself was struck with amazement, and his whole army also, which followed him on this expedition, and witnessed the miracle."[12] Scholars will no doubt continue to debate the integrity of Constantine's conversion. But it is at least clear that Constantine regarded the cross as a military symbol. He was able to interpret the cross this way because of the traditional Christus Victor theme of the atonement. Ian Gillman presents fascinating additional evidence from Eusebius that illustrates the connection between Constantine's understanding of the meaning of the cross and his military endeavors. After the vision Constantine reportedly sought Christian interpreters of it, who affirmed "that the sign which had appeared was the symbol of immortality, and the trophy of that victory over death which He had gained in time past when sojourning on earth."[13] Gillman concludes that "the cross was the meaningful symbol of the victory of Christ over the powers of darkness and death. It was the sign of the power of Christ still at work in the world, the symbol which caught up into itself all that theologians had struggled to express when dealing with soteriology. When Constantine referred to the cross, these are the connotations which must be kept in mind."[14]

9. D. H. Williams, *Retrieving the Tradition and Renewing Evangelicalism: A Primer for Suspicious Protestants* (Grand Rapids: Eerdmans, 1999), 111.

10. Ibid., 124.

11. Ibid., 130.

12. Eusebius, *The Life of Constantine,* in *Nicene and Post-Nicene Fathers,* Second Series, trans. Ernest Cushing Richardson, ed. Philip Schaff and Henry Wace (1890; repr., Peabody, Mass.: Hendrickson, 1994), 1:490 (I.28).

13. Ibid., 1:491 (I.32).

14. Ian Gillman, "Constantine the Great in the Light of the Christus Victor Concept," *Journal of Religious History* 1 (1961): 200.

Doctrinal development always displays both continuity and discontinuity. In the case of Constantine, it is evident that he retained a powerful link with the traditional Christus Victor theme of the atonement. Constantine, or at least the historian Eusebius, did not see a discrepancy between the Christus Victor theme of the atonement and an imperial embrace of the Christian faith. Weaver's claim that the Christus Victor theme depended on a situation of confrontation between Church and state[15] is simply not borne out by the facts. Constantine drew on the Christus Victor tradition to underwrite his imperial power. The Christus Victor theme does not lend itself to easy domestication in the service of a stance of nonviolent opposition to the existing structures of society. Constantine's use of the cross as a symbol of military victory and power illustrates that the danger of using the cross as a symbol of violence is by no means limited to the Anselmian strand of atonement theology.

Substitutionary Atonement before Anselm

A more balanced approach to the history of doctrine recognizes both that the Christus Victor theme continued well into the Middle Ages and beyond and that notions of sacrifice, satisfaction, and substitution did not originate with Anselm but followed a long tradition throughout the history of the Church. It is to the latter—the origins of Anselmian themes—that I briefly want to turn. To speak of "Anselmian themes" implies a broad categorization. Indeed, the common division of atonement theories into three main motifs—the Christus Victor, moral-influence (Abelardian), and satisfaction (Anselmian) theories—means that we lump together a large number of rather divergent themes into only three groups. While Anselm's own understanding of the atonement is best described as a satisfaction theory of the atonement, I take the broad umbrella of "Anselmian theories" to include most talk of sacrifice, satisfaction, vicarious suffering, punishment, and propitiation.[16] Many of these themes can function fairly independently from one another. Sacrifice does not necessarily involve punishment, and vicarious suffering does not imply satisfaction or propitiation. Still, the various Anselmian theories mostly share a God-ward direction. They regard the atoning death of Christ as itself reaching an objective purpose. The focus of reconciliation lies here not in the human subjects and in their response but in the death of Christ itself and in what it objectively accomplished. In this understanding the atonement does something for God: his honor or justice is upheld (satisfaction, punishment), or his anger

---

15. Weaver, *Nonviolent Atonement*, 86.
16. Anselm viewed satisfaction and punishment as mutually exclusive and thus had a nonpenal understanding of the cross.

and wrath are assuaged (propitiation). In other words, reconciliation involves some kind of economy of exchange.

It would be anachronistic to search for carefully articulated theories of the atonement among the early Fathers. Throughout this period the various strands of thought continued side by side, often in the writings of one and the same author. Gerard Sloyan rightly observes: "It can be seen from the variety of opinions . . . that there was no single, clear theory in the patristic era of how human redemption was accomplished."[17] It would be inappropriate to look for a careful elaboration of one of the three main strands of atonement theology in the early Church. In that sense Anselm was indeed somewhat of a milestone. The eleventh century marked the point at which the various themes became the subject of more explicit and intense discussion and controversy. As the theories became more articulated in detail and nuance, the tensions and incompatibilities between them became more pronounced as well.[18]

This is not to say there were no Anselmian themes in the early Church. They were present, and at times they were remarkably emphatic.[19] Already in the early second-century *Epistle to Diognetus,* we find the principle of substitution eloquently proclaimed in the description of God's Son as

> a ransom for us, the holy One for transgressors, the blameless One for the wicked, the righteous One for the unrighteous, the incorruptible One for the corruptible, the immortal One for them that are mortal. For what other thing was capable of covering our sins than His righteousness? By what other one was it possible that we, the wicked and ungodly, could be justified, than by the only Son of God? O sweet exchange! O unsearchable operation! O benefits surpassing all expectation! that the wickedness of many should be hid in a single righteous One, and that the righteousness of One should justify many transgressors![20]

17. Gerard S. Sloyan, *Jesus: Redeemer and Divine Word* (Wilmington, Del.: Glazier, 1989), 82–83. Cf. L. W. Grensted, *A Short History of the Doctrine of the Atonement* (Manchester: Manchester University Press, 1920), 86–87; Jaroslav Pelikan, *The Emergence of the Catholic Tradition (100–600),* vol. 1 of *The Christian Tradition: A History of the Development of Doctrine* (Chicago: University of Chicago Press, 1971), 148, 152, 258; H. D. McDonald, *The Atonement of the Death of Christ: In Faith, Revelation, and History* (Grand Rapids: Baker, 1985), 148.

18. Later theologians, however, also continued to combine various strands of atonement theology. Luther's Christus Victor theme, celebrated by Aulén, was accompanied by penal substitutionary notions. Calvin likewise combined the various theories of the atonement. See Robert A. Peterson, *Calvin's Doctrine of the Atonement* (Phillipsburg, N.J.: Presbyterian & Reformed, 1983).

19. Cf. Hugo Grotius's helpful list of "Testimonies of the Ancient" in *De satisfactione Christi adversus Faustum Socinum Senensem,* trans. Hotze Mulder, ed. Edwin Rabbie, vol. 1 of *Opera Theologica* (Assen, Neth.: Van Gorcum, 1990), 280–317.

20. *The Epistle of Mathetes to Diognetus,* in *The Ante-Nicene Fathers,* ed. Alexander Roberts and James Donaldson, rev. A. Cleveland Coxe (1885; repr., Peabody, Mass.: Hendrickson, 1994), 1:28 (IX). The context of this passage also refers to our deserved "punishment and death," so that it would not be too far-fetched to presume that the "sweet exchange" carried a penal element.

The notion of a "sweet exchange" (*antallagē*) reverberates throughout the period of the Fathers of the second, third, and fourth centuries. St. Gregory of Nazianzus (c. 325–89), who went on record to oppose his fellow Cappadocians' notion of God paying a ransom to the devil, commented:

> For He is made not only a Jew, and not only doth He take to Himself all monstrous and vile names, but even that which is most monstrous of all, even very sin and very curse; not that He it [*sic*] such, but He is called so. For how can He be sin, Who setteth us free from sin; and how can He be a curse, Who redeemeth us from the curse of the Law? But it is in order that He may carry His display of humility even to this extent, and form us to that humility which is the producer of exaltation.[21]

As this quotation from Nazianzen illustrates, the theme of substitution did not necessarily function by itself. For the Cappadocian father, Christ's vicarious suffering is closely tied to a "display of humility" meant to produce humility also in us. Nazianzen closely weds the themes of vicarious suffering and moral influence. Nonetheless, the element of substitution is present and is even connected to the idea of Christ suffering the curse of the Law. Similar statements expressing the vicarious character of the atonement can be found throughout the patristic period, both in the East and in the West.[22]

The idea of substitutionary suffering is fairly common in the early Church. Interestingly, the Fathers do not limit this substitution to Christ's *death*. One of the consistent criticisms against Anselmian atonement theories is that they undervalue the *life* of Christ. Whatever may be said of later theories of substitution, the early Fathers regarded not only Christ's death but also his life as redemptive. The notion of substitution is, of course, often associated particularly with the idea that Christ takes our place in his death, undergoing the wrath of God on our behalf. Thus, the cross becomes a place where sin is judged and punished, a place where God satisfies his justice or his wrath. It may be worthwhile to trace this notion, present already in Gregory of Nazianzus, in some more detail. The idea of Christ suffering the curse of the Law is often intimately associated with the scholastic Reformed tradition that began to develop in the late sixteenth century.[23] But penal substitution as such was not a Calvinist invention. Among the early Church fathers, we find references to the penal character of the cross.

21. Gregory Nazianzen, *Select Orations,* in *Nicene and Post-Nicene Fathers,* Second Series, trans. Charles Gordon Browne and James Edward Swallow, ed. Philip Schaff and Henry Wace (1894; repr., Peabody, Mass.: Hendrickson, 1994), 7:338 (XXVII.1).

22. The element of substitution is present in Tertullian, Origen, Cyril of Alexandria, Cyprian, Basil of Caesarea, Athanasius, Hilary, Ambrose, Augustine, Chrysostom, and Leo the Great. See Grensted, *Short History,* 75, 78; H. E. W. Turner, *The Patristic Doctrine of Redemption: A Study of the Development of Doctrine during the First Five Centuries* (London: Mowbray; New York: Morehouse-Gorham, 1952), 103–13; Pelikan, *Emergence,* 257–58; McDonald, *Atonement,* 147–62.

23. See, for example, Green and Baker, *Recovering the Scandal;* Snyder, *Protestant Ethic.*

There are elements in Irenaeus, for instance, that point beyond recapitulation of Adam's life. Recapitulation, as we have seen, also includes the tree of the cross.[24] The tree of knowledge in the Garden of Eden is a counter-type of the tree of the cross. And it is the blood of the cross that saves us from sin: Christ himself "points out the recapitulation that should take place in his own person of the effusion of blood from the beginning."[25] Throughout Irenaeus's writings we find some of the more objective atonement categories of later satisfaction theology, such as sacrifice and propitiation. When arguing that God has cancelled the Law of Moses, Irenaeus points out that people under the Old Covenant often wrongly thought that they could "propitiate" God by means of their sacrifices. They should have realized that the transcendent God "stands in need of nothing."[26] The working assumption that underlies Irenaeus's sentiment of the transcendent God not needing human sacrifices seems to be that there is a close connection between the Levitical sacrifices and the idea of propitiation.

Irenaeus even appears to assume that Christ's sacrificial death on the cross is propitiatory in character and so is meant to deal with the wrath of God.[27] To be sure, such references remain sparse. Robert J. Daly comments that in Irenaeus "the idea of the sacrifice of Christ seems to be presumed more often than explicitly stated."[28] This is quite true, and even this modest assertion remains mostly an argument from silence. The notion of Christ's death being sacrificial and propitiatory remains marginal in Irenaeus.[29] Christ's suffering

24. Cf. chapter 5 (the section titled "Irenaeus and Recapitulation").

25. *Irenaeus against Heresies* (hereafter *AH*), in *The Ante-Nicene Fathers,* ed. Alexander Roberts and James Donaldson (1885; repr., Peabody, Mass.: Hendrickson, 1994), 1:541 (V.14.1).

26. Ibid., 1:481 (IV.17.1). Interestingly, Irenaeus says that God does ask for mercy and compassion. One cannot help but wonder whether the transcendent God would "need" these any more than he needs sacrifices. Irenaeus seems to be aware of this tension in his argument when he comments (regarding the Eucharist): "Now we make offering to Him, not as though He stood in need of it, but rendering thanks for His gift, and thus sanctifying what has been created" (Ibid., 1:486 [IV.18.6]).

27. Both Aulén and Lawson deny the presence of sacrifice and propitiation in Irenaeus: Gustaf Aulén, *Christus Victor: An Historical Study of the Three Main Types of the Idea of the Atonement,* trans. A. G. Hebert (London: SPCK, 1970), 27, 33; John Lawson, *The Biblical Theology of Saint Irenaeus* (London: Epworth, 1948), 193. For a defense of the element of propitiation in Irenaeus, see Andrew J. Bandstra, "Paul and an Ancient Interpreter: A Comparison of the Teaching of Redemption in Paul and Irenaeus," *Calvin Theological Journal* 5 (1970): 58–61.

28. Robert J. Daly, *Christian Sacrifice: The Judaeo-Christian Background before Origen* (Washington, D.C.: Catholic University of America Press, 1978), 348.

29. Irenaeus does repeatedly refer to the "blood" of Christ and to the "cross" and the "tree," indicating an interest in the death of Christ. This death is, after all, part of Christ's work of recapitulation. An interesting example—also illustrative of Irenaeus's christological reading of the Old Testament—is found in *Fragments from the Lost Writings of Irenaeus,* in *The Ante-Nicene Fathers,* ed. Alexander Roberts and James Donaldson (1885; repr., Peabody, Mass.: Hendrickson, 1994), 1:23. Here Irenaeus depicts Balaam's donkey as a type of the body of Christ: "For the Saviour has taken up the burden of our sins." Cf. Irenaeus, *Proof of the Apostolic Preaching,* trans. Joseph P. Smith (New York: Paulist, 1952), 69.

as such is just not a central category for Irenaeus. He may comment that our Lord "by His passion destroyed death, and dispersed error, and put an end to corruption, and destroyed ignorance, while he manifested life and revealed truth, and bestowed the gift of incorruption"[30]—but such references to Christ's passion are rather incidental within the whole of Irenaeus's theology. Moreover, some of the passages that speak of Christ's death as a sacrifice do not make clear that this sacrifice has to do with the condemnation for sin,[31] and passages in which Irenaeus speaks of Christ "propitiating" the Father do not indicate whether it is Christ's obedience (in the face of temptation) or his death that propitiates the Father.[32]

Perhaps Irenaeus expresses the connection between Christ's sacrifice and propitiation most clearly when he says that the Lord "did not make void, but fulfilled the law, by performing the offices of the high priest, propitiating God for men, and cleansing the lepers, healing the sick, and Himself suffering death, that exiled man might go forth from condemnation, and might return without fear to his own inheritance."[33] There is a sense, however weakly expressed, in which Irenaeus regards Christ's death as a sacrifice that propitiates the Father. For Irenaeus, Christ gains the victory not *only* by means of his prophetic office. The priestly element also comes to the fore. Christ is only the victorious king because he is prophet *and* priest. Moral as well as penal elements are necessary to achieve the ultimate victory.

Origen (c. 185–253) is another Church father who argues that Christ is the sacrificial victim through whose death on the cross "propitiation" is made.[34] Similarly, Cyril of Alexandria (c. 375–444) argues that Christ "accepted the punishment of sinners."[35] These judicial elements were reinforced in the West through the writings of St. Hilary of Poitiers († 367) and St. Augustine (354–430). "Christ, though guiltless," comments Augustine, "took our punishment, that He might cancel our guilt, and do away with our punishment."[36] In the sixth century we find Gregory the Great (c. 540–604) explicitly discussing the question of God's justice in condemning the Mediator who "deserved not to be punished for Himself." Gregory answers the question with an eye to the outcome of Christ's death: "But if He had not Himself undertaken a death

30. Irenaeus, *AH,* 1:338 (II.20.3).

31. E.g., ibid., 1:467 (IV.5.4).

32. E.g., ibid., 1:544 (V.17.1).

33. Ibid., 1:471 (IV.8.2).

34. Origène, *Homélies sur les Nombres,* ed. Louis Doutreleau, Sources Chrétiennes, 461 (Paris: Les Éditions du Cerf, 2001), 3:162 (xxiv.i.6). Cf. Grensted, *Short History,* 62.

35. In line with his Alexandrian Christology (closely linking Christ's human and divine natures), Cyril emphasized that this punishment was punishment that God took upon himself (McDonald, *Atonement,* 152).

36. Augustine, *Reply to Faustus the Manichaean,* in *Nicene and Post-Nicene Fathers,* First Series, trans. Richard Stothert, ed. Philip Schaff and Henry Wace (1887; repr., Peabody, Mass.: Hendrickson, 1994), 4:208 (XIV.4).

not due to Him, He would never have freed us from one that was justly due to us. And so whereas 'The Father is righteous,' in punishing a righteous man, 'He ordereth all things righteously.'"[37]

Again, all of this is not to say that before the time of Anselm penal substitution formed the only, or even the dominant, strand of reflection on the meaning of the cross. What is more, I make clear in the remainder of this chapter that the emphatic presence of juridical elements throughout the Church's tradition (especially in the Western Augustinian segment of the Church) has by no means been uniformly positive. Nonetheless, it is important to recognize that penal substitutionary interpretations of the cross had a place from the beginning of the tradition of the Church, so that the Reformers and their successors did not originate an entirely novel understanding of the atonement. The consistent presence of juridical elements of the atonement in the history of the Church should caution us not to discard them too hastily. The tradition has some important theological insights to offer as we struggle with the penal elements in our interpretation of the cross.

The Violence of Atonement in Augustinian Theology

The historical pedigree of substitutionary and juridical elements of atonement theology means that perhaps we need another look at the possibilities that such elements may offer. I contend that it is not a penal understanding of the cross as such that endangers hospitality, but rather the juridicizing, individualizing, and de-historicizing of the cross that is responsible for an imbalanced approach that legitimizes unnecessary violence. In chapter 2 we noted that the Augustinian tradition—and particularly Calvin and later Calvinism—developed an understanding of predestination that was timeless, individual, and futuristic in orientation. These emphases correspond with tendencies in Reformed atonement theology that hark back to, and radicalize, traditional Augustinian readings of the atonement. In the following discussion, I explain some of these unfortunate emphases and developments.

The first and most fundamental of the difficulties is the juridicizing of the cross. Again, I wish to underline that legal or juridical concepts do have their place, both in biblical revelation and (as we have already seen) in the Church's understanding of the atonement. The problem with the development of atonement theology does not lie with the notion of punishment as such. Punishments are based on laws, and the concept of law obviously plays an important role in the biblical witness. To affirm a juridical element in the atonement does not mean, however, that we should *reduce* the atonement to

---

37. Gregory the Great, *Morals on the Book of Job* (Oxford: Parker, 1844), 1:149 (I.iii.14). Cf. Grensted, *Short History*, 98.

juridical elements, to law court scenes, or to notions of personal forgiveness of sins. When I speak about the juridicizing of the atonement, I have in mind a form of reductionism that limits the divine-human relationship to judicial categories, and that views the cross solely in terms of laws, infractions, judicial pronouncements, forgiveness, and punishments.

In a groundbreaking 1963 essay, Krister Stendahl, then New Testament professor at Harvard, lamented the "introspective conscience of the West." Stendahl maintained that ever since the time of Augustine, Western theologies have taken their starting point in St. Paul's sense of frustration expressed in Romans 7:19—"[T]he good thing I want to do, I never do; the evil thing which I do not want—that is what I do." By reading this complaint as an expression of a believer's struggle with his or her inability to live a righteous life, Christians have since the time of Augustine consistently focused on the interior state of affairs in their souls. Augustine, said Stendahl, "may well have been one of the first to express the dilemma of the introspective conscience."[38] According to Stendahl medieval Irish manuals for self-examination, fear of the Black Death, and a system of penance and indulgences all reinforced a sense of doubt and uncertainty that ultimately led to Luther's fearful question, "How can I find a gracious God?"—a question that was utterly alien both to the Jewish worldview and to the robust conscience of St. Paul, who was never in doubt about God's willingness to forgive, and who rarely speaks of salvation in terms of forgiveness.[39] Again, this is not to say that St. Paul does not speak about forgiveness at all, nor is it to deny the relative significance of law court metaphors in his theology of justification.[40] But St. Paul does not resort to a reductionism that limits our relationship with God to legal categories.

Within the Reformed tradition, this juridicizing has been exacerbated by the development of federal or covenant theology in the late sixteenth and seventeenth centuries. The word "covenant" is, of course, a biblical term. But this does not mean that the biblical notion of "covenant" is the interpretive lens through which all Scripture should be viewed. Old Testament theologian John Stek has drawn attention to the problem of "covenant overload" in the Reformed tradition. He argues that covenants occur in the biblical account only as ad hoc commitments, based on already existing relationships. Covenants, explains Stek, "were called into play only when circumstances *occasioned doubts* concerning desired or promised courses of action. The specific purpose of 'covenants' was to add a guarantee of fulfillment to commitments made."[41] The

---

38. Krister Stendahl, "The Apostle Paul and the Introspective Conscience of the West," in *Paul among Jews and Gentiles* (Philadelphia: Fortress, 1976), 83.

39. Ibid., 82.

40. As I explain in chapter 9, I believe that the loss of the sacrament of penance in the Protestant tradition has been a particularly unhelpful development.

41. John H. Stek, "Covenant Overload in Reformed Theology," *Calvin Theological Journal* 29 (1994): 25 (italics in the original).

idea of a covenant, in other words, is secondary and is built on a relationship that was already there prior to the establishment of the covenant. Covenants are simply "emergency measures" that are necessary until God's kingdom has fully come.

Just as later Calvinists went beyond Calvin in their theology of predestination, so they did in their covenant theology as well. It is generally acknowledged that Calvin was not a federal theologian.[42] No matter how important it may have been for him, the covenant concept did not dominate Calvin's theology. He only spoke of one covenant of grace, which God had established with Christ as Mediator to restore the relationship that was broken by sin. The covenant was God's redemptive means in a postlapsarian world marred by sin. It is not until the 1590s that we see the development of a "covenant of works" (*foedus operum*) or a "covenant of nature" (*foedus naturae*), used to describe the prelapsarian situation in the Garden of Eden. The real origin of federal theology has been connected to this development in the late sixteenth century.[43] A number of different theories circulate about the reason(s) behind this development of a covenant of works.[44] Whatever the historical impetus may have been, the result was an impressive theological system built on a thoroughgoing juridical basis. Reformed scholasticism maintained that there were certain laws of nature to which Adam (along with all subsequent humanity) had been bound. Moses positively promulgated these laws in the Ten Commandments at the time of the exodus. All humanity was bound by this covenant of works and was obliged to abide by its stipulations. Failure to do so would result in eternal death—the "curse of the Law." The fall of Adam and Eve, therefore, made the punishment

---

42. See, for instance, David A. Weir, *The Origins of the Federal Theology in Sixteenth-Century Reformation Thought* (Oxford: Clarendon, 1990); and James B. Torrance, "The Concept of Federal Theology: Was Calvin a Federal Theologian?" in *Calvinus Sacrae Scripturae Professor: Calvin as Confessor of Holy Scripture,* ed. Wilhelm H. Neuser (Grand Rapids: Eerdmans, 1994), 15–40. For a different view, see Peter A. Lillback, *The Binding of God: Calvin's Role in the Development of Covenant Theology* (Grand Rapids: Baker; Carlisle, UK: Paternoster, 2001).

43. See Weir, *Origins.*

44. Some of the reasons that have been suggested for the development of the covenant of works are:

(1) It gave Reformed theologians a counterbalance of human responsibility to their rigid predestinarianism (Weir, *Origins*).

(2) It was the result of the philosopher Peter Ramus (1515–72), who advocated bifurcating all theology into pairs of two, so that the covenant of grace logically demanded another covenant (W. Wilson Benton, "Federal Theology: Review for Revision," in *Through Christ's Word: A Festschrift for Dr. Philip E. Hughes,* ed. W. Robert Godfrey and Jesse L. Boyd III [Phillipsburg, N.J.: Presbyterian & Reformed, 1985], 180–204).

(3) By confining the curse of the law to the covenant of works, the covenant of grace was made to shine in all its glorious unconditionality (Michael McGiffert, "Grace and Works: The Rise and Division of Covenant Divinity in Elizabethan Puritanism," *Harvard Theological Review* 75 [1982]: 463–502; "From Moses to Adam: The Making of the Covenant of Works," *Sixteenth Century Journal* 19 [1988]: 131–55).

(4) It gave a theological rationale for sabbatarianism by making Sabbath observance a demand of the covenant of nature (Derk Visser, "The Covenant in Zacharias Ursinus," *Sixteenth Century Journal* 18 [1987]: 531–44).

of eternal wrath inevitable. Only by believing in Jesus Christ as the mediator or head of a new covenant (the covenant of grace) could one avoid the curse of the Law and become an heir to the blessings of God's grace.

The crown on the edifice of federal theology was the notion of an eternal "covenant of redemption" (*pactum salutis*) or "covenant of peace" between the Father and the Son. This concept, by a twist of irony first introduced by Arminius (1560–1609), was seized on and developed by his high Calvinist Puritan opponent, William Ames (1576–1633), and subsequently became a standard element of the scholastic federal package.[45] The introduction of the covenant of redemption meant that now the covenant notion was not only pulled back to the prelapsarian state of innocence but was also located in eternity itself as an agreement between the Father and the Son regarding the salvation of the elect. The Father promised "offspring" to the Son (Isa. 53:10)—that is to say, eternal salvation for the elect—on two conditions. The first was that the Son would perfectly obey the covenant of nature or of works, which Adam had failed to keep. This became known as Christ's active obedience. The second condition was that the Son would suffer eternal death as the punishment that Adam had deserved by breaking the covenant of works. This was referred to as Christ's passive obedience. In the covenant of redemption, the Son voluntarily agreed to the terms of the covenant, and so the stage for history was set. In federal theology, therefore, the world of God's eternal decrees overshadowed the historical covenant relationship and diminished its significance.[46] Put in different terms, the absolute will of God outmaneuvered his revealed will. Even the Trinitarian relationships themselves were now encapsulated in a juridical framework. God's eternal hospitality was bounded and regulated by strict legal arrangements and so lost the welcoming nature of absolute, pure hospitality.

The juridicizing of the divine-human relationship in the radical wing of the Augustinian tradition encouraged individualizing and de-historicizing tendencies in atonement theology. Again, individualizing notions of Western atonement theology are not limited to the followers of Anselm. Abelard's understanding of the atonement was no less individualistic than Anselm's. The problem lies with a Western mind-set that has overemphasized the relative importance of the individual. This is not to say that the individual and his or her responsibility are insignificant. But Western thought has suffered from a

45. For the development of the covenant of redemption, see B. Loonstra, *Verkiezing-Verzoening-Verbond: Beschrijving en beoordeling van de leer van het pactum salutis in de gereformeerde theologie* (The Hague: Boekencentrum, 1990).

46. For the Dutch theologian Klaas Schilder, history became a "substratum" for the sake of the realization of God's eternal decrees. See G. C. Berkouwer, *The Providence of God,* trans. Lewis B. Smedes (Grand Rapids: Eerdmans, 1952), 71; J. Douma, *Algemene genade: Uiteenzetting, vergelijking en beoordeling van de opvattingen van A. Kuyper, K. Schilder en Joh. Calvijn over 'algemene genade',* 4th ed. (Goes, Neth.: Oosterbaan & Le Cointre, 1981), 136, 162.

preoccupation with the individual that goes well beyond a biblical appreciation for individual responsibility. When Augustine's follower Gottschalk († c. 869) restricted the significance of the atonement to the elect, the result was that atonement was from then on related to the invisible Church, that is to say, to those individuals whom God had chosen from eternity. Vicarious substitution came to mean that Christ took the place of certain (elect) individuals. On the cross Christ bore the penalty of *my* particular sins that *I* have committed. Notions of corporate or institutional guilt cannot possibly have a place in such a scenario. The result has been a tendency toward a transactional or mercantile understanding of the atonement, in which my sins are transferred or imputed to Christ, while his righteousness is directly transferred or imputed to me. This understanding of immediate imputation became the hallmark of a Reformed understanding of the atonement.[47] It is a far cry from the Irenaean concept of recapitulation, in which Christ represented all humanity. When contemporary scholars argue that the emphasis has been too long on the individual and their personal sin and comment that "the emphasis now should be on the social,"[48] they make a valid point. Again, when they argue that our hymns and prayers reveal "an emphasis upon individual guilt, individual forgiveness, individual holiness, and an individual relationship with God,"[49] they alert us to a weakness that lies deeply embedded in the Augustinian—and especially in the Protestant and evangelical—mind-set.

Philip J. Lee, in his fascinating book *Against the Protestant Gnostics,* concludes his preface with the provocative comment, "As a Protestant, I believe I have identified the elusive modern gnostics, and they are ourselves."[50] According to Lee one of the characteristics of second-century Gnosticism was that it opposed the knowing self to the community. Salvation for the Gnostic is salvation from ignorance. "The significance of the Gospel, then, becomes solely that of illumination. And what is illuminated is the true *self.*"[51] Lee characterizes the spirituality of the Gnostics as narcissistic, egocentric, and escapist.

It would surely be erroneous to depict the whole of Western tradition as Gnostic in character. Nonetheless, certain tendencies within Western religious individualism are reminiscent of the ancient heresy of Gnosticism. In his classic study, *Habits of the Heart,* Robert Bellah has pointed out that radical individualism deeply permeates North American spirituality: "Most

---

47. Alister E. McGrath points to Philip Melanchthon as the originator of this new understanding of imputation ("Forerunners of the Reformation? A Critical Examination of the Evidence for Precursors of the Reformation Doctrines of Justification," *Harvard Theological Review* 75 [1982]: 219–42). For a careful critique of the idea of imputation, see Robert H. Gundry, "Why I Didn't Endorse 'The Gospel of Jesus Christ: An Evangelical Celebration,'" *Books & Culture* (January/February 2001): 6–9.

48. Ray, *Deceiving the Devil,* 85.

49. Snyder, *Protestant Ethic,* 59.

50. Philip J. Lee, *Against the Protestant Gnostics* (New York: Oxford University Press, 1987), xiv.

51. Ibid., 27 (italics in the original).

Americans see religion as something individual, prior to any organizational involvement."[52] This individualism has been abetted by the way in which the doctrine of the Church has developed in the West. Both Augustine and Calvin worked with the notion of an invisible Church (*ecclesia invisibilis*), which consisted of everyone whom God from eternity had chosen to everlasting life. To be sure, Augustine and the Catholic tradition following him strongly emphasized the need to belong to the visible Church, the community gathered around the eucharistic table of the Lord and under the hierarchical magisterial authority of the bishop. Calvin likewise had a deep appreciation for the nurturing function of Mother Church as a visible institution.[53] Later Calvinists, however, became far more introspective, and in their concern for the individual's eternal well-being, they made generous use of the Gnosticizing notion of an "invisible Church." One of the results in North America has been a denominationalism that has lost all appreciation for the salvific significance of the Church community. "With denominationalism," maintains Lee, "it has become quite obvious that individuals not only do choose Jesus, but choose him on their own terms."[54]

In addition to juridicizing and individualizing tendencies, Anselmian atonement theories have also inherited from the Augustinian tradition the inclination to de-historicize the cross.[55] By emphasizing double predestination, Augustinianism has always had the inherent tendency to emphasize the eternal and timeless rather than the historical. Heiko Oberman has correctly pointed out that there is a great deal of theological continuity between the Middle Ages and the period of the Reformation.[56] De-historicizing tendencies of Protestant scholasticism had their origin in a tradition that had long emphasized eternity at the expense of history. The Augustinian tradition had often worked with the idea that humanity was under a curse of eternal punishment because of Adam's primal sin in the Garden of Eden. The curse placed on Adam was the curse of eternal damnation. The Augustinian logic was impeccable: rejection of eternal bliss was deserving of eternal punishment. True wisdom would make people see "how great a wickedness was committed in that first transgression. The more enjoyment man found in God, the greater was his wickedness in abandoning Him; and he who destroyed in himself a good which might have been eternal, became worthy of eternal

52. Cf. Robert N. Bellah et al., *Habits of the Heart: Individualism and Commitment in American Life* (Berkeley: University of California Press, 1985), 226.

53. I suspect, however, that Calvin's appreciation for the invisible Church—corresponding to his theology of predestination—outweighs his love for the visible Church. See C. Graafland, *Kinderen van één moeder: Calvijns visie op de kerk volgens zijn Institutie* (Kampen, Neth.: Kok, 1989).

54. Lee, *Against the Protestant Gnostics*, 156.

55. Cf., for instance, Ray, *Deceiving the Devil*, 85; Snyder, *Protestant Ethic*, 55–73.

56. Heiko Augustinus Oberman, *Forerunners of the Reformation: The Shape of Late Medieval Thought*, 2nd ed. (Minneapolis: Fortress, 1981).

evil."[57] The logic may seem flawless, but Colin Gunton has somewhat of a point when he argues that in the Augustinian tradition "there has been both an overvaluing of abstract logical connections between ideas and an undervaluing of everything else."[58] God's dealings with the people of Israel came to be viewed merely as an incidental historical interlude until the time that God would send his Son to deal with the problem of Adam's sin, which had merited eternal death. Within this paradigm it was not easy to see how, for instance, Romans 9–11—dealing with God's election of Israel—fit with the apparently systematic theological setup of the overall letter. The three chapters often seemed like an odd historical interlude in a book dealing with ahistorical, eternal truths.

The juridicizing, individualizing, and de-historicizing of atonement theology led to some remarkable inner-Calvinist debates. For many scholastic Calvinists, Jesus' cry of dereliction—"my God, my God, why have you forsaken me?"—could only be interpreted in strictly literal fashion. Christ suffered eternal abandonment by God—the exact same punishment that human beings deserved. John Owen (1616–83), the brilliant Puritan preacher and scholar, insisted against the Dutch jurist Hugo Grotius (1583–1645) and the Kidderminster preacher Richard Baxter (1615–91) that Christ suffered the exact same punishment (*solutio eiusdem*) that humanity deserved.[59] In a discussion on the concept of satisfaction in his book *The Death of Death in the Death of Christ* (1647), Owen described the death of Jesus Christ as a commercial transaction, with God being the creditor and humanity the debtor. In Owen's scheme sin was the debt owed by humanity and death the compensation according to the agreement of the Law. Owen argued that Christ's ransom intervened with this judicial arrangement. "For to make satisfaction to God for our sins, it is required only that he undergo the punishment due to them; for that is the satisfaction required where sin is the debt."[60] Owen then discussed the views of Hugo Grotius. While accepting the notion of penal substitution, Grotius had argued that God did not judge "by the letter of the law" and had the freedom to extend some mercy.[61] As supreme ruler of the universe, God had his reasons to relax the Law. Strict punishment (*solutio eiusdem*) would not leave room for forgiveness, whereas

57. Aurelius Augustine, *The City of God*, in *Nicene and Post-Nicene Fathers*, First Series, trans. Marcus Dods, ed. Philip Schaff (1887; repr., Peabody, Mass.: Hendrickson, 1994), 2:463 (XXI.12).

58. Colin E. Gunton, *The Actuality of Atonement: A Study of Metaphor, Rationality, and the Christian Tradition* (Grand Rapids: Eerdmans, 1989), 17.

59. For an extended discussion of this issue, see Hans Boersma, *A Hot Pepper Corn: Richard Baxter's Doctrine of Justification in Its Seventeenth-Century Context of Controversy*, 2nd ed. (Vancouver, B.C.: Regent College Publishing, 2004), 245–54.

60. John Owen, *The Works of John Owen*, ed. William H. Goold (London: Banner of Truth, 1967), 10:266.

61. Grotius, *De satisfactione*, II.2.

in fact God had been lenient in accepting Christ's satisfaction. Therefore, Christ's payment, according to Grotius, was one that was similar—but not identical—to the punishment threatened in the Law (*solutio tantidem*). Owen was not convinced that God had exercised such leniency. Forgiveness, argued Owen, consists of the "laying of our sin on Christ," on the one hand, and the "gracious imputation of the righteousness of Christ to us," on the other. Both of these were acts of free grace and mercy.[62] In other words, in Reformed scholasticism forgiveness and strict punishment were not opposed to each other, because the former was for believers, while the latter was for Christ. Owen and others pushed the commercial metaphor to its limit.[63] The result was an abstract, logical system in which Christ's atoning death could have taken place anywhere at any point in history. In Reformed scholasticism the violence of an economy of exchange came to dominate the understanding of the cross. The conditionality of God's hospitality featured so prominently that it undermined his unconditional hospitality—both the origin and the goal of Christ's death on the cross.

St. Paul and the Possibility of Unconditional Hospitality

We all sense that there should be some kind of correspondence between the eschatological pure hospitality that beckons us and the divine means to get there. If there is no such correspondence, we end up with an entirely arbitrary God for whom the end justifies any means. When the cross is interpreted as a place of penal justice, it should, in fact, *be* a place of justice, regardless of the violence that accompanies it—just as a fine or a prison term may be termed an instance of justice despite the violence that they entail. So, how can we be sure that we recognize in the outstretched arms on the cross the arms of the Father running down the road? How can we be sure that this is just punishment rather than legalized criminality? In the remainder of this chapter, I want to work out a model of penal representative atonement that honors the death and resurrection of Jesus Christ as the climax of divine hospitality.

When Krister Stendahl wrote his 1963 essay on the "introspective conscience of the West," he revolutionized New Testament scholarship—both the study of the Gospels and Pauline studies. Perhaps one of the most significant results of this scholarship is a renewed appreciation for what is often called "the historical Jesus" as well as for the historical grounding of the writings of

---

62. Owen, *Works,* 10:268–69.

63. By contrast Grotius had strong reservations about the commercial metaphor: "For the right of absolute ownership, as well as a personal right, is secured for the sake of him who has this right, but the right of punishment does not exist for the sake of him who punishes, but for the sake of a community" (*De satisfactione,* II.16).

St. Paul.[64] For too long, people have read St. Paul through the eyes of a systematic theology that had little regard for his Jewish background and for the historical particularities of Israel's situation that inform his writings. Scholars have always agreed, of course, that the Pauline letters spoke to particular situations and were addressed to certain individuals or churches that had to deal with heretical notions or other difficulties. Nonetheless, it was commonly held that one could strip the Pauline letters of their historical context and arrive at the pristine, abstract systematic theology that functioned as a substratum, as it were, underneath each of the letters. Hence, it is understandable that the epistle that is least determined by the contextuality of particular addressees—the letter to the Romans—was thought to express the heart of Paul's theology most brightly and most directly.

The last twenty-five years have changed all this. There is a profound awareness among New Testament scholars today that Jesus came as the representative of Israel—the embodiment of the New Israel—and that as such he came as the culmination of a particular historical journey of fellowship (and the lack thereof) between Yahweh and the Abrahamic nation. To be sure, behind the Israelite history lies the story of all humanity. Jesus is not just the New Israel; he is also (and ultimately) the Second Adam (Rom. 5:12–21; 1 Cor. 15:45–49). But the role of Jesus as the messianic representative of Israel is so pervasive throughout the New Testament that we cannot ignore the history of God's chosen people. The cross is not simply an arbitrary divine punishment inflicted on God's Son, a punishment that could have taken place at any time and in any place, but is a historically dated expression of God's hospitality, accompanied by the type of violence (punishment) without which such hospitality cannot materialize.

An exegetical foray into St. Paul's letter to the Galatians may clarify the significance of this point. This letter centers on the question of the Church and its boundaries: Who belongs to the Church, and on what basis do they belong? Is ethnic descent or is the obedience of faith the deciding factor? Is it the "works of the law"—such as circumcision, kosher food, and Sabbath observance—or is it association with Jesus Christ that marks one as a member of the people of God? St. Paul argues that it is the latter, and he feels strongly that the heart of the gospel is at stake (Gal. 1:6–7). "You stupid people in Galatia!" he berates his readers in the opening verse of chapter 3. "After you have had a clear picture of Jesus Christ crucified, right in front of your eyes,

---

64. I have been influenced particularly by the writings of E. P. Sanders, N. T. Wright, and James D. G. Dunn. Those familiar with recent New Testament scholarship will recognize that I am gratefully making use of their insights. In doing so, I am concurring with Alister E. McGrath's lament of "the artificial divide that has opened up between New Testament scholarship and systematic theology" ("Reality, Symbol, and History: Theological Reflections on N. T. Wright's Portrayal of Jesus," in *Jesus and the Restoration of Israel: A Critical Assessment of N. T. Wright's Jesus and the Victory of God,* ed. Carey C. Newman [Downers Grove, Ill.: InterVarsity; Carlisle, UK: Paternoster, 1999], 160).

who has put a spell on you?" St. Paul closely ties the ecclesiological question, "What are the boundary markers of the Church?" to the soteriological issue, "How is it that God includes us among his people?"

After making an appeal to the presence of the Spirit (an Old Testament eschatological promise), the apostle continues with the following passage:

> ⁶*Abraham*, you remember, *put his faith in God*, and this was reckoned to him as uprightness [Gen. 15:6]. ⁷Be sure, then, that it is people of faith who are the children of Abraham. ⁸And it was because scripture foresaw that God would give saving justice to the gentiles through faith, that it announced the future gospel to Abraham in the words: *All nations will be blessed in you* [Gen. 12:3]. ⁹So it is people of faith who receive the same blessing as Abraham, the man of faith.
>
> ¹⁰On the other hand, all those who depend on the works of the Law are under a curse, since scripture says: *Accursed be he who does not make what is written in the book of the Law effective, by putting it into practice* [Deut. 27:26]. ¹¹Now it is obvious that nobody is reckoned as upright in God's sight by the law, since *the upright will live through faith* [Hab. 2:4]; ¹²and the Law is based not on faith but on the principle, *whoever complies with it will find life in it* [Lev. 18:5]. ¹³Christ redeemed us from the curse of the Law by being cursed for our sake since scripture says: *Anyone hanged is accursed* [Deut. 21:23], ¹⁴so that the blessing of Abraham might come to the gentiles in Christ Jesus, and so that we might receive the promised Spirit through faith. (Gal. 3:6–14)

In this discussion in Galatians 3, St. Paul enters into a debate on the relationship between Abraham, the Law, and the Christian life. Undoubtedly, he is stepping into well-known territory. His opponents had likely appealed to Genesis 15 and 12 for their position that one needed to belong to the Abrahamic nation—signified by Law adherence—in order to be part of the people of God. Abraham had received the promises of descendants and land (Gen. 15:5, 7). The only way in which the Gentiles could share in the blessing of Abraham was by attaching themselves to the ethnic people of God. He had indicated to Abraham, "[A]ll clans on earth will bless themselves *by you*" (12:3, italics added). The promises in these foundational passages in Genesis—descendants, land, and blessings for other nations—appeared to be ethnically based.

St. Paul, however, gives a radically new interpretation of these passages. He points out that God's promises of land and descendants (Gen. 15:5, 7) cannot be separated from the verse that says, "Abram put his faith in Yahweh and this was reckoned to him as uprightness" (15:6). From the start, therefore, God's relationship with Abraham was not based on a blood tie or on ethnic particularity, but on faith. Thus, St. Paul concludes: "Be sure, then, that it is people of *faith* who are the children of Abraham" (Gal. 3:7, italics added). And if it is faith that characterizes the people of God, then this is also the framework that needs to be applied to the earlier chapter, in which God called Abraham from Ur (Genesis 12). If all *nations* will bless themselves *by Abraham* (Gen.

12:3), and if—as St. Paul has just argued—Abraham's relationship with God was characterized by *faith,* then these three elements (nations, Abraham, and faith) belong together: "So it is people of faith who receive the same blessing as Abraham, the man of faith" (Gal. 3:9). The apostle to the Gentiles is of the opinion that the Law party has misconstrued the true meaning of Genesis 15 and 12, substituted ethnic descent for a faith relationship, and in the process redefined the boundaries of the Church. The covenant blessings, maintains St. Paul, are for Gentiles just as much as they are for Jews. Faith, rather than ethnicity, defines the boundaries of the Church.

At this juncture we arrive at one of the passages that has often played a key role in substitutionary interpretations of the atonement (Gal. 3:10–13). A traditional Protestant reading of this passage typically takes the following steps:

1. *Juridicizing:* The working assumption tends to be that St. Paul's negative reflections on the Law are caused by the legalism of his Judaizing opponents—the idea that one needs to earn one's salvation. Since no one is able to keep all the commandments perfectly, such attempts to live by the Law are futile. Any infraction of the Law necessarily invokes the curse of the Law (Gal. 3:10). Accordingly, St. Paul contrasts the Old Testament's demand to follow God's commandments (Lev. 18:5) with the New Testament's appeal to faith (based on Hab. 2:4). By bearing the curse of the Law for us, Christ effects this transition from the Old to the New Testament, from faith to works (Gal. 3:13).

2. *Individualizing:* The inability to keep the Law is not the inability of the nation Israel, but the inability of each individual. This reading emphasizes that St. Paul is quoting Deuteronomy 27:26 from the Septuagint, which contains the word "everything." Galatians 3:10 literally translates: "Cursed is everyone who does not abide by *everything* written in the book of the Law to do them." Traditional exegetes would point to other passages from St. Paul where he appears to assume that nobody is able to keep all the requirements of the Law (Gal. 5:3; Rom. 3:19–20).[65] The Law thus accuses people's individual conscience.

3. *De-historicizing:* All of this implies a timeless interpretation of the atonement: anyone who at any time would try to live by the Law would find that he or she was unable to do so perfectly. This counted for individual Jews before the birth of Christ and still counts for people today. The Law's timeless function is that of a tutor to convict people of sin and so lead them to Christ (Gal. 3:24).

65. Cf. Thomas R. Schreiner, *The Law and Its Fulfillment: A Pauline Theology of Law* (Grand Rapids: Baker, 1993), 41–71.

There are a number of serious problems with this type of reading. First, one of its consequences is a tendency to separate the Old and the New Testaments means of salvation. This reading assumes that salvation in the Old Testament was based on works (Lev. 18:5), while in the New Testament it is based on faith. It seems difficult to accept that in the Old Testament God would use a means of salvation that in New Testament times is considered erroneous, or even heretical: the presumed Judaizing (and Catholic!) error of works righteousness. Second, the assumption that St. Paul had an "introspective conscience" cannot withstand careful scrutiny of his letters. Throughout these letters we meet a confident St. Paul—confident not only after but even before his Damascus Road experience (cf. Phil. 3:6). This is not to say that Paul thought that he had been sinless or perfect in obeying the Law. But he took comfort from the fact that under the Law, Israelites could atone for their sins by means of repentance, sacrifice, and restitution; not all sins resulted in punishment.[66] Finally, and perhaps most seriously, the traditional Protestant reading belittles hospitality because it works with a strict economy of exchange. The covenantal relationship between God and human beings takes on strongly contractual connotations.[67] The stranger has secured a place in the home not by an unconditional gift but by means of a contractual agreement (with the elect being allotted to Christ on the basis of his agreement to suffer in their stead). Nouwen's notion that the father "cannot force, constrain, push, or pull" the prodigal appears to be lost.[68]

It seems to me that we need to opt for a national-historical reading of this passage, one that does not ignore its juridical and covenantal overtones—it plainly contains penal language—but that makes the judicial elements subservient to the hospitality that God extends in Jesus Christ. St. Paul's quotation of Deuteronomy 27:26 is highly significant, because this text is part of a larger covenant document (Deuteronomy 27–30) and needs to be read in that context. N. T. Wright explains the context as follows:

> It describes, and indeed appears to enact, the making of the covenant in Moab, the covenant which holds out blessing and curse. The blessing and curse are not merely "take-it-or-leave-it" options: Deuteronomy declares that Israel will in fact eventually make the wrong choice, and, as a result, suffer the curse of all curses, that is, exile (Deu-

66. E. P. Sanders, *Paul and Palestinian Judaism: A Comparison of Patterns of Religion* (Philadelphia: Fortress, 1977), 157–82; James D. G. Dunn, *The Epistle to the Galatians* (Peabody, Mass.: Hendrickson, 1993), 171; John H. Hayes, "Atonement in the Book of Leviticus," *Interpretation* 52 (1998): 10–12. This point is crucially important, because traditional substitutionary views of the atonement have often held that God's justice requires that all sins against God are deserving of eternal death and are, in fact, punished with eternal death on the cross (or, for others, in hell).

67. Cf. James B. Torrance, "Covenant or Contract? A Study of the Theological Background of Worship in Seventeenth-Century Scotland," *Scottish Journal of Theology* 23 (1970): 51–76.

68. Henri J. Nouwen, *The Return of the Prodigal Son: A Story of Homecoming* (New York: Image-Doubleday), 95.

teronomy 28.15–29.29). But that will not be the end of the story, or of the covenant. Deuteronomy 30 then holds out hope the other side of covenant failure, a hope of covenant renewal, of the re-gathering of the people after exile, of the circumcision of the heart, of the word being "near you, on your lips and in your heart" (30.1–14). In other words, Deuteronomy 27–30 is all about exile and restoration, *understood as* covenant judgment and covenant renewal.[69]

The Mosaic covenant was an arrangement that God made not with one individual but with an entire nation. This also means that the covenant curse of exile would fall on the entire nation. The Deuteronomic Law insists that Israel *as a whole*—despite the uprightness of individual believers—would consistently reject the very aim of repentance and sacrifice, namely, restoration of and growth in the relationship with Yahweh. The book of Deuteronomy leads up to the divine prediction of the rebellion of Israel, of its rejection of the monotheist confession of the Shema as the heart of the Law (Deut. 6:4–6). The book thus leads to the culmination of exile as the curse of the Law.[70] The Deuteronomic history books (Joshua–2 Kings) trace the apostasy of God's people, which finally results in the exilic curse.[71]

Significantly, exile is God's last option. He resorts to this climactic punishment only when it becomes clear that Israel as a whole has consistently refused to repent and so to obtain forgiveness and a restoration of the relationship with Yahweh.[72] God does not delight in punishment but keeps the violence of penal force at bay as much as possible. What is more, the punishment of exile as the curse of the Law serves to salvage the realization of monotheistic worship as the very heart of the Law. This punishment serves the purpose of pure, eschatological hospitality: the Father's eternal embrace of the prodigal son. "Punishment may be necessary . . . but it is not the pain of punishment itself that achieves justice, as though justice resides in creating equity of suffering, the pain of offenders' punishments compensating for the pain inflicted on victims. True justice resides in the restoring of relationships and the recreation of *shalom* (Romans 5)."[73]

When St. Paul quotes the Deuteronomic invocation of the curse, he is assuming that Israel has, in fact, suffered the curse of the Law in the historical punishment of exile. In other words, the "curse of the Law" is not some eternal

---

69. N. T. Wright, *The Climax of the Covenant: Christ and the Law in Pauline Theology* (Minneapolis: Fortress, 1992), 140.

70. Deut. 28:32, 36–37, 49–52, 63–68; 29:28; 31:16–22, 29. The Song of Moses that the Israelites are to sing (Deuteronomy 32) is to function as a judicial self-indictment.

71. Gordon McConville, *Grace in the End: A Study in Deuteronomic Theology* (Grand Rapids: Zondervan, 1993), 65–122.

72. Again, this is not to say that individual Israelites would not have had their relationship with God restored by the Old Testament means of reconciliation. Scripture (in particular the Psalms) calls many people "righteous." The point is that Israel as a whole did not abide by Torah and its means of reconciliation.

73. Marshall, *Beyond Retribution,* 69.

principle that results from any and every transgression of the commandment, but it refers to the historical judgment of exile against Israel because of its consistent rejection of divine hospitality. Despite the partial return of the Jews in the sixth century B.C., St. Paul saw the Jewish nation of his day still oppressed by foreigners and therefore still in exile.[74] According to a national-historical interpretation of Galatians 3, therefore, St. Paul maintains that in his death Christ has suffered Israel's exile: "Christ, as the representative Messiah, has achieved a specific task, that of taking on himself the curse which hung over Israel and which on the one hand prevented her from enjoying full membership in Abraham's family and thereby on the other hand prevented the blessing of Abraham from flowing out to the Gentiles. The Messiah has come where Israel is, under the Torah's curse . . . , in order to be not only Israel's representative but Israel's *redeeming* representative."[75] Christ not only suffered Israel's exile, however, but in the eschatological reality of his resurrection ("a new creation"—2 Cor. 5:17), he has also returned from exile and thereby restored Israel.[76] The resurrection of Jesus Christ is the inbreaking of the age to come and as such is the realization of God's pure, unconditional hospitality—which is not infinitely delayed, forever "to come" (*à venir*).[77] Thus, we can observe the objective pole of the atonement when we interpret the cross in the light of the open grave. Redemption is not simply the result of punishment, but is the result of a punishment that leads to the restoration and new life of the eschaton.

St. Paul's difficulty with the Galatians is that they refuse to live in anticipation of this eschatological hospitality that has, at least in principle, already brought them the blessing of covenant renewal and so of God's unconditional hospitality; the blessing of Abraham has now come to the Gentiles (Gal. 3:14). The Judaizers' wish to abide by the ethnic boundary markers of the Law means that they posit themselves under the old covenant and so put themselves back into a historical period that has proven to be a dead-end road. Life under the Law led to exile. By attempting to do "works of the Law," therefore, the people of Galatia would place themselves in the sphere of the curse. "This curse-threat looms overhead like the sword of Damocles, ever ready to fall and realize its full maledictory potential upon those who stand beneath it. This state of ex-

74. The idea that Paul saw Israel as being in exile is controversial but has received substantial support: N. T. Wright, *The New Testament and the People of God*, vol. 1 of *Christian Origins and the Question of God* (Minneapolis: Fortress, 1992), 268–72; Schreiner, *Law*, 47–49; N. T. Wright, *Jesus and the Victory of God*, vol. 2 of *Christian Origins and the Question of God* (Minneapolis: Fortress, 1996), 268–74; Craig A. Evans, "Jesus and the Continuing Exile of Israel," in *Jesus and the Restoration of Israel*, ed. Carey C. Newman (Downers Grove, Ill.: InterVarsity; Carlisle, UK: Paternoster, 1999), 77–100.

75. Wright, *Climax*, 151.

76. Ezekiel 37:1–14 depicts the return from exile as a resurrection from the dead.

77. Pace Derrida.

istence results from being 'under the law,' for it is the *torah* which pronounces the threat of curse."[78]

Overcoming the Economy of Exchange

This theological exposition of a key passage in Galatians leads to several conclusions. First, the traditional Protestant interpretation of Paul, based on the juridicizing, individualizing, and de-historicizing tendencies of Western atonement theology, unnecessarily accentuates an economy of exchange with an emphasis on the demands of the Law. It neither recognizes the flexibility of the Law nor God's consistently gracious hospitality that he extended to Israel throughout its history, despite Israel's failures and disobedience. One of the results of this position is a chasm between the violence of substitutionary atonement and the hospitable eschatological reality that it is supposed to open up. The justice and mercy of God appear to be at odds.

Second, a reappraisal of Pauline theology shows that penal representation is not a straightforward exchange between Christ and certain individuals. As Christopher Marshall puts it: "It is true . . . that Paul sees a *substitutionary dimension* to Christ's death. But it is substitutionary not in the sense of one person *replacing* another, like substitutes on a football team, but in the sense of one person *representing* all others, who are thereby made present in the person and experience of their representative. Christ died not so much instead of sinners as on behalf of sinners, as their corporate representative."[79] New Testament scholars today are pointing in a direction that is strikingly similar to the notion of recapitulation, first coined by the second-century Church father Irenaeus. Jesus Christ is the representative who acts as the head of Israel and of all humanity. Penal representation has a future when it is placed within an Irenaean framework. It is probably better, therefore, to refer to the penal aspect of the cross as "penal representation" than to speak of it as "penal substitution."

An Irenaean framework takes its starting point not in the penal aspect of the atonement but in the hospitable eschatology that is realized in principle in the resurrection of Jesus Christ. The violence of the penal aspect of the Law is always subservient to the eschatological future of God's unconditional hospitality. To be sure, because the cross is situated on a particular hill outside a certain city and is the result of humanity's (and Israel's) consistent refusal to accept divine hospitality, God finally comes with the violence of punishment. But this penal aspect comes to the fore only after a long history of divine patience and functions as the final step toward the eschatological reality of pure hospitality.

78. Joseph P. Braswell, "'The Blessing of Abraham' versus 'the Curse of the Law': Another Look at Gal 3:10–13," *Westminster Theological Journal* 53 (1991): 76–77.
79. Marshall, *Beyond Retribution,* 61 (italics in the original).

God's justice on the cross is a form of *restorative* justice.[80] The theodicy of God's violence in this justice is ultimately not found in rational arguments but in the eschatological reality of God's unconditional or pure hospitality—a hospitality that lies anchored in the resurrection of the sacrificial Lamb.[81] Through the resurrection we are able to recognize in the outstretched arms of Jesus the arms of the Father, welcoming home the prodigal son.

The parable of the prodigal son stands before us as a summons of pure hospitality. It is the beckoning of the infinity of the resurrection. In the light of the resurrection we may interpret the cross as God's act of hospitality, which as such "is paradigmatic for the Christian community in both its external and its internal affairs."[82] Human hospitality is the art of cruciformity, taught by the father's hospitable welcome of the prodigal.[83] In view of the reality of the resurrection, which is ours in hope through Christ, we are called on today to display God's unconditional hospitality. This summons lies at the heart of St. Paul's letter to the Galatians. But we cannot leave it at this. If we were to follow the Levinasian demand to the end, our identity would be crushed in our act of so-called hospitality. We would institutionalize a politics of violence and abuse if we did not accept any conditions on our hospitality. In Derrida's words, we would open the door not just for the good person but also for the devil to come in.[84] A politics of absolute hospitality and absolute nonviolence may seem appealing, but it is a recipe for a politics of the worst kind of violence.

The resurrection mandate of pure hospitality needs to be tempered, therefore, by the wisdom of conditional hospitality. Inasmuch as we are still constrained by current historical conditions, our welcome of the stranger and the prodigal will necessarily involve some restraint, conditionality, and even violence.

80. Colin Gunton rightly defends the notion of exchange as appropriate for atonement theology, and he then adds that we must conceive of punishment "as an interim measure, a holding action, in a fallen society, yet an institution that is eschatologically to be displaced by something else" ("Towards a Theology of Reconciliation," in *The Theology of Reconciliation*, ed. Colin E. Gunton [London: T&T Clark, 2003], 171; italics in the original).

81. The justification of divine violence on the cross is not *only* eschatological. The mystery of the Trinity and the mystery of the incarnation (Jesus Christ being both human and divine) can function as a complementary way of dealing with the question of divine violence on the cross: God himself visits us in Jesus Christ and offers up himself. The judge is judged in our place. Cf. Karl Barth, *Church Dogmatics*, trans. G. W. Bromiley (Edinburgh: T&T Clark, 1956), IV/1: 211–83; Miroslav Volf, "'The Trinity Is Our Social Program': The Doctrine of the Trinity and the Shape of Social Engagement," *Modern Theology* 41 (1998): 403–23. The mystery of the incarnation means that the violence in penal substitution is ultimately the violence of divine self-sacrifice, an act that stems from the pure hospitality that is the essence of God's being. God is therefore not a "bloodthirsty" God who punishes his innocent Son. Cf. Hans Boersma, "Eschatological Justice and the Cross: Violence and Penal Substitution," *Theology Today* 60 (2003): 186–99.

82. Michael J. Gorman, *Cruciformity: Paul's Narrative Spirituality of the Cross* (Grand Rapids: Eerdmans, 2001), 246.

83. In *Cruciformity*, Michael J. Gorman has made an impassioned plea for cruciform nonretaliation and hospitality. It will become clear that I believe that absolute nonviolence is neither possible nor judicious.

84. Cf. chapter 1 (the section titled "Levinas, Derrida, and the Impossibility of Pure Hospitality").

The penal element of the atonement offers some significant insights into the way we should act in our everyday social, economic, and political realities. Practicing hospitality is a difficult and painful task. It requires the wisdom of making decisions that always involve a certain degree of violence. But we dare not avoid the decision: we move on, our eyes fixed on the resurrection—the messianic future of pure hospitality.

8

Atonement, Violence, and Victory

Gustaf Aulén: A Lutheran Christus Victor

With the Christus Victor theme, we arrive at the third and final major atonement model. It may seem out of place to discuss Christus Victor as the last of the three traditional approaches. Many treatments of the atonement place it first—and certainly not without reason: for a number of Church fathers, atonement was the result, first and foremost, of Christ's defeat of Satan and his "powers and principalities." Still, there is reason to leave the Christus Victor theme until the end. We have already seen that it is historically questionable to regard the eleventh century (Anselm) as the very beginning of notions like satisfaction, substitution, and propitiation. At least some of these notions go back to the early Church. Also, moral-influence theories, often traced back to the twelfth century (Abelard), can claim strong support already in the second-century figure of Irenaeus.[1] The main reason I have reserved my treatment of the Christus Victor theme until the end, however, is that I believe it is, in a real sense, the most significant model of the atonement. The three models are not unrelated. Christ's victory over the powers of darkness is the telos and climax of his work of recapitulation. In other words, the victory is the *result* of the entire process of recapitulation. In my understanding of the Christus Victor theme, it does not explain *how* Christ gains the victory. Christ's obedient life and his teaching, as well as his representative punishment on the cross, are what

---

1. See chapters 5 and 7.

constitute the battle against Satan. It is by these means that Christ brings about victory. There is a sense, therefore, in which the Christus Victor theme is the ultimate metaphor. Moral influence and penal representation are subordinate to Christus Victor inasmuch as they are the means toward an end.

The notion of Christ's victory on the cross received a major new impetus with the 1931 publication of Gustaf Aulén's *Christus Victor: An Historical Study of the Three Main Types of the Idea of the Atonement.* In this book Aulén, a professor of systematic theology at the University of Lund in Sweden, presented a strong plea for the Christus Victor theme, to which he also referred as the "classic" or "dramatic" view of the atonement. To be sure, Aulén insisted that he had a far more modest purpose. His book, he said, "is strictly an historical study; it contains no personal statement of belief or theory of the atonement."[2] But I suspect that after reading Aulén's book, few people will be convinced by this disclaimer. It is clear that Aulén feels that we need a return to the Christus Victor theme and that both the Abelardian and the Anselmian theories have serious theological deficiencies.

What exactly happened to undermine the Christus Victor theme of the atonement? According to Aulén it was predominant throughout the early Church. While he pays special attention to Irenaeus, Aulén sees the notion of victory over Satan throughout the early Church. It is there in the Eastern fathers, such as Justin Martyr, Origen, Athanasius, Basil the Great, Gregory of Nyssa, Gregory of Nazianzus, Cyril of Alexandria, Cyril of Jerusalem, Chrysostom, and John of Damascus; as well as in the Western fathers, such as Ambrose, pseudo-Ambrose, Augustine, Leo the Great, Caesarius of Arles, Faustus of Rhegium, and Gregory the Great. Nonetheless, starting with Tertullian and Cyprian in the third century, atonement theology slowly but surely got off track, according to Aulén, with the introduction of legalistic notions, such as penance, merit, and satisfaction.[3] This resulted in the law-based juridical notions that have dominated the Western Church. Aulén holds Anselm particularly responsible for a legalistic understanding of the atonement. He regards it as Anselm's basic error that in the face of sin, human beings must make satisfaction. Thus, salvation is no longer the work of God from start to finish; Christ's death becomes "an offering made to God from man's side, from below."[4] Ever since Anselm, this juridical line has occupied the theological minds of the West. The only exception, argues Aulén, was Martin Luther, who through his study of Gregory the Great recovered the notion of Christus Victor. Unfortunately, with Luther's successor, Melanchthon, the juridical mind-set reasserted itself

2. Gustaf Aulén, *Christus Victor: An Historical Study of the Three Main Types of the Idea of the Atonement,* trans. A. G. Hebert (London: SPCK, 1970), xxi. Cf. ibid., 158.

3. Ibid., 38–39, 81–83. Aulén also notes Latin juridical tendencies in Gregory the Great, whom he sees as oscillating between the classic view and the Latin doctrine (ibid., 84).

4. Ibid., 88.

with a vengeance, resulting in the penal substitutionary view of the atonement that has been characteristic of Protestantism ever since. "Retributive justice thus becomes the essential element in this view of Law. It is not unjust to say . . . that Melanchthon is the real father of the 'rational nomism' of Protestant Orthodoxy."[5]

Many recognize Aulén's picture of the development of atonement theology as rather one-sided. The early Church is not nearly as consistent or single minded in its affirmation of the Christus Victor theme as Aulén would have us believe. And the alleged rift between Luther and later Protestantism has more to do with Aulén's own desire to appropriate Luther than with a real historical break with Luther since the time of Melanchthon. This is not to deny the rather strong presence of the Christus Victor theme in Luther. It is certainly there, and probably more prominently than in many other Lutheran and Reformed theologians. But several theologians have pointed out that the Latin position is present in Luther as well. Ted Peters, criticizing Aulén, comments that "Luther also holds a satisfaction perspective with regard to the work of Christ, and it has certain vital elements in common with Anselm."[6]

Despite these infelicities in Aulén's presentation of the development of the Christus Victor theme, he is right that Western theology has witnessed a juridicizing of the human-divine relationship.[7] It is true that the Christus Victor theme has not received the prominence in Western thought that it deserves according to the biblical witness and the testimony of the ancient Church. In this chapter, therefore, I address the question how we can incorporate the Christus Victor theme in our understanding of the atonement. I analyze some of the traditional and a few contemporary voices advocating the Christus Victor theme. In the process, I keep in mind questions surrounding divine hospitality and violence. At first glance, the Christus Victor theme may seem to do little to enhance our view of God as a hospitable God. It seems that instead we have God as the warrior, violently slaying the principalities and powers and so casting Satan himself into the pool of fire. I will argue, however, that the Christus Victor metaphor underwrites, rather than undermines, divine hospitality.

Aulén presents us with a concise overview of the various characteristics of the Christus Victor theme:[8]

---

5. Ibid., 128.

6. Ted Peters, "The Atonement in Anselm and Luther: Second Thoughts about Gustaf Aulén's *Christus Victor,*" *Lutheran Quarterly* 24 (1972): 309–10. Cf. Jaroslav Pelikan's similar criticism of Aulén in his foreword to the 1970 edition of the book (Aulén, *Christus Victor,* xvi).

7. Again, as I argued in chapter 7, this is not to say that the presence of the juridical element is an altogether negative feature. I believe rather that an overemphasis on judicial categories is responsible for the shortcomings of Western theories of the atonement.

8. The following is taken from ibid., 145–54. Aulén presents an overview of each of the three main types of the atonement. In the discussion here, I am particularly interested in the Christus Victor theme.

1. *Structure:* The classic view of the atonement shows a continuity of divine operation and a discontinuity in terms of merit and justice. In other words, God himself is the one who performs the work of atonement and in doing so is reconciled with the world. The Christus Victor theme is essentially dualistic, for it is divine warfare against the powers of evil that leads to victory and to the triumph of God's grace. Atonement is, therefore, a work of grace rather than justice or satisfaction.

2. *The idea of sin:* Sin, in the classic type of atonement, is an objective power of evil that holds people in its grip. Since God's claim on humanity is not simply a legal claim, the notion of satisfaction is impossible. God's full, personal claim on human beings implies that the notion of sin is not just objective, but also highly personal. Thus, the classic type can escape the criticism that it views the bondage of sin as an abstract, impersonal force. What is more, the classic view holds to a broad understanding of sin. It is not just transgression of the law but has to do with the evil powers of death, the devil, law, and the curse.

3. *Salvation:* Salvation is the victory gained by Christ and continued in the Church through the Holy Spirit. There is no difference between atonement and justification: "Justification is simply the Atonement brought into the present."[9]

4. *Christ and the incarnation:* The Christus Victor theme posits a close connection between the incarnation and the atonement, because the atonement is the work of God incarnate. God steps down to bring about reconciliation; people do not bring about their own salvation. Without denying the true manhood of Christ, the classic idea emphasizes that it is *God* who in Christ reconciles the world to himself.

5. *The conception of God:* The dualistic worldview of the Christus Victor theme penetrates the doctrine of God itself. On the one hand, there is a divine conflict with evil; on the other hand, God is the sovereign ruler, even over the powers of evil. Thus, there is an ambivalence that ultimately goes back to a tension between divine love and divine wrath. God's love overcomes his wrath through the divine self-sacrifice.

Several things stand out in Aulén's analysis of the Christus Victor theme. One is the fact that he interprets this theme through his Lutheran glasses. The emphasis on salvation as being solely God's work, the deep apprehension of notions of merit and penance, and the relative depreciation of the Old Testament as legalistic all point in the direction of Luther,[10] and, I might add, in

9. Ibid., 150.
10. Ibid., 69, 79. Cf. Henri Blocher's comment, "The idea that the legal order is broken (even exploded) when atonement takes place may suit Aulén's rather antinomian bent, but it would be difficult to find in any of the major witnesses of patristic thought and Reformation doctrine" ("*Agnus Victor:* The Atonement

many ways these very same notions point away from the early Church fathers and from their combination of the Christus Victor theme with legal categories. Eugene Fairweather has underscored Aulén's departure from the early Church by questioning "whether Aulén's treatment of the atonement is really compatible with a sound Christology."[11] Fairweather challenges the way in which Aulén closely connects the atonement and the incarnation, making the atonement strictly a movement from God to human beings rather than the other way around. By contrast, what Fairweather observes in the early Church is that it "is the divine Word who acts, but the Word has truly become flesh, and he acts *divine et humane*—in a divine and in a human manner."[12] Fairweather doesn't believe that Aulén does justice to Christ's work as man and sees the specter of docetism hovering over Aulén's theology.[13] Fairweather comments rather sharply that

> to forget that the atonement is actually consummated by the Godward movement of the human will of the God-Man is to lapse into that kind of partial denial of the incarnation against which the greatest teachers of the ancient church fought so long and so wisely. . . . No doubt Aulén is right in seeing in the whole story the triumph of God over the powers of evil, but he goes desperately wrong in failing to recognize that the very heart of this triumph is the conquest of sin by the perfect human obedience of the Word made flesh.[14]

Fairweather's criticisms are exactly right. Aulén's emphasis on divine monergism in salvation reflects more his own Lutheranism than the early Fathers' understanding of the Christus Victor theme. One wonders how hospitality can flourish if salvation becomes a divine fiat achieved on the cross without any input from the human side. A victory on the cross that has "vicarious efficacy" for "all mankind" seems like salvation for us and without us. Hospitality is not true hospitality if it does not leave room for the genuine acceptance and participation on the part of the guest.

as Victory and Vicarious Punishment," in *What Does It Mean to Be Saved? Broadening Evangelical Horizons of Salvation,* ed. John G. Stackhouse [Grand Rapids: Baker, 2002], 73).

11. Eugene R. Fairweather, "Incarnation and Atonement: An Anselmian Response to Aulén's Christus Victor," *Canadian Journal of Theology* 7 (1961): 167.

12. Ibid., 173. See also Youssouf Dembele, "Salvation as Victory: A Reconsideration of the Concept of Salvation in the Light of Jesus Christ's Life and Work Viewed as a Triumph over the Personal Powers of Evil" (Ph.D. diss., Trinity Evangelical Divinity School, 2001), 65–66.

13. Fairweather appeals to Rom. 5:17–19: "It was by one man's offence that death came to reign over all, but how much greater the reign in life of those who receive the fullness of grace and the gift of saving justice, through the one man, Jesus Christ. One man's offence brought condemnation on all humanity; and one man's good act has brought justification and life to all humanity. Just as by one man's disobedience many were made sinners, so by one man's obedience are many to be made upright." Fairweather also refers to 1 Tim. 2:5–6; Heb. 2:17; and Heb. 5:1.

14. Fairweather, "Incarnation and Atonement," 175.

My strongest criticism of Aulén concerns the fact that he treats the Christus Victor theme as the only real option in approaching the atonement. He regards the Anselmian or Latin view of the atonement as a moralistic deviation from the early Church: "The relation of man to God is treated by Anselm as essentially a legal relation, for his whole effort is to prove that the atoning work is in accordance with justice."[15] Similarly, Aulén rejects Abelard's view of the cross as awakening meritorious human love.[16] Aulén regards the further development of this subjective emphasis in Pietism and liberalism as the negative consequences of the Enlightenment. The Abelardian view abandoned the retributive punishment of objective atonement theology while exalting the benevolence of God. But the drawbacks outweigh the gains: "Man repents and amends his life, and God in turn responds by rewarding man's amendment with an increase of happiness. The ruling idea is therefore essentially anthropocentric and moralistic."[17] Both (penal) satisfaction theories and moral-influence theories fall under Aulén's judgment.

To be sure, Aulén acknowledges the presence of divine judgment. But the way in which he sees God handling this judgment is neither by means of human improvement (moral influence) nor by means of punishment (penal representation). Instead, it is God's defeat of the power of evil on the cross that removes judgment and reconciles us to God. Salvation from the power of Satan (the defeat of evil) is at the same time atonement or reconciliation (the removal of judgment):

> It is important, above all, at this point to see clearly that this work of salvation and deliverance is at the same time a work of atonement, of reconciliation between God and the world. It is altogether misleading to say that the triumph of Christ over the powers of evil, whereby he delivers man, is a work of salvation but not of atonement; for the two ideas cannot possibly be thus separated. It is precisely the work of salvation wherein Christ breaks the power of evil that *constitutes* the atonement between God and the world; for it is by it that He removes the enmity, takes away the judgment which rested on the human race, and reconciles the world to Himself, not imputing to them their trespasses (2 Cor. v. 18).[18]

By liberating us from the power of evil, God not only sets us free (i.e., gives salvation or deliverance) but also removes his judgment (i.e., makes atonement). In effect Aulén makes the former the instrument of the latter. It is not as though victory is achieved by means of judgment on sin; rather, judgment is taken away by means of victory. The result of this is an entirely nonpenal understanding of the cross: it is not punishment but victory that removes

15. Ibid., 90.
16. Ibid., 96.
17. Ibid., 135.
18. Ibid., 71 (italics in the original).

judgment and so achieves reconciliation. It seems to me that this is a truncated understanding of the atonement, which doesn't allow us at all to look beyond the Christus Victor theme.

Of course, the Christus Victor theme can flourish quite well without Aulén's weaknesses. His book itself, in fact, points to other elements in the Christus Victor theme, which I believe are worthwhile, and some of which I discuss later: its relative metaphysical dualism (between God and the forces of evil), its understanding of the "principalities and powers" as semipersonal beings, its appreciation of God as divine warrior, and its understanding of the cross as constitutive of divine victory. All these elements point us in the right direction and toward a positive appreciation of the Christus Victor theme.

Irenaeus: Recapitulation and Christus Victor

One of Aulén's main proponents of a Christus Victor theme of the atonement is Irenaeus. And indeed, we have already seen that for Irenaeus incarnation and recapitulation reconstitute humanity and so result in victory over death.[19] By recapitulating both Adam's life and his death, Christ retraced and in principle restored humanity to incorruptibility and immortality. While this means that Irenaeus's atonement theology has an objective component—Christ truly gained the victory through his life and his death—it also implies a subjective pole: Christ is now our perfect teacher, who rescues us from forgetfulness and imparts true knowledge, as well as our moral example, who persuades us to imitate him.

Perhaps Irenaeus's theology of recapitulation does not have the logical rigor and precision of some of the later expositions of the various strands of atonement theology.[20] It is clear, however, that the incarnation of the Word is God's own entry into the very lives of the victims of Satan's oppression and bondage. God's hospitality is redemptive not merely insofar as God waits for humanity's homecoming but insofar as God himself journeys into the far country. His hospitality submits to the historical and temporal particularities of human existence with all its limitations and exclusions, even to violence and death itself. God's hospitality is, for Irenaeus, a creational and incarnational hospitality.

19. See the discussion in chapter 5 (the section titled "Irenaeus and Recapitulation").

20. Just to add to the confusion, according to Irenaeus the reversal of disobedience takes place not only in Christ but also in Mary: Eve disobeyed as a virgin, while Mary obeyed as a virgin. Eve disobeyed an angel, while Mary obeyed an angel. As Adam was restored in Christ, so Eve was restored in Mary: "For what the virgin Eve had bound fast through unbelief, this did the virgin Mary set free through faith" (Irenaeus, *Irenaeus against Heresies* [hereafter *AH*], in *The Ante-Nicene Fathers,* ed. Alexander Roberts and James Donaldson [1885; repr., Peabody, Mass.: Hendrickson, 1994], 1:452 [III.21.4]. Cf. ibid., 1:547 [V.19.1]; 1:548–49 [V.21.1]; *Proof of the Apostolic Preaching* [hereafter *Dem.*], trans. Joseph P. Smith [New York: Paulist, 1952], 33). Irenaeus does not explain how Mary's recapitulation contributes to human redemption.

To speak about recapitulation is to also speak about Christus Victor. Although Irenaeus does not work out the Christus Victor theme in as much detail as some later Church fathers, such as Origen and Gregory of Nyssa, it is nonetheless key to Irenaeus's understanding of God's redemptive hospitality. When one traces the Christus Victor theme in Irenaeus, a dynamic picture emerges: Satan has abused Adam and Eve's moral immaturity, tempted them into disobedience, and thus captured and imprisoned the human race. Repeatedly, Irenaeus refers to Satan as the "strong man" whom Christ has bound and robbed (Matt. 12:29).[21] In a characteristic passage, Irenaeus comments:

> For as in the beginning he [the apostate angel of God] enticed man to transgress his Maker's law, and thereby got him into his power; yet his power consists in transgression and apostasy, and with these he bound man [to himself]; so again, on the other hand, it was necessary that through man himself he should, when conquered, be bound with the same chains with which he had bound man, in order that man, being set free, might return to his Lord, leaving to him (Satan) those bonds by which he himself had been fettered, that is, sin. For when Satan is bound, man is set free; since "none can enter a strong man's house and spoil his goods, unless he first bind the strong man himself."[22]

Irenaeus sees Adam's transgression as the "bonds" or the "chains" that Satan uses to bind human beings.[23] God in turn puts Satan in chains. Christ "robs" the strong man (Matt. 12:29), "crushes" the devil (Gen. 3:15),[24] and "destroys" death. There may seem to be a violent edge to Irenaeus's vocabulary here. But he immediately deals with this apprehension: whereas apostasy used deception and violence whereby "it insatiably snatched away what was not its own," God uses "persuasion" instead of "violent means" and does not infringe on "justice."[25] Emphasizing again the subjective element, Irenaeus states that only upon repentance are people loosed from these shackles of sin.[26]

This understanding of the Christus Victor theme has some notable strengths when compared to Aulén's approach. First, for Irenaeus it is but one aspect (albeit an important one) of the broader concept of recapitulation. This enables him to do more justice also to the prophetic and priestly elements of recapitulation. Second, Irenaeus's strongly antidocetic stance and his clear affirmation

21. Irenaeus, *AH*, 1:421 (III.8.2); 1:447–48 (III.18.6); 1:455–56 (III.23.1). Cf. 1:457 (III.23.7).

22. Ibid., 1:550 (V.21.3).

23. Ibid., 1:423 (III.9.3); *Dem.*, 31, 38; Irenaeus, *Fragments from the Lost Writings of Irenæus* (hereafter *Frag.*), in *The Ante-Nicene Fathers*, ed. Alexander Roberts and James Donaldson (1885; repr., Peabody, Mass.: Hendrickson, 1994), 1:575 (43).

24. See Irenaeus, *AH*, 1:457 (III.23.7); 1:548 (V.21.1).

25. Ibid., 1:527 (V.1.1). Cf. 1:456 (III.23.1).

26. Irenaeus, *Frag.*, 43.

of time and space in the face of his Gnostic detractors means that he takes the humanity and obedience of Christ far more seriously than Aulén is able to do. Whereas the latter needs to defend himself against the charge of docetism, it is hard to imagine anyone bringing such an accusation against Irenaeus. Third, because Irenaeus emphasizes the true humanity and obedience of Christ in the face of temptation, he can combine the cosmic struggle with the human struggle here on earth. Redemption is not something that plays itself out on a timeless, spiritual level only. It touches base in the human life of Christ and in the concrete existence of the Church today.

An additional intriguing element of Irenaeus's understanding of the Christus Victor theme is that he believes Christ gained the victory through nonviolent means. Although I believe Irenaeus overemphasizes the nonviolence of the atonement, it is nonetheless noteworthy that he does not push the battle imagery to extremes: respectful of human freedom and unwilling to take recourse to some kind of violent encounter between Jesus and Satan, Irenaeus interprets the battle by means of other metaphors. For Irenaeus it is incarnation and recapitulation, it is Christ's teaching and modeling, and it is his sacrificial death on the cross that constitute the battle leading to the victory of hospitality.

Gregory of Nyssa: Justification of Divine Deception

Several other Church fathers also looked at the Christus Victor theme not so much from the perspective of sin and punishment but more from that of slavery and freedom. Human beings were not primarily the *perpetrators* of violence but were first of all the *victims* of satanic tyranny. The Alexandrian theologian Origen (c. 185–253), in his commentary on Matthew 16:8, stated his belief that Christ gave his soul as a ransom, not to God, but to the evil one: "For he had us in his power, until the ransom for us should be given to him, even the life [or soul] of Jesus, since he (the evil one) had been deceived, and led to suppose that he was capable of mastering that soul, and he did not see that to hold Him involved a trial of strength . . . greater than he was equal to."[27] Origen pictures the situation in such a way that, afraid of Jesus' teaching, the devil wanted to put him to death, unaware that he was being tricked into doing this.[28] Unable to hold on to his divine victim in death, Satan was thus forced to admit defeat.

According to Gregory of Nyssa († 385), we had "voluntarily bartered away our freedom" to the devil. At this point, argued Gregory, it was right and just for God "to make over to the master of the slave whatever ransom he may

---

27. Origen, *In Matt.* xvi.8. Quoted from Hastings Rashdall, *The Idea of Atonement in Christian Theology* (London: Macmillan, 1919), 259.

28. Ibid., 262.

agree to accept for the person in his possession."[29] For Gregory redemption is a matter of "exchange." Attracted by the incredible power of Jesus Christ, Satan determined to choose him "as a ransom for those who were shut up in the prison of death."[30] The reason for Christ to appear in the flesh was so that Satan would not recognize the deity hidden in his humanity. This method of approach showed God's "supreme wisdom," according to Gregory.[31] Thus, for Gregory the justice of God came to the fore in the exchange, while his wisdom appeared in hiding Christ's divinity.

This wisdom of God worked itself out in an intriguing way. God's hiding of Christ's divinity had a particular purpose, according to Gregory: "[I]n order to secure that the ransom in our behalf might be easily accepted by him who required it, the Deity was hidden under the veil of our nature, that so, as with ravenous fish, the hook of the Deity might be gulped down along with the bait of flesh, and thus, life being introduced into the house of death, and light shining in darkness, that which is diametrically opposed to light and life might vanish; for it is not in the nature of darkness to remain when light is present, or of death to exist when life is active."[32] Gregory's well-known metaphor of the fish and the hook—with which he goes a step beyond Origen's notion of divine deception—is his way of demonstrating the wisdom of God. God ensured that Satan was unable to recognize the divinity of Christ.[33] Using the humanity of Christ as the bait, Satan bit into the hook of Christ's divinity and so overreached himself. The darkness of Satan's prison couldn't stand the light of Christ's divinity; his eternal life entered the domain of death, which so ceased to exist. For Gregory the atonement is a manifestation both of God's justice and of his wisdom. The exchange model (the ransom) ensures the former, while God hiding the divinity of Christ in the flesh of his humanity ensures the latter.

The combination of ransom and deception adds something to the Irenaean use of the Christus Victor theme. Irenaeus hints that it is through recapitulation itself that Christ gains the victory. Irenaeus does not use notions of ransom and deception to explain the victory. Gregory adds these two concepts. They imply, of course, that the devil has a (perhaps rightful?) ownership of the human

29. Gregory of Nyssa, *The Great Catechism*, in *Nicene and Post-Nicene Fathers*, Second Series, trans. William Moore and Henry Austin Wilson, ed. Philip Schaff and Henry Wace (1893; repr., Peabody, Mass.: Hendrickson, 1994), 5:493 (XXII).

30. Ibid., 5:493 (XXIII).

31. Ibid., 5:494 (XXIII).

32. Ibid., 5:494 (XXIV).

33. Gregory uses at least two additional images to emphasize the consubstantiality of Christ's humanity with ours: the Shepherd is both Shepherd and sheep; and the stalk of humanity, cut in half lengthwise at one end (Adam's) and so separated into body and soul through Adam's sin, is reunited at the other end (Christ's). See Peter Bouteneff, "Soteriological Imagery in Gregory of Nyssa's *Antirrheticus*," *Studia Patristica* 32 (1997): 81–86.

race. Gregory envisages God paying the devil, in fraudulent fashion, a ransom. In this Gregory is not alone. Ambrose (c. 345–407) follows him, speaking of Christ's death as a "pious fraud," even if he adds the notion of substitutionary punishment.[34] And also in Augustine there is a hint of this idea of divine fraud when he comments that "the blood of Christ was given, as it were, as a price for us, by accepting which the devil was not enriched, but bound: that we might be loosened from his bonds."[35]

The notion is fascinating, but I remain unconvinced of the deception theme and of the fishing analogy. In the Gospels the demons appear to have little doubt as to Christ's true identity (Mark 1:25, 34; 3:11).[36] At least in the Gospel of Matthew, the devil seems to do his utmost to keep Christ off the cross, rather than to get him crucified.[37] What is more, is Satan's ownership such that God had to pay him a ransom to be just?[38] While the ransom idea itself is indeed biblical, it would stretch the biblical data to infer that Satan is the recipient of the price. St. Gregory of Nazianzus (c. 325–89), Gregory of Nyssa's fellow Cappadocian, rightly objects to the idea that a ransom would have to be paid either to Satan or to God: "I enquire to whom was the blood of God poured out? If to the evil one—alas! that the blood of Christ should be offered to the wicked one! But if you say 'To God'—how shall that be, when it is to another (than God) that we were enslaved?"[39] St. John of Damascus (c. 675–c. 749) likewise objects to the idea of Satan being paid a ransom: "God forbid that the blood of the Lord should have been offered to the tyrant."[40]

The most common criticism of the deception theory is, of course, that it appears to morally implicate God. Not all would agree that the fishing analogy is a demonstration of God's wisdom and justice. Many would argue that the divine deception involved in the exchange seriously compromises God's

34. Ambrose, *In Luc. Exp.* iv.16. Quoted from Rashdall, *Idea,* 328.

35. Aurelius Augustine, *On the Trinity,* in *Nicene and Post-Nicene Fathers,* First Series, trans. Arthur West Haddan, ed. Philip Schaff (1887; repr., Peabody, Mass.: Hendrickson, 1994), 3:178 (XIII.xv.19).

36. Cf. Colin E. Gunton, *The Actuality of Atonement: A Study of Metaphor, Rationality, and the Christian Tradition* (Grand Rapids: Eerdmans, 1989), 63; Jonathan R. Wilson, *God So Loved the World: A Christology for Disciples* (Grand Rapids: Baker, 2001), 88.

37. In the temptation narrative (Matt. 4:1–11), the devil wants Christ to take control of the kingdoms of the world without first taking the road of suffering. After his confession at Caesarea Philippi, Peter resists the idea of Christ being put to death. Jesus interprets this again as a satanic temptation: "Get behind me, Satan!" (Matt. 16:23). On the cross Jesus is tempted to come off the cross three times: by the passers-by, the leaders of the people, and the bandits (Matt. 27:39–44). Two of the three times, he is addressed as the Son of God, which is the messianic designation that Satan had also used in the wilderness temptation.

38. Cf. Rashdall, *Idea,* 364; Aulén, *Christus Victor,* 4; Gunton, *Actuality,* 64.

39. Gregory of Nazianzus, *Poemata dogmatica* I.viii.65–69. Quoted from Rashdall, *Idea,* 309.

40. John of Damascus, *An Exact Exposition of the Orthodox Faith,* in *Nicene and Post-Nicene Fathers,* Second Series, trans. S. D. F. Salmond, ed. Philip Schaff and Henry Wace (1899; repr., Peabody, Mass.: Hendrickson, 1994), 9:72 (III.27). While John of Damascus keeps Gregory's notion of the bait analogy (quoting him almost verbatim), he argues that the ransom has been paid to the Father (ibid.).

justice. By using deception or violence God would use the same means that
Satan had initially used to introduce sin into the world. Undeniably, Gregory
is quite forthright about this when he argues that "the deceiver was in his
turn deceived."[41] Unfortunately, Gregory's theological justification in defense
of divine deception has rarely received attention, probably because historical
theologians have tended to focus on the crude imagery of the fishing analogy.
But it is worthwhile to have a brief look at his argument, for it is in essence an
argument that maintains that divine deception or violence does not necessarily
compromise the ultimate victory of God's hospitality.[42]

Gregory senses the theological difficulty involved when he acknowledges
a measure of divine "deception," "fraud," and "surprise." He justifies this,
however, with an appeal to the divine intent of human salvation:

> He who first deceived man by the bait of sensual pleasure is himself deceived by the pre-
> sentment of the human form. But as regards the aim and purpose of what took place, a
> change in the direction of the nobler is involved; for whereas he, the enemy, effected his
> deception for the ruin of our nature, He Who is at once the just, and good, and wise one,
> used His device, in which there was deception, for the salvation of him who had perished,
> and thus not only conferred benefit on the lost one, but on him, too, who had wrought
> our ruin. For from this approximation of death to life, of darkness to light, of corruption
> to incorruption, there is effected an obliteration of what is worse, and a passing away of
> it into nothing, while benefit is conferred on him who is freed from those evils.[43]

Whereas Satan's deception of Adam was for the ruin of human nature, God's
deception was for our salvation. It is, says Gregory, similar to those who visit
the doctor and who "for their cure are subjected to the knife and the cautery;
they are angry with the doctors, and wince with the pain of the incision; but
if recovery of health be the result of this treatment, and the pain of the cautery
passes away, they will feel grateful to those who have wrought this cure upon
them."[44] When everyone, even "the introducer of evil himself," will be freed,
the deception will be shown for what it truly is: supreme wisdom.[45]

Gregory's argument is essentially that the use of deception (or, we might
add, the use of violence) is not morally identical in every instance and that it

41. Gregory of Nyssa, *Great Catechism*, 5:495 (XXVI).

42. To be sure, Gregory expresses his hesitation about the use of divine violence in connection with the
cross: by using violence God "will clearly be acting unjustly in thus arbitrarily rescuing one who has been
legally purchased as a slave" (ibid., 5:492–93 [XXII]). Gregory's arguments in favor of divine deception,
however, can just as well be used in favor of divine violence.

43. Ibid., 5:495 (XXVI).

44. Ibid., 5:496 (XXVI).

45. Ibid. Gregory appears to have held to the notion that through a process of purification all rational
beings, including the devil, would be saved. See John R. Sachs, "Apocatastasis in Patristic Theology," *Theological Studies* 54 (1993): 634; Morwenna Ludlow, *Universal Salvation: Eschatology in the Thought of Gregory
of Nyssa and Karl Rahner* (Oxford: Oxford University Press, 2000), 80–81, 85.

cannot be evaluated uniformly regardless of the intent. Since God's intention is salvific in nature, he is justified in his deception. This proposition will not be quite convincing to everyone. Surely, the end does not justify all means. And the warning needs to be sounded that we often tend to rationalize abusive types of violence with the claim that it is for the other's own good. Still, in the Second World War many Dutch people hid Jewish people in their homes and lied to German soldiers who questioned them. In my view this type of deception was morally upright. By offering protection to potential victims and by lying about it to the forces of evil, these people were instinctively aware that the biblical notion of truth (ʾĕmet) was more akin to faithfulness than to verifiable correspondence. Similarly, just-war theorists have always maintained that the consideration of intent—particularly the purpose of reestablishing peace—is an important consideration in the justification of violence.[46] This does not necessarily answer the question of why this or that *particular* case of divine violence is justified. Nonetheless, it is difficult to see why there could not be at least *some* instances of divine violence that are justified in the interest of restorative justice and eternal hospitality.

Recovery of the Christus Victor Theme

The Christus Victor notion has not been a prominent one in the later history of the Church. To be sure, as Aulén points out, Luther was keenly aware of the spiritual battle that was fought in the life and death of Christ and that continues to be fought in the lives of Christians today. And also John Calvin, often pinpointed as the main proponent of the penal satisfaction theory, incorporated elements of the Christus Victor theme in his theology.[47] Nonetheless, the theme has suffered in comparison to the other two main streams of atonement theology. There are a number of reasons for this relative neglect.[48] One of the main ones is the influence of Enlightenment thought on the Western Church. The Enlightenment's myopic naturalism has made it difficult to accept any sort of supernatural influence in the realm of actual history. Notions of cosmic battle between God and the powers of evil have been hard to sustain in an environment where science and technology have held absolute sway. Theologically, this tendency is probably best summed up in Rudolf Bultmann's well-known comment, "We cannot use

---

46. Cf. James Turner Johnson, *Morality and Contemporary Warfare* (New Haven, Conn.: Yale University Press, 1999), 41–51; James Turner Johnson, "Can Force Be Used Justly? Questions of Retributive and Restorative Justice," 2001 Kuyper Lecture, Wenham, Mass.: Gordon College, 2001. http://downloads.weblogger.com/gems/cpj/2001KLJ.T.Johnson.pdf.

47. See Robert A. Peterson, *Calvin's Doctrine of the Atonement* (Phillipsburg, N.J.: Presbyterian & Reformed, 1983), 46–54.

48. See Aulén, *Christus Victor,* 7–15; Gregory A. Boyd, *God at War: The Bible and Spiritual Conflict* (Downers Grove, Ill.: InterVarsity, 1997), 61–72; Dembele, "Salvation as Victory," 12.

electric lights and radios and, in the event of illness, avail ourselves of modern medical and clinical means and at the same time believe in the spirit and wonder world of the New Testament."[49] There has been a strong tendency in New Testament studies to demythologize and depersonalize the demonology of the New Testament.[50] Within such an environment, it has been difficult to sustain the idea of a cosmic dualism between the powers of God and the powers of Satan. Also, the Enlightenment's emphasis on individual human autonomy and control has not been conducive to a theology that acknowledges the pervasive influence of demonic powers throughout the universe, affecting not just individuals but also relationships, communities, and the very structures of society. Finally, the emphasis on detailed providential control in the Augustinian tradition has been a factor in bracketing the significance of the relationship between supernatural spiritual beings and activities on the human level.[51] Where providence extends to every minute detail of human life, it may not be easy to see how real "warfare" is taking place in which Christ has won the principle battle.

The last few decades, however, have witnessed a renewed interest in the Christus Victor theme, particularly within evangelicalism.[52] It is an interest that goes hand in hand with an interest in spiritual warfare and exorcism. Gregory Boyd, in his elaborate study *God at War* (1997), combines his advocacy of open theism and libertarian human freedom with what he calls a "warfare worldview." He insists that throughout Scripture, God is in conflict with the powers of evil. This warfare climaxes in the death and resurrection of Jesus Christ. Christ offered up a sacrifice to atone for our sins, acknowledges Boyd, but "Christ did this only because he did something even more fundamental, as we have seen: he dealt a death blow to Satan and recaptured his rightful rule over the whole creation."[53] In similar fashion Robert Webber, in his *Ancient-Future Faith* (1999), insists that postmodern Christians are in need of an atonement theology that returns to the Christus Victor theme and, in particular, to Irenaeus's recapitulation theology.[54] With the modern Enlighten-

49. Rudolf Bultmann, *New Testament and Mythology and Other Basic Writings,* trans. and ed. Schubert M. Ogden (Philadelphia: Fortress, 1984), 4.

50. There are, of course, legitimate exegetical questions regarding the identity of the Pauline "powers and principalities": Are they power structures, or are they spiritual beings? Or could the terms refer to both? Cf. Oscar Cullmann, *Christ and Time: The Primitive Christian Conception of Time and History* (London: SCM, 1951), 191–210; G. B. Caird, *Principalities and Powers: A Study in Pauline Theology* (Oxford: Clarendon, 1956); H. Berkhof, *Christ and the Powers,* trans. John Howard Yoder, 2nd ed. (Scottdale, Pa.: Herald, 1977); Clinton E. Arnold, *Ephesians, Power, and Magic: The Concept of Power in Ephesians in Light of Its Historical Setting,* Society for New Testament Studies Monograph Series, no. 63 (Cambridge: Cambridge University Press, 1989); Boyd, *God at War,* 270–76.

51. Boyd, *God at War,* 56–57.

52. The earlier publication of Aulén's work in 1931 was an isolated occurrence.

53. Boyd, *God at War,* 267.

54. Robert E. Webber, *Ancient-Future Faith: Rethinking Evangelicalism for a Postmodern World* (Grand Rapids: Baker, 1999), 43–61.

ment worldview put in question, it seems that theologians are coming out of the closet and boldly reasserting the limitations of scientific naturalism.

While I appreciate these new efforts at integrating the Christus Victor perspective, they do not sufficiently take into account the serious apprehensions, harbored by many, of the imperialism, violence, and oppression afflicted in the past in the name of Christianity. The issue of the relationship between atonement and violence has hardly been discussed at all within the evangelical orbit. It is nonetheless an issue that we need to come to grips with, if we don't want the traditional models of the atonement simply to be written off as accommodating violence and abuse.[55]

J. Denny Weaver deals with the issue, from an Anabaptist perspective, in his recent book *The Nonviolent Atonement* (2001), in which he advocates a "narrative Christus Victor" approach to the atonement. Weaver echoes a great deal of the criticism of traditional atonement theology—presented by black theology, feminist theology, and womanist theology—arguing that the theological tradition of much of Christendom has accommodated patriarchy, military violence, slavery, and racism. In particular Weaver expresses his agreement with the description of penal substitution as divine child abuse.[56] The working assumption of his "narrative Christus Victor theory" is "that the rejection of violence, whether the direct violence of the sword or the systemic violence of racism or sexism, should be visible in expressions of Christology and atonement."[57] Weaver envisages a Christus Victor approach that excludes the theme of divine trickery or deception and instead focuses on the nonviolent life of Jesus of Nazareth. In his view the forces of evil are solely responsible for the death of Jesus. It is, therefore, not the death of Jesus that constitutes the victory; rather, it is the resurrection that overcomes death as the last enemy.[58] As individuals repent and perceive the saving work of Christ, they are "joining a reality already established by the resurrection of Jesus."[59]

It will be clear from my approach thus far that I do not espouse Weaver's nonviolent understanding of the life of Jesus. His radical exclusion of any divine purpose in the cross is an obvious break with the traditional Christus Victor theme with its notion of divine deception. He also excludes both the Anselmian and the Abelardian theme from his understanding of the atonement. The connection with the history of Christian thought becomes minimal in Weaver's theology. His search for a nonviolent atonement underwrites his

---

55. I am encouraged by the fact that at the 2002 annual American Academy of Religion convention in Toronto, the Evangelical Theology Group organized a session on the relationship between violence and the atonement.

56. J. Denny Weaver, *The Nonviolent Atonement* (Grand Rapids: Eerdmans, 2001), 127–29, 141, 151, 178.

57. Ibid., 7.

58. Ibid., 45, 54, 76.

59. Ibid., 219.

entire project and creates an imbalance in his approach to the Church's tradition. While a recovery of the Christus Victor theme is to be applauded, Weaver does not point us in a particularly helpful direction.

Darby Kathleen Ray: Feminism and Deception

Darby Kathleen Ray also appropriates the Christus Victor theme of the atonement in her book *Deceiving the Devil: Atonement, Abuse, and Ransom* (1998). Like Weaver she takes seriously the challenges to atonement theology from the side of feminist and liberation theologians. Also like Weaver she sharply criticizes the traditional Anselmian and Abelardian models, insisting that "together they have bequeathed contemporary Christians with a highly problematic doctrine of atonement."[60] Neither of these theories, says Ray, assists us in recognizing and confronting the power of evil in the lives of many women, men, and children. Feminist and liberation theologians believe that both models have "deadly consequences."[61] She points specifically to the genocide and the massacres of colonialism, which would not have been possible without a theology sustaining them.[62] In Latin America some of the dominant christological images have been those of "Christ the Conquering One" and "Christ the Conquered One":

> On the one hand, Christ is the Conquering One; the One whose power and might are emulated by those in positions of power; the One who sanctions their power. On the other hand, Christ is the Conquered One; the One who was falsely accused, brutally beaten, and tortured to death; the One with whom the poor and marginalized can identify; the One who sanctions their powerlessness. The former Christology ignores the suffering and death as unpalatable or inconvenient, while the latter embraces it so closely that suffocation seems inevitable. Together, these two sides of the same christological coin feed the violence of the few and the passivity of the many.[63]

Ray believes that under the "guise of neutrality and universality," Christian theology has in fact supported all types of oppression and violence, particularly against women, children, and Third World countries.[64] And indeed, Ray makes some valuable observations about the need to combat evil and injustice. She recognizes the serious character of evil and points out some painful elements in the history of Western imperialism. She rightly emphasizes that redemp-

---

60. Darby Kathleen Ray, *Deceiving the Devil: Atonement, Abuse, and Ransom* (Cleveland: Pilgrim, 1998), 2.

61. Ibid., 18.

62. Ibid., 77.

63. Ibid., 88.

64. Ibid., 72–73.

tion is not just an individual matter but that it is also something communal and institutional. These are all concerns on which she elaborates throughout her book.

Some feminist theologians are tempted to do away with atonement theology altogether in view of the violence in the history of the Christian Church. Ray does not want to go in that direction. Instead, she wants to outline an atonement model that deals with three major problems in the Anselmian and Abelardian models, which she believes have dominated Christian theology in the past.[65] The first is the traditional view of sin as rebellion and pride. This brings with it "guilt, blame, and self-hate for the one who dares to assert herself against authority; it also breeds a sense of powerlessness, since self-assertion is seen as problematic; and it justifies punishment of the willful."[66] Sin, argues Ray, is not simply rebellion against God; rather, it is "rebellion against God's care for the world, against the world as God's manifestation of creative love, against the world as God's body."[67] The second problem is the traditional God concept, which has valorized divine sovereignty and omnipotence, while infantilizing human beings as disobedient and helpless: "When divine sovereignty and omnipotence are combined with the model of God as father, as they are in most Anselmian and Abelardian strands of atonement thought, the abusive potential of these ideas becomes incontrovertible."[68] Finally, Ray critiques the romanticizing of death that she observes in the traditional atonement theories: "Romantic visions of a martyred Savior function in many cases to keep victims of abuse in their death-dealing situations."[69] In particular she feels that the notion of self-sacrifice is hardly appropriate for victims of violence. Victims are never able to live up to the requirement that they be as innocent as Jesus was. And the requirement to forgive often undermines true justice: "For abusers, forgiveness can become a means of avoiding accountability through cheap grace."[70]

In her attempt to find an atonement model that counters the power of evil and at the same time avoids what she considers to be structural problems in the Anselmian and Abelardian models, Ray turns to the Christus Victor model. To be sure, this theme also has certain problems: (1) its cosmic dualism between God and the devil may encourage Christians to demonize people with whom they disagree; (2) its tendency to depict redemption as a purely cosmic affair may undermine human responsibility; and (3) its portrayal of the atonement as a "done deal" may lead to a Christian triumphalism that doesn't recognize

---

65. Ray does see some positive elements in both of these models. The Anselmian model takes evil seriously, and the Abelardian affirms the continuity of Jesus' life and death (ibid., 142).

66. Ibid., 25.

67. Ibid., 34.

68. Ibid., 41.

69. Ibid., 57.

70. Ibid., 68.

the need to resist the dehumanizing effects of evil.[71] But on the positive side the Christus Victor theme looks at sin as not just an individual thing, but as an institutional problem as well. Sin thus becomes identified with abuse of power. Moreover, the Christus Victor theme takes liberation from bondage seriously. Here, to be saved is to be freed from enslavement to evil. And despite the excesses of cosmic dualism, the Christus Victor theme at least entails a serious view of human evil and recognizes that human effort alone won't make it disappear.

It will be clear from the previous chapters that I am not enamored with Ray's objections to the Abelardian and Anselmian models. I am not at all convinced that her objections require us to abandon these theories. Instead of entering into a discussion of Ray's criticism, however, I want to have a closer look at her use of the Christus Victor model. She has an interesting approach to the traditional notion of divine deceit, which we saw especially in the thought of Gregory of Nyssa. She argues that divine deceit is not immoral. Instead, "it points to the reality that any struggle against oppression and injustice that seeks to avoid violent means or that emerges from a context of relative powerlessness must rely on cunning and ingenuity rather than ascribed authority or power."[72] By employing "playful imitation" it is possible to "expose the absurdity" of the dominant or normative discourse.[73] "Paradoxically," says Ray, Christ's "suffering and death do not signal defeat but reveal the righteousness of his cause, the moral persuasiveness of his praxis, for they bring into clear public view the violence and injustice of the reigning powers."[74] Like Gregory of Nyssa, Ray wants to rescue the notion of divine deceit because it offers possibilities to resist the powers that are in control.

Yet, Ray does not use Gregory's line of defense. She does not justify deceit in the interest of the greater good. In that case we might analogously justify violence for the sake of ultimate peace. Instead she interprets deceit as a form of nonviolence and hence as justifiable. Thus, like Weaver she understands Jesus' life as a life of complete nonviolence.[75] While her solution is intriguing (particularly her willingness to use deceit in the struggle for justice), it is unclear why Ray would unequivocally reject the use of violence. Why would deceit (if used by the powerless in the struggle against evil) be justified, while (physical) violence needs to be unequivocally rejected? This distinction is questionable especially because Ray adopts what she calls a "tragic view" of reality, which holds that there is no universal morality grounded in absolute foundations, and which acknowledges

71. Ibid., 126–29.

72. Ibid., 138–39.

73. Ibid., 139.

74. Ibid., 141. There is an intriguing similarity at this point between Ray's thinking and Girard's mimetic theory of the atonement (see chapter 6).

75. Ibid., 141, 144.

the "moral ambiguity" of the world in which "none of our decisions or actions is innocent."[76] A tragic view of reality can hardly uphold nonviolence as an absolute or nonnegotiable standard but would have to recognize that violence lies at the heart of things and cannot possibly be avoided.

Ray's theology has serious shortcomings. It is not clear, for instance, how Christ's death is unique or decisive for her in any meaningful way. In her defense it should be said that she opposes Rita Nakashima Brock's idea that the atoning import of the cross lies in the community rather than in Christ himself. Countering Brock, Ray insists that Jesus is not "just one among many."[77] Nonetheless, in her conclusion to the book, she comments that "redemption is not a thing of the past effected for us by another, but a constant challenge, a real possibility."[78] For Ray the patristic model of the atonement claims that the "way of resistance and compassion illuminated by Jesus has the potential, when followed, to liberate from evil, to reveal a way of confronting our evil and the evil of others, which exposes the moral perversity of injustice and offers a clear alternative."[79] I would agree. But is this all? In what way, we must wonder, is the cross of Christ unique in this description?[80] In the end Ray's Christus Victor doesn't offer sufficient help. First, she is unsuccessful in making a moral distinction between divine deceit and divine violence. Thus she is unable to deal with the question of divine violence. Her objections seem hollow in the light of her justification of deception. Second, the lack of objectivity in terms of what the cross actually accomplishes by way of guarantee for the future means that the eschaton of God's unconditional hospitality is in serious jeopardy.

Conclusion

The rediscovery of the Christus Victor theme is a positive element in the recent developments of atonement theology. The scrutiny and critique of some of the more negative impulses of the Enlightenment have brought a healthy suspicion of a naturalist worldview and of individual human autonomy. The result is an increased appreciation of both divine and satanic or demonic influences. The Christus Victor theme cannot function without at least some degree of metaphysical or cosmic dualism. Gregory Boyd and others are right in reclaiming this dualism as part of the Christian heritage. This is not to say that

76. Ibid., 112; cf. 141–42.
77. Ibid., 108.
78. Ibid., 145.
79. Ibid.
80. Cf. the similar criticism of Joel B. Green and Mark D. Baker, *Recovering the Scandal of the Cross: Atonement in New Testament and Contemporary Contexts* (Downers Grove, Ill.: InterVarsity, 2000), 182–83.

such dualism is ultimate or eternal. We need to heed Anselm's warning when he shows his displeasure with the ransom theories of the early Church. The devil, maintains Anselm, did not have just possession over human beings but was simply a servant of God who had become a thief and a traitor: "[N]either the Devil nor man does belong to anyone except to God, and . . . neither of them exists outside the domain of God's power."[81] Indeed, the ultimate control is God's, and the future of hospitality has already been ascertained by means of the cross and the resurrection. At the same time the biblical imagery of divine warfare and the metaphors of ransom and of victory are pervasive in Scripture, and we should neither ignore them nor domesticate them.[82] A biblical perspective requires a relative cosmic dualism that affirms real warfare, both in Christ's life and in ours, while at the same time insisting on ultimate divine sovereignty.

Few theologians have been as successful as Irenaeus in presenting us with a cautious, yet useful, presentation of the Christus Victor theme. First, Irenaeus avoids the more speculative notion of the devil having the rightful ownership of humanity, as well as the more graphic "fishhook" theology developed by Gregory of Nyssa and others. Second, while insisting on a cosmic element in the divine struggle against Satan, Irenaeus does not for a moment lose sight of the humanity of Christ and the importance of his obedience in the particularities of the reality of human history. Third, Irenaeus is aware that the Christus Victor theme does not exhaust our understanding of Christ's redemptive significance. While we must indeed incorporate this royal aspect, we cannot afford to lose sight of the prophetic (Abelardian) and priestly (Anselmian) elements, for they contain important features that uphold the genuine hospitality of God and the need to maintain justice in the face of evil and violence. Thus, the genius of Irenaeus's theology is that he encapsulates elements of each of the three atonement models within his understanding of recapitulation. For Irenaeus, Christ is ultimately the Second Adam, the reconstituted humanity, in whom we can all find our renewed identity and so achieve reconciliation with God.

Underlying much of the discussion so far has been the question: Do we need to fear the violent imagery involved in the Christus Victor theme? I believe that instead we have sufficient reason to trust the Christus Victor theme as a warrant of divine hospitality. We need to keep in mind that the three models of the atonement are not independent of one another. While victory is the aim in the atonement and as such constitutes a significant metaphor, the

---

81. Anselm of Canterbury, *Why God Became Man (Cur Deus Homo),* trans. and ed. Jasper Hopkins and Herbert Richardson (n.p.: Edwin Mellen, 1980), 56 (I.7). Cf. Anthony W. Bartlett, *Cross Purposes: The Violent Grammar of Christian Atonement* (Harrisburg, Pa.: Trinity, 2001), 82.

82. For the notion of ransom, see Matt. 20:28; Mark 10:45; 1 Tim. 2:6; Heb. 9:28; 1 Pet. 1:18–19. For the idea of divine victory by means of the cross, see especially John 12:31–33; Col. 2:13–15; Heb. 2:14–15; Rev. 5:5–6.

Anselmian and Abelardian models present us with the means by which God ultimately defeats evil and upholds his eternal and unconditional hospitality. It is his priestly and prophetic work that enthrones Christ as King. This means that we need not resort either to a deal with the devil or to divine deception in describing the battle leading to the victory of Christ. By adopting an Irenaean framework of the Christus Victor, therefore, it becomes possible to avoid the moral ambiguity often associated with this model of the atonement. Furthermore, Gregory of Nyssa rightly points out that even if we do have recourse to divine deception (or to divine violence, as in the case of moral-influence and penal views of the atonement), this is not necessarily immoral and need not conflict with God's loving intent and with the realization of the full glory of his love. Divine violence is not always opposed to divine hospitality but may well be a suitable instrument in ascertaining the hope of the entire cosmos being embraced by the hospitable love of God. It is the resurrection—the eschatological future of absolute hospitality—that allows us to call the atonement an act of unprecedented hospitality.

PART 3

The Public Face
of Hospitality

9

The Church as the Community
of Hospitality

The Church as the Presence of Christ

At this point we might consider our treatment of atonement theology finished. Having dealt with each of the three major theories of the atonement, we might wonder, what else is there to discuss? Such a restriction does not seem entirely satisfactory, however. All theology has a relationship to the Church in the sense that it originates in the Church and is accountable to the Church. While theologians are no less tempted than other academics to consider themselves autonomous, such an approach would be an illusion. If theology is, to use the Augustinian dictum, "faith seeking understanding," then theology arises from and points back to the liturgical practices and to the life of the Church. There is no doctrine or theology (*lex credendi*) without a worshipping community (*lex orandi*).

The centrality of the Church for theology is by no means universally accepted. The modern period has seriously compromised the centrality of the Church, and the lack of appreciation for the role of the Church is endemic among the heirs of the Enlightenment, both those of the liberal and of the evangelical stripe. This chapter is thus an appeal for the position of the Church as the primary place where reconciliation takes shape and as the place where the atonement—accomplished in principle and decisively through the recapitulation or representation of Israel in the historical figure of Jesus Christ—finds

205

its focus and telos. As especially the moral-influence theory reminds us, the process of reconciliation is not complete without the subjective pole of human acceptance and reconciliation.

Each of the three aspects of the atonement—the prophetic, the priestly, and the royal—have their place in the life of the Church. The theological rationale for this is not simply that the Church imitates Jesus Christ in his threefold office. More profoundly, the Church, in a real sense, *is* the presence of Christ in the world. The Pauline notion of the Church as the "body of Christ" invites our reflection on the nature of the continuation of Christ's presence in and through human agency. Catholic theology has contributed some significant theological insights into the way in which Christ continues to be present in and through the Church. To be sure, Hans Küng has rightly cautioned against an overidentification between Christ and his Church. While Christ is present in the Church, he is not wholly contained in the Church, and the Church must develop in obedience to Christ. Speaking of J. A. Möhler's 1832 notion of the Church as the "continued incarnation of Christ," Küng comments sharply, "Such a Church has no option but to usurp for itself the prerogative of God, infallibly."[1] There is nonetheless a sense in which the Church continues the life (as well as the suffering!) of Christ. If perhaps the Catholic temptation is an overidentification between Christ and the Church, Protestants need to come to a renewed appreciation of the intimate unity between the two.

A more helpful way forward than Möhler's "continued incarnation" can perhaps be found in an understanding of the Church as the continuation of Jesus' presence through the Church's sharing in his anointing with the Spirit.[2] The threefold office of Christ as prophet, priest, and king stems, after all, from his Spirit baptism, in which the Church shares through faith. This emphasis on the work of the Spirit allows us, on the one hand, to avoid a static ecclesiology, which closes the Church to any correction or development and which may obscure the Spirit-guided response in our reception of the Word and the sacraments. This approach affirms, on the other hand, the close connection between Christ and the Church as his body, which means that the structures,

---

1. Hans Küng, *The Church* (Garden City, N.Y.: Image-Doubleday, 1976), 311. Cf. the criticism of Yves M.-J. Congar, *Tradition and Traditions: The Biblical, Historical, and Theological Evidence for Catholic Teaching on Tradition,* trans. Michael Naseby and Thomas Rainborough (San Diego: Basilica; Needham Heights, Mass.: Simon & Schuster, 1966), 312–13. For in-depth discussions of Möhler's incarnational ecclesiology, see Michael J. Himes, *Ongoing Incarnation: Johann Adam Möhler and the Beginnings of Modern Ecclesiology* (New York: Crossroad Herder, 1997); Michael J. Himes, "Divinizing the Church: Strauss and Barth on Möhler's Ecclesiology," in *The Legacy of the Tübingen School: The Relevance of Nineteenth-Century Theology for the Twenty-first Century,* ed. Donald J. Dietrich and Michael J. Himes (New York: Crossroad Herder, 1997), 95–110; Bradford E. Hinze, "The Holy Spirit and the Catholic Tradition: The Legacy of Johann Adam Möhler," in *The Legacy of the Tübingen School,* 75–94.

2. Cf. Veli-Matti Kärkkäinen, *Pneumatology: The Holy Spirit in Ecumenical, International, and Contextual Perspective* (Grand Rapids: Baker, 2002), 73–74, who refers to the work of Catholic theologian H. Mühlen.

the offices, and the sacraments of the Church are not indifferent, but are the God-given means to continue his work of reconciliation in the world.[3]

I suspect that evangelicals, in particular, are nervous about any sort of identification between Christ and the Church, even if the Spirit is the one who mediates this identification. But there is solid warrant for such identification, not just in the tradition but also in the Scriptures themselves. The notions of recapitulation (Irenaeus) and of reconstitution (N. T. Wright) go back to the biblical idea of Jesus as the representative of Israel, so that the entire history of Israel finds its culmination in the life and death of Jesus Christ. At the same time, the recapitulation or reconstitution of Israel in Christ implies that Jesus not only stands at the end of the Old Testament people of God, but that he also forms the nucleus of the New Testament people of God, comprised of Jews and Gentiles. In other words, the Pauline notions of the believers being "in Christ" and so along with him being the seed of Abraham (Gal. 3:16, 29) are ways of saying that the life of the Church is more than people looking up to a Savior in order to imitate him. Union with Christ means that, in a real sense, the Church has been raised up with Christ and has received a place in heaven at the right hand of God (Eph. 2:6; Col. 2:12; 3:1–4). A recovery of the Spirit-given identity between Christ and his Church enables us to identify the continued presence of the prophet, priest, and king in the world and so to explore the continuation of atonement and reconciliation in the life of the Church.

In this chapter I present some of the implications of the centrality of the Church as the continuation of Jesus' presence by focusing on the Word of God, on the sacraments, and on the Church's suffering, all from the angle of the hospitality theme. This implies a centrality of theology and the Church that may be unsettling to some.[4] I am not apologizing for this. I want to comment, however, that my focus on the Church as a community of hospitality is not meant to take away from the practice of hospitality outside the realm of the Church. While the Church, in and through Jesus Christ, is both the sign and the initial presence of the kingdom of God, the two should not be equated.[5]

3. In his discussion on the role of tradition, Jaroslav Pelikan attempts to avoid the extremes of using images, on the one hand, as idols (which purport to be the embodiment of what they represent) and, on the other, as mere tokens (which are mere accidental representations pointing beyond themselves). Instead, he asks us to look at images as icons, which are what they represent, but which invite us to look through themselves to a living reality. Pelikan insists that we need to regard tradition as a kind of icon rather than as a static idol or a mere token (*The Vindication of Tradition* [New Haven, Conn.: Yale University Press, 1984], 55–57).

4. See Hans Boersma, "The Relevance of Theology and Worldview in a Postmodern Context," in *Living in the LambLight: Christianity and Contemporary Challenges to the Gospel,* ed. Hans Boersma (Vancouver, B.C.: Regent College Publishing, 2001), 1–13.

5. Radical Orthodoxy, by viewing the Church as counterpolis to the state, would seem to fall prey to such identification. See Miroslav Volf, "Against a Pretentious Church: A Rejoinder to Bell's Response," *Modern Theology* 19 (2003): 281.

The Church, though constituted as a public through its various practices of hospitality that are ultimately geared toward the telos of the absolute hospitality of the resurrection, is not the only public.[6] We also need to look for the public face of hospitality outside the visible Church. The Spirit-mediated presence of Christ is also found outside the boundaries of the ecclesial community. In the next chapter I focus on the implications of atonement theology beyond the immediate context of the Church.

This chapter is a plea for the place of the Church as the community of reconciliation. The Church, as the presence of Christ in the world, proclaims and celebrates the hospitality of the gospel (which I will call "evangelical hospitality"). This Church is a community forged by the bond of baptism, which is meant for Christians as they receive divine forgiveness and renewal. (I refer to this as "baptismal hospitality.") The Church extends the grace of God's forgiveness by inviting all baptized believers into the fellowship of the Lord's Supper ("eucharistic hospitality"). This visible Church community is sufficiently concerned about its identity as the restored people of God that it continuously invites its members to confess their sins before God and one another ("penitential hospitality"). Finally, as the Church shares in the life of Christ and lives in obedience to him, it may expect to share in the suffering of Christ, in anticipation of the fullness of the hospitable kingdom of God ("cruciform hospitality").

The need for boundaries implies that the hospitality of divine forgiveness and reconciliation cannot be absolute or unconditional. The divine means of embodying hospitality in the world—primarily the preaching of the gospel and the sacraments—cannot escape the tension between hospitality and the violence that exists in all of human life. That being said, I also argue that in Christ the Church is the primary agent of God's forgiveness in the world, and that the resurrection life—the practice of forgiveness and reconciliation—must especially be evident in the liturgy and life of the Church. Only to the degree that the Church is a community of hospitality and reconciliation can she also play a role in opening the doors of the kingdom of God.

Evangelical Hospitality

The past few decades have witnessed a surge of both popular and scholarly literature in the area of forgiveness and reconciliation, much of it focusing on an analysis of the process of human forgiveness. While I certainly do not

6. Reinhard Hütter, drawing on Hannah Arendt, suggests as the two main constitutive features of a "public" (1) a specific telos and (2) mutually binding principles expressed in distinct practices, laws, and doctrines (*Suffering Divine Things: Theology as Church Practice,* trans. Doug Stott [Grand Rapids: Eerdmans, 2000], 161).

want to downplay the importance of such reflection, I believe that it is time that we focus not primarily on the human process of forgiveness, but that we view this process as intimately connected with—indeed, as an aspect of—the divine initiative of hospitality in Christ and his Church. The Church is a divine institution and as such both receives and mediates God's reconciling initiative by the preaching of the gospel and by means of the sacraments. It is only through this vertical relationship that forgiveness and reconciliation among human beings make any sense at all.

The concepts of forgiveness and reconciliation have unfortunately been coopted to a large extent by a self-absorbed culture that tends to be more concerned about experiencing the feeling of being forgiven than about extending divine forgiveness and reconciliation to others. In his bold study on forgiveness, L. Gregory Jones takes to task our therapeutic culture that encapsulates even the notions of forgiveness and reconciliation in its quest for self-fulfillment. Underlying our internalization and privatization of forgiveness, says Jones, lies a "preoccupation with individual feelings and thoughts at the expense of analyses of culpability, responsibility and repentance. The unrelenting focus on isolated individuals suggests that forgiveness is important because of its effects on my feelings . . . not because of a need to discern whether there are tragic misunderstandings or culpable wrongdoing and brokenness that need to be dealt with through practices of forgiveness and repentance."[7] Jones asks us to move away from a focus on the therapeutic and emotional effects that forgiveness may have on ourselves when we forgive others. With such concerns we end up with the idea that we might even need to forgive God: "It does not matter that God is not culpable; what matters are my own feelings and health."[8]

Patrick R. Keifert describes this danger of a betrayal of authentic hospitality in his book *Welcoming the Stranger: A Public Theology of Worship and Evangelism.* Drawing on Richard Sennett and Parker Palmer, Keifert laments the "ideology of intimacy" that has taken hold of the North American Church. This ideology, says Keifert, has three main tenets: "First, it posits that an enduring, profound human relationship of closeness and warmth is the most—or even the only—valuable experience that life affords. Second, the ideology supposes that we can achieve such an intimate, meaningful relationship only through our own personal effort and will. Third, it assumes that the purpose of human life is the fullest development of one's individual personality, which can take place only within such intimate relationships. This ideology of intimacy distorts contemporary understanding and evaluation of Christian public worship."[9] The "ideology of intimacy" in Christian worship fails to recognize the need

7. L. Gregory Jones, *Embodying Forgiveness: A Theological Analysis* (Grand Rapids: Eerdmans, 1995), 50.
8. Ibid., 52.
9. Patrick R. Keifert, *Welcoming the Stranger: A Public Theology of Worship and Evangelism* (Minneapolis: Fortress, 1992), 24.

to retain permeable boundaries that enable others to join the community in worship. The focus on the development of one's individual personality implies a disregard for those outside the Church precisely because it implies a disregard for the Church's own identity as a public identified by divine and cruciform hospitality.

Hospitality reaches outside the boundaries of the community. It runs counter, therefore, to a second ideology that Keifert identifies in the North American Church: the "ideology of individualism." If the significance and impact of forgiveness are measured by the effect it has on the emotional stability of the individuals in the relationship (or perhaps mainly on the emotional well-being of the person offering the forgiveness), then the preaching of the gospel loses its public claim. In this context Keifert draws attention to the current pervasiveness of the family as a metaphor for the Church. The Church is seen as a private group of people who give one another pastoral and emotional support in the private sphere.[10] Since the Church has lost its public character, the liturgy is construed as an extended family gathering. This loss of the Church as a public is not as innocuous as it may first appear: "The extended family can become a small clique that establishes the norms for worship; its needs and interests become the focus of worship. For the inner circle, worship therefore seems very warm, open, and intimate. To other members, it appears exclusive."[11] This tendency to downplay the public character of worship services means that we are in danger of losing their hospitable character. Keifert rightly insists that if we are to recover hospitality in worship, we need to keep in mind that "God is the host of public worship, whose presence is often revealed in and through the stranger" and that the God who is present in worship "is essentially a gracious God who gives to the stranger."[12]

As we saw in chapter 1, Derrida has shown the near ubiquity of an economy of exchange, in which our gift of hospitality turns out to be a selfish quest for recognition. Too often we open the door to others and extend forgiveness to others not primarily out of concern for their well-being, but because of the effects that our gift of hospitality (and forgiveness) ultimately has on ourselves. Derrida's analysis purports to have universal applicability; he interprets all so-called acts of forgiveness as ultimately narcissistic in character. I am not

10. Ibid., 8.

11. Ibid., 29. All of this is not to say that the family metaphor is inherently problematic. As Scott Hahn has pointed out, it is an important biblical metaphor (*First Comes Love: Finding Your Family in the Church and Trinity* [New York: Doubleday, 2002]). The difficulty lies in the disappearance of the public invitation of the gospel and so the loss of the church as a public.

12. Keifert, *Welcoming the Stranger,* 58. It is important to recognize here that the public character of worship does not simply lie in the fact that this worship is meant for everyone, including nonmembers. While this is certainly true, the appeal of evangelical hospitality to outsiders lies precisely in the fact that the church itself is a public, constituted in its liturgical practices of hospitality and in the telos of eschatological absolute hospitality.

convinced he is correct. A more charitable reading would allow for more genuine hospitality, for true forgiveness and reconciliation. Derrida is right, however, to draw our attention to the fact that our practices of forgiveness and reconciliation are easily incorporated into an economy of exchange from which true grace and hospitality have all but disappeared. Therapeutic notions of forgiveness, which focus on the privacy of individual emotions and on self-fulfillment, fall prey to an abusive economy of exchange in which one extends forgiveness for one's own sake rather than for the sake of the other. A focus on the private emotional effects of forgiveness at the expense of a concern for truthful responsibility and repentance puts up stiff barriers around the self, or at least around the community, and so endangers true hospitality. Derrida's warning needs to be heard, therefore, in a culture that is overly concerned about what "I get out of it" when I forgive somebody else.

There is something insidious about such therapeutic notions of forgiveness, which seem to infiltrate our evangelical churches today. Hospitality that is truly evangelical does not have the feelings of well-being of individual Church members as its first concern. True hospitality reaches out to the other and can never be satisfied with erecting impermeable boundaries. The gospel (*euangelion*) is the true antidote to the self-enclosed economy of exchange that characterizes a therapeutic view of forgiveness. The good news of the gospel, in its very nature, expands boundaries as it reaches out to those beyond the Church. The gospel is the Word of God that invites everyone to repent and accept the lordship of Jesus Christ. The Sunday morning preaching of the gospel has an open or public aspect. Every Church is at heart a "seeker Church," seeking out and extending hospitality to those beyond its boundaries. With Jones I am concerned that repentance is being lost from our vocabulary and, therefore, that hospitality loses its association with the public divine invitation for all to return to God. The North American Church needs to recover the notion that inasmuch as hospitality has a place in the liturgy, it is the hospitality of the *gospel*. It is literally an *evangelical* hospitality, in which God offers everyone his hospitality of forgiveness and reconciliation.[13] It is, therefore, the gospel itself that constitutes the Church as a public with a distinct telos. When the hospitality of the gospel loses its centrality, the Church loses its public space and so its distinctive character. The good news is a public invitation to repent

13. This is not to say that preaching is a Derridean sort of absolute or unconditional hospitality (which is our eschatological hope). There is of necessity a preferential hospitality (see chapter 3) that limits and excludes, even in the preaching. This is true in several ways. First, time and space, language, and culture are among the factors limiting the reach of the preaching. Second, the specificity of the gospel message implies the demand for conformity to the gospel and ultimately even the possibility of exclusion from this community. The hospitality of the proclamation of good news is only possible against the backdrop of boundaries that identify the church as a community that is shaped by the gospel. Reinhard Hütter appropriately describes the paradox of the christological "center" of the Church being the "one 'boundary' the church never transcends" (*Suffering Divine Things*, 165; italics omitted).

and to abandon our narcissism in favor of genuine altruism and so become a hospitable community that models the evangelical practice of other-focused forgiveness and reconciliation. Such evangelical hospitality invites others into the eternal kingdom of God.[14]

The preaching of the gospel has often, and to my mind rightly, been viewed as God's primary means of grace. The public proclamation of God's Word is the way in which he liberally extends good news; it is truly *evangelical* hospitality. We need to have a keen eye for the importance of preaching as God's public gift of hospitality to the world. By recovering the significant place of the expository sermon in the liturgy, the Church will be able to recover the communal, public invitation of God among the "company of strangers."[15] In this way the Church will in turn be equipped to demonstrate and extend forgiveness and reconciliation to other strangers, who will no longer feel excluded from a privatized and closed intimate family fellowship. Our congregations will more and more tend to lose their social homogeneity; they will no longer be "lifestyle enclaves."[16] The preaching of the gospel—evangelical hospitality—is the expression of God's desire for everyone to be saved (1 Tim. 2:4).

Baptismal Hospitality

Baptism is the sacrament through which one enters into the Church and is united to Jesus Christ. As the prime sacrament of initiation, baptism does not simply signify the universal call or promise of the gospel, but it actually incorporates one into Christ and at the same time into the eschatological community of hospitality. We might be tempted to make fine logical distinctions here, in the hope of establishing the correct order of things. But the Scriptures do not seem concerned about which comes first: our personal union with Christ or our membership in the Church (cf. Acts 2:41; 1 Cor. 12:13). Karl Rahner has rightly cautioned against an individualized understanding of baptism.[17] It is the individual person who is baptized, but this person is baptized into the people of God. To belong to Christ means to belong to his Church and

14. For an insightful analysis of the self-affirming individualism in contemporary Protestantism, see Marsha G. Witten, *All Is Forgiven: The Secular Message in American Protestantism* (Princeton, N.J.: Princeton University Press, 1993).

15. Cf. Parker J. Palmer, *Company of Strangers: Christians and the Renewal of America's Public Life* (New York: Crossroad, 1983).

16. This term originates with Robert Bellah. L. Gregory Jones employs the term in his discussion on "Eucharistic Hospitality: Welcoming the Stranger into the Household of God," *Reformed Journal* 39 (May 1989): 13.

17. See Peder Nørgaard-Højen, "Baptism and the Foundations of Communion," in *Baptism and the Unity of the Church,* ed. Michael Root and Risto Saarinen (Grand Rapids: Eerdmans; Geneva: WCC, 1998), 63–64.

vice versa. Since Christ is the representation of Israel, who recapitulates her life, death, and resurrection, faith and baptism unite us to Christ and lead us into the Church.

We should resist the temptation, therefore, to prioritize between being united to Christ and joining his Church. Doing so leads too easily to a denigration of the significance of the Church as the visible communion of believers. Baptism, as the primary sacrament of initiation, rebuffs such attempts to play out faith in Christ against fellowship with the Church of Christ. Danish theologian Peder Nørgaard-Højen rightly comments that there exists "an essential relationship between being a Christian and the community of believers (the *communio sanctorum*) as the place in which the faith becomes concrete and the implications of baptism become visible."[18] It is impossible to belong to Christ without at the same time belonging to the Church of Christ. Believing is never an isolated activity.[19] To accept the invitation of the host implies that one is willing to share in the feast together with everyone who has accepted the same invitation. Baptismal hospitality is by definition corporate in character.

Baptism into Christ and into his Church implies a bond of unity with everyone who likewise has been baptized into Christ and his Church. We can only deny this objective bond of fellowship (*koinōnia*) if we radically limit the implications of baptism to the local Church. Such a limitation hardly seems justified. To be sure, the local congregation and the baptized person's life in and participation with it are of supreme importance. But to be incorporated into the local Church means to be incorporated into Christ and so to become part of his universal body as well. Walter Kasper puts it well when he says that

> baptism is more than inclusion in a local congregation and also more than inclusion in a particular confession. Baptism incorporates us in the one and only body indivisible of Christ (1 Cor. 12:13 and 1:13). Thus for the New Testament, the one church of Jesus Christ is present in each local congregation (1 Cor. 1:2; 2 Cor. 1:1), and the "church" is both the local church and the church universal in one. Thus baptism makes us a member of a local congregation but also a member of the one, holy, catholic and apostolic church (*una sancta, catholica et apostolica ecclesia*). From its inmost nature baptism has an importance that goes beyond this or that local or confessional church.[20]

Baptism forges a unity that resists the sinful divisions that we have erected. Baptism tells us that divine hospitality reaches far beyond denominational walls and calls those very boundaries into question. The 1982 Lima document of the World Council of Churches, *Baptism, Eucharist and Ministry*, is quite right,

18. Ibid., 64.
19. Cf. *Catechism of the Catholic Church* (Mahwah, N.J.: Paulist, 1994), 44–45 (§ 166).
20. Walter Kasper, "Ecclesiological and Ecumenical Implications of Baptism," *Ecumenical Review* 52 (2000): 530–31.

therefore, to refer to baptism as "a sign and seal of our common discipleship" and as a "basic bond of unity."[21]

Recognizing this unity established through baptism, most churches in the Orthodox, Catholic, and Protestant traditions accept the validity of one another's baptism. All ecumenical dialogue partners are in agreement that rebaptism is a schismatic act that severs the unity of the Church and as such needs to be rejected.[22] When baptism is administered with water in the name of the Triune God and with the intention of doing what the Church does, this is generally considered a sufficient basis for ecumenical recognition of a bond of unity.[23] The essentials of the faith, as expressed in the creeds of the early Church, constitute what the seventeenth-century Puritan Richard Baxter referred to as "mere Christianity."

Of course, even a "mere Christianity" implies a community centered on a particular gospel message. The Trinitarian creeds of the Church belong to the very core of the faith. Baptism is not extended indiscriminately to believers and unbelievers alike. It is not an unconditional or absolute form of hospitality. As a sacrament of initiation, baptism is a rite that takes place on the very boundary of the Church. Baptism includes particular people in the Church. Only those who are willing to have their identities shaped by the gospel are baptized into Christ and his Church. Baptizands throughout the centuries have renounced the devil and his works upon their entry into the Church. The works of the powers of darkness have no place in the community of light. The hospitality of baptism implies the necessary exclusion of everything that does not belong to the Church of Jesus Christ.

Despite this exclusion it is right to speak of "baptismal hospitality." I have coined this term for several reasons. First, it indicates that *God* reaches out to his people with genuine hospitality, extends to them his grace, and places them within the boundaries of his Church. Second, the corporate character of this baptismal hospitality implies recognition of baptism across the various boundaries that we have erected and that detract from the witness of the visible community of faith. Baptismal hospitality as *our* mutual recognition of one

---

21. *Baptism, Eucharist and Ministry*, Faith and Order Paper, no. 111 (Geneva: WCC, 1982), 3 (B6). Vatican II also recognizes the basic sacramental bond of unity established through baptism (André Birmelé, "Baptism and the Unity of the Church in Ecumenical Dialogues," in *Baptism and the Unity of the Church*, ed. Michael Root and Risto Saarinen [Grand Rapids: Eerdmans; Geneva: WCC, 1998], 104).

22. The rejection of rebaptism is not unambiguous. Churches that only accept adult baptism may readily agree to reject rebaptism, but they may still insist on baptizing people who come to them from other churches on the grounds that they don't recognize infant baptism as a true baptism in the first place. From a completely different perspective, some of the Orthodox churches also do not recognize the baptism of other churches (see Kasper, "Ecclesiological and Ecumenical Implications," 532–34).

23. For a balanced discussion on the relationship between Church and baptism in Cyprian, Optatus, and Augustine, see J. Faber, *Vestigium Ecclesiae: De doop als 'spoor der kerk' (Cyprianus, Optatus, Augustinus)* (Goes, Neth.: Oosterbaan & Le Cointre, 1969).

another's baptismal practices thus counters our divisions and implies unity of the baptizand with the universal Church. Finally, baptismal hospitality issues a call. Baptism is often referred to as both a gift and a call.[24] God not only gives us his grace by incorporating us into Christ and into his Church, but he also calls on us to accept the responsibility of this gift. Baptism is a call to continue in faith; it is a call to respond to God's hospitable invitation both now by joining the Church and in the future by continuing in the meal of the host and by a life of fellowship with Christ and with one's fellow believers. This aspect of the call or invitation to the obedience of faith is a positive element in recent ecumenical dialogue. The Scriptures regard baptism as inextricably connected with the human response of faith in Christ.[25] Divine hospitality only reaches its purpose of eternal fellowship through the continual faithful response of the believer. Baptismal hospitality therefore implies the need for a continual acceptance of the promise of forgiveness and life.[26]

Eucharistic Hospitality

In a real sense God's hospitality finds its climax in the celebration of the Eucharist. As the anticipation of—and indeed, the first participation in—the eschatological wedding banquet, the Eucharist suits the metaphor of hospitality better than either the preaching of the gospel or the sacrament of baptism. Evangelical hospitality and baptismal hospitality are terms that I have employed in line with the common notion of "eucharistic hospitality." While I have thus tried to emphasize the unity of these three means of grace, it is clear that the Eucharist conjures up the imagery of hospitality more naturally than either preaching or baptism.

Even in our North American fast-food culture, the connection between meals and hospitality has not been completely severed. To invite people to a meal continues to be a sign of fellowship and unity. It is understandable, therefore, that the term "eucharistic hospitality" has come to denote the willingness of churches to accept people from other denominations to share with them in the celebration of the communion meal. The theological rationale for this practice of eucharistic hospitality toward those of different confessional backgrounds is the baptismal unity that transcends denominational walls. If we recognize

---

24. *Baptism, Eucharist and Ministry,* p. 3 (B8): "Baptism is both God's gift and our human response to that gift."

25. Cf. J. van Bruggen, *Het diepe water van de doop* (Kampen, Neth.: Kok, 1997).

26. This emphasis on the call for faith does not necessarily imply a rejection of infant baptism. It is possible to speak of a common faith of the church (or of the parents) in which children participate. Richard Baxter (1615–91) defended infant baptism on the grounds that children were associated with their parents' faith as their "appendages." See Hans Boersma, *Richard Baxter's Understanding of Infant Baptism* (Princeton, N.J.: Princeton Theological Seminary, 2002).

the baptism administered in other churches as establishing a common bond of unity, shouldn't we also accept all baptized Christians—regardless of denominational background—at the Lord's Table?

I believe there is something fundamentally right about this argument, and I will elaborate on it later in this discussion. At the same time, the expression is not without danger. Eucharistic hospitality is hospitality that *we*—the people of God—extend to others. But if such horizontal fellowship is justified at the communion table, then surely it must have its basis in a prior vertical relationship. Divine hospitality must precede human hospitality. As Monika Hellwig puts it, the Lord's Supper is "in the first place the celebration of the hospitality of God shared by guests who commit themselves to become fellow hosts with God. It is the celebration of divine hospitality as offered in the human presence of Jesus as word, wisdom and outreach of God."[27] Eucharistic hospitality is always first God's gracious invitation to find forgiveness and life in unity with Christ and with his Church. The Eucharist is, after baptism, the second sacrament of initiation into the Church. When I speak of "eucharistic hospitality," therefore, I am not simply referring to the common idea of accepting fellow believers from other confessional traditions at the Eucharist. I am also, and primarily, referring to God's gracious invitation to share in his feast of absolute hospitality in eternal life.

Both of these elements—divine and human hospitality—are prominent in the Gospel of Luke. Its theme of hospitality has frequently been noted, with a recent commentary aptly carrying the title *The Hospitality of God*.[28] John Koenig goes so far as to say, "The very structure of Luke's work witnesses to a conviction on his part that some deep link exists between the verbal content of God's good news and its historical embodiment in boundary situations involving guests and hosts."[29] Throughout this Gospel, the place of the stranger (along with that of other outcast figures, such as tax collectors and sinners) figures prominently. In Jesus, God reaches out especially to these strangers who fall outside the purview of the ruling elites, and he invites them into fellowship with him. As a result Luke weaves much of his Gospel around occasions of fellowship at festal meals.[30] After Jesus called Levi, the tax collector, to be his

---

27. Monika K. Hellwig, *The Eucharist and the Hunger of the World,* rev. ed. (Kansas City, Mo.: Sheed & Ward, 1992), 18. Cf. Monika K. Hellwig, "The Eucharist and World Hunger," *Word & World* 17 (1997): 65.

28. Brendan Byrne, *The Hospitality of God: A Reading of Luke's Gospel* (Collegeville, Minn.: Liturgical, 2000).

29. John Koenig, *New Testament Hospitality: Partnership with Strangers as Promise and Mission* (Philadelphia: Fortress, 1985), 86. Koenig's entire chapter on Luke-Acts presents a helpful elaboration on the hospitality theme.

30. Simon Morrison Steer lists fifty-one occurrences of the food motif in Luke's Gospel ("Eating Bread in the Kingdom of God: The Foodways of Jesus in the Gospel of Luke" [Ph.D. diss., Westminster Theological Seminary, 2002], 151–53).

disciple, "Levi held a great reception in his house" (Luke 5:29). And when Jesus told Zacchaeus, another tax collector, to come out of the sycamore fig tree, he "hurried down and welcomed him joyfully" (19:6). Jesus' hospitality is symbolic. It indicates that God's hospitality breaks the patterns of human imagination. What is more, Jesus' association with tax collectors and sinners means that God's hospitality is now more extravagant than ever before. Those who always knew themselves to be on the outside are now invited to share in the eschatological feast of the kingdom of God. As Jonathan Wilson puts it: "When God welcomes us, he does not do so because we are worthy of hospitality: 'God proves his love for us in that while we were still sinners Christ died for us' (Rom. 5:8). If, while we were still sinners and enemies, Christ reconciled us to God, then the hospitality of God's love does not depend on our worthiness."[31]

It is fitting, therefore, that Jesus should use parables to demonstrate a divine hospitality that is infinitely greater than any human hospitality and that serves both as a model for human hospitality and as an indication of what the future of divine eschatological fellowship will look like. At the same time, these parables expose illegitimate human limitations on hospitality, with which the ruling classes (the Pharisees and the scribes) are operating. In his parables Jesus depicts God as the master who will take the place of a servant at the table, while God's faithful servants may recline as the honored guests (Luke 12:35–38). Jesus speaks of the rejection of God's invitation by those who are self-assured of their place in the kingdom, so that instead he has "the poor, the crippled, the blind and the lame" and even those who live by "the open roads and the hedgerows" invited to the great banquet (14:15–24). While the prodigal son is feasting on the fattened calf with his father and the rest of the household, the older son becomes angry and refuses to come in (15:11–31). Lazarus, separated from the rich life by a forbidding gate, longs to eat what falls from the rich man's table, only to find himself reclining at table with Father Abraham in the hereafter, while the rich man ends up in agony in Hades (16:19–31).

The parables are illuminating in that they illustrate God's immeasurable hospitality for those who, by human reckoning, are entirely undeserving of our care and attention. At the same time, the parables indicate that the divine hospitality reaching out into the humdrum of human existence has its boundaries. Those who are self-serving and live profligate lives at the cost of those in need of hospitality end up being excluded from the feast (Luke 12:45–48; 14:24; 16:22–24). This is not to say that divine hospitality is not extended to them. *All* servant managers are able to prepare for their master's return; it is

---

31. Jonathan R. Wilson, *Gospel Virtues: Practicing Faith, Hope, and Love in Uncertain Times* (Downers Grove, Ill.: InterVarsity, 1998), 175. Cf. Steer: "The celebratory meals in the homes of Levi and Zacchaeus are joyful expressions of the OT emphasis on hospitality and vivid foreshadowing of the eschatological banquet" ("Eating Bread," 255).

just that some take advantage of his absence to follow their selfish inclinations (12:42–48). Many guests have received an invitation to the great banquet; the problem is that those initially invited come up with flimsy excuses why they cannot show up (14:18–20). Till the very end of the parable of the prodigal son, the older brother continues to be the object of his father's love; the last words of the parable constitute an impassioned plea by the father for the older brother to join in the celebration (15:31–32). It appears that while there are boundaries to the kingdom, they are troublesome only to those who refuse to accept the hospitality of God.

On three occasions in Luke's Gospel, the Pharisees extend hospitality to Jesus and invite him to dinner with them (7:36; 11:37; 14:1).[32] Interestingly, Jesus never rejects their invitations, despite the clear presence of ulterior motives. Each time, however, he uses the opportunity to expose the Pharisees' hypocrisy and their violent rejection of the stranger, while he himself takes the place of the host and welcomes outcasts, forgiving the prostitute who pours perfume on Jesus' feet and kisses them (7:36–50) and healing the man who is suffering from dropsy (14:2–4). Indeed, Jesus narrates the three parables of the lost sheep, the lost coin, and the lost son all in response to the Pharisees' anger and frustration with Jesus: "This man welcomes sinners and eats with them" (15:2). The increasing rift between Jesus and the Pharisees comes about not because of a lack of hospitality on Jesus' part but is the result of a nongenuine hospitality on the part of the Pharisees, which is accompanied by a disdain for all who are not part of the religious and social class to which they themselves belong.

Questions surrounding eucharistic hospitality receive fresh impetus when viewed in the light of Luke's depiction of divine and human hospitality throughout his Gospel. Jesus' hospitality and the fellowship surrounding the meals indicate the kind of hospitality with which God invites everyone to the eschatological feast. The Lord's Supper, like the meals in Luke's Gospel, is celebrated in anticipation of the eternal banquet. There is a close tie between the Eucharist and eucharistic hospitality, on the one hand, and Luke's fellowship meals and the hospitality that Jesus displays there, on the other. This is not to say that there are no differences between common meals and the Eucharist. But there is good reason why God has chosen to give himself to us in the Eucharist in the context of a meal, in bread and wine.

Miroslav Volf tells the childhood story of a visitor who used to join his family every month for a Sunday meal after the celebration of Holy Communion. As a young boy Miroslav had his reservations about the intruding stranger's monthly visits. Now realizing the connection between the common meal and the Eucharist, Volf comments:

---

32. For an extended discussion of each of the three passages, see Steer, "Eating Bread," 168–228.

Had I objected—"But must *we* invite him *every* time he comes!?"—they [i.e., Volf's parents] would have responded, "As the Lord gave his body and blood for us sinners, so we ought to be ready to share not only our belongings, but also something of our very selves, with strangers." The circle of our table was opened up by the wounds of Christ, and a stranger was let in. Had I continued to protest, they would have reminded me of that grand eschatological meal whose host will be the Triune God, a meal at which people of every tribe and tongue will be feasting. I had better be ready to sit next to him at *that* meal, they would have insisted.[33]

Gabriel Axel's 1987 film, *Babette's Feast,* likewise posits a link between the common meal and the Lord's Supper. Through the circumstances of the French-German war of 1870–71, the French cook Babette ends up in a reclusive and ingrown Lutheran sect on the Danish island of Jutland. While she comes to the community as a stranger, she ends up organizing a lavish feast for them, which throws into disarray their ingrained asceticism. The sumptuous feast becomes the occasion for the villagers to deal with their mutual grievances and to offer one another forgiveness and reconciliation. What is more, the extravagance of the feast turns the stranger and guest, Babette, into the host for the entire community. In self-denying love she gives every last penny of her fabulous wealth to express her gratitude to this small group of people. The meal is truly a eucharistic meal, a meal of thanksgiving.[34] Much of the film is taken up by the intricacies of the meal itself, where the eleven disciples of the community are undergoing their transformation. There is also one outsider who joins them: General Löwenhielm. Throughout the meal this twelfth guest clearly behaves as a stranger. Familiar with the intricacies of Parisian cuisine, he is the only one who truly appreciates the generous character of the meal. This outsider is needed to complete the community (as a community of twelve) and to assist them in their transformation, even as he himself also comes to see his life in an entirely new perspective.

The story of *Babette's Feast* is reminiscent of Luke's account of the two travelers on the road to Emmaus (24:13–35).[35] They, like the small Danish

33. Miroslav Volf, "Theology for a Way of Life," in *Practicing Theology: Beliefs and Practices in Christian Life,* ed. Miroslav Volf and Dorothy C. Bass (Grand Rapids: Eerdmans, 2002), 249 (italics in the original). Christine D. Pohl also comments on the connection in her essay in the same volume, "A Community's Practice of Hospitality: The Interdependence of Practices and of Communities," 135.

34. Clive Marsh, "Did You Say 'Grace'? Eating in Community in *Babette's Feast,*" in *Explorations in Theology and Film: Movies and Meaning,* ed. Clive Marsh and Gaye Ortiz (Oxford: Blackwell, 1997), 213; Lloyd Baugh, *Imaging the Divine: Jesus and Christ-Figures in Film* (Kansas City, Mo.: Sheed & Ward, 1997), 140–41; Bryan P. Stone, "'The Communion of Saints': *Babette's Feast,*" in *Faith and Film: Theological Themes at the Cinema* (St. Louis: Chalice, 1999), 162–63. Robert A. Flanagan refers to *Babette's Feast* as "a cinematic icon of the Eucharist" in "Babette's Feast: The Generosity of God," *Jacob's Well* (spring/summer 1998). The article can be found on the Web: www.jacwell.org/reviews/1998–Spring-Babette's%20Feast.htm.

35. For a wonderful exposition of this story, against the background of Psalms 42 and 43, see N. T. Wright, *The Challenge of Jesus: Rediscovering Who Jesus Was and Is* (Downers Grove, Ill.: InterVarsity, 1999), 150–73.

sect, are joined by a stranger, the grace of whose presence they are unable to recognize, wrapped up as they are in their grief. After they have kindly taken Jesus into their home, Jesus turns from a mere stranger into the host: "Now while he was with them at table, he took the bread and said the blessing; then he broke it and handed it to them" (24:30).[36] Significantly, it is in the breaking of the bread that Cleopas and his friend recognize Jesus (24:31, 35). It is the meal with the stranger that transforms them and makes them recognize their Lord. The meal is not actually a eucharistic celebration. There is nonetheless a close connection between this meal on the evening of the resurrection day and the Lord's Supper itself. Jesus' fourfold pattern of taking bread, giving thanks, breaking it, and giving it to his disciples is reminiscent both of his feeding of the five thousand (9:16) and of the Last Supper, which he celebrated with his disciples when he instituted the Eucharist (22:19).

The Eucharist is the place where God extends his lavish hospitality to his disciples. Some of them don't quite seem to fit within the community's boundaries. Neither Babette, the Christ figure of the movie, nor General Löwenhielm seems to belong. Both are outsiders. But as the community welcomes them, they are able to turn the community toward grace and celebration. The Eucharist, like the common meal, asks for our hospitality. Since it is God's hospitality that all guests experience at the Lord's Table, eucharistic hospitality toward people from different denominational backgrounds can hardly be an option. Eucharistic hospitality is based on the baptismal hospitality that God himself has extended to all who come to him in faith.[37]

To be sure, the extension of eucharistic hospitality to all who are baptized introduces a dilemma. How is it possible to be united around the communion table without fully extending this unity toward a denominational merger of the various churches? Faced with this dilemma, we might be tempted to look at eucharistic fellowship as the end of ecumenical discussions rather than as the means. To sit around the same table implies full fellowship, and so we would rather not share the Eucharist until we have arrived at full visible Church unity. The Roman Catholic Church, for instance, tends to be quite hesitant about eucharistic hospitality and only allows it under certain circumstances. To be sure, Vatican II has recognized that the bond of baptism creates "some, though imperfect, communion with the Catholic Church."[38] But this imperfect communion only implies eucharistic fellowship in situations of

---

36. Amy G. Oden points out that the Fathers of the early Church noticed the fluidity between the identities of stranger/guest and host: "Because the guest is actually more than just a guest, but is Christ, then there is another surprise as well. Christ becomes the host and the host becomes the guest" (*And You Welcomed Me: A Sourcebook on Hospitality in Early Christianity* [Nashville: Abingdon, 2001], 51).

37. The limitation of eucharistic hospitality to those who are baptized indicates again that the Church has boundaries and that the Church's hospitality cannot be absolute if the Church wants to remain Church.

38. "Decree on Ecumenism," in *The Conciliar and Postconciliar Documents*, vol. 1 of *Vatican Council II*, ed. Austin Flannery, rev. ed. (Northport, N.Y.: Costello; Dublin: Dominican, 1975), 455.

"urgent necessity," such as danger of death, persecution, or imprisonment.[39] The Orthodox churches tend to be even more categorical in their rejection of eucharistic hospitality. Paulos Mar Gregorios makes his point quite forcefully when he comments that "the term hospitality is quite offensive to us in this context, since it implies that those who do not do what some Western churches are now doing are being downright inhospitable. I personally feel offended by that implication and therefore by the term 'eucharistic hospitality', which should be expunged from the ecumenical vocabulary for the sake of good relations."[40]

There is a sense in which I can appreciate the Catholic and Orthodox reservations. They stem from an ecclesiology that takes the visible communion of believers seriously, and wants to retain the unity of believers under the office of the apostolic ministry.[41] Such an ecclesiology is a reminder that even the Church's hospitality is not yet an absolute eschatological hospitality. The Eucharist is not distributed to all. Those who are incorporated into the visible body through baptismal boundary crossing are those who receive the sacrament of the Eucharist.[42] Indeed, these more restricted practices should serve as reminders to evangelicals that visible unity is important and that eucharistic hospitality is no panacea for the fragmentation of our churches and does not justify the continuation of denominational divisions. By refusing to extend eucharistic hospitality to believers from other denominations, however, we end up with a static ecclesiology. We need to keep in mind that

39. "Declaration on the Position of the Catholic Church on the Celebration of the Eucharist in Common by Christians of Different Confessions," in *Conciliar and Postconciliar Documents,* 505. Cf. Geoffrey Wainwright, "Towards Eucharistic Fellowship," *Ecumenical Review* 44 (1992): 7; Susan K. Wood, "Baptism and the Foundations of Communion," in *Baptism and the Unity of the Church,* ed. Michael Root and Risto Saarinen (Grand Rapids: Eerdmans; Geneva: WCC, 1998), 44–45.

40. Paulos Mar Gregorios, "Not a Question of Hospitality," *Ecumenical Review* 44 (1992): 46. Cf. also Robert G. Stephanopoulos, "Implications for the Ecumenical Movement," *Ecumenical Review* 44 (1992): 18–28.

41. Cf. John Paul II, "Ecclesia de eucharistia," 44: "Precisely because the Church's unity, which the Eucharist brings about through the Lord's sacrifice and by communion in his body and blood, absolutely requires full communion in the bonds of the profession of faith, the sacraments and ecclesiastical governance, it is not possible to celebrate together the same Eucharistic liturgy until those bonds are fully re-established. Any such concelebration would not be a valid means, and might well prove instead to be *an obstacle, to the attainment of full communion,* by weakening the sense of how far we remain from this goal and by introducing or exacerbating ambiguities with regard to one or another truth of the faith" (italics in the original).

42. This chapter does not elaborate on questions surrounding excommunication. Suffice it to say that I regard discipline and excommunication essentially as acts of hospitality in that they constitute a final call to return to the fold of the Church. William T. Cavanaugh rightly observes: "Excommunication by the community clarifies for the sinner the seriousness of the offense, and, if accompanied by a proper penitential discipline, shows the sinner the way to reconciliation with the body of Christ while shielding the sinner from the adverse effects of continued participation in the Eucharist in the absence of true reconciliation. As an invitation to reconciliation, then, excommunication done well is an act of *hospitality*" (*Torture and Eucharist: Theology, Politics, and the Body of Christ* [Oxford: Blackwell, 1998], 243; italics in the original).

Christ is still in the process of gathering his Church.[43] Bernard Thorogood rightly concludes, therefore, that eucharistic hospitality can indeed be a means to promote the end of further unity: "There can be no actions of the church on earth which are the end of the pilgrimage road, for that is the gift of glory, the ingathering of the whole body, the completion of God's gracious road. . . . So to downgrade 'means' appears to me a lack of the eschatological dimension in worship. What we are and do cannot ever be the end. . . . We need not be ashamed of eucharistic hospitality as a means toward God's hospitality."[44] By rejecting communion with other believers we appropriate too eagerly the characteristics of catholicity and apostolicity, as though they had no extension beyond our own particular denomination. Baptism forms a common bond that calls for eucharistic hospitality. The table is that of the Lord, who himself extends hospitality to those who belong to his Church. The two sacraments of initiation belong together.[45]

Penitential Hospitality

The connection between confession and hospitality may not be as self-evident as the connection between preaching, baptism, the Eucharist, and hospitality. Confession, more immediately than any other means of grace, draws our attention to the fact that divine hospitality is not without its boundaries. Instead of focusing our attention on the liberality of hospitality, confession—and in particular the practice of penance—tends to make us think of reluctantly owning up, of punishments, and of burdens imposed by the clergy on the laity.[46] We are more likely to associate confession with violence than with hospitality. Whereas preaching, baptism, and the Lord's Supper all have positive connotations, penance tends to have a negative ring to it. To speak of

43. Miroslav Volf goes so far as to argue that on "this side of the eschatological gathering of the whole people of God, there can be no church in the singular" (*After Our Likeness: The Church as the Image of the Trinity* [Grand Rapids: Eerdmans, 1998], 157–58). He calls openness to all other churches an "interecclesial minimum" (157) and an "indispensable condition of ecclesiality" (156).

44. Bernard Thorogood, "Coming to the Lord's Table: A Reformed Viewpoint," *Ecumenical Review* 44 (1992): 12–13.

45. Susan K. Wood, "Baptism as a Mark of the Church," in *Marks of the Body of Christ*, ed. Carl E. Braaten and Robert W. Jenson (Grand Rapids: Eerdmans, 1999), 43. As Wood points out, the connection between baptism and Eucharist as rites of initiation has implications also for infant communion, which is recognized more in the Eastern than in the Western tradition.

46. The terms "confession" and "penance" are ambiguous. In this discussion I take "confession" to mean both the private confession of sins in front of a clergy and the public communal confession of sins in the liturgy. The sacrament of penance, in the Catholic tradition, consists of contrition (repentance), confession (of sins), absolution (pronouncement of forgiveness), and satisfaction (doing certain works of reparation to repair the harm done and restore Christian habits). Sometimes the word "penance" is reserved for the aspect of satisfaction only. Here I take penance to refer to the entire process of private auricular confession.

"penitential hospitality" may well seem to be a contradiction in terms. Penance and hospitality seem to belong to two different worlds.

It is not altogether wrong to distinguish preaching, baptism, and the Eucharist from confession. Preaching is first and foremost the proclamation of good news. Baptism is an expression of God's love drawing us into eternal fellowship. The Eucharist is an advance celebration of the eternal wedding feast of the Lamb. The celebratory character of each of these means of grace is at the very least dimmed when we face the fact that we need to admit our wrongdoings. The immediate occasion for confession lies in human sin. Where no sin has been committed, nothing needs to be confessed. Apprehension and shame about having to admit one's wrongdoings to someone else is a natural attitude when going to confession. Several of the Church fathers were so concerned with the horrible situation that gives rise to the need for confession that they insisted that after baptism it could only be done once in a lifetime.[47] To enter into the "order of penitents" during Lent and receive absolution at Easter was a serious matter that made clear to everyone that in this sinful world God used boundaries and conditions in practicing his hospitality.

It would nonetheless be theologically incorrect and pastorally ill advised to reserve the term "hospitality" for preaching, baptism, and the Eucharist and to associate confession and penance with violence. We have already seen that on this side of eternity hospitality is never extended without the violence of exclusion. Indeed, even the practices of evangelical, baptismal, and eucharistic hospitality are impossible without the recognition of boundaries. God's work of reconciliation in and through the Church takes place in concrete, circumscribed activities. Confession may be more emphatically and directly concerned with boundaries, but by no means exclusively so: God's Word is the good news about the victory of Jesus Christ, but this victory implies a lordship that rejects false worship and idolatry as incompatible with the gospel. Baptism speaks of the union between the believer and Christ and his Church, but this union loses its meaning when baptism is extended also to those who do not belong to the *communio sanctorum.* The Eucharist is the celebration of reconciliation and of new life, but to extend the Eucharist to those who are not baptized or to those who willfully reject the hospitality of God is to endanger the very character of the Church as the eschatological community of the resurrection. Preaching, baptism, and the Eucharist are means of grace. Grace turns into cheap grace

47. Tertullian, *On Repentance,* in *The Ante-Nicene Fathers,* trans. S. Thelwall, ed. Alexander Roberts and James Donaldson, rev. Cleveland Coxe (1885; repr. Peabody, Mass.: Hendrickson, 1994), 3:662–63 (VII); Hermas, *The Pastor,* in *The Ante-Nicene Fathers,* trans. F. Crombie, ed. Alexander Roberts and James Donaldson, rev. Cleveland Coxe (1885; repr., Peabody, Mass.: Hendrickson, 1994), 2:21 (II.iv.1); Clement of Alexandra, *Stromata,* in *The Ante-Nicene Fathers,* ed. Alexander Roberts and James Donaldson, rev. Cleveland Coxe (1885; repr., Peabody, Mass.: Hendrickson, 1994), 2:360 (II.xiii). Cf. Edward J. Hanna, "Penance," in *The Catholic Encyclopedia,* ed. Charles G. Herbermann et al. (New York: Gilmary, 1913), 11:631.

when we refuse to say of particular actions that they have no place in a forgiven community. Hospitality loses its character when it admits everyone—perhaps even the devil—to come in.

Confession and discipline should not be viewed, therefore, as something that clouds the hospitality of God, as a negative holdout from a sin-obsessed past. Penance—acknowledging one's sin and receiving divine absolution from the pastor or priest—is a practice inscribed on the very boundary between inclusion and exclusion. Without penance our sins exclude us from the community of reconciliation and turn us into strangers exiled from home. The Church can only function as a witness to God's eschatological hospitality if, in fact, the believers commit themselves to practices of conversion and penance. Forgiveness without penance means hospitality without boundaries and an invitation to the worst kind of violence: an invitation to Satan, sin, and death to take over the community of grace. It is by no means a contradiction in terms to speak of "penitential hospitality." Penitence is one means of guarding the hospitable character of the community of the Church.

Why is it that we have such difficulty acknowledging the beneficial and hospitable character of confession? Why is it that we tend to identify confession with legalistic Christianity, with authoritarian clergy, and with an anxious, fearful type of Christianity? I suspect that much of this stems from the psychologizing of the faith that characterizes so much of contemporary evangelicalism. In his monumental study *Sin and Confession on the Eve of the Reformation,* Thomas N. Tentler traces the medieval attempt to hold the twin aspects of consolation and discipline in a balance, despite the tension that existed between the two.[48] I am afraid that contemporary evangelicalism has decisively opted for the former at the cost of the latter. With Christian bookstores catering to the insatiable desire of the laity to be consoled, evangelical communities are becoming more and more concerned with pragmatic self-help strategies for people trying to cope in our late modern society.

The result of this overemphasis on consolation at the cost of discipline means that it has become difficult for evangelical churches to display any kind of real, alternative morality. The desire to uphold Christian standards of ethics is labeled as legalism or works righteousness, while immoral practices are defended as at least tolerable within the Church under the guise of Christ-like inclusivity. Discussing the rise of a therapeutic model in Western society, J. Daryl Charles comments: "In contrast to the traditional mode of morality, informed by Christian religion and expressed through varying degrees of self-restraint and self-accountability, the new model was permissive, allowing the self to be indulged. Whereas the religious person was born to be saved, the psychological person is born to be pleased. *How one feels,* not *what one believes,*

---

48. Thomas N. Tentler, *Sin and Confession on the Eve of the Reformation* (Princeton, N.J.: Princeton University Press, 1977).

was now understood to be the spiritual and ethical guide."[49] Charles is quite right. Consolation has trumped discipline; hospitality has been redefined as absolute hospitality. The result for evangelicalism is an inability to appreciate the value of confession and penance.

The situation hasn't always been such in the history of Protestantism. We have a tendency to assume that our negative attitudes toward confession in general—and to personal penance in particular—is part and parcel of what it means to be a Protestant. A careful reading of the Reformers, however, reveals a far more nuanced appreciation of the role of confession than is prevalent among evangelicals today. To be sure, the Reformers were united in their sharp criticism of the development of the doctrine of confession and especially of medieval scholastic approaches to the sacrament of penance. But their critique did not result in a wholesale rejection of the need for confession.[50] It is perhaps not very well known that Martin Luther believed that there were three rather than two sacraments. He continued to view penance as a sacrament, even though he did not think it originated in a command from the Lord himself.[51] In his Shorter Catechism (1529), Luther discussed the sacrament of penance between the sacraments of baptism and the Eucharist and described it as consisting of two parts: "one, that we confess our sins; the other, that we receive absolution or forgiveness from the father confessor, as from God himself, in no wise doubting, but firmly believing that our sins are thereby forgiven before God in heaven."[52] Melanchthon's *Apology of the Augsburg Confession* (1531) likewise referred to penance as a sacrament, indicating that "most people in our churches use the sacraments—absolution and the Lord's Supper—many times during the course of a year."[53]

John Calvin's discussion of penance leaves little doubt as to his dislike of the Catholic practice of auricular confession, "a thing so pestilent and in so many

---

49. J. Daryl Charles, *The Unformed Conscience of Evangelicalism: Recovering the Church's Moral Vision* (Downers Grove, Ill.: InterVarsity, 2002), 29. Charles's comments are part of a discussion of Philip Rieff, *The Triumph of the Therapeutic: Uses of Faith after Freud* (New York: Harper & Row, 1966).

50. Cf. Ronald K. Rittgers, "Private Confession and Religious Authority in Reformation Nürnberg," in *Penitence in the Age of the Reformations,* ed. Katharine Jackson Lualdi and Anne T. Thayer (Aldershot, UK: Ashgate, 2000), 49–55.

51. See Jean-Jacques von Allmen, "The Forgiveness of Sins as a Sacrament in the Reformed Tradition," in *Sacramental Reconciliation: Religion in the Seventies,* ed. Edward Schillebeeckx (New York: Herder & Herder, 1971), 113; Scott Hahn, *Lord, Have Mercy: The Healing Power of Confession* (New York: Doubleday, 2003), 168.

52. Philip Schaff, ed., *The Evangelical Protestant Creeds,* vol. 3 of *The Creeds of Christendom,* rev. David S. Schaff (1931; repr., Grand Rapids: Baker, 1983), 87. To be sure, Luther was not always consistent. Toward the end of *The Babylonian Captivity of the Church* (1520), he returns to his earlier discussion of the sacrament of penance and comments that it lacks a "divinely instituted visible sign," so that "strictly speaking" there are only two sacraments, baptism and the Eucharist (in *Luther's Works,* trans. A. T. W. Steinhäuser, ed. Helmut T. Lehmann [Philadelphia: Fortress, 1959], 36:124).

53. Robert Kolb and Timothy J. Wengert, eds., *The Book of Concord: The Confessions of the Evangelical Lutheran Church,* trans. Charles Arand et al. (Minneapolis: Fortress, 2000), 186.

ways harmful to the church."[54] But this does not allow us to view Calvin as a forerunner of contemporary evangelicalism, rejecting the importance of doing confession. Whereas the therapeutic mind-set of evangelicalism has elevated today's psychologist to the former position of the priest, Calvin argued that the duty of mutual admonition and rebuke "is especially enjoined upon ministers." He even goes so far as to suggest that "although all of us ought to console one another and confirm one another in assurance of divine mercy, we see that the ministers themselves have been ordained witnesses and sponsors of it to assure our consciences of forgiveness, to the extent that they are said to forgive sins and to loose souls."[55] When a person "lays open his heart's secret to his pastor, and from his pastor hears that message of the gospel specially directed to himself, 'Your sins are forgiven, take heart' [Matt. 9:2 p.], he will be reassured in mind and be set free from the anxiety that formerly tormented him."[56] Despite his grave objections to the Catholic sacrament of penance, Calvin would stand aghast at our inability to combine consolation and discipline by means of private confession.[57] The Reformers understood that consolation cannot function without discipline and that the practice of hospitality can only take root if we also exercise a concern for boundaries.

All of this is not to say that there are no continuities between the Reformation and contemporary evangelicalism. The Reformers were concerned to alleviate the uncertainty and fear of the laity that they felt the medieval scholastics had introduced. The scholastics' demand for full contrition or repentance prior to penance and their insistence on punishment (or satisfaction) following the confession seemed to the Reformers to deprive the faithful of hope and assurance. How could one know whether one's repentance and confession was complete? And how could one ever satisfy God by completing the acts of penance imposed by one's priest?[58] Indeed, the very idea that human beings would have to undergo punishment and make satisfaction seemed to the Reformers to endanger God's free gift of grace and the unique role of Christ's satisfaction.[59] The *sola fide* of the Reformation was at stake in the doctrine of penance.

54. John Calvin, *Institutes of the Christian Religion,* trans. Ford Lewis Battles, ed. John T. McNeill, 2 vols. (Philadelphia: Westminster, 1960), III.iv.19.

55. Ibid., III.iv.12.

56. Ibid., III.iv.14.

57. Of course, many of our evangelical churches have done away not only with private or secret penance but also with communal liturgical confession, thus eliminating confession almost entirely from the life of the Church.

58. Ibid., III.iv.2, 17–18, 27. Cf. Steven E. Ozment, *The Reformation in the Cities: The Appeal of Protestantism in Sixteenth-Century Germany and Switzerland* (New Haven, Conn.: Yale University Press, 1975), 52; B. A. Gerrish, *Grace and Gratitude: The Eucharistic Theology of John Calvin* (Minneapolis: Fortress, 1993), 91–92.

59. Calvin, *Institutes,* III.iv.26. Cf. Thomas H. Groome's comment about the Reformers' desire to highlight the gratuity of God's grace: "This was much needed over against Catholic freneticism about performing

The Reformers lashed out particularly strongly against the compulsory character of auricular confession, something they viewed as a novelty introduced by Pope Innocent III at the Fourth Lateran Council (1215).[60] Although the sacrament of penance goes back to the early Church, and although various forms of it had been practiced throughout the history of the Church, the requirement of annual penance was not introduced until the thirteenth century. The Reformers' objection here went beyond the mere charge of novelty. What was at stake was the authority of the Church to impose requirements that went beyond the prescriptions of Scripture itself. For Calvin "it [was] not our task to bind with new bonds consciences that Christ most sternly forbids to enslave."[61] The liberty of the Christian needed to be protected, so Calvin thought, against illicit intrusions of the clergy. The authority of the clergy to pronounce absolution was strictly tied to the Word itself. The power of the keys to bind and to loose did not belong to the clergy in an absolute sense, apart from the gospel.[62] Calvin considered the idea of a priest forgiving someone's sins an "intolerable sacrilege, because there is no function more proper to God than the forgiveness of sins."[63] For the clergy to assume an authority that reached beyond the Word itself and to absolve sins, in the proper sense of the term, would be for them to assume the place of God himself.

The continuity between the sixteenth-century Reformers and contemporary evangelicalism is obvious. The Reformers' concern to protect the free grace of God (*sola fide*) and the freedom of the laity to be judged by the Word of God alone (*sola Scriptura*) are also hallmarks of evangelicalism. These underlying concerns lay at the heart of the Protestant objections to penance. I suggest, however, that our theological and pastoral context is quite different from that which the Reformers faced in the late Middle Ages. Our context is not one of theological scholasticism (with all its drawbacks) but one that has taken the Reformation principles of *sola fide* and *sola Scriptura* to extremes, so that an emphasis on morality and discipline are immediately viewed with suspicion. Ironically, the very pastoral concern of anxiety and fear that Calvin had about auricular confession as it functioned in the sixteenth century should lead to a reconsideration of the practice today. Evangelical consciences are often troubled by the heavy burden of unconfessed sins. Penance provides an opening to confess sin and to receive the forgiveness of God.

In a thought-provoking essay Barbara Brown Taylor likens the practice of penance to the concept of "restorative justice":

---

pious practices as if we need to earn salvation by our own efforts" (*What Makes Us Catholic: Eight Gifts for Life* [New York: HarperSanFrancisco, 2001], 57).

60. Calvin, *Institutes*, III.iv.7.

61. Ibid., III.iv.14. Speaking about Chrysostom, Calvin comments that "he dare not require as necessary what he understands never to have been prescribed by the Word of God" (III.iv.8).

62. Ibid., III.iv.14, 21–22.

63. Ibid., III.iv.24; cf. III.iv.15.

Just for a lark, imagine going to your pastor and confessing your rampant materialism, your devotion to things instead of people, and your isolation from the poor whom Jesus loved. Then imagine being forgiven and given your penance: to select five of your favorite things—including perhaps your Bose radio and your new Coach book bag—and to match them up with five people who you know would turn cartwheels to have them. Then on Saturday, put your lawn mower in your trunk, drive down to that transitional neighborhood where all the old people live and offer to mow lawns for free until dark. Discerning sinners will note that none of this is standard punishment. It is penance, which is not for the purpose of inflicting pain but for the much higher purpose of changing lives by restoring relationships.[64]

Penance, argues Taylor, is justice in the interest of restoring relationships. We usually associate restorative justice with a particular approach to criminal justice, not with the Church's role of offering forgiveness and restoration to the sinner. But Taylor is quite right to link the two. Just as we cannot do without the penal aspect in our judicial system, so it is wrong-headed to exclude the practice of confession and penance from the life of the Church. Confession and penance are not an unjust violent imposition on the conscience of the individual. Instead, they constitute one of the ways in which the Church safeguards and protects its character as a hospitable community.

Cruciform Hospitality: *Salvifici Doloris*

As a community of hospitality, the Church receives God's forgiveness and restoration through preaching as well as through baptism, Eucharist, and penance. The Church is in turn called upon to serve as God's messianic agent in this world. This means that the Church continues the suffering role of Christ. Jesus Christ, as we saw in chapter 7, took Israel's exilic curse on himself. As Israel's representative he suffered in the place of and on behalf of Israel and all humanity. Expelled from Jerusalem, Christ endured Israel's exile from the Promised Land and suffered Adam and Eve's expulsion from the garden. In this (all too brief) section I explore what it means for the Church to continue the suffering of Jesus Christ and so to be an agent of hospitality for the world.

The idea that suffering can be interpreted as sacrificial self-giving is not uncontested. Feminist and liberation theologians often prefer the element of protest to that of voluntary suffering. Darby Kathleen Ray, for example, objects

---

64. Barbara Brown Taylor, *Speaking of Sin: The Lost Language of Salvation* (Cambridge: Cowley, 2000), 93–94. R. A. Duff discusses punishment meted out by the state in terms of the religious practice of penance in *Trials and Punishments* (Cambridge: Cambridge University Press, 1986). Brenda M. Baker, however, is correct in pointing out the limitations of this analogy: penance is primarily concerned with the restoration of the offender, while criminal justice has the larger interests of the community at stake ("Penance as a Model for Punishment," *Social Theory and Practice* 18 [1992]: 322).

to traditional atonement theories because they perpetuate the evil of abuse in the lives of many people. "For me," says Ray, "the issue of atonement is the issue of confronting human evil."[65] Jon Sobrino, likewise, insists that "suffering in today's world means primarily the sufferings of the people who are being crucified, and the purpose of theology is to take these people down from the cross."[66] Prophetic protest holds out the hope of a transformation of suffering. Such protest challenges evil and hopes for a change in the miserable conditions of life. Protest, therefore, may seem a more suitable reaction to injustice than self-sacrificial suffering.

Confrontation and protest in the face of evil and suffering have much to be commended. Unjust situations are not to be blindly accepted; they need critical evaluation in the light of the gospel's demand for justice. It is the Church's task to be the Church for the poor. In the following discussion, therefore, my primary concern is not to object to theology's task of presenting a prophetic protest against the powers of evil.[67] Rather, I wish to question whether it is enough or even possible for the Church to raise its voice in protest without at the same time encountering the reality of cruciform suffering, which is the result of prophetic protest and, I argue, the Church's emphatic calling, to be embraced with joy and thanksgiving. Cruciform suffering, I believe, is one significant way in which God makes us share in Christ's redemptive mission for the sake of the world.

The boldness of this claim would be entirely unjustified were it not that the biblical witness presents similar and even more shocking statements about the importance and the value of suffering. "It makes me happy to be suffering for you now," comments St. Paul, "and in my own body to make up all the hardships that still have to be undergone by Christ for the sake of his body, the Church" (Col. 1:24). For a Protestant this passage presents a twofold challenge. First, the passage connects suffering and joy, raising suspicions like the ones expressed earlier in this chapter. St. Paul appears to be suggesting that suffering is not a universally negative experience, that it is possible somehow to rejoice in one's suffering. Does this not confirm the worst fears of those who see the cross as Christendom's primary instrument of violence? Doesn't it illustrate that the New Testament itself justifies the status quo of institutionalized violence? Second, the passage suggests that Christ's suffering is yet to be complemented by others. Something appears to be lacking in his sufferings. Doesn't this necessarily entail a devaluation of the unique and all-sufficient character of Christ's

65. Darby Kathleen Ray, *Deceiving the Devil: Atonement, Abuse, and Ransom* (Cleveland: Pilgrim, 1998), 6.

66. Jon Sobrino, *The Principle of Mercy: Taking the Crucified People from the Cross* (Maryknoll, N.Y.: Orbis, 1994), 29.

67. I defend the need for prophetic protest in chapter 10 (the section titled "Restorative Justice and the Hospitality of Forgiveness").

suffering? Does it not mean that we exalt human merit, in the sense that we earn our own salvation—even if it is by means of suffering?

It is one thing to maintain that Christ redeemed us *through* suffering *from* suffering; it is something else to argue that Christ redeemed us *through* suffering *for* suffering. The idea that we are redeemed for suffering does not sit well in our late-modern Western culture, which has little time for any sort of discomfort. I suspect that one of the main reasons is that by means of technological and economic progress we have been able to remove many of the physical discomforts of life. Assuming that we have taken the sting out of suffering, we are more impatient than ever when our comfortable lives are intruded on. In his analysis of the spirituality of the Gen X culture, Tom Beaudoin discusses what he calls the suffering of the Gen Xers. After rightly insisting that expressing a sense of suffering is different from whining, Beaudoin describes the suffering of our young people: "It is one thing to whine about not being able to pay for a new skateboard, bike, or car. It is entirely another to point out that Xers earn 20 percent less in real income than people our age a generation ago. . . . It is one thing to whine about political correctness on college campuses, and quite another to protest the average Xer's college debt, which reaches into tens of thousands of dollars, mortgaging our young adult years (even though many of us work part-time during college)."[68] I cannot help but think that this quotation illustrates an inability to distinguish between material discomfort and suffering. Does Beaudoin really mean to argue that the Gen Xers' decline in material prosperity constitutes suffering? Perhaps the experience of true suffering would open us up to the possibility that suffering may have redemptive value. Without such value we can only cry out for the resurrection, and even then we are left with the nagging question of how this suffering itself could possibly be justified.[69]

Traditional atonement theology has, of course, always insisted on the redemptive value of suffering. The basis for this lies not just in the Colossians passage but is found throughout the pages of Scripture. In many places St. Paul expresses his joy in the midst of suffering and boasts of it.[70] He is not engaged here in abstract, timeless meditations on the possibility of joining the two apparently contradictory notions of joy and suffering. His suffering went well beyond a 20 percent drop in income or a heavy college debt (cf. 2 Cor. 11:23–33). Indeed, by expressing his joy in suffering he is placing himself in

68. Tom Beaudoin, *Virtual Faith: The Irreverent Spiritual Quest of Generation X* (San Francisco: Jossey-Bass, 1998), 97.

69. To be sure, the resurrection is part of an overall Christian theodicy of suffering. As I have argued, it is in the light of the absolute hospitality of the resurrection that we find the justification for God's use of violence as an instrument of hospitality.

70. E.g., Rom. 5:3; 2 Cor. 1:5–7; 4:1–18; 7:4; 11:23–27; Gal. 6:17; 1 Thess. 1:6. Cf. James D. G. Dunn, *The Epistles to the Colossians and to Philemon: A Commentary on the Greek Text,* New International Greek Testament Commentary (Grand Rapids: Eerdmans; Carlisle, UK: Paternoster, 1996), 114.

the larger story of the suffering of the people of God. Circumstances in the centuries before the birth of Christ forced them to reflect on their suffering—in particular the suffering of continuous oppression and domination. How could it be that while being faithful to the Torah, they were nonetheless oppressed by powers hostile to the kingdom of God? Why did God not have mercy on his people?

In this situation the Jewish people developed a martyrdom theology.[71] Without necessarily seeking out suffering, they began to realize that through suffering they were obtaining a place in God's plan of redemption: "These then, having consecrated themselves for the sake of God, are now honored not only with this distinction but also by the fact that through them our enemies did not prevail against our nation, and the tyrant was punished and our land purified, since they became, as it were, a ransom for the sin of our nation. Through the blood of these righteous ones and through the propitiation of their death the divine providence rescued Israel, which had been shamefully treated" (4 Macc. 17:20–22).[72] The Jewish martyrs came to regard themselves not just as enduring foreign oppression by way of punishment from God or as suffering injustice inflicted on them by their enemies, but as participating in the redemption of God's people.[73]

Especially since Albert Schweitzer's 1906 publication on the historical Jesus, New Testament scholars have often pointed out the significance of this suffering of the "messianic woes" that are the birth pangs of the new age of the kingdom of God.[74] They constitute a time of concentrated, redemptive suffering of certain individuals on behalf of the entire nation and so give birth to the messianic age. Without this suffering the dawning of the new age would be impossible, because God would continue to be angry with his people. And so the martyrs prayed, "Be merciful to your people and let our punishment be a satisfaction on their behalf. Make my blood their purification and take my life as a ransom for theirs" (4 Macc. 6:27–29).

The early Jewish Christians interpreted Christ's messianic suffering in the light of this overall picture of the "messianic woes" that would introduce

---

71. Cf. John S. Pobee, *Persecution and Martyrdom in the Theology of Paul* (Sheffield: JSOT, 1985), 13–46.

72. Translations of 4 Maccabees are taken from James H. Charlesworth, ed., *The Old Testament Pseudepigrapha*, vol. 2 (Garden City, N.Y.: Doubleday, 1985).

73. For more extensive elaborations of this theme in intertestamental literature, see N. T. Wright, *The New Testament and the People of God*, vol. 1 of *Christian Origins and the Question of God* (Minneapolis: Fortress, 1992), 276–79; N. T. Wright, *Jesus and the Victory of God*, vol. 2 of *Christian Origins* (Minneapolis: Fortress, 1996), 577–84. Cf. Manfred T. Brauch, *Hard Sayings of Paul* (Downers Grove, Ill.: InterVarsity, 1989), 234–39; Leonardo Boff, *Passion of Christ, Passion of the World: The Facts, Their Interpretation, and Their Meaning Yesterday and Today*, trans. Robert R. Barr (Maryknoll, N.Y.: Orbis, 1987), 60, 75–78.

74. Albert Schweitzer, *The Quest for the Historical Jesus: A Critical Study of Its Progress from Reimarus to Wrede*, trans. W. Montgomery, 3rd ed. (London: Black, 1954), 385–86. Cf. Pobee, *Persecution*, 38–39; Wright, *Jesus*, 578.

the new age of the resurrection. The "hardships" of Christ, suggests Peter T. O'Brien, need to be understood against "the OT and Jewish background with its apocalyptic conception of the afflictions of the end time, the woes of the Messiah."[75] When St. Paul comments that he is happy to make up in his own body all the hardships that still have to be undergone by Christ, his joy stems not from the sufferings in themselves, but from the fact he is able to share in the messianic suffering of Christ. James D. G. Dunn rightly comments:

> The claim is not megalomaniac. . . . It is rather the most striking expression of a convic-tion which Paul seems to have had from the beginning of his apostolic ministry, namely that his mission was to fulfill or complete that of the Servant of Yahweh, that is, also of the suffering Servant of deutero-Isaiah. This underlines in turn the degree to which Paul understood his apostleship in eschatological terms as the last act on the stage of this world before (as we would say) the final curtain (particularly 1 Cor. 4:9). It was because Paul saw himself as a major actor in the final drama of God's reconciling purpose that he could also see his all too real sufferings as somehow bringing to completion what was still outstanding of the sufferings of Christ ("crucified with Christ") by which the world was redeemed and transformed.[76]

The Pauline notion of Christians being crucified with Christ is not an abstract theological idea but rather an expression of a historical reality of human suf-fering. The "hardships" of Christ speak of actual circumstances in which St. Paul experiences the physical, mental, and spiritual hardships of cruciformity. His life of hardship is being conformed to that of Christ.

In his book *Cruciformity: Paul's Narrative Spirituality of the Cross,* Michael J. Gorman insists that this pattern of cruciformity reaches beyond St. Paul to all Christian believers. The metanarrative of Pauline theology is "an ongoing pattern of living in Christ and of dying with him that produces a Christ-like (cruciform) person. Cruciform existence is what being Christ's servant, in-dwelling him and being indwelt by him, living with and for and 'according to' him, is all about, for individuals and communities."[77] For Gorman this implies that cruciform suffering is an integral part of the life of the Chris-tian community. This cruciformity is more than mere imitation of Christ: "Cruciformity misunderstood as the human imitation of Christ is indeed an impossibility. However, cruciformity is the initial and ongoing work of Christ himself—by his Spirit sent by God—who dwells within each believer and believing community, shaping them to carry on the story (Phil. 4:13)."[78] On this reading of St. Paul, the Church is the continuation of Christ's presence

---

75. Peter T. O'Brien, *Colossians, Philemon,* Word Biblical Commentary, 44 (Waco, Tex.: Word, 1982), 78.

76. Dunn, *Colossians, Philemon,* 116–17.

77. Michael J. Gorman, *Cruciformity: Paul's Narrative Spirituality of the Cross* (Grand Rapids: Eerdmans, 2001), 49.

78. Ibid., 400.

in the world. Because of the work of the Spirit in believers, their sufferings for the sake of the coming of the kingdom are in a real sense the sufferings of Christ himself.[79] This explains how St. Paul is able to say that it is Christ himself who still needs to undergo more sufferings. In the believers' sufferings Christ himself is suffering.

Viewed as a continuation of the very work of Christ himself, the suffering cruciformity of the Church is a sharing in all the characteristics of Christ's own suffering. The entire Christian community (not just Paul himself) shares in the "messianic woes" of Jesus. When Paul says that there are "things lacking" (*ta husterēmata*) in Christ's hardships, neither the unique character nor the sufficiency of Christ's passion is at stake. Instead, the apostle places his suffering (and that of the Christian community) in the light of the overall redemptive history. In this historical understanding Christ as representative takes on himself the suffering of Israel and through the suffering and pain of birth pangs brings about the age of the resurrection. Aware that the old age continues even though the new age has already come, St. Paul makes clear that the redemptive suffering on behalf of others cannot but continue until the birth of the new age has been completed. The gates of the kingdom open up through the suffering of Christ. This hospitable suffering continues in the suffering of the Church.

Pope John Paul II, himself no stranger to suffering, published an apostolic letter on redemptive suffering six weeks after meeting with his would-be assassin, Mehmet Ali Agca, two days after Christmas 1983.[80] The title of the apostolic letter, *Salvifici doloris* ("Of Salvific Suffering"), as well as its content, makes all the more sense in the light of the preceding discussion. In this letter the pope first argues that it is "[p]recisely *by means of his suffering*" that Christ must accomplish the work of salvation.[81] He then speaks of our suffering: "In bringing about the Redemption through suffering, Christ *has* also *raised human suffering to the level of the Redemption*. Thus each man, in his suffering, can also become a sharer in the redemptive suffering of Christ."[82] For the pontiff,

79. Dunn makes the point quite strongly in commenting on Gal. 2:19 and 6:14: "Paul did not think of the crucifixion with Christ as a once-for-all event of the past. Nor was he thinking in these passages of the believer as already taken down from the cross with Christ and risen with Christ. On the contrary, 'I have been crucified with Christ'; that is, I have been nailed to the cross with Christ, and am in that state still; *I am still hanging with Christ on that cross*" (James D. G. Dunn, *The Theology of Paul the Apostle* [Grand Rapids: Eerdmans, 1998], 485; italics in the original).

80. See George Weigel, *The Truth of Catholicism: Inside the Essential Teachings and Controversies of the Church Today* (New York: Perennial-HarperCollins, 2001), 115–17.

81. John Paul II, "Salvifici doloris" (apostolic letter, February 11, 1984; www.vatican.va/holy_father/ john_paul_ii/apost_letters/documents/hf_jp-ii_apl_11021984_salvifici-doloris_en.html; italics in the original), 16.

82. Ibid., 20; italics in the original. This theological insight has important implications for our understanding of moral issues, such as physician-assisted suicide. See J. Daryl Charles, "Protestant Reflections on Salvifici doloris," *National Catholic Bioethics Quarterly* 2 (2002): 211–20.

as for St. Paul, it is the unity between Christ and his Church that makes the Church share in the redemptive suffering of Jesus Christ.

It seems to me that the evangelical high regard for the authority of Scripture and the Catholic high regard for the place of the Church can meet in this notion of redemptive suffering. *Salvifici doloris* is a lengthy biblical exposition on the place of suffering in the Pauline letters and goes a long way to overcome Protestant fears that Catholics might underestimate the unique role of Christ and introduce works righteousness in its place. "The sufferings of Christ," comments John Paul, "created the good of the world's redemption. This good in itself is inexhaustible and infinite. No man can add anything to it."[83] At the same time, just as Paul shares in the messianic woes that bring about the fullness of the new age, so also Christian believers have a share in this redemptive work. After all, when Christians suffer, their suffering is not a suffering independent from that of Christ. Believers share in the very suffering of Christ. "[T]here is a sense," therefore, Dunn rightly comments, "in which Christ's passion is incomplete. . . . The transition from old age to new age is long-drawn-out and those in transit from one to the other are caught 'with Christ' in the overlap."[84] The work of atonement has its climactic and decisive moment in the crucifixion of Jesus Christ. He continues his work in the redemptive mission of the Church for the world.

The joy of suffering comes about at different levels. When faced with suffering, Christians rejoice at being counted worthy to share in Christ's hardship. They rejoice at the evidence of being united to Christ. More than anything, they rejoice in the opportunity to share in the hospitality of the kingdom that opens up through the suffering Christ, continued also in their lives.[85] In many ways suffering remains an enigma; there is no conclusive rational theodicy of suffering. There is nonetheless meaning in suffering, because it plays a role in the hospitality that God offers in Christ. Our suffering is not senseless; it is redemptive. The divine host himself makes it part of the suffering of Christ and so opens the gates of the kingdom for a suffering world.

83. John Paul II, "Salvifici doloris," 24.
84. Dunn, *Theology*, 486.
85. With these claims I in no way want to question the fact that individuals who are suffering need time and space to make these claims their own.

10

Public Justice and the Hospitality of Liberation

Justice as a Public Category

The idea that the Christian faith might contribute to a more peaceful or hospitable society is by no means universally acknowledged. Christianity is often seen as a source of violence rather than as a contributor to public justice. It is fairly commonplace to argue that the more passionate people are about their Christian commitments, the more likely they are to resort to violence.[1] The history of Christianity, promoters of this view argue, contains numerous examples of Christians taking up arms to defend and promote their faith—witness the numerous witch hunts and pogroms, the Crusades, the Spanish Inquisition, and the conquest of the Americas. The outcome of the Christian faith in all these cases appears to be injustice rather than justice. Even many of those who wish to defend Christianity against the charge of violence often tend to agree that at least since Constantinianism turned the Church into the chaplain for the state, the gospel of hospitality has been compromised, and Christianity has become an agent of violence.[2] And as conflicts reemerge all across the globe

1. See, for example, Mark Juergensmeyer, *Terror in the Mind of God: The Global Rise of Religious Violence* (Berkeley: University of California Press, 2000). Juergensmeyer's thesis concerns religion in general, not just Christianity.

2. For the imagery of the Church as the state's chaplain, see Rodney Clapp, *A Peculiar People: The Church as Culture in a Post-Christian Society* (Downers Grove, Ill.: InterVarsity, 1996), 16–18.

235

between Islamic and Christian (or, perhaps, Western) values, the question of the relationship between violence and religion becomes ever more pressing.[3] Should Christians let go of some of their passion about their faith commitments in order to alleviate concerns about possible violence? Should they abandon the public beyond the Church? Jacques Derrida, we saw in chapter 1, asks us to replace the particularities of the messianic religions with an indeterminate messianicity, not polluted by the stains of the violence of the historic manifestations of messianism, witnessed most poignantly in the war for the "appropriation of Jerusalem."[4] The only way to ensure absolute hospitality (if there is such a thing for Derrida) would be to replace the actual messianisms of the monotheistic religions, including Christianity, with a structural messianicity from which the actual contents of the faith have been removed.

In actual fact, of course, Derrida's "indeterminate messianism" isn't as radical and indeterminate as he makes it out to be. His insistence on equality, justice, and democracy are more than just a faint echo of the liberal democracy that is spreading throughout the world and demanding that the world religions leave behind the violence of their fundamentalist fringes. Liberal democracy, it could be argued, is quite capable of encapsulating or domesticating the apparently radical message of postmodernism. The United States' grip on Afghanistan and the Middle East (through the recent invasion of Iraq) seems like a belated validation of Francis Fukuyama's "end of history."[5] We cannot help but wonder: Will we end up with a worldwide liberal democratic society, after all, as the way to deal with issues of religion-induced violence? And, perhaps more importantly, how do Christians, who learn their practices of hospitality at the foot of the cross, react to the hegemony of liberal democracy?

The plea for liberal democracy as the option guaranteeing a reliable roadmap to peace, hospitality, and the end of history is not new. The seventeenth-century wars of religion between Catholics and Protestants were a small-scale European version of the interreligious conflicts that we witness today, and fears of those earlier wars of religion resulted in ideological attempts to stifle disagreement that are not dissimilar to what we are witnessing in liberal democracy's ascent to power. The 1648 Peace of Westphalia may serve as a symbol for the rationalist foundationalism that attempted to establish peace by looking for a common religious foundation to overcome the divisions of revealed religions. This foundationalism, wedded to the idea of "common notions" (*notitiae communes*) as the eighteenth-century version of an empty "messianicity," still

3. For the growing confrontation between Islamic and Christian values, see Samuel P. Huntington, *The Clash of Civilizations and the Remaking of World Order* (New York: Simon & Schuster, 1997); Philip Jenkins, *The Next Christendom: The Coming of Global Christianity* (Oxford: Oxford University Press, 2002).

4. Jacques Derrida, *Specters of Marx: The State of the Debt, the Work of Mourning, and the New International*, trans. Peggy Kamuf (New York: Routledge, 1994), 58.

5. Francis Fukuyama, "The End of History?" *The National Interest* 16 (summer 1989): 3–18; and the author's elaboration in *The End of History and the Last Man* (New York: Free-Macmillan, 1992).

insisted on retaining some kind of natural religion.[6] But the retreat to "common notions" proved unable to stem the tide of a more far-reaching naturalism and materialism that rejected altogether the idea that hospitality in the natural world depended ultimately on eternal or supernatural hospitality.

The effects of this secularism would be far reaching. Attempts to sustain hospitality now came to rely entirely on the goodwill of human beings, who no longer had a teleological transcendent horizon giving concrete shape to their practices of hospitality.[7] The loss of a common teleological horizon has resulted in a normative pluralism that relies on the empty messianicity of what Richard J. Neuhaus has termed "the naked public square."[8] And although both modern and postmodern accounts stem from a laudable desire for peace, it is not at all clear that attempts to reduce the world religions to their lowest common denominators, such as equality, democracy, and justice, will be successful in keeping violence at bay. Friedrich Nietzsche was keenly aware that the only way to oppose the Christian faith was by unmasking it as a hidden will to power and to counter it in the name of power.[9] The utter indeterminacy of the naked public square stands as an open invitation to anybody's will to power to assert itself and give shape to society.[10] Absolute hospitality not only makes it possible for the devil to come in (Derrida); it makes his arrival unavoidable. An ontology of violence is the natural outcome of the public foreclosing of the telos of eschatological hospitality that sustained the Christian vision throughout the Middle Ages and the time of the Reformation.

Some readers may feel that in this book I myself have fallen prey to an ontology of violence. I have started off by granting Levinas and Derrida that all our practices of hospitality necessarily have a violent edge. Absolute hospitality (hospitality without violence), I have argued, remains an eschatological horizon that should influence our ethical decisions today but must be tempered by the wisdom of erecting and enforcing boundaries. Boundaries are notoriously violent places, and many Christians, especially those within so-called peace traditions, will likely be disillusioned by my unwillingness to assert the desirability of unconditional or absolute hospitality in our world today. But my

6. Already in 1624, in *De veritate,* Lord Herbert of Cherbury insisted on five universally held "common notions" that served as the interpretive key to which revealed religions had to conform: (1) there exists one supreme God; (2) this God is chiefly to be worshipped; (3) the principal part of this worship consists in piety and virtue; (4) we must repent of our sins, and if we do, God will pardon us; and (5) there are rewards for good people and punishments for evil people both here and hereafter (James C. Livingston, *Modern Christian Thought,* vol. 1, 2nd ed. [Upper Saddle River, N.J.: Prentice Hall, 1997], 16).

7. I criticize Derrida's loss of transcendence (in the traditional theistic sense) in "Irenaeus, Derrida, and Hospitality: On the Eschatological Overcoming of Violence," *Modern Theology* 19 (2003): 163–80.

8. Richard John Neuhaus, *The Naked Public Square: Religion and Democracy in America* (Grand Rapids: Eerdmans, 1984).

9. Friedrich Nietzsche, *Thus Spoke Zarathustra: A Book for All and None,* trans. Walter Kaufmann (New York: Viking, 1966), 113–16.

10. Cf. Neuhaus, *Naked Public Square,* 78–93.

insistence on "good violence" does not imply a Derridean ontology of violence. To the contrary, my argument throughout this book has been that the cross is a supreme instance of divine hospitality despite God's involvement with violence. I have argued that it is only for the sake of the telos of eschatological hospitality that some degree of violence is necessary and justifiable. In other words, I have argued that the necessity of violence does not result from an ontology of violence but is entirely dependent on the Christian vision of the coming of the fullness of the *civitas Dei,* the city of God.

The Church is, of course, the public locale in and through which God extends his hospitality most directly. As the previous chapter makes clear, the Church as a place of hospitality is a testimony to the fullness of God's coming reign. As such, the Church, with its public proclamation of the gospel, is the primary space where we witness the public face of hospitality. The expression "public justice" in the title of the present chapter does not mean to convey, therefore, a false dualism between the private character of the Church and the public character of, say, the state or the economic realm; the Church is the primary public space in which divine hospitality and justice are pursued. In this final chapter, however, I want to move beyond the Church and ask whether public justice can be pursued also beyond the boundaries of the Church in other public spaces and whether this can be viewed as an extension of divine hospitality in the interest of the eternal kingdom of peace.[11] More specifically, I ask the question, Can we look to the cross as providing an impetus for public justice that reaches beyond the boundaries of the Church into the political, social, and economic arenas? By answering this question in the affirmative, I am putting myself on a collision course with those who are satisfied with an indeterminate structural religiosity and am asking modern theology to abandon its fatal disease of false humility.[12] Throughout the Middle Ages and the Reformation period, theology connected public justice to the vision of the eschatological kingdom of peace. To abandon this connection for the sake of a "neutral" democratic pluralism would mean to allow a rival ontology to take control

11. Reinhard Hütter strikes just the right balance. On the one hand, he insists strongly on the Church as public ("The Church as Public: Dogma, Practice, and the Holy Spirit," *Pro Ecclesia* 3 [1994]: 334–61; *Suffering Divine Things: Theology as Church Practice,* trans. Doug Stott [Grand Rapids: Eerdmans, 2000], 158–71). On the other hand, he recognizes the existence of a "multiplicity of different publics" (*Suffering Divine Things,* 159). From a Christian perspective, the different publics must all be oriented toward the telos of absolute eschatological hospitality. This will cause tensions when some publics refuse to accept this telos. This does not, however, turn the Church into a "contrast community": "That under certain circumstances the church as public can indeed or even must assume the form of a 'contrast community' is a question of ecclesial *judgment,* that is, an answer—to be determined in each given case—to the question of how under changing circumstances the church can itself remain a public" (ibid., 171).

12. The terminology is from John Milbank, who rightly insists on a central place for theology (*Theology and Social Theory: Beyond Secular Reason* [Oxford: Blackwell, 1993], 1).

and to ignore that all public spaces ought to submit to the telos of God's eschatological hospitality.

At the same time, I have quite deliberately not included this discussion in the previous chapter on the Church. Even though I believe that the loss of the centrality of theology and the visible Church has done untold damage to social and political developments in the Western world, I am convinced that Augustine and Aquinas were essentially right in giving a distinct place to the *civitas terrena*.[13] The implementation, however provisionally, of peace and justice beyond the boundaries of the Church seems to me a laudable endeavor. I do not mean to suggest that it is possible to attain the ultimate telos of eschatological hospitality through economic, social, and political means. Nor am I tempted by the modern assertion of the irrelevance of theology and the Church in proffering implications of the vision of unconditional hospitality for public justice in the earthly city. I do, however, insist both that it is immoral to leave the realms of civil government and economics to the nonecclesial society and that it is supercilious to claim that the Church is the true polis and the only place in which God's hospitality and justice have any impact at all. A Christian perspective will recognize that Christ's work of recapitulation has implications also for justice in the other public realities, beyond the boundaries of the Church.

By making the hospitality of public justice the focus of this last chapter, I may seem to make a connection particularly with the penal representative view of the atonement. It is the Calvinist model that has traditionally insisted most strongly that the atonement needs to be viewed from a judicial angle and that the cross satisfies the justice of God. And indeed, legal categories do have a place both in atonement theology and in a proper view of public justice. But just as penal elements do not have the final say with regard to the atonement, so also public justice cannot rely on legal categories alone. The dangers of juridicizing, individualizing, and de-historicizing that I discussed in chapter 7 are real also in the area of public justice. Calvinist attempts to set up a social, political, and economic order do not have an overly positive track record, and I believe this is related to the limitations that Reformed theologies of the atonement place on divine hospitality.[14] Public justice needs to connect not just with a penal representative view of the atonement but also needs to look for implications of the moral-influence and Christus Victor views of the atonement.

In an attempt to come to a positive view of justice as a public category, I will discuss some of the implications of redemption as liberation from bondage. In

13. Readers of John Milbank will notice my not too subtle criticism of his attempt to go back beyond Augustine and especially Aquinas to a patristic view of the Church as the only true polis (*Theology and Social Theory*, 398–422).

14. John Calvin's Geneva, Oliver Cromwell's England, and Hendrik Verwoerd's South Africa all suffered the effects of a theology that in many respects was less than hospitable.

other words, my focus is especially (though not exclusively) on the Christus Victor theme. Most of my exposition takes the shape of an extended interaction with Radical Orthodoxy and its analysis of liberation theology. I adopt what I regard as some of Radical Orthodoxy's positive features—notably its high regard for theology and its recognition of the importance of the Church for the development of public justice. That being said, I want to guard against an ecclesiology that refuses to recognize the boundaries of the Church and the distinct place of other public spheres. I argue that liberation theology, despite some of its problematic elements, has fulfilled a prophetic role both internally in the Church and externally toward the social, economic, and political order. By connecting public justice with elements of the moral-influence and Christus Victor theories of the atonement, I demonstrate that theology makes a contribution to the political, social, and economic realms and that this public justice, pursued with a view to the telos of God's eschatological hospitality, is a liberating category.

Radical Orthodoxy and the Hospitality of Public Justice

The recent movement of Radical Orthodoxy has made a plea for an ontology of peace. John Milbank, the most prominent spokesperson of this group, argues for a "participationist" account of reality that strongly emphasizes our human participation in the eternal life of the Triune God as the way to achieve both harmonious difference and a common purpose.[15] Milbank insists that the only way to offer hope of peaceful coexistence is to regain the vision of the *civitas Dei* as the eternal city of peace that guides our actions today. Milbank's vision is by no means inhibited or shy. He refuses to settle for the naked public square of liberal democracy and unmasks the totalizing violence that threatens contemporary politics. Faced with the dual loss of the supernatural and of metanarratives, contemporary politics has come to rely on power and violence as ultimate categories. Milbank wants to counter this postmodern nihilism with an alternative Christian vision. Unabashedly reaffirming theology as the queen of the sciences, he insists: "Theology purports to give an ultimate narrative, to provide some ultimate depth of description, because the situation of oneself within such a continuing narrative is what it means to belong to the Church, to be a Christian. However, the claim is made by faith, not a reason which seeks foundations. Surrendering this gaze to the various gazes of 'methodological atheism' would not prove to be any temporary submission."[16] Milbank makes a case for the role of theology and of the Church in providing

---

15. Cf. R. R. Reno, "The Radical Orthodoxy Project," in *In the Ruins of the Church: Sustaining Faith in an Age of Diminished Christianity* (Grand Rapids: Brazos, 2002), 68–72.

16. Milbank, *Theology and Social Theory,* 249.

the true metanarrative. In today's postmodern climate, this is nothing short of revolutionary. Milbank wants to take us beyond secular reason toward an overarching ontology of peace capable of sustaining our society. As such, it is a remarkably bold attempt to present the Christian faith as the true divine warrant for hospitality in a violent society.

There is much in Milbank's brilliant account that has my warm endorsement. Here is an unapologetic defense of the Christian narrative as the one story that is able to deconstruct postmodern nihilism and to present a viable alternative. Radical Orthodoxy offers renewed hope for the future of theological studies and, indeed, for the future of the Church. What is more, as an alternative, Radical Orthodoxy avoids the rationalist foundationalism that has bedeviled so much theology in its shameless capitulation to the naturalist assumptions of the modern era. It seems to me, therefore, that we need to enter into a dialogue with Radical Orthodoxy as it attempts to provide an ontology of peace that clearly derives from the Christian tradition. Radical Orthodoxy is radical at least in the sense that it locates resources in the Christian tradition that can draw us to the eternal and absolute hospitality of God.

This is not to say that I endorse the Radical Orthodoxy project without reservations. I want to make two critical observations, one with regard to the understanding of violence and one with regard to the role of the Church. First, by radically opposing the Church as the community of peace to the state as the realm of violence, Milbank depreciates both the pervasive character of violence and the positive role that it can play. In many ways, his view is similar to the pacifist tradition of John Howard Yoder and Stanley Hauerwas. All these accounts rely on a vision of the Church as the alternative political community. Also the concern for peace and nonviolence is something that Milbank shares with the "peace tradition." Milbank sees Jesus as the embodiment of God's participatory peace. Jesus teaches a new way of life founded on "non-rivalry, non-retaliation and mutual sharing."[17] It is Jesus' nonviolent practice of forgiveness that the Church continues in her life. The Church repeats and continues the narration of Jesus' "utter refusal of selfish power."[18] The Church, therefore, is a community of forgiveness that gives shape to the eschatological peace that characterizes the divine life. This implies that violence, for Milbank, is inherently problematic. He insists that "all violence is evil"[19] and that peace, as a transcendental, is opposed by violence as an "anti-transcendental."[20] Accordingly, Milbank criticizes Augustine for asserting the possibility of a "legitimate, non-sinful, 'pedagogic' coercion . . . because it makes some punishment positive

17. John Milbank, *The Word Made Strange: Theology, Language, Culture* (Cambridge, Mass.: Blackwell, 1997), 146.

18. Ibid., 153.

19. John Milbank, *Being Reconciled: Ontology and Pardon* (London: Routledge, 2003), 26.

20. Ibid., 28.

and ascribes to it the action of divine will."[21] For Milbank all talk about God punishing, and hence all talk of divine violence, is deeply problematic.

It would seem, then, that Milbank fits squarely in the Yoder-Hauerwas tradition. But this would be a mistaken conclusion. In a recent essay Hauerwas jokingly comments that "in another time Milbank might make the case why my kind should be burned at the stake."[22] Jokes aside, Milbank does indeed make the case that coercive power may justifiably be used in the interest of peace. It is simply that he is hesitant to apply the term "violence" to such coercive power. How do we judge whether to call a particular act violent? Milbank suggests that "violence is never simply *evident,* because we have to *judge* whether a substantive good has been impaired. . . . Much apparent violence may be exonerated, while much occulted violence must be disinterred."[23] Violence in the name of a "substantive *telos*" may well be justified, argues Milbank. "Thus in certain circumstances, the young, the deluded, those relatively lacking in vision require to be coerced as gently as possible."[24]

Milbank clearly doesn't like to refer to necessary coercive power as violence. Still, on occasion he does exactly that. He insists that we should not patronize our Christian ancestors by apologizing on their behalf, because "we cannot as human beings suppose that violence is entirely unavoidable, in so far as it runs the educative risks of redemption."[25] Milbank puts it unequivocally: "We *should* defend—even sometimes with violence—what we believe in."[26] And he ends up sharply criticizing the pacifist position: by gazing at violence the pacifist cannot avoid the "trace of the non-intervening *voyeur,*" and by averting the gaze the pacifist demonstrates "signifiers of indifference or embarrassment."[27]

Milbank's tiptoeing around the question of whether or not necessary coercive power is actually violence stems from a broader tension in his thinking. Lucy Gardner says:

---

21. Milbank, *Theology and Social Theory,* 419–20. Milbank has since moderated his criticism of Augustine by commenting: "I think now even more strongly that he [i.e., Augustine] was right to see [the use of force] as inescapable. You can tell that I have had children since I wrote *Theology and Social Theory*" ("Testing Pacifism: Questions for John Milbank," in *Must Christianity Be Violent? Reflections on History, Practice, and Theology,* ed. Kenneth R. Chase and Alan Jacobs [Grand Rapids: Brazos, 2003], 204).

22. Stanley Hauerwas, "Explaining Christian Nonviolence: Notes for a Conversation with John Milbank," in *Must Christianity Be Violent? Reflections on History, Practice, and Theology,* ed. Kenneth R. Chase and Alan Jacobs (Grand Rapids: Brazos, 2003), 173.

23. Milbank, *Being Reconciled,* 28; italics in the original. Cf. ibid., 80: "[T]here is violence in one case and peace in another in relation to the justice of the ends pursued—*not* as extrinsic means, but as embryonic ends (this has nothing to do with ends justifying means). But this is the point: claims to see violence are always diagnostic, in relation to accounts of the political, collective Good" (italics in the original).

24. Milbank, *Being Reconciled,* 38; cf. Milbank, *Theology and Social Theory,* 418.

25. Milbank, *Being Reconciled,* 38.

26. Ibid., 39; italics in the original.

27. Ibid., 29.

> Put bluntly, the problem is this: at the heart of Radical Orthodoxy I find a call for
> non-oppositional opposition, or, more properly speaking, an undoing of opposition
> in a non-oppositional way. . . . At the same time, however, Radical Orthodoxy exhibits
> the rhetoric and the exercise of a very powerful *oppositional* opposition, which talks of
> this undoing not only, as one would expect, in terms of a refusal of the oppositions of
> secularised discourse (including most modern theology), but also in terms of an efface-
> ment and a blurring of those oppositions.[28]

Milbank cannot have it both ways. He cannot have both participation in the
nonviolent practice of Jesus' forgiveness *and* the requirement of tragic violence
to attain the telos of the peaceful *civitas Dei*. He needs to give up either his
opposition to divine violence or his opposition to pacifism. One cannot both
disapprove and approve of violence at the same time.

I suspect that Milbank would defend his rejection of pacifism and his defense of violence by saying not that violence can be a good thing or by saying
that it can be redemptive (which is the line I have taken in this book), but by
insisting that the necessity of violence is simply a *tragic* necessity.[29] But this
runs into insuperable problems in connection with the obvious presence of
divine violence in the biblical account, as well as in the traditional theories of
the atonement. It seems to me, therefore, that Milbank's critique of Augustine's
nonsinful violence is an unfortunate inconsistency in his otherwise lucid and
helpful critique of pacifism. Milbank's exposition would gain in consistency
if he were to recognize the pervasive character of violence and were to state
unequivocally that violence can be positive or negative depending on its relationship to the telos of absolute eschatological hospitality.[30]

Second, Radical Orthodoxy, in its attempt to reassert the central place of
the Church, confuses the *centrality* of the Church (a helpful category) with the
monopoly of the Church (a far less innocuous idea). In the previous chapter I
discussed the Church as the community of hospitality. Certainly, for Milbank the
Church functions as the hospitable community. It is not clear to me, however,
that he makes room for anything *beyond* the Church. In other words, I'm not
convinced that Milbank's theology truly allows for the type of discussion on
which I am embarking in this chapter, a discussion of the hospitality of public
justice beyond the Church. Justice, for Milbank, is always necessarily *ecclesial*

---

28. Lucy Gardner, "Listening at the Threshold: Christology and the 'Suspension of the Material,'" in *Radi-cal Orthodoxy: A Catholic Enquiry*, ed. Laurence Paul Hemming (Aldershot, UK: Ashgate, 2000), 127–28.

29. Cf. Milbank's comment: "A measure of resignation to the necessity of this *dominium* can also not
be avoided. But with, and beyond Augustine, we should recognize the tragic character of this resignation"
(*Theology and Social Theory*, 422).

30. For a more elaborate critique, see Hans Boersma, "Being Reconciled: Cultural-Ecclesial Practice
as Atonement in Radical Orthodoxy," in *Creation, Covenant, and Participation: Radical Orthodoxy and the
Reformed Tradition*, ed. James H. Olthuis and James K. A. Smith (Grand Rapids: Baker, forthcoming).

justice. He insists, after all, that the Church is the true polis, the alternative city, of which the state is but the false parody:

> Whereas the *civitas terrena* inherits its power from the conqueror of a fraternal rival, the "city of God on pilgrimage through this world" founds itself not in a succession of power, but upon the memory of the murdered brother, Abel slain by Cain. The city of God is in fact a paradox, "a nomad city" (one might say) for it does not have a site, or walls or gates. It is not, like Rome, an *asylum* constituted by the "protection" offered by a dominating class over a dominated, in the face of the external enemy. This form of refuge is, in fact, but a dim archetype of the real refuge provided by the Church, which is the forgiveness of sins.[31]

In Milbank's vision the Church as "a nomad city" monopolizes the practice of hospitality—an apparently absolute hospitality that knows no "site, or walls or gates." It will be clear from the previous chapter that I am not convinced any such nonlocality without boundaries is either possible or desirable this side of the eschaton. What is more, by restricting hospitality to the Church, Milbank effectively reduces everything in the *civitas terrena* to the rule of arbitrary power and violence. "The realm of the merely practical, cut off from the ecclesial, is quite simply a realm of sin," insists Milbank. This is true insofar as the Church is central and has something to say about the realm of the practical. But he then goes on to argue: "In fact the only thing that *can* place it [i.e., the merely practical realm] outside the Church, or the true commonwealth, is the use of a coercive force that is inherently arbitrary or excessive."[32] Here Milbank goes beyond simply maintaining a close connection between the Church and other publics. Here the Church becomes the *only* locale of true politics. And indeed, he insists that "[a]ll 'political' theory, in the antique sense, is relocated by Christianity as thought about the Church."[33] Nicholas Lash rightly comments that throughout Milbank's book runs a "strand according to which the citizens of God's new *civitas* have simply left the world of politics behind them, and must refuse to be drawn back into its compromises and entanglements."[34]

The result of Milbank's sharp division between the polis as the realm of power and violence and the Church as the realm of justice and peace implies an inherently negative evaluation of any sort of politics beyond the Church. Nothing just or peaceful can be found outside the Church, which as a result becomes an unavoidably pretentious institution.[35] And while nothing good can be found

---

31. Ibid., 392; italics in the original.
32. Ibid., 406; italics in the original.
33. Ibid.
34. Nicholas Lash, "Not Exactly Politics or Power?" *Modern Theology* 8 (1992): 362.
35. I am borrowing from Miroslav Volf in his debate with Daniel M. Bell, another proponent of Radical Orthodoxy: "Above all, I am contesting Bell's awfully pretentious church: it threatens to make God dispensable because it has inserted God into the workings of its own 'technology' and it wants to abolish everything (society, state, and economy) but itself to the extent that it sees itself as a full-fledged 'social, political, and

outside the Church, the Church itself becomes the city in which all true politics is practiced. But if there is no politics outside the Church, then Church and kingdom are, for all intents and purposes, equated. Milbank fails to appreciate that the absolute hospitality of the kingdom is an eschatological reality that we are still anticipating in its fullness and of which the Church is merely an advance outpost.[36] Milbank wants to retain a vision of social justice. He does not believe, however, that this justice can ever be a public justice that extends beyond the Church. By contrast, in the remainder of this chapter I outline how the (atonement) theology of the Church influences a vision of public justice as freedom and restoration also beyond the boundaries of the Church.

Public Justice and a Theology of Liberation: Hospitality and Freedom

The aim of liberation theology, which arose in the 1960s in reaction to the oppression of the poor in Latin America, is aptly summarized by the words of one of its prominent spokespersons, Ignacio Ellacuría: we must take the crucified people down from the cross.[37] Behind this intent lie a number of unspoken assumptions about the place of theology, the nature of the atonement, and the role of justice, which I want to explore in some detail. This discussion is necessarily limited. I cannot give any sort of complete description or analysis of liberation theology here. And by restricting myself to liberation theology, I certainly do not mean to limit the relevance of atonement theology in the public sphere to questions of liberation alone. But I concentrate on the relationship between liberation and public justice because it puts into sharp focus the question of theology's contribution of justice and hospitality in the various public spaces against the backdrop of the telos of God's eschatological hospitality.

Theology, for liberationists, bases itself directly on the praxis of the faith community. Gustavo Gutiérrez's groundbreaking 1973 publication, *A Theology of Liberation,* defines theology as an activity that in the light of God's Word takes its starting point in a critical attitude toward economic and sociocultural issues in the life of the Church.[38] Theology, in other words, is concerned with

---

economic formation in its own right'" ("Against a Pretentious Church: A Rejoinder to Bell's Response," *Modern Theology* 19 [2003]: 284–85).

36. Cf. Mark C. Mattes: "Milbank seems too quick to deny God's work at all in the 'city of man', despite the fact that people can be vehicles of God's creative and healing work whether they have allegiance to God or not. In so doing, he inflates the concept of the church, such that one almost thinks that it is no longer a 'creature of the word', a vessel of the divine that is hidden from the world, but as somehow the kingdom already come or coming in its fullness" ("A Lutheran Assessment of 'Radical Orthodoxy,'" *Lutheran Quarterly* 15 [2001]: 363).

37. Cf. Jon Sobrino, *The Principle of Mercy: Taking the Crucified People from the Cross* (Maryknoll, N.Y.: Orbis, 1994).

38. Gustavo Gutiérrez, *A Theology of Liberation: History, Politics, and Salvation,* trans. and ed. Caridad Inda and John Eagleson (Maryknoll, N.Y.: Orbis, 1973), 11.

issues of hospitality and justice in society.[39] The coming kingdom of God is, like none other, a kingdom of justice and hospitality. God's eschatological or unconditional hospitality contains none of the elements of injustice that still pertain to today's legal constructs and judicial pronouncements. Of course, when we try to uphold justice in our everyday affairs, we face the question, Is there a relationship between this public justice and God's eternal perfect eschatological justice? Or are liberationists merely pursuing a futile dream? Should they keep their dreams to the Church, where theology can ponder abstract questions about the relationship between God's justice in Jesus Christ and the eternal justice that is to come? Should the Church be the only place where justice is at all relevant? Certainly, this option is tempting. The conditions under which we labor to implement social and economic justice today are less than favorable, and to assume an eschatological horizon behind our efforts at public justice may seem as if we were out of touch with reality.

The liberationists' vision of public justice arose in reaction to Jacques Maritain's political theory of the New Christendom in the 1920s and 1930s. The old Constantinian Christendom had envisioned a close relationship between Church and state, and at the very least both were supposed to act in the interests of eschatological hospitality. Maritain's New Christendom wanted to give greater autonomy to the temporal sphere of the *civitas terrena*. No longer was the Church supposed to uphold and defend a Christian civil order. Maritain asked the Church to acknowledge the changes of modernity, to take a step back, and to recognize the existence of two planes: both the spiritual and the temporal. Daniel M. Bell aptly summarizes Maritain's approach when he comments that "the New Christendom model accords the temporal end a legitimacy or validity that precludes its instrumental use. In other words, the ends of the temporal order, namely the earthly and perishable goods of our life here below, are no longer simply to be dismissed out of hand by the spiritual."[40] Maritain was intent on giving natural or temporal ends their own significance. Building on Thomas Aquinas, the New Christendom meant a reassertion of the relative independence of the natural vis-à-vis the supernatural.

---

39. The prominent place of the historical socioeconomic and political context, particularly as this context has tended to be interpreted by means of Marxist categories, has naturally raised questions of priority in terms of the relationship between revelation and historical context. While I am sympathetic to these concerns, liberationists have rightly reminded us of the impact that the Christian faith ought to have on the social and economic spheres. See further Miroslav Volf, "Doing and Interpreting: An Examination of the Relationship between Theory and Practice in Latin American Liberation Theology," *Themelios* 8 (3) (April 1983): 11–19; Stanley J. Grenz and Roger E. Olson, *Twentieth-Century Theology: God and the World in a Transitional Age* (Downers Grove, Ill.: InterVarsity, 1992), 222–24. Cf. Christian Smith, *The Emergence of Liberation Theology: Radical Religion and Social Movement Theory* (Chicago: University of Chicago Press, 1991), 27–31.

40. Daniel M. Bell, *Liberation Theology after the End of History: The Refusal to Cease Suffering* (London: Routledge, 2001), 48.

Maritain's vision was hugely influential, both in continental Europe and in Central America. He initiated a progressive movement that wanted to enable the laity of the Church to speak out and to act on social and political issues. With religion and politics separated into two distinct spheres, lay people could now organize themselves in Catholic Action cells that would be directly involved in practical matters of social and political significance. The Church's effect on politics thus became indirect, limited to its religious and moral teaching of the laity. In the 1931 encyclical, *Quadragesimo anno,* Pope Pius XI began this educational process when for the first time he explicitly referred to "social justice" as a significant concern.[41] The practical effects of this shift in Catholic thought were enormous. Among others, it resulted in the Church's withdrawal of support from the German Catholic Center Party, in the loss of the Papal States in Italy, and in the separation between Church and state in Chile.[42] Whether secularism was partially the result of the New Christendom or whether the New Christendom was merely the recognition of a new secular reality is difficult to tell. What is clear, however, is that the Thomist appeal did not increase the impact of the Church in social and political affairs. The awakening of the Church's conscience to issues of social justice not only meant a reassertion of the role of nature but also implied a retreat of the Church from the social and political realms.

Liberation theologians, aware that Maritain's progressive New Christendom could easily be coopted by those in power and could thus be turned against the Church's social concerns, objected to the distinction between the two planes.[43] In reaction Gutiérrez radicalized Maritain's relative autonomy of the temporal sphere and pushed its boundaries to the point of eliminating any room at all for a distinct religious sphere. Appealing to Dietrich Bonhoeffer, Gutiérrez insisted that the world had become secular and thus had come of age.[44] Rejecting the Thomist distinction between the natural and the supernatural, he argued that "there are not two histories, one profane and one sacred, 'juxtaposed' or 'closely linked'. Rather there is only one human destiny, irreversibly assumed by Christ, the Lord of history."[45] And just as there is only one history, so there is only one call to salvation:

---

41. Charles E. Curran, *Catholic Social Teaching 1891–Present: A Historical, Theological, and Ethical Analysis* (Washington, D.C.: Georgetown University Press, 2002), 189.

42. William T. Cavanaugh, *Torture and Eucharist: Theology, Politics, and the Body of Christ* (Oxford: Blackwell, 1998), 124–41.

43. See, for instance, Gutiérrez, *Theology of Liberation,* 65: "The distinction of planes banner has changed hands. Until a few years ago it was defended by the vanguard; now it is held aloft by power groups, many of whom are in no way involved with any commitment to the Christian faith. Let us not be deceived, however. Their purposes are very different. Let us not unwittingly aid the opponent."

44. Ibid., 67.

45. Ibid., 153.

> The most immediate consequence of this viewpoint is that the frontiers between the life
> of faith and temporal works, between Church and world, become more fluid. . . . But
> there is another important consequence. This affirmation of the single vocation to salva-
> tion, beyond all distinctions, gives religious value in a completely new way to the action
> of man in history, Christian and non-Christian alike. The building of a just society has
> worth in terms of the Kingdom, or in more current phraseology, to participate in the
> process of liberation is already, in a certain sense, a salvific work.[46]

Gutiérrez nearly eliminated the realm of the supernatural by insisting that
grace suffused all history and all life. Just as sin was "the root of a situation of
injustice and exploitation" and was "evident in oppressive structures,"[47] so also
Christ's salvation was "not something otherworldly."[48]

Whether or not one agrees with this near-elimination of the supernatural
sphere (which I do not), Gutiérrez, along with other liberation theologians, rightly emphasized freedom from oppression as a central theme in
Scripture. The Christus Victor theme of the atonement is in a real sense
the most significant model of the atonement.[49] The result of Christ's work
of recapitulation is victory over the powers of oppression. In other words,
God's hospitality aims at the freedom of humanity and all creation. The
whole creation is waiting to "be freed from its slavery to corruption and
brought into the same glorious freedom as the children of God" (Rom.
8:21). This freedom no doubt includes freedom from social and political
bondage. The concrete language with which the Old Testament prophets
describe the peace and justice of the coming kingdom of God precludes all
spiritualizing that seals off salvation from our concrete historical contexts.
To be sure, it is not the Church's responsibility to come with specific solutions to each and every political issue. Charles E. Curran wisely observes:
"Because our Christian and human values are mediated in and through all
of the relevant empirical and scientific data and analysis, people who share
the same general values and faith commitments often find themselves in
disagreement about the approach to a particular issue."[50] The Church must
of necessity be careful in asserting its authoritative voice in the particularities
of social and political issues. Nonetheless, there are situations of egregious
evil and injustice where the Church must speak as Church in order to effect redemptive liberation. What is more, even when the Church cannot
speak as Church on specific issues, it nonetheless directs the religious and
moral lives of the believers, who cannot but make social, economic, and

46. Ibid., 72.
47. Ibid., 175.
48. Ibid., 151.
49. See p. 181.
50. Curran, *Catholic Social Teaching*, 111.

political judgments that ultimately stem from faith commitments that speak of redemption and liberation.[51]

The Christus Victor model is the basis of attempts to implement public justice beyond the realm of the Church: we are called to take the crucified peoples from the cross. But Christus Victor is not the only model that is relevant to the question of public justice. When liberationists reach for atonement theology in defense of their social and political praxis, they often appeal to the moral-influence theory as well. Jon Sobrino, for instance, insists that the crucified peoples of the Third World, as the continuation of Christ in this world, are the ones who reveal God's love, hope, and forgiveness to the First World: "Simply from a human viewpoint, changing a heart of stone into a heart of flesh—conversion—is a fundamental problem for the First World. And this is what the Third World offers it as a possibility. Above all, the Third World portrays in its own flesh the existence of an immense sin that brings slow or violent death to innocent human beings. To express it in inescapable terms, it holds the power for conversion."[52] For Sobrino the hope of the First World lies paradoxically in the crucifixion of the Third World. In a typically Abelardian move, Sobrino finds in the suffering of the crucified peoples the emotive power to bring about conversion.

We see a similar emphasis on moral influence in Leonardo Boff's *Passion of Christ, Passion of the World.* Although he discusses several different models of the atonement, he sees the relevance of each of the models in the way they offer human beings the possibility of imitation. With regard to Christ's death as a sacrifice, Boff comments that just as Christ's life was sacrificial, so can ours be. "He was a being-for-others to the last extreme. Not only his death, but his whole life was a sacrifice: it was wholly surrender."[53] Since, according to Boff, human life has an ontological structure of sacrifice, he argues: "Sacrifice . . . accomplishes our complete hominization and total salvation. Jesus Christ accomplished this himself, and he invites others, with whom he is in ontological solidarity, to do so as well."[54] Shifting to the ransom model, Boff again argues that just as Christ paid the price of liberty, so can we: "His attitude maintains its irresistible 'pro-vocative' value even today. It is still capable of rousing the slumbering conscience, of inspiring the enslaved to take up the process of liberation over and over."[55] And despite his strenuous objection to atonement models that turn God into a judge demanding the death of his Son, Boff nonetheless continues to see value in the model of vicarious satisfaction: "Christ our savior

51. It will be clear that I am rather sympathetic to Maritain's neo-Thomist approach, which is structurally similar to Abraham Kuyper's view of common grace and sphere sovereignty.

52. Sobrino, *Principle of Mercy,* 79.

53. Leonardo Boff, *Passion of Christ, Passion of the World: The Facts, Their Interpretation, and Their Meaning,* trans. Robert R. Barr (Maryknoll, N.Y.: Orbis, 1987), 94.

54. Ibid.

55. Ibid., 96.

stirs us, to achieve what he has achieved. We are redeemed, we are satisfied, only to the extent that we are earnest in satisfying our basic human calling."[56] In each of these cases, it is the subjective dimension that renders salvation and liberation. Without actually putting it this way, Boff turns each metaphor and model into a subsection of the moral-influence theory.

Sobrino's and Boff's views of the atonement are not impervious to criticism. In particular their one-sided emphasis on the moral-influence theory fails to do full justice to the role of the other atonement models. Nonetheless, they are right that the cross constitutes an appeal to oppressor (Sobrino) and victim (Boff) alike. Suffering caused by economic or social oppression ought to awaken oppressors to the hideous character of injustice, whether it is the result of individual actions or violent structures. And there is little doubt that we are called to imitate Jesus Christ in his prophetic role of insisting on hospitality and freedom for the poor and oppressed, and that such a prophetic attitude will meet with resistance and at times can lead to sacrifice and a violent death. In short, while the Church is not called to denounce the public spheres of statecraft and economic exchange as such, there is a need for Christians—and, on occasion, for the Church itself—to speak prophetically into situations of injustice. As I indicated in chapter 9, by voluntarily taking on themselves the suffering that results, Christians continue the suffering of Christ, so that their suffering is also redemptive in nature.

Recent voices within the Radical Orthodoxy movement have criticized not only Maritain's New Christendom and its neo-Thomist distinction of the two planes but also the liberationists' radicalizing of Maritain's approach. John Milbank objects to the liberationist identification between salvation and liberation. After baptizing secular society, Milbank insists, liberation theologians go on to affirm this secular social justice as salvation: "The social realm is thought to possess its own immanent ethical principles, which are those of an emergent 'humanity' and which cannot be qualified by theology. All that theology can do is to give these principles of liberation another name: 'salvation'. Theology is able to declare that natural, human ethics is approved of by God."[57] William Cavanaugh similarly insists that with Gutiérrez "[t]he world has absorbed the church into itself" and this has resulted in the loss of the Church as a social and political body and as a "contrast society."[58] Finally, Daniel Bell, in a sustained critique of liberation theology, insists that liberationists fall into the dual trap of

56. Ibid., 98.
57. Milbank, *Theology and Social Theory,* 233.
58. Cavanaugh, *Torture and Eucharist,* 180. Cavanaugh is right that, at least in theory, Gutiérrez undermines the role of the Church and of the irruption of grace in and through the Church by insisting on only one history, a history that is essentially secular in nature. But this does not entirely disqualify his insistence on one history and one call to salvation. Gutiérrez is right to suggest that political and economic structures (i.e., not those of the Church) do matter a great deal and that some are more hospitable and more just than others. Insofar as they are more just, they reflect at least some of the intended result of Christ's redemption through his life, death, and resurrection. It is simply not clear to me how the celebration of the Eucharist

continuing Maritain's separation between the temporal and the spiritual and of identifying politics with statecraft: "The result of the liberationists' maintaining the distinction of planes and endorsing the Church's retreat to the apolitical space created by such a distinction is that the state assumes control of the temporal realm. . . . The state surfaces as the principal agent of social and political order. Politics becomes a matter of statecraft."[59] These criticisms of liberation theology do not concern the idea of social justice as such. At issue is the location of the public and the social *beyond the Church*. In other words, Radical Orthodoxy feels that neither the Thomist idea of the two planes nor the liberationist appeal to the unity of secular history does justice to the centrality of the Church as the one place that is able to counter violence and implement true hospitality and justice. Radical Orthodoxy's expansionist ecclesiology is what causes it to oppose the legacy of the nature/grace theology of the Western Church. Not satisfied with the Church being central, Radical Orthodoxy insists that it is the *only* place in which hospitality and justice have any role to play at all.

By exclusively appropriating the rights to hospitality and justice, Radical Orthodoxy's *ecclesia* is the result of an all-or-nothing approach that is unable to recognize even a limited degree of justice and hospitality outside the boundaries of the Church. Bell consistently regards the temporal spheres of politics and economics as driven by a deviant "technology of desire" and counters it with forgiveness—including practices of confession, repentance, and penance—as the Church's alternative technology of desire.[60] Cavanaugh insists that the state's liturgical use of torture (an atomizing dismembering) needs to be countered by the Church's liturgy of the Eucharist (a communal remembering of Christ).[61] The echoes of Yoder and Hauerwas come through loud and clear—and with them, unfortunately, the spiritualizing tendencies of the Radical Reformation. Fascinating and tempting as this approach may be, it does not allow for the relative good of justice and hospitality to take shape outside the ecclesial boundaries of the eucharistic community.

Restorative Justice and the Hospitality of Forgiveness

Liberation theology rightly insists that hospitality and justice can also be pursued in other public areas, even if the Church is the primary incarnation

---

could be an adequate political answer to the tortures under Pinochet's regime, as Cavanaugh insists. Salvation, in the biblical sense of the term, penetrates also beyond the boundaries of the Church.

59. Bell, *Liberation Theology*, 63; cf. ibid., 3. I will not enter into a discussion of Bell's first point of criticism (the alleged liberationist separation between the two planes). Let it suffice that I think his reading of Gutiérrez is at best one-sided. In *Theology of Liberation*, 53–77, Gutiérrez vehemently critiques Maritain's distinction of planes.

60. Bell, *Liberation Theology*, 171–84.

61. Cavanaugh, *Torture and Eucharist*, 229–34.

of God's presence in the world.[62] Christ's victory on the cross and his teaching and modeling of God's hospitality have social, political, and economic implications, even if Christians are not always in agreement on what exactly those implications are. Liberationists insist that for public justice to flourish, it is necessary to denounce prophetically what the 1968 Episcopal Conference at Medellín called "institutionalized violence," a situation of injustice that has crept into many of our societal structures.[63] Liberation theology wants to pursue public justice and rightly insists on erecting boundaries against the greed and oppression that enslave many people in the Third World. This need for boundaries raises difficult questions. Should justice be pursued to the point of civil disobedience and perhaps armed insurrection? Dare Christians ever take up arms against violent dictators? Would this be consistent with a Christian attitude of forgiveness in imitation of God's forgiveness? Although I cannot deal with each of these questions in detail, I want to offer some foundational comments regarding the relationship between justice and forgiveness.

Liberationists remind us of the need to set and maintain boundaries for the sake of hospitality and justice. They do not all agree on *how* to set these boundaries. Some argue that Jesus has shown us a way of nonviolent persuasion, and that we are to imitate this nonviolence as we strive for public justice. Leonardo Boff, for instance, insists that Jesus "attempts only to persuade, to state his arguments clearly, to appeal to good sense and reason. His assertions are not 'authoritative', but persuasive. He always leaves the other a space for freedom. . . . Jesus never employs violence to make his ideas prevail. He appeals to, and speaks to consciences."[64] As we have already seen, the notion of persuasion figures prominently also in Irenaeus.[65] It is a term that alludes to the likely presence in the background of some kind of moral-influence model. For Boff moral influence is closely connected with the nonviolent pursuit of public justice.

It is not at all clear to me, however, that the hospitality of persuasion precludes all redemptive violence. And to other liberationists Boff's persuasive methodology is not nearly radical enough. Gutiérrez, in his landmark study, argues that the unjust violence of the oppressors is quite different from the just violence of the oppressed.[66] And he insists that "the Church must place itself squarely within the process of revolution, amid the violence which is present in different ways."[67] Sobrino, for similar reasons, questions the common phrase,

---

62. I certainly endorse Bell's appropriation of the Thomist vision of public justice as pursuing the common good rather than merely pursuing commutative and distributive justice. Bell's critique of Catholic social thought as abandoning the telos of the common good in favor of the modern discourse of rights is extremely perceptive (*Liberation Theology*, 102–10).

63. Gutiérrez, *Theology of Liberation*, 108. Cf. Smith, *Emergence of Liberation Theology*, 34–36.

64. Boff, *Passion of Christ*, 18; cf. ibid., 59, 64.

65. See chapter 5.

66. Gutiérrez, *Theology of Liberation*, 108–9.

67. Ibid., 138.

"Hate the sin and love the sinner." He feels that the statement is not nearly radical enough, since

> we must not only hate the sin but eradicate it, and objectively this is a violent action against the sinner. Liberation from oppression also means destroying the person oppressing, in his formal capacity as oppressor. And although this task is difficult and dangerous, it cannot be abandoned for love of the oppressed.
>
> The spirituality of forgiveness must integrate this tension between love and destruction, and this can only be done with a great love which comprehends the destruction of the sinner as love. Through love, we have to be prepared to welcome the sinner and forgive him. We have to be prepared to make it impossible for him to continue with his deeds, which dehumanize others and himself.[68]

For Sobrino violence can function as a paradoxical form of hospitality. Accordingly, he sees forgiveness and mercy not as opposites of justice but defines them precisely in terms of implementing justice. Forgiveness, he insists, is more than a legal acquittal. Since forgiveness has reconciliation as its purpose, forgiveness itself means the transformation of social injustice: "In a sinful reality, there are sinners. In the first place, these are the idols who bring death. Forgiving them means fundamentally eradicating them."[69]

One does not need to adopt Sobrino's unconventional understanding of forgiveness as transformation to appreciate his insistence on the goal of the destruction of evil and the ultimate reconciliation between offender and victim. Justice should be restorative in nature. Likewise, Sobrino is right that the hospitality of forgiveness entails judgment and boundaries, because these help us avoid the chaotic open spaces of cheap grace. Liberation implies that we are willing to counter evil social structures and to promote actively just relationships. This is not to say that I endorse Gutiérrez and Sobrino's willingness to engage in revolutionary activities. Not all activities that pursue justice—not even all those that involve violence—need necessarily be revolutionary in character. Different functions and a variety of situations call for uniquely distinct responsibilities.[70] But both authors are right to suggest that liberation and reconciliation call for opposition to injustice and for an active endorsement of public justice beyond the Church.

68. Sobrino, *Principle of Mercy*, 65.

69. Ibid., 62. L. Gregory Jones holds to a similar understanding of forgiveness as a "way of life" or a "habit" that must be practiced (*Embodying Forgiveness: A Theological Analysis* [Grand Rapids: Eerdmans, 1995], 66–67, 163). I critique this definition of forgiveness in "Being Reconciled."

70. The question of the right to revolt has a long history of debate. Particularly within the Reformed tradition, there has always been an appreciation for the role of "lesser magistrates" versus an oppressive dictatorial leadership. Even such an appeal to a right to revolt, however, would not justify a blanket endorsement of revolutionary activity against oppressive political or economic structures of power.

Daniel Bell has sharply criticized liberationists for their activist stance. He believes that capitalism should be opposed not by means of violence but by means of "the refusal to cease suffering." Bell insists that only when we continue Christ's crucified suffering in our lives and so offer forgiveness to our oppressors can we have hope for reconciliation. He makes a plea for the "crucified power" of the "crucified people gathered as the Church of the poor."[71] Bell argues that justice can only blossom if we resist violence by means of forgiveness: "Justice does not, as the liberationists suggest, set things right and then forgiveness steps in to squelch the flames of vengeance and resentment. On the contrary, it is forgiveness that sets things right, and then in the soil that forgiveness has prepared, justice blossoms. Forgiveness is the condition of possibility for justice."[72]

I am certainly sympathetic to Bell's notion of cruciform power, which has unmistakable biblical warrant. The suffering of martyrdom that results from oppressive violence is, as I have indicated in the previous chapter, redemptive in character.[73] Still, there are several caveats that Bell overlooks. First, the suffering of martyrdom is the result not only of the Church's practices of forgiveness but is often the result of a prophetic stance that denounces injustice. Archbishop Oscar Romero's murder in 1980 was the result not of a passive stance that invites suffering but of his increasingly vocal opposition to Salvadorian economic and political power structures. Christian martyrdom and active social and political engagement are not each other's opposites; the former can often result from the latter. Bell's protestations notwithstanding, I do not believe that he avoids the dangers of cheap grace and fatalistic resignation to suffering.[74] To avoid these dangers, we need more than the identification of those who suffer injustice as the crucified people of God. We also need an active social and political engagement that erects beneficial boundaries against the oppressors' practices of injustice.

Second, because Bell adopts Radical Orthodoxy's monopolizing understanding of the Church, he fails to appreciate the positive role that governments can play in countering injustice. In particular, because the state has the power of the sword, it has the duty to protect the weak and to promote structures that are more reflective of God's eschatological hospitality. As indicated in chapter 7, the theory of penal representation draws our attention to the potentially restorative function of punishment.[75] Of course, not all punishment is restorative

---

71. Bell, *Liberation Theology,* 191.

72. Ibid., 186.

73. See chapter 9 (the section titled "Cruciform Hospitality: *Salvifici Doloris*").

74. See Bell, *Liberation Theology,* 173–74; 191. I realize, of course, that many who take a nonviolent stance can be quite prophetic and activist in their approach (e.g., Stanley Hauerwas and Walter Wink). My point here is Bell's lack of nuance in opposing his "refusal to cease suffering" to liberationist activism.

75. As mentioned earlier, in line with his negative view of the state, John Milbank regards it as "problematic to talk about 'God punishing'" and insists that all punishment is a tragic risk that cannot escape the taint of sin (*Theology and Social Theory,* 420).

in character. Punishment can be abusive, and advocates of restorative justice rightly oppose the vindictive spirit that very much supports our retributive judicial system.[76] But just as God exercised penal justice on the cross in the interest of eschatological hospitality, so our judicial systems should go beyond mere retribution and must strive for the restoration of relationships. In terms of criminal justice, this will imply judicial structures that offer hope for all parties involved: victims, offenders, and the community. The last thing that Christians should do is to abandon the judicial system with the illusion that the Church is the only place in which justice is found. Instead, they should be involved in attempts at reforming our justice system to make it reflect more clearly God's hospitality on the cross. What our society needs is not just a Church that models hospitality to the world, but also a Church with a theology of public justice that gives space to the state to curb injustice and to promote hospitality.

The demand to abandon the quest for a public justice beyond the Church and informed by Christian theological commitments is ill founded. Voices advocating such a disavowal of Christian public justice come from different quarters: some speak out of fear that Christianity's involvement leads to violence and injustice; others from the conviction that the Church, as opposed to the state, is the proper public sphere. As I hope to have shown in this final chapter, each of the three traditional atonement models has the potential to contribute positively in a search for public justice. I am not arguing that atonement theology has never been used to counter hospitality or to advance injustice. It is clear, however, that a combination of the inspiration of Christ's love (moral influence) and a carefully delineated understanding of restorative justice (penal representation) may already today contribute to some measure of liberation from bondage (Christus Victor). Public justice may already today function as a signpost of the resurrection and the end to violence.

76. See, for example, Charles W. Colson, *Justice That Restores* (Wheaton, Ill.: Tyndale, 2001); William C. Placher, *Jesus the Savior: The Meaning of Jesus Christ for Christian Faith* (Louisville: Westminster John Knox, 2001), 150–56.

Epilogue

The End of Violence

Eschatology and Deification

Underlying much of this study has been the appeal to paradox: all acts of hospitality in history share in the limited and conditional character of creation and require, as such, some degree of violence. I have argued that this violence can be redemptive and does not need to detract from the hospitable character of these acts. I have made the case that God's hospitality on the cross implies such redemptive violence, and that human hospitality requires a certain degree of violence as well. I have also maintained that it is only in the eschatological resurrection of Christ, completed on the last day, that this violence comes to an end and God ushers in his unconditional or absolute hospitality. Only the telos of this resurrection is sufficient justification for all good violence, whether divine or human.

If it is true, however, that all human practices of hospitality are in a paradoxical relationship with violence, precisely ultimately to overcome violence, what does this do to our humanity in the eschaton? Will the boundaries of time and space no longer hold at that point? Would that not mean that we cease to be human? And would it not imply that the telos of the resurrection amounts to a negation of the very structures of God's good creation? These are important questions, which stem directly from my desire to affirm both that there is an intimate connection between hospitality and violence in the world as we know it and that the resurrection overcomes all limitations of conditionality and violence.

Also here Irenaeus proves eminently helpful. The bishop of Lyons insists that the crossing of the eschatological boundary forces us to maintain two seemingly contradictory approaches and that we should keep a careful and precarious balance between the two.[1] On the one hand, he maintains that without question we would not cease to be human. The creaturely categories of time and space that we know today will be maintained in the hereafter. In the kingdom of God, says Irenaeus,

> neither is the substance nor the essence of the creation annihilated (for faithful and true is He who has established it), but "the *fashion* of the world passeth away;" that is, those things among which transgression has occurred, since man has grown old in them. . . . But when this [present] fashion [of things] passes away, and man has been renewed, and flourishes in an incorruptible state, so as to preclude the possibility of becoming old, [then] there shall be the new heaven and the new earth, in which the new man shall remain [continually], always holding fresh converse with God. . . . And as the presbyters say, Then those who are deemed worthy of an abode in heaven shall go there, others shall enjoy the delights of paradise, and others shall possess the splendour of the city; for everywhere the Saviour shall be seen according as they who see Him shall be worthy.[2]

Irenaeus insists on the continuation of the created order beyond the eschatological boundary. This created order is seen in the various "mansions" of the righteous—descending in levels of glory: heaven itself, paradise, and the city of Jerusalem. This eternal glory shall "ever continue without end."[3] Immortality, it seems, is not entry into a timeless eternity but is simply time without end.

One of the results of this affirmation of an eternal continuation of time and matter is that the linguistic structures of human existence will also continue. The creaturely activities of learning and interpretation will carry on in the eternal kingdom of God.[4] Irenaeus says that we must leave certain matters of interpretation "in the hands of God, and that not only in the present world, but also in that which is to come, so that God should for ever teach, and man should for ever learn the things taught him by God."[5] Human beings will never have the perfect knowledge that God has. The continuation of learning and interpretation is an affirmation of the limited nature of creaturely existence and seems to imply that the human activities of searching, discerning, and discriminating will continue.

1. See Hans Boersma, "Irenaeus, Derrida, and Hospitality: On the Eschatological Overcoming of Violence," *Modern Theology* 19 (2003): 163–80.

2. Irenaeus, *Irenaeus against Heresies* (hereafter *AH*), in *The Ante-Nicene Fathers*, ed. Alexander Roberts and James Donaldson (1885; repr., Peabody, Mass.: Hendrickson, 1994), 1:566–67 (V.36.1); italics in the original.

3. Ibid., 1:567 (V.36.1).

4. For a carefully argued defense of the continuation of temporality and language in eternal life, see James K. A. Smith, *The Fall of Interpretation: Philosophical Foundations for a Creational Hermeneutic* (Downers Grove, Ill.: InterVarsity, 2000).

5. Irenaeus, *AH*, 1:399 (II.28.3).

On the other hand, Irenaeus realizes that the hospitality of God is such that we cannot possibly comprehend it by means of categories taken from this side of the eschatological equation. He insists that the world of "temporal things" will disappear.[6] He realizes, in other words, that this-worldly categories are inadequate to describe the situation of God's eschatological hospitality. Repeatedly, the bishop of Lyons refers to the idea of *theosis,* or divinization.[7] To be sure, he mostly speaks of humans attaining "incorruptibility" or "immortality."[8] Nonetheless, several times he makes use of Psalm 82 ("I have said, Ye *are* gods; and all of you *are* children of the most High"—v. 6 KJV), which he interprets as speaking of our adoption as sons.[9] Irenaeus says not only that adoption means that we will become sons of God, but he also states that we were "at first merely men, then at length gods"[10] and comments that in the end we will "pass into God."[11]

We see a similar approach in Irenaeus's understanding of *visio Dei* as the ultimate purpose of the history of redemption.[12] Throughout history there has been a gradual increase in this vision of God, ranging from the manifestation of God in creation, to prophetic visions in the Old Testament, to the vision of the Lord in his incarnation, and to the eschatological vision of God in eternal life. It is the vision of God that will ultimately render people immortal: "For as those who see the light are within the light, and partake of its brilliancy; even so, those who see God are in God, and receive of His splendour. But [His] splendour vivifies them; those, therefore, who see God, do receive life. . . . Men therefore shall see God, that they may live, being made immortal by that sight, and attaining even unto God."[13] These references to deification and *visio Dei*

6. The tension in Irenaeus's theology at this point leads to the paradoxical affirmation in one and the same paragraph of the disappearance of the world of "temporal things" and of the continuation of time "without end" (ibid., 1:566–67 [V.36.1]).

7. For Irenaeus's views on deification, see F. Altermath, "The Purpose of the Incarnation according to Irenaeus," *Studia Patristica* 13 (1975): 63–68; Demetrios J. Constantelos, "Irenaeos of Lyons and His Central Views on Human Nature," *St. Vladimir's Theological Quarterly* 33 (1989): 351–63; Denis Minns, *Irenaeus* (Washington, D.C.: Georgetown University Press, 1994), 56–82.

8. In order to protect the creational integrity of human beings in the kingdom of God—against all Gnostic spiritualizing—Irenaeus only hesitantly affirms the language of deification. H. E. W. Turner's classic study puts it well: "The idea of deification is clearly present, but it is almost as if a reverential glottal-stop prevents the use of the actual term" (*The Patristic Doctrine of Redemption: A Study of the Development of Doctrine during the First Five Centuries* [London: Mowbray; New York: Morehouse-Gorham, 1952], 76–77). Cf. also Trevor A. Hart, "Irenaeus, Recapitulation, and Physical Redemption," in *Christ in Our Place: The Humanity of God in Christ for the Reconciliation of the World,* ed. Trevor A. Hart and Daniel P. Thimell (Exeter: Paternoster; Allison Park, Pa.: Pickwick, 1989), 153.

9. Irenaeus, *AH,* 1:419 (III.6.1–3); 1:522 (IV.38.4).

10. Ibid., 1:522 (IV.38.4).

11. Ibid., 1:507 (IV.33.4).

12. See especially Mary Ann Donovan, "Alive to the Glory of God: A Key Insight in St. Irenaeus," *Theological Studies* 49 (1988): 283–97.

13. Irenaeus, *AH,* 1:489 (IV.20.5–6).

are indicative of Irenaeus's awareness that the eschaton breaks the barriers of the limitations and conditions that constitute our human nature today.

All of this implies a sharp tension in Irenaeus's thinking. On the one hand, over against the Gnostic refusal to recognize the conditions and limitations of the created order as good, Irenaeus insists that time, matter, and interpretation will continue in the eschaton. On the other hand, the deification that results from the resurrection means that time will be no more and that the conditions and limitations of creation will disappear in the presence of the immortal God. Irenaeus thus acknowledges that the eschatological hospitality of God introduces a mystery.[14] The eschaton is a future in which the Father will bestow "in a paternal manner those things which neither the eye has seen, nor the ear has heard, nor has [thought concerning them] arisen within the heart of man." Even the angels "are not able to search out the wisdom of God, by means of which His handiwork, confirmed and incorporated with His Son, is brought to perfection."[15] This acknowledgment of mystery is hardly an abdication of epistemic responsibility; rather, it is an admission of an epistemic fissure between the conditions of our present existence and those of the eschatological kingdom of peace.[16]

The end to violence with the arrival of God's unconditional hospitality does not mean that we will cease to be human—despite our inability to picture a humanity that is no longer dependent on boundary maintenance. Rather, it means that on the day of the resurrection God will transform our human bodies. The Church has traditionally followed Irenaeus in his appeal to the notion of deification.[17] This notion stems from the duality of the biblical testimony regarding Christ's own resurrection body. On the one hand, it has true physical integrity: the disciples really see Jesus (Luke 24:39); he continues to

14. In chapter 1, I acknowledged with Derrida that violence is inherent in the creational structures as we know them (and as such not necessarily sinful), while at the same time this violence wasn't there before the Fall in the garden. Also, because of our epistemic limitations, we cannot explain how we can affirm the full creational integrity (with its limitations and exclusions) in the garden while at the same time affirming the absolute nonviolence of the Edenic state. See chapter 1, n. 40.

15. Irenaeus, *AH,* 1:567 (V.36.3).

16. The combination of deification and of the continuation of creational categories seems structurally similar to the mysteries of paradox in other doctrines, such as the Trinity and the hypostatic union of the two natures in Christ. All of these affirm mysteries of faith (in which the transcendent or eschatological reaches into our world), without involving logical contradictions.

17. For the notion of deification, especially prominent in Eastern Orthodox theology, see Timothy Ware, *The Orthodox Church,* rev. ed. (London: Penguin, 1964), 231–38; Vitaly Borovoy, "What Is Salvation? An Orthodox Statement," *International Review of Mission* 61 (1972): 38–45; Vladimir Lossky, "Redemption and Deification," in *In the Image and Likeness of God,* ed. John H. Erickson and Thomas E. Bird (Crestwood, N.Y.: St. Vladimir's Seminary Press, 1985), 97–110; Michael C. D. McDaniel, "Salvation as Justification and Theosis," in *Salvation in Christ: A Lutheran-Orthodox Dialogue,* ed. John Meyendorff and Robert Tobias (Minneapolis: Augsburg, 1992), 67–83; Ron Dart, "The Oxford Movement and the Politics of Deification," *Fellowship Papers* (winter 1996–97): 10–21; Michael Azkoul, *Ye Are Gods: Salvation according to the Latin Fathers* (Dewdney, B.C.: Synaxis, 2002).

eat with his disciples (Luke 24:30; John 21:9–14); and, perhaps most significantly, the marks of his suffering have not disappeared from his resurrection
body (John 20:27). On the other hand, several of his intimates seem to have
difficulty recognizing him (Luke 24:16; John 20:14; 21:7), and Jesus appears
and disappears suddenly (Luke 24:31; John 20:19). It is the resurrection and
the arrival of the eschaton that mark this change in Jesus' physicality. St. Paul
argues that a similar transformation will also take place in those who will be
raised with Christ, and he speaks of them receiving a "glorious" or a "spiritual"
body (Phil. 3:21; 1 Cor. 15:44), which will be "imperishable" (1 Cor. 15:42).
The eschatological future, according to St. Paul, means the transformation of
the body so that it becomes capable of incorruptibility and immortality.[18]

The discontinuity implied by this deification can hardly be explained rationally.[19] The limited character of our creaturely existence as we know it today
simply does not allow for such epistemological access. The apostle alludes
to a future of which we have only the vaguest inkling (cf. 1 John 3:2) and at
which we can only marvel. All we can do is confess that our human nature will
continue in its physical and bodily nature, while at the same time acknowledge that it will be deified—made capable of entering into the glory of God's
unconditional, absolute hospitality. It is at this point of deification that the
atonement will have reached its ultimate end. Redemption is only complete
when the resurrection ushers in God's pure hospitality and makes us capable
of enjoying it to the full. The fullness of the kingdom of peace—the Church
and all creation brought to their final telos—will witness deified human beings
participating in the unconditional hospitality of God: "For the glory of God
is a living man; and the life of man consists in beholding God."[20]

---

18. N. T. Wright uses the term "transphysicality" to describe the early Christians' view of the resurrection body as "a body which was still robustly physical but also significantly different from the present
one" (*The Resurrection of the Son of God*, vol. 3 of *Christian Origins and the Question of God* [Minneapolis:
Fortress, 2003], 477–78).

19. Of course, much more could be said (in a rational fashion) about deification than I am able to discuss
within the limited confines of this epilogue.

20. Irenaeus, *AH*, 1:490 (IV.20.7).

Bibliography

Abdul-Masih, Magi. "The Challenge of Present-Day Palestine to Contemporary Theology." *Studies in Religion* 29 (2000): 439–51.

Altermath, F. "The Purpose of the Incarnation according to Irenaeus." *Studia Patristica* 13 (1975): 63–68.

Armstrong, Brian G. *Calvinism and the Amyraut Heresy: Protestant Scholasticism and Humanism in Seventeenth-Century France*. Madison: University of Wisconsin Press, 1969.

Aulén, Gustaf. *Christus Victor: An Historical Study of the Three Main Types of the Idea of the Atonement*. Translated by A. G. Hebert. London: SPCK, 1970.

Bailey, Kenneth E. *Poet and Peasant; and, Through Peasant Eyes: A Literary-Cultural Approach to the Parables of Luke*. Grand Rapids: Eerdmans, 1983.

Bailie, Gil. *Violence Unveiled: Humanity at the Crossroads*. New York: Crossroad, 1995.

Baker, Brenda M. "Penance as Model for Punishment." *Social Theory and Practice* 18 (1992): 311–31.

Bandstra, Andrew J. "Paul and an Ancient Interpreter: A Comparison of the Teaching of Redemption in Paul and Irenaeus." *Calvin Theological Journal* 5 (1970): 43–63.

Baptism, Eucharist and Ministry. Faith and Order Paper, no. 111. Geneva: WCC, 1982.

Barbour, Ian G. *Myths, Models, and Paradigms: A Comparative Study in Science and Religion*. New York: Harper & Row, 1974.

Bartlett, Anthony W. *Cross Purposes: The Violent Grammar of Christian Atonement*. Harrisburg, Pa.: Trinity, 2001.

Beachy, Alvin J. *The Concept of Grace in the Radical Reformation*. Nieuwkoop, Neth.: De Graaf, 1977.

Beaudoin, Tom. *Virtual Faith: The Irreverent Spiritual Quest of Generation X*. San Francisco: Jossey-Bass, 1998.

Begbie, Jeremy S. *Theology, Music, and Time*. Cambridge: Cambridge University Press, 2000.

Bell, Daniel M. *Liberation Theology after the End of History: The Refusal to Cease Suffering*. London: Routledge, 2001.

Bellah, Robert N., et al. *Habits of the Heart: Individualism and Commitment in American Life*. Berkeley: University of California Press, 1985.

Benson, Bruce Ellis. *Graven Ideologies: Nietzsche, Derrida, and Marion on Idolatry.* Downers Grove, Ill.: InterVarsity, 2002.

Benton, W. Wilson. "Federal Theology: Review for Revision." In *Through Christ's Word: A Festschrift for Dr. Philip E. Hughes,* edited by W. Robert Godfrey and Jesse L. Boyd III, 180–204. Phillipsburg, N.J.: Presbyterian & Reformed, 1985.

Bingham, D. Jeffrey. *Irenaeus' Use of Matthew's Gospel in* Adversus Haereses. Traditio Exegetica Graeca, no. 7. Louvain: Peeters, 1998.

Birmelé, André. "Baptism and the Unity of the Church in Ecumenical Dialogues." In *Baptism and the Unity of the Church,* edited by Michael Root and Risto Saarinen, 104–29. Grand Rapids: Eerdmans; Geneva: WCC, 1998.

Blocher, Henri. "*Agnus Victor*: The Atonement as Victory and Vicarious Punishment." In *What Does It Mean to Be Saved? Broadening Evangelical Horizons of Salvation,* edited by John G. Stackhouse, 67–91. Grand Rapids: Baker, 2002.

Boersma, Hans. "Being Reconciled: Cultural-Ecclesial Practice as Atonement in Radical Orthodoxy." In *Creation, Covenant, and Participation: Radical Orthodoxy and the Reformed Tradition,* edited by James H. Olthuis and James K. A. Smith. Grand Rapids: Baker, forthcoming.

———. "Calvin and the Extent of the Atonement." *Evangelical Quarterly* 64 (1992): 333–55.

———. "The Disappearance of Punishment: Metaphors, Models, and the Meaning of the Atonement." *Books & Culture* 9 (2) (March/April 2003): 32–34.

———. "Eschatological Justice and the Cross: Violence and Penal Substitution." *Theology Today* 60 (2003): 186–99.

———. "Hospitality and Violence: The Role of Punishment in the Atonement." *Psyche en Geloof* 13 (2002): 12–23.

———. *A Hot Pepper Corn: Richard Baxter's Doctrine of Justification in Its Seventeenth-Century Context of Controversy.* 2nd ed. Vancouver, B.C.: Regent College Publishing, 2004.

———. "Irenaeus, Derrida, and Hospitality: On the Eschatological Overcoming of Violence." *Modern Theology* 19 (2003): 163–80.

———. "Liturgical Hospitality: Theological Reflections on Sharing in Grace." *Journal for Christian Theological Research* 8 (2003): 67–77.

———. "Penal Substitution and the Possibility of Unconditional Hospitality." *Scottish Journal of Theology* 57 (2004): 80–94.

———. "Redemptive Hospitality in Irenaeus: A Model for Ecumenicity in a Violent World." *Pro Ecclesia* 11 (2002): 207–26.

———. *Richard Baxter's Understanding of Infant Baptism.* Princeton, N.J.: Princeton Theological Seminary, 2002.

Boff, Leonardo. *Passion of Christ, Passion of the World: The Facts, Their Interpretation, and Their Meaning.* Translated by Robert R. Barr. Maryknoll, N.Y.: Orbis, 1987.

Borovoy, Vitaly. "What Is Salvation? An Orthodox Statement." *International Review of Mission* 61 (1972): 38–45.

Bottum, J. "Girard among the Girardians." *First Things* 61 (March 1996): 42–45.

Bouteneff, Peter. "Soteriological Imagery in Gregory of Nyssa's *Antirrheticus.*" *Studia Patristica* 32 (1997): 81–86.

Boyd, Gregory A. *God at War: The Bible and Spiritual Conflict.* Downers Grove, Ill.: InterVarsity, 1997.

Braaten, Carl E. *Mother Church: Ecclesiology and Ecumenism.* Minneapolis: Fortress, 1998.

Brasswell, Joseph P. "'The Blessing of Abraham' versus 'the Curse of the Law': Another Look at Gal 3:10–13." *Westminster Theological Journal* 53 (1991): 73–91.

Brock, Rita Nakashima. *Journeys by Heart: A Christology of Erotic Power.* New York: Crossroad, 1988.

Brock, Rita Nakashima, and Rebecca Ann Parker. *Proverbs of Ashes: Violence, Redemptive Suffering, and the Search for What Saves Us.* Boston: Beacon, 2001.

Brown, Joanne Carlson. "Divine Child Abuse?" *Daughters of Sarah* 18 (3) (1992): 24–28.

Brown, Joanne Carlson, and Rebecca Parker. "For God So Loved the World?" In *Christianity, Patriarchy, and Abuse,* edited by Joanne Carlson Brown and Carole R. Bohn, 1–30. New York: Pilgrim, 1989.

Brown, Robert F. "On the Necessary Imperfection of Creation: Irenaeus' *Adversus Haereses* IV, 38," *Scottish Journal of Theology* 28 (1975): 17–25.

Brueggemann, Walter. *Theology of the Old Testament: Testimony, Dispute, Advocacy.* Minneapolis: Fortress, 1997.

Brümmer, Vincent. *The Model of Love: A Study in Philosophical Theology.* Cambridge: Cambridge University Press, 1993.

Burt, Donald X. *Friendship and Society: An Introduction to Augustine's Practical Philosophy.* Grand Rapids: Eerdmans, 1999.

Burt, Robert A. "Reconciling with Injustice." In *Transgression, Punishment, Responsibility, Forgiveness,* edited by Andrew D. Weiner and Leonard V. Kaplan, Graven Images, vol. 4, 106–22. Madison: University of Wisconsin Law School, 1998.

Caputo, John D. *On Religion.* London: Routledge, 2001.

———. *The Prayers and Tears of Jacques Derrida: Religion without Religion.* Bloomington: Indiana University Press, 1977.

Cavanaugh, William T. *Torture and Eucharist: Theology, Politics, and the Body of Christ.* Oxford: Blackwell, 1998.

Charles, J. Daryl. "Protestant Reflections on Salvifici doloris." *National Catholic Bioethics Quarterly* 2 (2002): 211–20.

———. *The Unformed Conscience of Evangelicalism: Recovering the Church's Moral Vision.* Downers Grove, Ill.: InterVarsity, 2002.

Clapp, Rodney. *A Peculiar People: The Church as Culture in a Post-Christian Society.* Downers Grove, Ill.: InterVarsity, 1996.

Cole, Darrell. "Good Wars." *First Things* 116 (October 2001): 27–31.

Collins, Robin. "Girard and Atonement: An Incarnational Theory of Mimetic Participation." In *Violence Renounced: René Girard, Biblical Studies, and Peacemaking,* edited by Willard M. Swartley, 132–53. Telford, Pa.: Pandora; Scottdale, Pa.: Herald, 2000.

Colson, Charles W. *Justice That Restores.* Wheaton, Ill.: Tyndale, 2001.

Cone, James H. *God of the Oppressed.* Rev. ed. Maryknoll, N.Y.: Orbis, 1997.

Congar, Yves M.-J. "Classical Political Monotheism and the Trinity." *Concilium* 143 (1981): 31–36.

———. *Tradition and Traditions: The Biblical, Historical, and Theological Evidence for Catholic Teaching on Tradition.* Translated by Michael Naseby and Thomas Rainborough. San Diego: Basilica; Needham Heights, Mass.: Simon & Schuster, 1966.

Constantelos, Demetrios J. "Irenaeos of Lyons and His Central Views on Human Nature." *St. Vladimir's Theological Quarterly* 33 (1989): 351–63.

Cottrell, Jack W. "Conditional Election." In *Grace Unlimited,* edited by Clark H. Pinnock, 51–73. Minneapolis: Bethany, 1975.

Coward, Harold, and Toby Foshy, eds. *Derrida and Negative Theology.* New York: State University of New York Press, 1992.

Critchley, Simon. *The Ethics of Deconstruction: Derrida and Levinas.* 2nd ed. West Lafayette, Ind.: Purdue University Press, 1999.

Crysdale, Cynthia S. W. *Embracing Travail: Retrieving the Cross Today.* New York: Continuum, 1999.

Curran, Charles E. *Catholic Social Teaching 1891–Present: A Historical, Theological, and Ethical Analysis.* Washington, D.C.: Georgetown University Press, 2002.

Daly, Gabriel. "Theology of Redemption in the Fathers." In *Witness to the Spirit: Essays on Revelation, Spirit, Redemption,* edited by Wilfrid Harrington, 133–48. Dublin: Irish Biblical Association; Manchester: Koinonia, 1979.

Daly, Robert J. *Christian Sacrifice: The Judaeo-Christian Background before Origen.* Washington, D.C.: Catholic University of America Press, 1978.

Dawn, Marva J. *Powers, Weakness, and the Tabernacling of God.* Grand Rapids: Eerdmans, 2001.

De Bruijne, A. L. Th. "Hermeneutiek en metaforie." In *Woord op schrift: Theologische reflecties over het gezag van de bijbel,* edited by C. Trimp, 109–60. Kampen, Neth.: Kok, 2002.

De Jong, Peter Y. *Crisis in the Reformed Churches: Essays in Commemoration of the Great Synod of Dort, 1618–1619.* Grand Rapids: Reformed Fellowship, 1968.

Dembele, Youssouf. "Salvation as Victory: A Reconsideration of the Concept of Salvation in the Light of Jesus Christ's Life and Work Viewed as a Triumph over the Personal Powers of Evil." Ph.D. diss., Trinity Evangelical Divinity School, 2001.

Den Heyer, C. J. *Jesus and the Doctrine of the Atonement: Biblical Notes on a Controversial Topic.* Translated by John Bowden. Harrisburg, Pa.: Trinity, 1998.

Derrida, Jacques. *Deconstruction in a Nutshell: A Conversation with Jacques Derrida.* Edited by John D. Caputo. New York: Fordham University Press, 1997.

———. "Faith and Knowledge: The Two Sources of 'Religion' at the Limits of Reason Alone." In *Religion,* translated by Samuel Weber, edited by Jacques Derrida and Gianni Vattimo, 1–78. Stanford, Calif.: Stanford University Press, 1998.

———. "Force of Law: The 'Mystical Foundation of Authority.'" In *Deconstruction and the Possibility of Justice,* edited by Drucilla Cornell, Michel Rosenfeld, and David Gray Carlson, 3–67. London: Routledge, 1992.

———. "Hospitality, Justice and Responsibility: A Dialogue with Jacques Derrida." In *Questioning Ethics: Contemporary Debates in Philosophy,* edited by Richard Kearney and Mark Dooley, 65–83. London: Routledge, 1999.

———. *Of Hospitality: Anne Dufourmantelle Invites Jacques Derrida to Respond.* Translated by Rachel Bowlby. Stanford, Calif.: Stanford University Press, 2000.

———. *Points . . . : Interviews, 1974–1994.* Translated by Peggy Kamuf et al. Edited by Elisabeth Weber. Stanford, Calif.: Stanford University Press, 1995.

———. *Specters of Marx: The State of the Debt, the Work of Mourning, and the New International.* Translated by Peggy Kamuf. New York: Routledge, 1994.

Derrida, Jacques, with Alexander Garcia Düttmann. "Perhaps or Maybe." In *Responsibilities of Deconstruction,* edited by Jonathon Dronsfield and Nick Midgley, *PLI: Warwick Journal of Philosophy* 6 (1997): 1–69.

Donovan, Mary Ann. "Alive to the Glory of God: A Key Insight in St. Irenaeus." *Theological Studies* 49 (1988): 283–97.

Dooley, Mark. "The Politics of Exodus: Derrida, Kierkegaard, and Levinas on 'Hospitality.'" In *Works of Love,* edited by Robert L. Perkins, 167–92. Macon, Ga.: Mercer University Press, 1999.

Driver, John. *Understanding the Atonement for the Mission of the Church.* Scottdale, Pa.: Herald, 1986.

Duff, R. A. *Trials and Punishments*. Cambridge: Cambridge University Press, 1986.

Dulles, Avery. *Models of the Church*. Rev. ed. New York: Image-Doubleday, 1987.

Dunn, James D. G. *The Theology of Paul the Apostle*. Grand Rapids: Eerdmans, 1998.

Evans, C. Stephen. *The Historical Christ and the Jesus of Faith: The Incarnational Narrative as History*. Oxford: Clarendon, 1996.

Evans, Craig A. "Jesus and the Continuing Exile of Israel." In *Jesus and the Restoration of Israel: A Critical Assessment of N. T. Wright's Jesus and the Victory of God,* edited by Carey C. Newman, 77–100. Downers Grove, Ill.: InterVarsity; Carlisle, UK: Paternoster, 1999.

Faber, Alyda. "Wounds: Theories of Violence in Theological Discourse." Ph.D. diss., McGill University, 2001.

Fairweather, Eugene R. "Incarnation and Atonement: An Anselmian Response to Aulén's *Christus Victor*." *Canadian Journal of Theology* 7 (1961): 167–75.

Finger, Thomas. "Christus Victor and the Creeds: Some Historical Considerations." *Mennonite Quarterly Review* 72 (1989): 31–51.

Frear, George L. "René Girard on Mimesis, Scapegoats, and Ethics." *The Annual of the Society of Christian Ethics* (1992): 115–33.

Froehlich, Karlfried. "Justification Language and Grace: The Charge of Pelagianism in the Middle Ages." In *Probing the Tradition: Historical Studies in Honor of Edward A. Dowey, Jr.,* edited by Elsie Anne McKee and Brian G. Armstrong, 21–47. Louisville: Westminster John Knox, 1989.

Fukuyama, Francis. *The End of History and the Last Man*. New York: Free-Macmillan, 1992.

Gardner, Lucy. "Listening at the Threshold: Christology and the 'Suspension of the Material.'" In *Radical Orthodoxy: A Catholic Enquiry,* edited by Laurence Paul Hemming, 126–46. Aldershot, UK: Ashgate, 2000.

Gerrish, B. A. *Grace and Gratitude: The Eucharistic Theology of John Calvin*. Minneapolis: Fortress, 1993.

Gillman, Ian. "Constantine the Great in the Light of the Christus Victor Concept." *Journal of Religious History* 1 (1961): 197–205.

Girard, René. *Deceit, Desire, and the Novel: Self and Other in Literary Structure*. Translated by Yvonne Freccero. Baltimore: Johns Hopkins University Press, 1965.

———. *The Girard Reader*. Edited by James G. Williams. New York: Crossroad, 1996.

———. *I See Satan Fall like Lightning*. Translated by James G. Williams. Maryknoll, N.Y.: Orbis; Ottawa: Novalis; Leominster, UK: Gracewing, 2001.

———. *The Scapegoat*. Translated by Yvonne Freccero. Baltimore: Johns Hopkins University Press, 1986.

———. *Things Hidden since the Foundation of the World*. Translated by Stephen Bann and Michael Metteer. Stanford, Calif.: Stanford University Press, 1987.

———. *Violence and the Sacred*. Translated by Patrick Gregory. Baltimore: Johns Hopkins University Press, 1977.

Godfrey, William Robert. "Tensions within International Calvinism: The Debate on the Atonement at the Synod of Dort, 1618–1619." Ph.D. diss., Stanford University, 1974.

Gorman, Michael J. *Cruciformity: Paul's Narrative Spirituality of the Cross*. Grand Rapids: Eerdmans, 2001.

Gorringe, Timothy. *God's Just Vengeance: Crime, Violence, and the Rhetoric of Salvation*. Cambridge: Cambridge University Press, 1996.

Graafland, C. *Kinderen van één moeder: Calvijns visie op de kerk volgens zijn Institutie*. Kampen, Neth.: Kok, 1989.

———. *Van Calvijn tot Barth: Oorsprong en ontwikkeling van de leer der verkiezing in het Gereformeerd Protestantisme*. The Hague: Boekencentrum, 1987.

———. *Van Calvijn tot Comrie: Oorsprong en ontwikkeling van de leer van het verbond in het Gereformeerd Protestantisme*. Vol. 1. Zoetermeer, Neth.: Boekencentrum, 1992.

Green, Joel B., and Mark D. Baker. *Recovering the Scandal of the Cross: Atonement in New Testament and Contemporary Contexts*. Downers Grove, Ill.: InterVarsity, 2000.

Grensted, L. W. *A Short History of the Doctrine of the Atonement*. Manchester: Manchester University Press, 1920.

Grenz, Stanley J. *Theology for the Community of God*. Nashville: Broadman & Holman, 1994.

Grenz, Stanley J., and John R. Franke. *Beyond Foundationalism: Shaping Theology in a Postmodern Context*. Louisville: Westminster John Knox, 2001.

Gunton, Colin E. *The Actuality of Atonement: A Study of Metaphor, Rationality, and the Christian Tradition*. Grand Rapids: Eerdmans, 1989.

———. "Towards a Theology of Reconciliation." In *The Theology of Reconciliation*, edited by Colin E. Gunton, 167–74. London: T&T Clark, 2003.

Gutiérrez, Gustavo. *A Theology of Liberation: History, Politics, and Salvation*. Translated by Caridad Inda and John Eagleson. Maryknoll, N.Y.: Orbis, 1973.

Hahn, Scott. *First Comes Love: Finding Your Family in the Church and Trinity*. New York: Doubleday, 2002.

———. *Lord, Have Mercy: The Healing Power of Confession*. New York: Doubleday, 2003.

Hall, Basil. "Calvin against the Calvinists." In *John Calvin*, edited by G. E. Duffield, 19–37. Grand Rapids: Eerdmans, 1966.

Hamerton-Kelly, Robert G. *The Gospel and the Sacred: Poetics of Violence in Mark*. Minneapolis: Fortress, 1994.

———. "Religion and the Thought of René Girard." In *Curing Violence*, edited by Mark I. Wallace and Theophus H. Smith, 3–24. Sonoma, Calif.: Polebridge, 1994.

———. *Sacred Violence: Paul's Hermeneutic of the Cross*. Minneapolis: Fortress, 1992.

Hardin, Michael. "Sacrificial Language in Hebrews: Reappraising René Girard." In *Violence Renounced: René Girard, Biblical Studies, and Peacemaking*, edited by Willard M. Swartley, 103–19. Telford, Pa.: Pandora; Scottdale, Pa.: Herald, 2000.

———. "Violence: René Girard and the Recovery of Early Christian Perspectives." *Brethren Life and Thought* 37 (1992): 107–20.

Hart, Trevor A. "Irenaeus, Recapitulation, and Physical Redemption." In *Christ in Our Place: The Humanity of God in Christ for the Reconciliation of the World*, edited by Trevor A. Hart and Daniel P. Thimell, 152–81. Exeter: Paternoster; Allison Park, Pa.: Pickwick, 1989.

Hatch, Edwin. *The Influence of Greek Ideas and Usages upon the Christian Church*. Edited by A. M. Fairbairn. 5th ed. Peabody, Mass.: Hendrickson, 1995.

Hauerwas, Stanley. "Explaining Christian Nonviolence: Notes for a Conversation with John Milbank." In *Must Christianity Be Violent? Reflections on History, Practice, and Theology*, edited by Kenneth R. Chase and Alan Jacobs, 172–82. Grand Rapids: Brazos, 2003.

Hayes, John H. "Atonement in the Book of Leviticus." *Interpretation* 52 (1998): 5–15.

Heard, Chris. "Hearing the Children's Cries: Commentary, Deconstruction, Ethics, and the Book of Habakkuk." *Semeia* 77 (1997): 75–89.

Hellwig, Monika K. *The Eucharist and the Hunger of the World*. Rev. ed. Kansas City, Mo.: Sheed & Ward, 1992.

Hoekema, Anthony. "The Covenant of Grace in Calvin's Teaching." *Calvin Theological Journal* 2 (1967): 133–61.

Holtrop, Philip C. *The Bolsec Controversy on Predestination from 1551 to 1555: The Statements of Jerome Bolsec, and the Responses of John Calvin, Theodore Beza, and Other Reformed Theologians.* Lewiston, N.Y.: Edwin Mellen, 1993.

Huber, Wolfgang. *Violence: The Unrelenting Assault on Human Dignity.* Translated by Ruth C. L. Gritsch. Minneapolis: Fortress, 1996.

Huntington, Samuel P. *The Clash of Civilizations and the Remaking of World Order.* New York: Simon & Schuster, 1997.

Hütter, Reinhard. "The Church as Public: Dogma, Practice, and the Holy Spirit." *Pro Ecclesia* 3 (1994): 334–61.

————. "Hospitality and Truth: The Disclosure of Practices in Worship and Doctrine." In *Practicing Theology: Beliefs and Practices in Christian Life,* edited by Miroslav Volf and Dorothy C. Bass, 206–27. Grand Rapids: Eerdmans, 2002.

————. *Suffering Divine Things: Theology as Church Practice.* Translated by Doug Stott. Grand Rapids: Eerdmans, 2000.

Jenkins, Philip. *The Next Christendom: The Coming of Global Christianity.* Oxford: Oxford University Press, 2002.

John Paul II. *The Encyclicals of John Paul II.* Edited by J. Michael Miller. 2nd ed. Huntington, Ind.: Our Sunday Visitor, 2001.

Johnson, James Turner. *Morality and Contemporary Warfare.* New Haven, Conn.: Yale University Press, 1999.

Jones, L. Gregory. *Embodying Forgiveness: A Theological Analysis.* Grand Rapids: Eerdmans, 1995.

————. "Eucharistic Hospitality: Welcoming the Stranger into the Household of God." *Reformed Journal* 39 (May 1989): 12–17.

Juergensmeyer, Mark. *Terror in the Mind of God: The Global Rise of Religious Violence.* Berkeley: University of California Press, 2000.

Kärkkäinen, Veli-Matti. *Pneumatology: The Holy Spirit in Ecumenical, International, and Contextual Perspective.* Grand Rapids: Baker, 2002.

Kasper, Walter. "Ecclesiological and Ecumenical Implications of Baptism." *Ecumenical Review* 52 (2000): 526–41.

Kässmann, Margot. *Overcoming Violence: The Challenge to the Churches in All Places.* Geneva: WCC, 1998.

Keifert, Patrick R. "The Other: Hospitality to the Stranger, Levinas, and Multicultural Mission." *Dialog* 30 (1) (1991): 36–43.

————. *Welcoming the Stranger: A Public Theology of Worship and Evangelism.* Minneapolis: Fortress, 1992.

Kendall, R. T. *Calvin and English Calvinism to 1649.* Rev. ed. Carlisle, UK: Paternoster, 1997.

Kennedy, Kevin Dixon. *Union with Christ and the Extent of the Atonement in Calvin.* New York: Lang, 2002.

Kerr, Fergus. "Rescuing Girard's Argument?" *Modern Theology* 8 (1992): 385–99.

Kirk-Duggan, Cheryl. *Misbegotten Anguish: A Theology and Ethics of Violence.* St. Louis: Chalice, 2001.

————. *Refiner's Fire: A Religious Engagement with Violence.* Minneapolis: Fortress, 2001.

Koenig, John. *New Testament Hospitality: Partnership with Strangers as Promise and Mission.* Philadelphia: Fortress, 1985.

Lane, Tony. "The Quest for the Historical Calvin." *Evangelical Quarterly* 55 (1983): 95–113.

————. "The Wrath of God as an Aspect of the Love of God." In *Nothing Greater, Nothing Better: Theological Essays on the Love of God,* edited by Kevin J. Vanhoozer, 138–67. Grand Rapids: Eerdmans, 2001.

Lascaris, A. F. "De verzoeningsleer en het offerchristendom: Anselmus, Calvijn en Girard." *Nederlands Theologisch Tijdschrift* 42 (1988): 222–42.

Lash, Nicholas. "Not Exactly Politics or Power?" *Modern Theology* 8 (1992): 353–64.

Lawson, John. *The Biblical Theology of Saint Irenaeus.* London: Epworth, 1948.

Lee, Philip J. *Against the Protestant Gnostics.* New York: Oxford University Press, 1987.

Lefebure, Leo D. *Revelation, the Religions, and Violence.* Maryknoll, N.Y.: Orbis, 2000.

————. "Victims, Violence, and the Sacred: The Thought of René Girard." *The Christian Century* 113 (December 11, 1996): 1226–29.

Levinas, Emmanuel. *Basic Philosophical Writings.* Edited by Adriaan T. Peperzak, Simon Critchley, and Robert Bernasconi. Bloomington: Indiana University Press, 1996.

————. *Otherwise than Being: Or Beyond Essence.* Translated by Alphonso Lingis. Pittsburgh: Duquesne University Press, 1998.

————. *Totality and Infinity: An Essay on Interiority.* Translated by Alphonso Lingis. Pittsburgh: Duquesne University Press, 1969.

Lillback, Peter A. *The Binding of God: Calvin's Role in the Development of Covenant Theology.* Grand Rapids: Baker; Carlisle, UK: Paternoster, 2001.

Loewe, William P. "Irenaeus' Soteriology: *Christus Victor* Revisited." *Anglican Theological Review* 67 (1985): 1–15.

————. "Irenaeus' Soteriology: Transposing the Question." In *Religion and Culture: Essays in Honor of Bernard Lonergan, S.J.,* edited by Timothy P. Fallon and Philip Boo Riley, 167–79. Albany: State University of New York Press, 1987.

————. "Myth and Counter-Myth: Irenaeus's Story of Salvation." In *Interpreting the Tradition: The Art of Theological Reflection,* edited by Jane Kopas, 39–54. Chico, Calif.: Scholars, 1983.

Lossky, Vladimir. "Redemption and Deification." In *In the Image and Likeness of God,* edited by John H. Erickson and Thomas E. Bird, 97–110. Crestwood, N.Y.: St. Vladimir's Seminary Press, 1985.

Ludlow, Morwenna. *Universal Salvation: Eschatology in the Thought of Gregory of Nyssa and Karl Rahner.* Oxford: Oxford University Press, 2000.

MacCormac, Earl R. *Metaphor and Myth in Science and Religion.* Durham, N.C.: Duke University Press, 1976.

Maimela, Simon S. "The Atonement in the Context of Liberation Theology." *International Review of Mission* 75 (1986): 261–69.

Marshall, Christopher D. *Beyond Retribution: A New Testament Vision for Justice, Crime, and Punishment.* Grand Rapids: Eerdmans; Auckland: Lime Grove House, 2001.

Mattes, Mark C. "A Lutheran Assessment of 'Radical Orthodoxy.'" *Lutheran Quarterly* 15 (2001): 354–67.

McDaniel, Michael C. D. "Salvation as Justification and *Theosis.*" In *Salvation in Christ: A Lutheran-Orthodox Dialogue,* edited by John Meyendorff and Robert Tobias, 67–83. Minneapolis: Augsburg, 1992.

McDonald, H. D. *The Atonement of the Death of Christ: In Faith, Revelation, and History.* Grand Rapids: Baker, 1985.

McFague, Sallie. *Metaphorical Theology: Models of God in Religious Language.* Philadelphia: Fortress, 1982.

————. *Models of God: Theology for an Ecological, Nuclear Age.* Philadelphia: Fortress, 1987.

McGiffert, Michael. "From Moses to Adam: The Making of the Covenant of Works." *Sixteenth Century Journal* 19 (1988): 131–55.

———. "Grace and Works: The Rise and Division of Covenant Divinity in Elizabethan Puritanism." *Harvard Theological Review* 75 (1982): 463–502.

McGrath, Alister E. "The Anti-Pelagian Structure of 'Nominalist' Doctrines of Justification." *Ephemerides Theologicae Lovanienses* 57 (1981): 107–19.

———. "Forerunners of the Reformation? A Critical Examination of the Evidence for Precursors of the Reformation Doctrines of Justification." *Harvard Theological Review* 75 (1982): 219–42.

———. "Reality, Symbol, and History: Theological Reflections on N. T. Wright's Portrayal of Jesus." In *Jesus and the Restoration of Israel: A Critical Assessment of N. T. Wright's Jesus and the Victory of God,* edited by Carey C. Newman, 159–79. Downers Grove, Ill.: InterVarsity; Carlisle, UK: Paternoster, 1999.

McHugh, John. "A Reconsideration of Ephesians 1.10b in the Light of Irenaeus." In *Paul and Paulinism: Essays in Honour of C. K. Barrett,* edited by M. D. Hooker and S. G. Wilson, 302–9. London: SPCK, 1982.

McIntyre, John. *The Shape of Soteriology: Studies in the Doctrine of the Death of Christ.* Edinburgh: T&T Clark, 1992.

Middleton, J. Richard, and Brian J. Walsh. *Truth Is Stranger Than It Used to Be: Biblical Faith in a Postmodern Age.* Downers Grove, Ill.: InterVarsity, 1995.

Milavec, Aaron. "Is God Arbitrary and Sadistic? Anselm's Atonement Theory Reconsidered." *Schola* 4 (1981): 45–94.

Milbank, John. *Being Reconciled: Ontology and Pardon.* London: Routledge, 2003.

———. "Testing Pacifism: Questions for John Milbank." In *Must Christianity Be Violent? Reflections on History, Practice, and Theology,* edited by Kenneth R. Chase and Alan Jacobs, 201–6. Grand Rapids: Brazos, 2003.

———. *Theology and Social Theory: Beyond Secular Reason.* Oxford: Blackwell, 1993.

———. *The Word Made Strange: Theology, Language, Culture.* Cambridge, Mass.: Blackwell, 1997.

Miller, Marlin E. "Girardian Perspectives and Christian Atonement." In *Violence Renounced: René Girard, Biblical Studies, and Peacemaking,* edited by Willard M. Swartley, 31–48. Telford, Pa.: Pandora; Scottdale, Pa.: Herald, 2000.

Minns, Denis. *Irenaeus.* Washington, D.C.: Georgetown University Press, 1994.

Muller, Richard A. "Calvin and the 'Calvinists': Assessing the Continuities and Discontinuities between the Reformation and Orthodoxy." *Calvin Theological Journal* 30 (1995): 345–75; 31 (1996): 125–60.

Nessan, Craig L. "Violence and Atonement." *Dialog* 35 (1996): 26–34.

Neuhaus, Richard John. *The Naked Public Square: Religion and Democracy in America.* Grand Rapids: Eerdmans, 1984.

Newbigin, Lesslie. *The Gospel in a Pluralist Society.* Grand Rapids: Eerdmans; Geneva: WCC, 1989.

Newman, Elizabeth. "Hospitality and Christian Education." *Christian Scholar's Review* 33 (2003): 75–93.

Nielsen, J. T. *Adam and Christ in the Theology of Irenaeus of Lyons: An Examination of the Function of the Adam-Christ Typology in the Adversus Haereses of Irenaeus, against the Background of the Gnosticism of His Time.* Assen, Neth.: Van Gorcum, 1968.

Nørgaard-Højen, Peder. "Baptism and the Foundations of Communion." In *Baptism and the Unity of the Church,* edited by Michael Root and Risto Saarinen, 61–77. Grand Rapids: Eerdmans; Geneva: WCC, 1998.

Oberman, H. A. *The Dawn of the Reformation: Essays in Late Medieval and Early Reformation Thought.* Grand Rapids: Eerdmans, 1986.

————. *Forerunners of the Reformation: The Shape of Late Medieval Thought.* 2nd ed. Minneapolis: Fortress, 1981.

————. *The Harvest of Medieval Theology: Gabriel Biel and Late Medieval Nominalism.* 1963. Reprint, Grand Rapids: Baker, 2000.

Oden, Amy G., ed. *And You Welcomed Me: A Sourcebook on Hospitality in Early Christianity.* Nashville: Abingdon, 2001.

Oden, Thomas C. *The Rebirth of Orthodoxy: Signs of New Life in Christianity.* New York: HarperSanFrancisco, 2002.

Ogletree, Thomas W. *Hospitality to the Stranger: Dimensions of Moral Understanding.* Philadelphia: Fortress, 1985.

Ozment, Steven E. *The Reformation in the Cities: The Appeal of Protestantism in Sixteenth-Century Germany and Switzerland.* New Haven, Conn.: Yale University Press, 1975.

Palmer, Parker J. *Company of Strangers: Christians and the Renewal of America's Public Life.* New York: Crossroad, 1983.

Peels, H. G. L. *The Vengeance of God: The Meaning of the Root NQM and the Function of the NQM-Texts in the Context of Divine Revelation in the Old Testament.* Translated by William Koopmans. Leiden: Brill, 1995.

Pelikan, Jaroslav. *The Christian Tradition: A History of the Development of Doctrine.* 5 vols. Chicago: University of Chicago Press, 1971–89.

————. "The Mirror of the Eternal." In *Jesus through the Centuries: His Place in the History of Culture,* 157–67. New Haven, Conn.: Yale University Press, 1985.

Peperzak, Adriaan. *To the Other: An Introduction to the Philosophy of Emmanuel Levinas.* West Lafayette, Ind.: Purdue University Press, 1993.

Peters, Ted. "Atonement and the Final Scapegoat." *Perspectives in Religious Studies* 19 (1992): 151–81.

————. "The Atonement in Anselm and Luther: Second Thoughts about Gustaf Aulén's *Christus Victor.*" *Lutheran Quarterly* 24 (1972): 301–14.

Peterson, Erik. "Der Monotheismus als politisches Problem." In *Theologische Traktate,* 45–147. Munich: Kösel, 1951.

Peterson, Robert A. *Calvin's Doctrine of the Atonement.* Phillipsburg, N.J.: Presbyterian & Reformed, 1983.

Placher, William C. "Christ Takes Our Place: Rethinking Atonement." *Interpretation* 53 (1999): 5–20.

————. *Jesus the Savior: The Meaning of Jesus Christ for Christian Faith.* Louisville: Westminster John Knox, 2001.

Pobee, John S. *Persecution and Martyrdom in the Theology of Paul.* Sheffield: JSOT, 1985.

Pohl, Christine D. *Making Room: Recovering Hospitality as a Christian Tradition.* Grand Rapids: Eerdmans, 1999.

Preuss, Horst Dietrich. *Old Testament Theology.* Vol. 1. Translated by Leo G. Perdue. Louisville: Westminster John Knox, 1995.

Rainbow, Jonathan H. *The Will of God and the Cross: An Historical and Theological Study of John Calvin's Doctrine of Limited Redemption.* Allison Park, Pa.: Pickwick, 1990.

Rashdall, Hastings. *The Idea of Atonement in Christian Theology.* London: Macmillan, 1919.

Rausch, Thomas P., ed. *Catholics and Evangelicals: Do They Share a Common Future?* Downers Grove, Ill.: InterVarsity, 2000.

Ray, Darby Kathleen. *Deceiving the Devil: Atonement, Abuse, and Ransom.* Cleveland: Pilgrim, 1998.

Reimer, A. James. "Trinitarian Orthodoxy, Constantinianism, and Radical Protestant Theology." In *Mennonites and Classical Theology: Dogmatic Foundations for Christian Ethics,* 247–71. Kitchener, Ont.: Pandora; Waterloo, Ont.: Herald, 2001.

Reno, R. R. "The Radical Orthodoxy Project." In *In the Ruins of the Church: Sustaining Faith in an Age of Diminished Christianity,* 63–79. Grand Rapids: Brazos, 2002.

Rittgers, Ronald K. "Private Confession and Religious Authority in Reformation Nürnberg." In *Penitence in the Age of the Reformations,* edited by Katharine Jackson Lualdi and Anne T. Thayer, 49–70. Aldershot, UK: Ashgate, 2000.

Russell, Brian. "Developing Derrida: Pointers to Faith, Hope, and Prayer." *Theology* 104 (2001): 403–11.

Sachs, John R. "Apocatastasis in Patristic Theology." *Theological Studies* 54 (1993): 617–40.

Sanders, E. P. *Paul and Palestinian Judaism: A Comparison of Patterns of Religion.* Philadelphia: Fortress, 1977.

Schroeder, Christoph. "'Standing in the Breach': Turning Away the Wrath of God." *Interpretation* 53 (1999): 16–23.

Schwager, Raymund. *Jesus in the Drama of Salvation: Toward a Biblical Doctrine of Redemption.* Translated by James G. Williams and Paul Haddon. New York: Crossroad, 1999.

———. *Must There Be Scapegoats? Violence and Redemption in the Bible.* Translated by Maria L. Assad. San Francisco: Harper & Row, 1987.

Schwartz, Regina M. *The Curse of Cain: The Violent Legacy of Monotheism.* Chicago: University of Chicago Press, 1997.

Sloyan, Gerard S. *Jesus: Redeemer and Divine Word.* Wilmington, Del.: Glazier, 1989.

Smith, Christian. *The Emergence of Liberation Theology: Radical Religion and Social Movement Theory.* Chicago: University of Chicago Press, 1991.

Smith, Christopher. "Chiliasm and Recapitulation in the Theology of Ireneus." *Vigiliae Christianae* 48 (1994): 313–31.

Smith, James K. A. "Determined Hope: A Phenomenology of Christian Expectation." In *The Future of Hope: Essays on Christian Tradition amid Modernity and Postmodernity,* edited by Miroslav Volf and William Katerberg. Grand Rapids: Eerdmans, forthcoming.

———. "Determined Violence: Derrida's Structural Religion." *Journal of Religion* 78 (1998): 197–212.

———. *The Fall of Interpretation: Philosophical Foundations for a Creational Hermeneutic.* Downers Grove, Ill.: InterVarsity, 2000.

Snyder, T. Richard. *The Protestant Ethic and the Spirit of Punishment.* Grand Rapids: Eerdmans, 2001.

Sobrino, Jon. *The Principle of Mercy: Taking the Crucified People from the Cross.* Maryknoll, N.Y.: Orbis, 1994.

Soskice, Janet Martin. *Metaphor and Religious Language.* Oxford: Clarendon, 1985.

Steer, Simon Morrison. "Eating Bread in the Kingdom of God: The Foodways of Jesus in the Gospel of Luke." Ph.D. diss., Westminster Theological Seminary, 2002.

Stek, John H. "Covenant Overload in Reformed Theology." *Calvin Theological Journal* 29 (1994): 12–41.

Stendahl, Krister. "The Apostle Paul and the Introspective Conscience of the West." In *Paul among Jews and Gentiles,* 78–96. Philadelphia: Fortress, 1976.

Stephanopoulos, Robert G. "Implications for the Ecumenical Movement." *Ecumenical Review* 44 (1992): 18–28.

Suchocki, Marjorie Hewitt. *The Fall into Violence: Original Sin in Relational Theology.* New York: Continuum, 1994.

Taylor, Barbara Brown. "Preaching the Terrors." In *Exilic Preaching: Testimony for Christian Exiles in an Increasingly Hostile Culture,* edited by Erskine Clarke, 83–90. Harrisburg, Pa.: Trinity Press International, 1998.

———. *Speaking of Sin: The Lost Language of Salvation.* Cambridge: Cowley, 2000.

Taylor, Mark Lewis. *The Executed God: The Way of the Cross in Lockdown America.* Minneapolis: Fortress, 2001.

Tentler, Thomas N. *Sin and Confession on the Eve of the Reformation.* Princeton, N.J.: Princeton University Press, 1977.

Thomas, G. Michael. *The Extent of the Atonement: A Dilemma for Reformed Theology from Calvin to the Consensus.* Carlisle, UK: Paternoster, 1997.

Thorogood, Bernard. "Coming to the Lord's Table: A Reformed Viewpoint." *Ecumenical Review* 44 (1992): 10–17.

Tiessen, Terrance L. *Irenaeus on the Salvation of the Unevangelized.* ATLA Monograph Series, no. 31. Metuchen, N.J.: Scarecrow, 1993.

Torrance, James B. "The Concept of Federal Theology: Was Calvin a Federal Theologian?" In *Calvinus Sacrae Scripturae Professor: Calvin as Confessor of Holy Scripture,* edited by Wilhelm H. Neuser, 15–40. Grand Rapids: Eerdmans, 1994.

———. "Covenant or Contract? A Study of the Theological Background of Worship in Seventeenth-Century Scotland." *Scottish Journal of Theology* 23 (1970): 51–76.

Torrance, Thomas F. *Divine Meaning: Studies in Patristic Hermeneutics.* Edinburgh: T&T Clark, 1995.

Trible, Phyllis. *Texts of Terror: Literary-Feminist Readings of Biblical Narratives.* Philadelphia: Fortress, 1984.

Turner, H. E. W. *The Patristic Doctrine of Redemption: A Study of the Development of Doctrine during the First Five Centuries.* London: Mowbray; New York: Morehouse-Gorham, 1952.

Vanhoozer, Kevin J. "The Atonement in Postmodernity: Of Guilt, Goats, and Gifts." In *The Glory of the Atonement: Biblical, Theological, and Practical Perspectives,* edited by Charles E. Hill and Frank A. James, 367–404. Downers Grove, Ill.: InterVarsity, 2004.

Van Veluw, A. H. *'De straf die ons de vrede aanbrengt': Over God, kruis, straf en de slachtoffers van deze wereld in de christelijke verzoeningsleer.* Zoetermeer, Neth.: Boekencentrum, 2002.

Visser, Derk. "The Covenant in Zacharias Ursinus." *Sixteenth Century Journal* 18 (1987): 531–44.

Volf, Miroslav. *After Our Likeness: The Church as the Image of the Trinity.* Grand Rapids: Eerdmans, 1998.

———. "Against a Pretentious Church: A Rejoinder to Bell's Response." *Modern Theology* 19 (2003): 281–85.

———. *Exclusion and Embrace: A Theological Exploration of Identity, Otherness, and Reconciliation.* Nashville: Abingdon, 1996.

———. "Theology for a Way of Life." In *Practicing Theology: Beliefs and Practices in Christian Life,* edited by Miroslav Volf and Dorothy C. Bass, 245–63. Grand Rapids: Eerdmans, 2002.

———. "'The Trinity Is Our Social Program': The Doctrine of the Trinity and the Shape of Social Engagement." *Modern Theology* 41 (1998): 403–23.

Von Allmen, Jean-Jacques. "The Forgiveness of Sins as a Sacrament in the Reformed Tradition." In *Sacramental Reconciliation: Religion in the Seventies,* edited by Edward Schillebeeckx, 112–19. New York: Herder & Herder, 1971.

Von Rohr, J. *The Covenant of Grace in Puritan Thought.* Atlanta: Scholars, 1986.

Vriezen, Th. C. *De verkiezing van Israël volgens het Oude Testament.* Amsterdam: Bolland, 1974.

Wainwright, Geoffrey. "Towards Eucharistic Fellowship." *Ecumenical Review* 44 (1992): 6–9.

Warrior, Robert Allen. "A Native American Perspective: Canaanites, Cowboys, and Indians." In *Voices from the Margin: Interpreting the Bible in the Third World*, edited by R. S. Sugirtharajah, 287–95. Maryknoll, N.Y.: Orbis, 1991.

Weaver, J. Denny. *The Nonviolent Atonement.* Grand Rapids: Eerdmans, 2001.

Webber, Robert E. *Ancient-Future Faith: Rethinking Evangelicalism for a Postmodern World.* Grand Rapids: Baker, 1999.

Weigel, George. *The Truth of Catholicism: Inside the Essential Teachings and Controversies of the Church Today.* New York: Perennial-HarperCollins, 2001.

Weir, David A. *The Origins of the Federal Theology in Sixteenth-Century Reformation Thought.* Oxford: Clarendon, 1990.

Wendel, François. "Justification and Predestination in Calvin." In *Readings in Calvin's Theology*, edited by Donald K. McKim, 153–78. Grand Rapids: Baker, 1984.

Westerhoff, Caroline. *Good Fences: The Boundaries of Hospitality.* Cambridge: Cowley, 1999.

White, Peter. *Predestination, Policy, and Polemic: Conflict and Consensus in the English Church from the Reformation to the Civil War.* Cambridge: Cambridge University Press, 1992.

Williams, D. H. *Retrieving the Tradition and Renewing Evangelicalism: A Primer for Suspicious Protestants.* Grand Rapids: Eerdmans, 1999.

Williams, George Huntston. "Christology and Church-State Relations in the Fourth Century." *Church History* 20 (3) (1951): 3–33; 20 (4) (1951): 3–26.

Williams, James G. *The Bible, Violence, and the Sacred: Liberation from the Myth of Sanctioned Violence.* Valley Forge, Pa.: Trinity, 1995.

Wilson, Jonathan R. *God So Loved the World: A Christology for Disciples.* Grand Rapids: Baker, 2001.

———. *Gospel Virtues: Practicing Faith, Hope, and Love in Uncertain Times.* Downers Grove, Ill.: InterVarsity, 1998.

Wink, Walter. *Engaging the Powers: Discernment and Resistance in a World of Domination.* Minneapolis: Fortress, 1984.

Witten, Marsha G. *All Is Forgiven: The Secular Message in American Protestantism.* Princeton, N.J.: Princeton University Press, 1993.

Wood, Susan K. "Baptism and the Foundations of Communion." In *Baptism and the Unity of the Church,* edited by Michael Root and Risto Saarinen, 37–60. Grand Rapids: Eerdmans; Geneva: WCC, 1998.

———. "Baptism as a Mark of the Church." In *Marks of the Body of Christ,* edited by Carl E. Braaten and Robert W. Jenson, 25–43. Grand Rapids: Eerdmans, 1999.

Wright, N. T. *The Climax of the Covenant: Christ and the Law in Pauline Theology.* Minneapolis: Fortress, 1993.

———. *Jesus and the Victory of God.* Vol. 2 of *Christian Origins and the Question of God.* Minneapolis: Fortress, 1996.

———. *The New Testament and the People of God.* Vol. 1 of *Christian Origins and the Question of God.* Minneapolis: Fortress, 1992.

———. *The Resurrection of the Son of God.* Vol. 3 of *Christian Origins and the Question of God.* Minneapolis: Fortress, 2003.

———. *What Saint Paul Really Said: Was Paul of Tarsus the Real Founder of Christianity?* Grand Rapids: Eerdmans, 1997.

Yoder, John Howard. *Preface to Theology: Christology and Theological Method.* Grand Rapids: Brazos, 2002.

Subject Index

Author Index

281

Scripture Index